One of the Family:
The Englishman and the Mafia

Also by John Pearson

Previous Publications

Non-fiction

Bluebird and the Dead Lake
The Persuasion Industry (with Graham Turner)
The Life of Ian Fleming
Arena: The Story of the Colosseum
The Profession of Violence
Edward the Rake
Facades: Edith, Osbert and Sacheverell Sitwell
Stags and Serpents: The Cavendish Dukes of Devonshire
The Ultimate Family: The Making of the House of Windsor
Citadel of the Heart: Winston and the Churchill Dynasty
Painfully Rich: J. Paul Getty and His Heirs
Blood Royal: The Story of the Spencers and the Royals
The Cult of Violence
The Gamblers

Fiction

Gone to Timbuctoo
The Life of James Bond
The Kindness of Dr. Avicenna

One of the Family:
The Englishman and the Mafia

John Pearson

arrow books

Published by Arrow Books in 2004

3 5 7 9 10 8 6 4

First published in the United Kingdom in 2003 by Century

Arrow Books
The Random House Group Limited
20 Vauxhall Bridge Road, London, SW1V 2SA

www.randomhouse.co.uk

Addresses for companies within The Random House Group Limited
can be found at:
www.randomhouse.co.uk/offices.htm

The Random House Group Limited Reg. No. 954009

A CIP catalogue record for this book
is available from the British Library

ISBN 9780099457787

The Random House Group Limited makes every effort to ensure that the
papers used in its books are made from trees that have been legally
sourced from well-managed and credibly certified forests. Our paper
procurement policy can be found at: www.randomhouse.co.uk/paper.htm

Mixed Sources
Product group from well-managed
forests and other controlled sources
www.fsc.org Cert no. TT-COC-2139
© 1996 Forest Stewardship Council
FSC

Typeset by SX Composing DTP, Rayleigh, Essex
Printed and bound in Great Britain by
Cox & Wyman Limited, Reading, Berkshire

I dedicate this book to Ros
'for being there'

Contents

Contents

Acknowledgements

For obvious reasons it might be unwise or inappropriate to mention some of the people who have helped me with this book. But among those I can mention I would like to thank the following – Dave Farley, Lesley Goodman, John Hannam, Clive Jenkins, Alan Jones, Colin and Joan Marden, Rose Milano, Sylvia and Mike Moody, Carmine de Noia, Andy Shire, Pippa Walker, and especially, Sean Pine. As always, I am deeply indebted to my wife, Lynette, whose cheerfulness and cleverness sustained me when lesser women would have faltered. Ted Green, though sometimes worried, also made his contribution.

But my greatest thanks must go to Wilf Pine himself, for the tale he had to tell and the genuine pleasure of his company. He himself would personally like to thank Don and David and the Arden family, Patrick Meehan Jr., and Tony, Bill, Ozzy and Geezer, otherwise known as 'Black Sabbath'. As he says, but for these people who became involved in various periods of his life, 'things would have been a lot different.'

Acknowledgements

I am immensely grateful to many colleagues who helped bring this book to completion, and I wish to thank them here.

1

The Man with the Gucci Walking Stick

WHEN I SAW Wilf Pine standing among the principal mourners at Charlie Kray's funeral, I sensed at once that he was different from the others. It was odd enough seeing all those top London criminals gathered together on that blustery April morning in the bright, hymn-happy interior of St Matthew's Church, Bethnal Green.

All the old 'aristocracy of crime' was on parade. Even Charlie Richardson was present, looking as usual like an elderly law professor despite his twenty-five-year stretch awarded at the so-called Old Bailey 'torture trial' in the mid-1960s. So, too, was 'Mad' Frankie Fraser, the only man alive to have been flogged twice with the cat o'nine tails, who now makes a living from Rotarian lunches, where he entertains his listeners by telling them how he extracted his victims' teeth with golden pliers; and beside him stood the Krays' old friend, impassive Freddie Foreman, who got a twelve-year sentence for disposing of the body of Jack the Hat McVitie on their behalf, and later confessed on prime-time television to having helped murder Frank Mitchell, the 'Mad Axeman', for them as a favour.

As these ageing villains took their places near Charlie's beautifully polished coffin, it was obvious to me that each one of them was regarding Wilf with a certain wary respect. What wasn't so obvious was why, and I left the funeral without discovering the answer. Nor was I much the wiser six months later when I attended another of these gangster funerals – this time of the second Kray twin, Reg himself, who had been released from Wayland Prison to die of cancer in a Norwich hotel a few weeks later.

Ever since Reg's death, resentment had been growing between his young widow, Roberta, who wanted him remembered as a gentle, loving husband, and these old criminals who felt that his funeral should emphasise his role as the most famous gangster in Britain and their own importance as his closest friends, and leaders of London's so-called 'criminal fraternity'. By the morning of the funeral, their resentment was smouldering since they had just discovered that, although they insisted that before he died Reg had told them that he wanted them to be his pallbearers, Roberta was now denying them this honour. This was taken as a dreadful insult. Charlie Richardson was not at the funeral. Joe Pyle chose to sit in his car outside the church throughout the service. Freddie Foreman found he had a prior engagement at New Scotland Yard, and Dave 'Lock, Stock and Two Smoking Barrels' Courtney left a wreath at the cemetery but wasn't at the funeral. By the time the twenty-two flower-decked limousines had snaked their way through the old East End to Chingford Mount Cemetery bearing the humbler mourners to the burial, trouble would almost certainly have erupted had Wilf Pine not been there to greet them at the graveside, holding the hand of the grieving widow.

The sprawling cemetery at Chingford Mount has been receiving the East End's dead for burial since the days of Queen Victoria, and shortly after their imprisonment for murder back in 1969 the Kray twins bought themselves a plot among the marble angels and the Victorian granite mausoleums, so that one day they could lie at peace together with their parents and their close relations in what someone had inevitably christened 'Kray Corner'. With Reg's burial, 'Kray Corner' was now full, and for this last farewell several hundred of the toughest characters in London had gathered here with but a single thought in mind – whatever his widow wanted, they intended to give their man a proper send-off. But even when the priest had solemnly intoned the service for the dead, and white-faced Roberta threw a single rose on to her husband's coffin, not a whisper of protest or dissent arose from anyone. And while the London clay was being shovelled over all that now remained of Reg, and Wilf led

Roberta to her limousine through that hostile but quiescent crowd, I wondered to myself how he had done it.

In his late fifties now, Wilf Pine was a solitary, dignified figure. His close-cropped beard and the expensively tailored dark grey suit, which he wore with a black polo-neck sweater, somehow combined a touch of showbiz with an air of authority it would have been hard to argue with.

But there was somehow more to Wilf than that. Until I got to know him better, I found him more threatening in his understated way than any of the old-time criminals around him; but once again I find it hard to say exactly why. In spite of seeming so controlled, it was as if something dangerous lingered around him from the past. Perhaps it was his hands. During what must have been some very painful sessions with a needle and a bottle of Indian ink many years before, the backs of each hand and every finger from the knuckle to the first joint had been heavily tattooed with letters and geometric signs. He never told me what they meant, but they reminded me of illustrations I had seen of similar tattoos practised by old-time convicts on France's 'Devil's Island'. This again was puzzling since, as far as I could discover, Wilf Pine had never been in prison.

But there was something else that foxed me. By the time of Reg's funeral I had learned that standing for even a short period caused him agony, and when he walked he did so with a painful limp.

'Chronic arthritis in the hip, and the base of the spine's disintegrating', he said. 'The doctors say there's nothing to be done. I say my sins are catching up with me at last. Whatever the cause, it's a bastard, and I'd be lost without this stick of mine.'

I had recognised that walking stick the first time I saw it. I had seen similar walking sticks in Rome back in the 1960s when no well-dressed Italian of a certain age would venture forth without carrying an expensive cane. This one was of highly polished amber-coloured malacca, encircled at the top with a band of gold. The handle was of old ivory, carved like the talon of a bird, and just below the gold band was a small gold button bearing a logo of unbeatable discretion. Engraved in small capitals were two words which used to be a testimonial to the ultimate in male elegance. GUCCI ITALY.

I asked Wilf how he came by it, but as usual in those days he was cagey.

'All in good time,' he said. 'All in good time. Let's say it once belonged to someone who was the closest thing I ever had to a real father. One day, if I'm still around, I'll tell you who he was.'

I had been introduced to Wilf by Reg Kray in a telephone call from Wayland Prison several months before the death of his brother Charlie. By then I was working on the sequel to *The Profession of Violence*, the 'authorised' biography I wrote about the twins in the early 1970s.

Reg was a man of few words on the telephone, having learned from experience that one could never be quite sure who might be listening.

'There's this old friend of me an' Ron's I think you ought to see. He's an interestin' character and could be useful for the book.' He gave me a telephone number and made me promise I would ring him. Not that I needed much encouraging. When Reg said somebody was 'interestin'' I rarely found him wrong. But when I realised he'd given me a Bournemouth number, that did surprise me. Whenever I thought of Bournemouth – which I rarely did – it was as home to retired army officers and sturdy bridge-playing widows rather than as an address for an old friend of the Krays.

I rang that evening and had my first experience of the inimitable voice of Wilf, a deadpan London accent strained through a bed of gravel. Like Reg, he was very guarded, but we arranged to meet for lunch in two days' time in a pub near Chichester, which had no greater significance than being halfway between Bournemouth and where I live in Sussex.

One of life's mysteries to which I've never found the answer is why one gets on with certain people from the start. Whatever the reason, get on I did that day with Wilf. He was a great raconteur, with an outrageous vocabulary, an unexpected warmth and a line in black humour which never failed to make me laugh. Much of this concerned his old friend, Ron Kray – 'the smartest madman I have ever known' – whom he visited for years in Broadmoor. He gave me the feeling that he wasn't all that fond of Reg, but his real friend was poor, sad, charming Charlie Kray, who had stupidly allowed himself to get involved in a highly suspect drugs scam, which had left him at the age of seventy-two as Britain's oldest prisoner in maximum security – where currently he was dying. Now that Charlie was terminally ill with heart disease, Wilf was visiting him almost every day in hospital, and would be with him when he died.

But as Wilf and I chatted so amiably over a fairly lousy lunch in that country pub, I ended up more mystified about him than when we started. He made it crystal clear that he was closely involved, if not in actual crime, at least with an awful lot of major criminals in addition to the Krays. But although he talked so knowledgeably about big-time crime, he left me in total ignorance about his own role, if there was one, in these exciting goings-on. All I remember afterwards is the feeling that for all Wilf Pine's apparent openness and ready conversation, there had to be another life that he was keeping very strictly to himself.

For once I was absolutely right, and it was at the conclusion of Charlie's funeral that I got my first real hint of what Wilf's 'other life' might be.

I remember looking at the great mass of wreaths and floral tributes to Charlie which had come from 'friends' all over the United Kingdom. By chance I noticed two that had come from New York, backing rumours I had always heard that Charlie had been mixed up with organised crime in the USA. I happened to mention this to Wilf, saying that I might include this in my book. One of the wreaths was from John Gotti and the other from somebody called Danny Pagano. 'They're both friends of mine,' said Wilf. 'Be careful. They can be touchy if you get things wrong. Everyone knows John Gotti's boss of the Gambino crime family, but if you mention Danny best to say that he's "*reputed* to be a high-ranking capo with the Genovese," according to the FBI.'

It was Reg's death that seemed to cement my friendship with Wilf. He'd told me that he'd promised Ron before his death that he'd look after his twin brother and, true to his word, had been deeply involved in his agonised and agonising last months. One day, shortly after finishing my book, I casually remarked to Wilf, 'Now I can start writing yours.'

I really meant this as a joke, but Wilf took it seriously.

'Not on your life,' he said, and for some reason this became a sort of joke between us. But it was one of those jokes that crop up so regularly that you end up taking it for granted. This happened with us, and gradually, from what had been intended as a joke, this book was born. We had many more meals together, with lots of stories and lots of endless discussions over what could and what emphatically could not be said. Gradually the mists began to clear, and as they did one of the saddest, wildest and utterly improbable stories I have ever heard started to unfold. But I always found that whenever I checked out even the most improbable of Wilf Pine's stories, it invariably proved absolutely true. And as the stories continued, I even discovered who had given him the Gucci walking stick.

2

Lessons for Life

WILF PINE WAS born in the proud city of Newcastle upon Tyne on 23 February 1944, but even now it's not something that he likes to dwell on. 'Had I known what life had in store for me in my early years and had it been possible to climb back into my mother's womb, I'd have done just that,' he says. 'And stayed there,' he adds.

The war was raging at the time, Newcastle was suffering almost daily bombing by the Germans, and it was typical of Wilf to arrive in the middle of an air raid. While the Nazi bombers were trying to blast the shipyards down the road to kingdom come, his birth nearly killed his mother.

Since the family was poor, there could be no question of the confinement taking place in hospital, or even with a doctor in attendance. Home was one of countless tiny terraced houses in a maze of streets behind the shipyards, and the nearest thing to a midwife was his Great-Aunt Betty and the next-door neighbour. The labour had been long and complicated, and when a doctor finally turned up he did not stay for long. He said that Wilf's mother would probably recover, but didn't give much for the chances of the baby.

Auntie Betty wasn't having that. Thanks to the air raids, no ambulances were available so she gathered up the sickly child, wrapped him in a blanket and hurried him off to the Royal Victoria Infirmary a mile or so away. This time two doctors examined him, but they gave the same verdict as before. There was little to be done, as the child was born with tuberculosis on the lungs. This was not unusual among poor families in the neighbourhood, and in those days few children born with TB survived.

What made this baby's prospects even worse was that he was unable to take his mother's milk, and for several weeks the infant Wilf was kept alive on a diet of sugar and water administered by Auntie Betty on the end of her finger. Then, as if determined to prove the doctors wrong, the sickly baby did survive. Within a year he was growing fast and showing signs of full recovery. His mother, a warm-hearted Newcastle girl who had been christened Mildred but was fortunately known by one and all as Millie, adored him. So did her two sisters, Aunt Mary and Aunt Katie. Briefly, in this cosy little world of women, Wilf and his eighteen-month-old brother Bernie flourished.

Then the war ended and the horror story that makes up the first seventeen years of Wilf Pine's life began.

Throughout the war his father, Able Seaman Bernard Pine, had been serving with the Royal Navy and spending long periods away from home. He was popular aboard ship, a great drinker and the life and soul of every party. Millie was still Millie Brigham, a twenty-three-year-old auburn-haired Newcastle girl, when her brother John brought his shipmate, Bernard, home on ten days' leave. Predictably, Millie and Bernard fell in love, with John encouraging the courtship, as did the Brighams when they discovered that the Pines were fellow Catholics.

As with most wartime romances, the wedding was a hurried business that took place in the spring of 1940 in the local Catholic church, and when Millie produced a son nine months later he was christened Bernard after his absent father. Not until 1945, when the war ended and Able Seaman Pine was demobilised, did Millie really get to know him. She soon discovered a darker side to her husband than the cheerful matelot she had fallen in love with. Like many working-class fathers in this period, Bernard found his relaxation after work drinking in the pub, and on returning home he could turn violent.

Bernard Pine's demob from the Royal Navy coincided with another all-important change in his family's way of life. Since Wilf was still considered delicate, Millie had decided it would do him good to move from the north to the gentler climate of the Isle of

Wight, where her mother-in-law was already living. Grandma Pine's husband had been a coastguard in Northumberland before ending up as a Customs and Excise man in Somerset, where he died in 1939. His daughter, Wilf's Aunt Cis, once told Wilf that his grandfather had been a quiet, family-loving man, 'unlike the son he sired', says Wilf, adding: 'I only wish I'd known him.'

After her husband's death and because she liked living in the south and was a lively woman with a taste for company, Grandma Pine decided to supplement her pension by taking on a pub, The Prince of Wales, in the seaside town of Ryde which, with its leafy esplanade and prosperous villas, was one of the favourite holiday havens of the Victorians. But Millie had to find a little house in the poorer part of Ryde called Oakfield, and when Bernard was demobbed he joined them there. From now on it would be the Isle of Wight, not his native Newcastle, that Wilf would look upon as home.

Few realise today how much poverty there was behind the apparent prosperity of the Isle of Wight in those post-war years. Visitors flocked to popular summertime resorts like Bembridge, Sandown and Shanklin, while Cowes during Cowes Week still attracted fashionable international society – royalty included – drawn by the exclusive clientele of the Royal Yacht Squadron. On the edge of Cowes Prince Albert had built Osborne House, where Queen Victoria chose to live after his death in 1861. This meant that for the last forty years of the nineteenth century the Isle of Wight was effectively the centre of the court of England.

But none of this had much effect on Oakfield in the 1940s, which in those days would have been classified as a deprived area. The housing was poor and primitive, mainly two-up, two-down terraced houses with outside lavatories and no bathrooms, and many of the men were unemployed. According to Wilf, 'You could always tell which houses had a regular income; they were the ones with Izal toilet paper. But most families, which included ours, had a nail hammered on the back of the door, with the previous day's newspaper, cut into squares, stuck on to it.'

Like most men after the war, Bernard Pine was in and out of work, finally settling as a cinema projectionist until the cinema burned down in the late 1960s. But he found employment almost

9

immediately upon being demobbed working on the railways. According to Wilf, 'his only reason for working was to put beer in his belly', leaving Millie to support the family by taking in washing and ironing and cleaning other people's homes. By now her husband had graduated to what Wilf calls 'indoor sports' – battering his wife on returning from the pub, then keeping his hand in by beating up his growing sons.

'I know some fairly rough behaviour went on in many working-class homes in those days,' Wilf says, 'but it was only when I started visiting my friends that I realised that my old man was something special.'

He denies, however, that his mother was the downtrodden victim of a brutal husband. 'She was a lively, feisty lady who could look after herself, but no one could cope with him.' What Bernard Pine indulged in was drunken brutality for its own sake, and Wilf's older brother Bernie had to bear the brunt of it. By the time he was nine, young Bernie was being beaten up so regularly that the neighbours had begun reporting what was happening to the authorities and Bernie was finally taken to a home in Southampton for 'care and protection'. This left seven-year-old Wilf from now on the chief target for his father's 'indoor sports'.

While Wilf was learning all about domestic violence at home, at school he came in contact with a different sort of cruelty. When his Brigham grandparents decided to follow their daughter from Newcastle to the Isle of Wight, they ended up in a nearby house in Oakfield. This meant that, with two devout Catholic grandmothers to contend with, Wilf was soon being taken to Mass not once but twice each Sunday, and at the age of six he was naturally entrusted to the nuns at nearby St Mary's Roman Catholic primary school.

Bearing in mind the words of Jesus on treating little ones, one might have thought the holy sisters would have recognised the plight of this badly abused small boy, but this didn't happen. The headmistress, Sister Paula, was a firm believer in hell and original sin and reinforced the power of prayer with corporal punishment. So ruthlessly did she wield her ruler on her children's hands that Wilf remembers one occasion when a local mother, angry at the way her child had been hurt, accosted Sister Paula in the playground and, as

Wilf says, 'ended up giving Sister Paula a taste of her own medicine with a good right-hander to the jaw'.

As for 'suffering the little children to come unto Him', whenever the parish priest visited Sister Paula when she was taking class, she would ask the priest, before leaving, if he would bless the children. But only after she had ordered Wilf to leave the room.

This meant that the two forces of authority Wilf encountered as a child – his father and his Catholic school – both started by abusing him and then rejected him. Hardly surprisingly, his one thought was a longing to escape, which generally meant playing truant from his home and school and enjoying the life that went on in the local streets. The streets were the one place where he felt happy and secure. An old scrap-metal yard around the corner from his house was a permanent adventure playground and became headquarters for a small boys' gang who got up to any devilment going. Meanwhile two more children had appeared at home – Wilf's sisters Maureen and Margaret – so that Millie had to struggle more than ever just to keep her family together. As a good Catholic wife and mother, she believed that however badly she was treated her duty always lay in obedience to her husband and producing children. Divorce was unthinkable, and since the family depended largely on her slender earnings for its food, the staple diet was lentils stewed with a ham bone and vegetables grown by her husband in the back garden. Most of the children's clothes were bought in jumble sales.

Wilf was eleven when he finally escaped from Sister Paula and the nuns, for the less painful world of Ryde Secondary Modern School. Soon after he arrived he remembers being tapped on the shoulder in the playground by a bigger boy who asked him how he was, and for a moment he failed to recognise him. It was his brother Bernie, who had been back on the island for a month already, living in another children's home at Ryde. Now it had been decided to reunite him with the family, so after their years apart the two boys had to get to know each other over again.

For Wilf this was no problem, since he hero-worshipped his elder brother. But Bernie Pine's return brought fresh trouble with their father. 'My father was as good as gold with the two girls, but he really was a bastard to us boys. I still hate remembering the beatings Bernie got from him,' says Wilf.

Inevitably Bernie started following the same pattern as before, rebelling against his father in the only way he had – by escaping into petty crime. Soon Wilf was following him. Wilf was a bright child, but years of abuse by his father had made him rebel against authority, like Bernie, and teachers soon gave up on him. Rather than have him in the classroom he was often sent to work in the school garden, which did little for his reputation with the smarter children, who began to make fun of his dirty appearance.

Wilf was thirteen by the time Bernie was caught and sent to an approved school. This left Bernie something of an outcast – from his home, his school and from the love of God.

Wilf remembers the year 1959 as 'a good year for Cliff Richard and a bad one for me. Cliff reached number one in the charts with "Living Doll", while for me it was the beginning of a living nightmare,' he says.

He was fifteen and was trapped in a cycle of petty crime and getting caught. It was as if he wanted to be arrested. He was even caught stealing a cyclist's crash helmet, which he didn't need because he hadn't got a bike, and the local magistrate in his wisdom thought the solution was to sentence him to three years in an approved school.

The one person sufficiently interested in Wilf to realise there was a problem here was his probation officer, and when he interviewed Bernard Pine his suspicions were confirmed that Wilf was more a victim than a potential villain. From the police reports, he knew already what went on in the Pine household and felt sorry for this teenage boy, whose father insisted he was out of control and that he didn't want him in the house. But this interview also gave the probation officer an idea of how to help him. Bernard Pine had said that as a boy he was sent to a naval training school at Greenwich before entering the navy. It might be possible to do something similar for Wilf instead of condemning him to the rough and tumble of an ordinary approved school. He had heard of a place which, although a Home Office approved school for young delinquents, was run on naval lines. It was at Blyth, near Whitley Bay in Northumberland;

once he knew that Wilf was born in Newcastle and that his father had been a sailor, he was able to get him into the Blyth Wellesley Nautical School.

This seemed to offer Wilf an opportunity to redeem himself. A brutal father and the jealous God of Sister Paula may have rejected him but, thanks to his probation officer, the Wellesley Nautical School now had its chance to make a man of him.

The school at Blyth was run exactly like a ship, and although the staff were actually prison officers employed by the Home Office, they all wore naval uniform and played the part of naval officers. The headmaster held the rank of captain, his deputy that of a commander, and the masters ranked as first and second lieutenants. The rules were strict, but, as in the navy, discipline was not directly enforced by the officers but by prefects chosen from the boys, who were also given the naval rank of leading hands and petty officers. Reveille was sounded at six each morning by a bugler, and every Sunday the school paraded to salute the flag, led by the boys' brass band.

As for the boys themselves, there was no silly nonsense here about psychiatrists or mollycoddling and discipline was enforced exactly as it would have been afloat. The boys had little contact with their families. Millie wrote to Wilf each month but could not afford to come to visit him, since naturally her husband would never have given her the money for the fare to Northumberland – still less would he have ever visited his son himself.

From the moment Wilf arrived at Blyth one autumn morning in 1959, no time was lost in introducing him to the regime that he would follow. Still concerned on his behalf, his probation officer accompanied him for the three-hundred-mile journey from the Isle of Wight and took him in person to the school reception office. Wilf has never forgotten every detail of what happened next:

I was greeted by these two characters in uniform. One, about forty-five had gold rings around his cuffs, showing that he was an officer; the other, a boy a couple of years older than me, had the crossed anchors on his sleeve of a petty officer. Everything

13

seemed very businesslike, and the officer told me not to worry, as my petty officer would look after me. Then while the probation officer had a cup of tea with the officer and sorted out the paperwork, which stated that henceforth my body and soul belonged entirely to the school, my new protector marched me off to collect my kit and bedding from the stores.

It was actually no distance, but to me the place appeared enormous, with rows of stone-built barrack blocks set around an enormous playing field, and a white ensign fluttering in the breeze. As we entered a building, my escort shoved me ahead of him down the corridor leading to the stores. To reach it I found I had to pass two older boys standing on each side of the corridor, and as I went to pass them they stretched out their legs, forcing me to stop. I asked as politely as I could if I could pass. But instead of answering they drew back their legs, then as I walked between them they hit me so hard in the face and around the head that I went down like a sack of shit, and got a further kicking as I lay on the floor. Then they stopped, and one of them asked, 'What're you doing there, moron? Feeling tired?' With that they lifted me to my feet, dusted me down and pushed me off along the corridor. My 'protector' totally ignored their behaviour, and ordered me to carry on and stand outside the door marked STORES while he had a friendly chat with my attackers. They all seemed quite amused by what had happened, and when they had finished laughing my escort joined me, knocked on the door and in we went.

I was told to take off my clothes and hand them over to the quartermaster, who simply guessed the size of what he gave me in return. In fact, the only things that fitted properly were the boots and shoes, because he took the trouble to ask what size I took. Soon I was loaded up with bedding, work clothes, uniform and, crowning everything, an official toothbrush, looking like a wire brush, and a tin of tooth-powder which took the enamel off my teeth.

As I staggered from the stores, loaded up with all these new possessions, the same two boys were standing in the corridor, and as I went to pass them they started on the same routine as before – except that this time they worked me over more thoroughly, leaving me with a split lip, a bloody nose and the beginnings of a badly blackened left eye. Then without a word they walked away, and my escort started yelling at me. 'Pick up your belongings, wanker. Don't just leave them getting dirty on the floor. And for fuck's sake don't start dripping blood all over them.'

With that, he led me to the dormitory, which from now on was to be my home, telling me to stow my gear in the locker room. 'Wash the blood off your fucking face. You look a disgrace. And for Christ's sake get a move on. They're waiting for us in the office.'

When I looked in the washroom mirror I could see my face was red and puffy and my eye was closing up. My nose had stopped bleeding, but as nothing would stop the blood oozing from my lip he gave me a cigarette paper, telling me to put a piece of it on the cut. This seemed to do the trick, and after marching me to the office at the double my escort had me standing with him at attention in front of the officer. On seeing the state that I was in, my probation officer nearly had a fit and jumped up from his chair.

'What on earth's happened to you, Wilf?' he said. But before I could explain, my escort answered, sweet as pie.

'I'm afraid, sir, that he fell over on the gravel while carrying all his bits and pieces from the stores.'

The officer, who was looking somewhat bored by now, asked, 'That correct, Pine?'

'Yes, sir,' I answered. 'It happened like he said.'

Turning to my probation officer, the officer smiled and said, 'Ah, well, these things do happen here from time to time.' Then, since the probation officer was just about to leave, he told me to see him to the main gate, then report back to the office.

As we walked down the drive, my probation officer asked me what had really happened, but I gave him the same answer as before. Obviously he didn't believe me, and he seemed genuinely upset, saying he didn't like leaving me there. I almost said, 'I wish to God you wouldn't', but I knew it would have made no difference, and I remember watching him cross the road and how I envied him as he caught the bus back to Newcastle – and the peace and tranquillity of the Isle of Wight.

The rest of the morning passed with a tour of the school in the company of a school lieutenant who, in contrast to his petty officer, Wilf found 'civilised and easy to talk to'. He showed him the workshops where the boys were taught useful trades for the future, like metalwork, painting and carpentry. He also mentioned that, if Wilf behaved himself, he might be considered for release before the expiry of his three-year sentence. Then a bugle sounded, and a hundred boys or more appeared as if from nowhere and began lining up in squads across the parade ground, each squad under the command of its own petty officer. When everything was in order, someone shouted the command, 'Attention. Right turn, quick march', and Wilf and the lieutenant watched as the whole school marched in strict parade-ground style to the dining room. Wilf and the lieutenant followed, and in the dining room he was told to get himself something to eat and report back to the office after lunch.

Life seemed to be improving. Wilf spent the afternoon doing nothing very much apart from sitting around and, when required, filling in yet further forms. Then at 4.30 he was ordered to the dining room, where he was served a mug of tea and bread and jam. Some of the boys he talked to seemed quite friendly, but on emerging from the dining room he found his petty officer 'protector' lining up his squad and checking that nobody was missing. Wilf joined them and did his best to march in step as they proceeded to the barrack block, where he had left his things that morning. While the rest of the squad was ordered to fall out, Wilf was told to go to the locker room to collect his kit and then wait outside the dormitory until he was summoned.

When he was, he saw that everybody in the dormitory was standing by his bed. The petty officer, who was at the far end of the aisle in front of a small stone platform, ordered Wilf to march towards him then halt. 'Now turn around,' he said.

Wilf turned. The whole dormitory was staring at him now, and

16

for a moment he wondered if he was in for some ceremony of welcome. But he also noticed a trail of muddy footprints which he had left down the length of the dormitory floor. It was the most highly polished floor he had seen in his life, and the next moment the petty officer was standing right in front of him, screaming in his face.

'You piece of shit. Just look what you've done. Do you know how hard these guys here work to keep the floor polished like that, and you think you have a right to walk all over it in those filthy fucking boots of yours. But we know how to deal with shit like you, don't we, boys?'

Wilf never saw the petty officer's head coming as he butted him straight between the eyes, knocking him to the floor. Then he grabbed him by his hair and dragged him to his feet again. 'Boys,' he said, 'you know what would happen to any of you if you'd done a thing like this. So you have my full permission to kick the shit out of him.' Which they did, one by one, taking turns until he finally passed out. Such was the welcome Wilf received from his shipmates on arriving at the Wellesley Nautical School.

'God knows how long I was unconscious,' he says, 'but when I came to I found myself in bed. How I got there I have no idea. I could just manage to see out of one eye, but later someone told me that when I tried sitting up I let out a scream loud enough to wake the dead. The pain made me pass out again, and I must have slept the rest of that night, as the next thing I knew was feeling my tormentor, the petty officer, prodding at me with his stick and telling me to get up, so that I'd be in shape for reveille when the bloody bugle sounded. He ordered two guys to take me to the washroom and make me presentable for parade. The boys must have been used to this sort of thing since, when they removed my pyjamas and saw my whole body was a mass of bruises, all that one of them remarked was: "For fuck's sake, look at the state of him." Apparently the one part of me that hadn't suffered too badly from the kicking was my head. When I hit the floor I'd instinctively rolled up in a ball and brought my arms up to shield my face. That was one of the few things in my life that I owed my father. I'd learned to do it instinctively when he started on

17

his larks, and it may have saved me getting seriously hurt. Thanks, Dad.'

Wilf always makes the point that there was nothing unusual in his treatment on arriving at the school. Some sort of beating up was part of the initiation of every new arrival, and as the school was run according to what he calls 'the law of the jungle' every boy received his share of the same sort of bullying and brutality that he endured. Just one thing might have made his punishment that much worse – the fact that he had muddied the sacred dormitory floor.

He realised the importance of that wretched floor next morning when reveille sounded. Between the early-morning roll call and being marched off for breakfast, everybody in the squad started beavering away, preparing the dormitory for inspection. Beds were shifted to the side of the room, and soon fifteen boys were on their knees in a dead straight line across the width of the dormitory. Each held a polishing rag, and the squad's 'leading hand' – 'after the petty officer the second toughest bastard in the division' – gave the orders. 'Arms straight, by the right, start polishing,' he shouted, and the fifteen boys began moving their arms in unison, with the leading hand counting out from one to twelve. This ritual continued until the length of the dormitory floor was gleaming.

While they were polishing the floor, the other boys in the dormitory were hard at work cleaning windows, scrubbing out the lavatories and polishing the brasswork for the officer's inspection later in the day. By 7.30 everything was shipshape, and the squad assembled outside to be marched to breakfast.

Wilf had never marched like this before and can't remember how he did it. What he does remember is that the agony of moving after being beaten up the night before nearly made him pass out again. Hot strong tea revived him, and from what the boys were saying he discovered that he might be lucky. This was the one Saturday in the month when school work stopped and the few boys who had earned the privilege were allowed out on town leave to Blyth. The others could relax around the school.

Then Wilf had a further stroke of luck. While at breakfast, someone had taken pity on him and made his bed up for him. This was as well, since bed-making was another of the complicated rituals that he would have to master before he could be accepted in the school. The sheets and blankets needed to be taken off and folded with mathematical precision, then the mattress doubled over so that each bed looked identical.

By now he was feeling so battered and unwell that all he could think of was spending the weekend lying down. But as this would have meant unrolling the mattress and untidying his bed, he knew he couldn't do this without somebody's permission.

'Ask the petty officer,' suggested one of the boys who had asked him how he felt. 'You never know how the bugger will react.'

Feeling he had little left to lose, Wilf walked over to where the PO was standing.

'Ah, Pine,' he said as he approached. 'I was going to send for you. How're you feeling?'

'How was I feeling? Ten years later if I'd had a gun I'd have blown his fucking head off. Instead, quick as you like I had the sense to say, "Not bad, but if I could lie down when everyone else is out it would really help my ribs and legs, which are killing me".'

Sweet as sugar he replied, 'Fine,' then added that he was getting Wilf excused next morning's Sunday church parade. 'The state your face is in after falling over yesterday wouldn't look too good to the rest of the congregation,' he explained. 'Oh, and while you're lying down, make sure you keep your body covered just in case the duty officer comes around. We wouldn't want him getting any wrong ideas about you, would we? Now fuck off.'

'Bloody hell,' I thought. 'Perhaps there is a God.'

After a weekend more or less recovering in bed, on Monday morning Wilf began the lessons that were officially intended to provide him with a useful trade for the future when his sentence finally ended. Since he lacked any ordinary skills, he was assigned to the paint shop where the elderly officer in charge gave him the task of cleaning and making good fifty or so old paintbrushes left behind by others who hadn't bothered to clean them. It was such boring work that Wilf says that he could understand why they hadn't done so, and hasn't cleaned a paintbrush himself from that day since, but at the time the work suited him. It meant he didn't have to bend or to exert himself, and he was able to spin out the work for two whole days, at the end of which the brushes looked like new and the instructor said that a conscientious boy like him would make a good painter and decorator if he stuck at it.

So Wilf stayed on in the paint shop, while in the dormitory he joined the others polishing the floor each morning, and the deadening routine began to make him feel as if he'd been in the school for ever. Even the bugle call became part of his existence. He hated it in the morning when it dragged him out of bed, but he enjoyed it when it summoned him to eat and told him it was time to finish work.

Apart from polishing the dormitory floor, which he always loathed, he began accepting the routine of daily life. Even now he insists that one emotion that he didn't feel was homesickness. 'As long as my father was in the house, all I wanted was to be as far away as possible.' When it came to it, he could cope with the brutality which formed the basis of the strict discipline of the school. Having put up with beatings from his father all his life, he could even accept the routine violence of the petty officers and leading hands against the boys as part of his existence.

He started making friends among a few members of his dormitory. As he says, it's not easy finding friends in this sort of environment, so he counted himself lucky to end up with three. 'We were very close,' he says, 'and the bond between us helped to see us through.'

Like his friends, he soon came to the conclusion that in the long run the only way to get away from the school as soon as possible was 'to play the authorities' game' and go along with whatever was on offer. One thing they all enjoyed was walking and rock-climbing in places like the nearby Cheviot Hills, and for the first time in his life Wilf found himself loving nature and being in the open air. 'The only downside came when you returned and had to face another fucking Monday morning.'

Once back at school there was something else he never did get used to and finally refused to accept. This was the bullying that was rife throughout the school, and the day dawned when he decided he would make a stand against it.

It happened when a pair of petty officers picked on me as a victim when they were having bets on who could knock a boy the furthest with a single punch. It was the sort of bloody silly thing they often did. Most of the lads got caught up in their games at some time or other, and I just happened to be passing when this pair decided they would use me for a bit of sport.

To tell the truth, I didn't mind too much about being punched by now. It hurt, of course, but I'd had so many beatings in my time that being punched around was like water off a duck's back. I took it as a fact of life. But this time everything was different. While those two bastards were having their spot of fun with me, I realised I'd had enough. That night I lay in bed and for a long time couldn't sleep. By the time I did I'd made my mind up. Rather than be kicked around like this for the rest of my life, I was going to do something about it.

But what? Wilf had fantasies of stabbing one of them or smashing his head in with a chunk of wood, but he also knew that there was really no way of striking back at these bullies without being beaten to a pulp himself and getting into serious trouble with the school authorities. As he says, the one reason everyone accepted this sort of bullying was simple – fear and the instinct of self-preservation.

But as he lay in bed plotting his revenge, it struck him that there *was* one way of getting even. He'd seen how, when the petty officers got bored or felt like showing off, they'd pick on somebody they didn't like, go to an officer and say they wanted a grudge fight with their victim.

Grudge fights went back to the early days of the Royal Navy as a way of settling arguments below decks. The rules were simple. Provided both parties agreed to it, the fight took place before the whole ship's company – in this case the entire school, assembled in the gym. There were no rounds, no seconds or timekeepers, and the fight had to end with a knockout. The referee was one of the officers whose job was simply to ensure that whoever ended up on the canvas was well and truly out for the count.

Since arriving at the school, Wilf had witnessed several of these fights. They always followed the same pattern, with the victim virtually defeated before he even entered the ring. Nobody wanted trouble with a petty officer, and for the sake of a peaceful life the victim would usually act like a punch-bag during the fight and end up on the canvas as quickly as possible. But none of this worried Wilf by now, and when as luck would have it another petty officer picked on him for a bit of sport, he went straight to the duty officer and told him he wanted a grudge fight in return.

'Are you taking the piss or are you raving mad?' the officer said. 'Just do yourself a favour and get out of my sight before I tell him what you've said.'

But Wilf repeated his request, and the officer realised that he was serious.

'On your head be it, then,' he muttered, 'But don't say I didn't warn you.'

Wilf had psyched himself up to make the challenge, but now that he'd done it he was seized by the enormity of what he'd done, particularly when the duty officer appeared together with the petty officer, having just told him about the challenge. The petty officer suddenly looked bigger than he remembered.

'You want to fight with me?' he said. 'For what reason, or has someone been putting you up to it?'

Wilf shook his head but didn't answer.

'Well, if that's what you want, you prick, I'm willing to oblige. But remember one thing: it was your choice.'

One of the rules of grudge fights was that they took place as soon as possible to stop the grudge continuing, and by the time Wilf had returned to his own dormitory his petty officer and the leading hand had already got wind of what he'd done. Neither could believe it.

'Is it true?' they asked, and when he said it was they burst out laughing. They told the rest of the dormitory, most of whom joined in the laughter, which increased when the duty officer appeared announcing that the fight would be held in the gym between teatime and recreation. Just a few of Wilf's close friends stuck by him, offering advice on how to fight, none of which he could remember. Then during tea the jokes went on when someone shouted out: 'It's Pine's last supper.'

But none of this mattered now. As there was no going back, all he could think of was that whatever happened he would give the contest everything he'd got and make sure that his opponent knew he'd been in a real fight by the end of it.

When the school was assembled in the gym, someone rang a bell, the referee shouted, 'Come out fighting', and Wilf in shorts and gym shoes went into the attack. He lacked experience as a boxer and was smaller than his opponent,

'So he took me for a pushover and wasn't concentrating when I went for him and caught him with a body shot. I could tell I'd hurt him from the look in his eyes, which gave me such a rush of adrenalin that it spurred me on. The trouble was it did the same for him, and he caught me with a dandy of a left hook, but I hardly felt it. Then I started catching him and hurting him and vice versa, and I was starting to enjoy myself until we went into a clinch and he nutted me above my right eye and the blood started pissing everywhere. Not that I even really minded that. By now we were slamming lefts and rights at each other and I felt I could go on for ever.

'They always say you never see the knockout blow coming, but afterwards someone told me it was the sort of perfect right cross to the chin that if properly delivered you don't get up from. I didn't. When I came round the last of the boys was filing out of the gym and one of the officers was trying to patch the cut above my eye.'

After the fight Wilf expected something to happen, but nothing did. The school was, after all, a penal institution and as he says 'all penal institutions are run on the same rigid lines of boredom, monotony and a strict regime'. This meant that one day was much like any other, and the only things that seemed to change at Blyth were the seasons. After the Isle of Wight, winter on the north-east coast was cold and bitter. Spring wasn't that much better – cold and windy with bursts of sunshine if you were lucky – and the few summer days passed all too quickly.

One gets some idea of the crucifying boredom of his life from one event that happened now and brought him more pleasure and excitement than anything since his arrival at the school.

One morning shortly after reveille Wilf was down on his knees, as he was at this time every morning of his life, not praying but polishing the dormitory floor. The petty officer was walking past and, for no reason Wilf could think of, ordered him to his feet, then shouted to one of the other boys who was polishing the windows.

"You there, you're back on deck [as the floor was called] and you, Pine, will take his place on window duty from now on. And jump to it, both of you.'

'At that moment,' says Wilf, 'I could believe that God had sent an angel to sit on my shoulder. My months of slavery to that fucking floor were over. Later, I worked out that I had spent six months and thirteen days polishing the bloody floor each morning of my life, and to this day I have the knees to prove it.'

But before Wilf could enjoy his freedom from bondage to the floor, he was hit by a tragedy involving one of the very few people in the school whom he was fond of. This was a nervous, white-faced boy of about his own age who had joined the school ahead of him. To start with, Wilf had thought him far too weak and sensitive to survive. But the more he talked to him, the more he learned how wrong he was and that, unlike Wilf, he was a genuine rebel who wouldn't knuckle under to anybody in authority. Wilf admired him for that.

He told Wilf that after the break-up of his parents' marriage he had been sent to a children's home for being out of control, but he ran away and lived by petty thieving until he was caught and, this time, was sent to an approved school from which he also ran way. From then on, escape and capture formed the pattern of his life until he ended up at Blyth, which was as far away as possible from contact with any member of his family who might have helped him. He told Wilf that since arriving he had 'done a bunk' twice already, but said he didn't really care what happened to him any more. All he did know was that he 'wasn't taking any more shit from anybody in the school', and that when he had the chance he'd be off again. A few days after Wilf was freed from the dormitory floor, he went. As Wilf recalled:

> None of us had an inkling that he was going over the fence that night, and even if we had I don't think we could have talked him out of it. For two or three days after he went missing none

of us knew what had become of him. Then when daily orders were being read out, as they always were following morning parade, it was announced that he'd been captured and that an officer and escort were already on their way to bring him back. But, as he intended all along, he never did come back.

All that day we waited for further news, but none came. All I knew was that by that evening after recreation, when we were back in the dormitory, one of my pals called out: 'Where the fuck's his bedding?' All there was was the bare metal bedstead where he had always slept. I checked his personal locker above his bed. It was empty. So was the locker by his bedside, where he kept his pyjamas and his washing things. It was as if he'd never been there at all.

True to form, while we were discussing what had happened, our petty officer told us all to shut up and get our beds made as the lights would soon be going out. But next morning we learned what had occurred. The whole school was assembled after breakfast, and the captain solemnly informed us that my pal would not be returning to the school, as he had taken his life before the escort arrived to bring him back.

Did I cry? Yes, buckets full. It was the only time throughout my stay in that godforsaken place that I ever shed a tear. So did a lot of us. We'd all known him and admired him and he was one of us. He was just sixteen.

During the days that followed, the school buzzed with rumours over how he died. No one seemed to know for sure, and there were umpteen versions, including one that the police had killed him. Later an officer told us what seemed to be the truth – that he had hanged himself in a police cell the night after they caught him. When he was discovered, they tried to resuscitate him – but to no avail. He was certified dead on arrival at the hospital.

In the days following his death we often discussed among ourselves why he did it. Ultimately, of course, nobody knew the answer. But there was one thing I did know, having witnessed it myself. This was what happened to an escapee like him when he was caught and brought back to the school.

It was another of those fixed routines that never changed. First, he would be taken to the main office, where he would have been informed in front of the captain that he was charged with escaping. Had he anything to say? They never had because there was no arguing against what they'd done. So the captain would pass sentence there and then, which once again never varied – so many strokes on the bare backside with a wicked-looking cane. The captain might increase or diminish the exact number of strokes, depending on how he was feeling and whether this was a first offence. As my friend had gone missing twice already, he'd have known that he'd be facing up to a severe caning, administered there and then over a chair in the captain's office by a guy we all knew to be the toughest, meanest officer in the school.

But that wouldn't be the end of it. There was more to come which, knowing my friend as I did, would have been harder to stomach than the flogging, and it was something he had gone through twice already. As soon as the punishment was over, the offender had to face one final humiliation which, like the sentence, never varied. Once he had pulled up his trousers he would be marched out of the captain's office to the parade ground, where the whole school would be standing at attention. Then in front of us all he would be made to stand and apologise for what he'd done and for letting down his schoolmates and his teachers and bringing disrepute upon the good name of the school.

Knowing this, I could understand why he preferred to top himself rather than go through with it again.

This was Wilf's first, but not his last, experience of suicide, which always affected him more deeply than any other sort of death. In this case he was tormented by all manner of unanswered questions to which he knew there was no answer. But as he brooded over his friend's death, his mood turned sullen and he took to heart one lesson it had taught him.

He says that what he learned was that, death apart, there was no escape from his situation. 'However hard you try, the bastards always catch you in the end. So instead of trying to escape, I made up my mind to do the opposite. I'd stay and fight and let the future take care of itself.'

After that first grudge fight, I found I'd made a lot of new and unexpected enemies apart from the petty officers. They were what I called 'the up and comings', would-be bullies who fancied themselves as fighters and joined the petty officers' 'crew', as they called it.

A week or so after my pal's death, I was put on painting the outside toilet block. I had just come from the paint shop, when one of these so-called tough guys started taking the piss out of me. As he had a couple of crew members with him I ignored him and carried on into the shit-house when, Bang! – my head hit the wall. I spun round and grabbed the bastard, only to see an officer standing right behind him. Before anyone could start any fancy tricks, I started shouting at the officer that I wanted a grudge fight with this bastard. And the bastard started screaming back that it was OK with him. Permission was granted there and then, and the fight was fixed for the usual period after tea.

So here I was in the same situation as I had been a few weeks earlier with the petty officer. But by now I'd learned a thing or two and used my brain as well as my fists. And in the end it wasn't me lying on the canvas being counted out. It was my opponent.

Once I'd started I began to see these grudge fights as my way of fighting back. With every fight I became that much better, and every time I won I felt I was avenging that dead friend of mine. I'd nothing to lose and began enjoying the excitement. Before long I became a serial grudge-fighting lunatic with three or four more fights within a six-week period, all of which ended with KOs by yours truly. All involved members of the petty officers' crew, and to be honest I started most of them myself. For the first time in my life I was getting something I had never ever known before – respect from those around me – and I must admit it tasted very sweet.

The only exceptions were, of course, the officers, who started getting worried over what I was up to, and in the end one of them took me before the captain after I requested permission for yet another fight. My request was turned down, and I was told that from now on this would always happen. Enough was enough; my days as a serial grudge-fighting lunatic were over, and the captain said that if I knew what was good for me I'd keep my head down and stay out of trouble.

As my old friend Freddie Foreman once told me after serving a twelve-year stretch, there is one thing the prison authorities can never stop: the clock ticking and time passing. Time even passed at Blyth, and over the next few months it seemed that most of the petty officers and leading hands who had given me such grief were nearing the end of their sentences and being released on licence. They were the worst of the school bullies and when they went things changed and the atmosphere was no longer as oppressive as before. Of course, the fights and the dramas continued, but on nothing like the scale they had earlier. I took the advice of the captain, said as little as possible to the officers and stayed out of trouble. But I also had the sense to cash in on the reputation my brief career as a gladiator had earned me, and actually earned the congratulations of the captain when I boxed successfully for my division.

But to my amazement there was more to come. A few days later I was summoned to his office and offered the job of petty officer. Did I want it? You can bet your life I did. And did I become a bastard? Yes, I did. But did I bully and terrify some poor sod who'd just arrived like me, terrified and hardly knowing where he was? NO WAY!

When you've been punched and kicked around by others for the hell of it, unless you're really sick you don't start doing it to others when you get the chance. I've always hated bullies and I've never been one myself. But now I had my little bit of power I made the most of it. The truth was that the school *had* actually taught me something. It wasn't what the authorities intended, but it was something which has stayed with me for life.

This lesson is that weakness never pays, any more than trying to escape. For guys like me, life is a battle from the day you're born and there's no alternative except to go on fighting. But you must also use your intelligence, never resort to bullying, and try to earn respect from those around you.

I say all this because of the strange way my time at the school came to an end. As I've said, I was due to serve three years, thanks to that kindly magistrate, but at the beginning of February 1961 I was summoned once again to the captain's office. I remember him as a big fat man, and that day he was in a kindly mood. He had some faceless character in a blue suit sitting beside him, and the captain introduced him as a gentleman from the Home Office, who wished to see me. He also wished to hear my school's report, which would now be read out in my presence.

When my report was read out, I was frankly amazed. Apart from the usual shit that everybody gets about bits of trouble I'd got into, the assessment of my work and what they called my 'attitude' wasn't bad at all. There was something about the way I'd boxed for my division, and how conscientiously – I liked that: conscientiously, indeed! – I had performed my duties as a petty officer.

'Any comments, Pine?' the captain asked.

'None, sir.'

'Then I take it you're happy with that report?'

'Yes, sir. Very happy, sir.'

With that I was marched out and told to wait in the lobby until I was summoned. I still hadn't the faintest idea what was going on, but knowing the school I guessed it was probably something unpleasant. I may have been kept waiting twenty minutes or so, but it felt like for ever before the captain's door opened and I was marched back in.

It was one of the few occasions when I saw the captain actually smiling.

'Pine, I am pleased to inform you that, subject to you being found gainful employment and a suitable place of residence, you are to be released immediately on licence. Congratulations, Pine.'

'Thank you, sir,' I said, about-turned, and marched out of the office, wondering if I was dreaming.

I asked one of the officers in the outer office if it was all for real. He said it was. That night I wrote home, telling my mother of the day's events and that all being well she could expect me back within a week or two. WRONG AGAIN!

Once more my old man was the spanner in the works. I heard nothing from my mother and weeks began to pass without a word about my fate. I started to worry, but whenever I asked one of the officers what was happening about my release I always got the same reply: 'Pine, you must understand. These things take time.'

March arrived and still no news, not even from my mother. Normally she instantly replied to my letters, but she hadn't answered the last two I had sent, and I really began to worry. So one evening during recreation, when we had one of the rare visits of the captain in our midst, I took my courage in my hands and actually asked him what was going on. I realised that I was very much out of order doing this and expected him to tell me to speak to my divisional officer – but he didn't.

'Come outside,' he said. 'There's too much noise in here to talk properly.' And once outside the recreation room he broke the news to me. 'We've been in touch with your family, Pine, trying to explain that as a condition of your licence you have to have a permanent abode and regular employment. I've personally written several letters to your father on the subject and the day before yesterday I finally received a reply. I've been trying to decide how to break the news to you.'

He looked so grim that I remember asking the first thing that came into my head. 'Is there something wrong with my mother, sir ?'

'No, Pine, I'm glad to say there's nothing like that. It's your father. I'm afraid he says he doesn't want you living in his house, nor will he help in any way to find you an employer. All I can say is that I'm very sorry, and that if you want us to, the school will try to find you a job and somewhere to live. Sleep on it and let your divisional officer have your decision in the morning.'

Back in the recreation room, my pals started asking me what my conversation with the boss had been about, but all I said to them was, 'Fuck off!'

I wasn't in the mood to speak to anyone. Nor did I imagine I would ever get to sleep as I couldn't believe this, even of my father. But somehow I dropped off, and the next thing I knew was that bloody bugle starting up again telling us all to rise and shine and face another day. I think it was the thought of this that made my mind up for me. Rather than go on with that boring, soul-destroying routine, I'd do absolutely anything, sweep the roads, clean out the public lavatories, and live in a tin hut at the end of somebody's back yard. Anything. So I found the duty officer and asked him to tell the captain I'd accept his offer.

A few days later I was interviewed by a probation officer from Newcastle. He struck me as a decent sort of fellow and said that if I was prepared to work in the Newcastle area he thought he could find work and accommodation for me. I was so desperate to get away that I'd have accepted a job in a coal-mine in Alaska if he'd offered it.

What he did come up with two weeks later was the offer of a job as a foundry-hand in a local engineering company and a bed in a hostel in Newcastle. It was only later I discovered just how hard he'd worked on my behalf, and I'll always be grateful, especially as he'd arranged with the school bursar to set th wheels in motion so I could leave the school for ever first th Saturday morning.

During the next two days I was kitted out in civilian cl and finally given the terms of my licence, together wit itinerary, telephone numbers and the address of the hoste my place of work, which that wonderful probation off prepared for me. After I'd said goodbye to one final person I had to see – th

I must say he was ver the school. me the stand in good stead for the fut

But what had I learned? Just a few things which I'm sure the captain wouldn't have thought about. First and foremost, I had learned how to fight and to survive in a world in which I'd also learned that dog eats dog. But more important still I'd vowed I would never let anyone ever lay a hand on me again, without them receiving even worse from me in return. I also learned a lot about body-art. When I entered the school, the identifying marks on my body were two small scars, one on each knee. On leaving the school, both hands and a great deal of my body was covered in tattoos.

Of course, I didn't say this to the captain. Instead we shook hands and I thanked him and we wished each other well. Then as I started walking down the drive carrying the cheap suitcase containing everything I owned, I couldn't help remembering how I'd walked my old probation officer from the Isle of Wight down that same drive on the day that I arrived to catch the next bus back to Newcastle and the peace and tranquillity of the island. Now it was March 1961, and it was me crossing the road to catch the bus to Newcastle, but sadly not to the Isle of Wight.

CHEERS DAD!

3

Return to the Island

WILF HAD NEVER seen a blast furnace in his life and was awe-struck by his first sight of the place where he would work. As high as a six-storey house, and spewing out white-hot molten iron, the furnace reminded him of pictures he had seen as a child of an erupting volcano with the lava flowing out of it. The heat in the foundry was intense, as groups of men stood waiting for the moment when the molten iron was ready to be poured.

While they waited, the foreman introduced him to the man he would be working with. A short, stocky man in his early forties, his name was Tom, and Wilf remembers him as 'a man with a smile big enough to light up Blackpool pier'.

As Wilf discovered, Tom was as kind-hearted as he was cheerful. So were his workmates, who made him welcome in a way he'd never really known before. As he spent the morning helping to prepare the moulds to take the molten iron, he was struck by the contrast between them and the staff at Blyth, who, although dressed up as naval officers, were little more than glorified prison warders. 'These were rock-hard men, working all day on a dirty, dangerous job, but what they gave out was an air of laughter and togetherness. Nothing ever seemed to get them down,' says Wilf, and he soon caught something of their spirit.

But at lunchtime he became uneasy. Someone produced a crate of beer. Because of the heat, each man received a bottle apiece from the management, and everyone had his own lunch box. No one at the hostel had mentioned anything to Wilf about taking sandwiches to work, so he asked Tom where he could buy something to eat.

'Sit your arse down, bonny lad, and share mine,' was the reply.

33

And soon it wasn't only Tom who was offering him something. 'Suddenly it seemed that everyone in hearing distance had been given too many sandwiches by his wife.' No sooner had he finished one than another was shoved into his hand, followed by the offer of a drink. This was Wilf's first taste of the brew that made his native city famous – Newcastle's own Brown Ale, or 'Nukey Brown', as beer-drinkers the world over call it. It was also the first alcoholic drink he'd tasted in his life.

But it wasn't just Nukey Brown that impressed him. It was the character of the Geordies, the ordinary people of Newcastle, with their combination of courage and generosity and their never-failing sense of humour. 'Over the weeks to come I found myself wondering what was the secret ingredient that makes Geordies what they are. I never could discover, but if anybody knows he should bottle it along with Nukey Brown,' says Wilf. 'He'd make a fortune.'

He was to get a foretaste of Geordie kindness when work was over. He'd been working hard all day, preparing the moulds and lugging around the heavy iron containers in which the foundry-men carried the molten ore from the furnace. It was hot, heavy work, and afterwards, when Tom and his workmates went as usual to the local pub, they took Wilf with them and offered him a drink. Still not certain whether he really liked the taste of beer, he settled for a pint of orange juice instead, and in the easy atmosphere of the pub someone asked the question he'd been dreading from the start. Where did he work before he came to Newcastle?

Something told him it would be unwise to lie, so he blurted out the truth, and for an uncomfortable few moments a stony silence settled on the bar. Then Wilf saw that Tom was grinning. "Just as well you told us, bonny lad, because we knew already,' he said drily and everybody started laughing.

That evening, for the first time in his life Wilf realised what it meant to be accepted by everyone around him, and it was much the same when he returned to the hostel, covered in dust and grime from his first day's work. Almost everyone staying in the hostel was a white-collar worker, but far from anyone remarking on Wilf's appearance, they couldn't have been more welcoming – this despite the fact that, as he discovered later, everyone already knew where he had come from.

But for real warmth and kindness, Tom and his fellow foundry-workers had no rivals in the way they looked after this unknown seventeen-year-old who'd just been thrust on them from an approved school. As well as continuing to take him for a drink most evenings after work, they invited him to their homes, introduced him to their families, and on Saturdays even shared with him the highlight of their week – watching Newcastle United when they were playing on their home ground at St James's Park. But however hard Wilf tried enjoying soccer, his real interests lay elsewhere. Having had little experience of girls, at seventeen he was getting anxious to make up for lost time and was grateful when his younger workmates offered to introduce him to some local girls.

This led to another new experience – his first real girlfriend. Her name was Ann, she was a miner's daughter from a village called Ashington, and Wilf still remembers her as 'gorgeous'. Soon she too was asking him home to meet her family, and this in turn led to what he calls 'a real eye-opener'. Arriving in time for Saturday lunch, he was greeted by Ann and her mother, a dainty little woman who barely reached his chest. She was extraordinarily warm and welcoming and said that unfortunately Ann's father had had to work an extra shift down the pit, but would be back in time for tea at four. At 3.15 Ann and her mother started boiling water on the fire which Ann said was for her father's bath. In those days miners' cottages didn't run to bathrooms and when the water was ready a tin bath was produced, set before the roaring fire and filled with water. At four on the dot, in walked the master of the house, and as they shook hands he apologised to Wilf for meeting him like this and asked to be excused while he took off his clothes and had his bath.

Until now, Wilf had always thought that *he* got dirty, slaving away all day in the heat and grime of the foundry, but when Ann's father had removed his clothes and climbed into the bath, Wilf saw that every inch of his body was engrained with coal-dust. Then, while Ann's mother started scrubbing the coal-dust off his back, he began chatting to Wilf as if he'd known him for years.

That evening, after a full roast dinner in his honour, Wilf slept on a put-you-up in the front room, and by the time the weekend was over he was in love, not just with Ann but with the whole family, who were so hospitable that they were already inviting him to come again. But this was not to be, for, as Wilf hastened to explain, he was about to leave Newcastle for good, despite the kindness of his many new-found friends, including Ann and her family.

What had happened was that, almost from the moment when he walked down the drive at Blyth for the last time and sniffed the precious air of freedom, he was overcome by a longing for the south. Although by birth a Geordie, the fact was that he was a southerner by adoption, and despite the warmth he had discovered in his native city the call of the south increasingly obsessed him. On his first night in the hostel, the first thing he had done was ring his mother. Since it would be many years before the Pine household could run to the expense of a telephone, he got her at the bar in Ryde where she still worked six days a week as a cleaner. It was the first time they had spoken for a year and a half, and although she was thrilled to hear him she had no idea that he had even been recommended for release, still less that he was actually free.

She soon realised what must have happened and explained why she had not replied to his recent letters. Again his father was to blame. Each morning, on his way to work, the old man would always meet the postman and take the mail so that Millie would be lucky to see anything addressed to her later that evening when he returned from the pub. But since he always read each letter first, regardless of who it was addressed to, he must have thrown Wilf's away, rather than be bothered with him any more.

Wilf and his mother, on the other hand, were thrilled to be in touch at last and couldn't wait to see each other. But there were problems. There was his job in the foundry, and there were his new-found friends, including Ann; above all, Wilf had to have permission from his probation officer before he could leave Newcastle. All of this took time to organise, but the longer he had to wait the more Wilf realised he had to go. He had been happier during his few months in Newcastle than he had for years, and had he been different he could obviously have made a successful life there, settled down, finally married Ann or someone like her, and the extraordinary life that lay in wait for him would not have happened.

Instead, it was as if the Isle of Wight, together with his father's cruelty, his status as an outcast from his school and from his Church, and the brutal lessons he had learned so well at Blyth, was part of the destiny life had in store for him. These separate influences, along with memories of friends and hopes of fresh adventures, had made the seventeen-year-old Wilf Pine unalterably what he was. And by the time he had finally obtained permission from his probation officer to return to Ryde, said goodbye to the men at the foundry and promised Ann that they would meet again (which, of course, they never did), he was ready for the next act in the violent drama of his life.

As he made the four-hour journey from Newcastle Central to King's Cross, Wilf had much to look forward to. As well as the precious 'peace and tranquillity' of the island, the thought of which he said had haunted him during his first days at Blyth, there was his mother and the two young sisters whom he barely knew. Besides this, Millie had told him that his brother Bernie was back from the sea after two years with the merchant navy, following *his* period in the approved school. Wilf couldn't wait to see him. Millie also told him 'she had squared things with the old man', who had grudgingly agreed to let him live at home, while Bernie, who was now working for the local council, had fixed him an interview the following Monday for a job working alongside him.

So one can understand why Wilf was in such good spirits as he took the familiar ferryboat across the Solent and found himself in good old Ryde again. The town looked more prosperous than he remembered, and he was taking it for granted that after the welcome he received from so many strangers in Newcastle he would be in for something even better from his friends and relatives in the town where he grew up.

Wrong again! In the first place he discovered that his parents had moved from the old neighbourhood, and instead of the friendly neighbours he remembered the new lot seemed unpleasantly suspicious from the start. Of course, it was wonderful seeing his mother and Bernie, who was now a strapping nineteen-year-old and could no longer be kicked around by their father. Nor could Wilf, after graduating with honours from his survival course at Blyth. 'But although the old man couldn't get up to his tricks any more, he remained his unpleasant self to me and Bernie, except that now he could only attack us with abuse,' says Wilf.

That same evening he got a clearer notion still of how far things had changed when Bernie took him to the local pub for a drink to celebrate his return. 'I think the reputation of the Pine brothers must have preceded us,' he says. 'As soon as we entered, you could have cut the atmosphere in the saloon bar with a knife. Not that Bernie took much notice. Bernie, as anyone who knew him will tell you, was never at a loss for words, nor was he scared of anyone. "Has someone died?" he asked in a loud voice. And when no one answered, he announced: "This is my brother, Wilf. We'd like a drink." At his words, the landlord couldn't have moved faster to take their order if he'd tried, and everybody in the bar suddenly became noticeably polite.

After this uneasy homecoming, Wilf was surprised that his interview the following Monday morning at the local council offices went so well and that he got the job he wanted working with his brother. This pleased him in more ways than one, for as well as being able to pay Millie a contribution to the household budget, and still have money of his own, it also meant that he could inform his probation officer that he was now in regular employment. This was important, for having been released on licence from an approved school before the completion of his sentence, he could have been packed off back to Blyth if he hadn't found himself a job.

The job itself was also to his liking. Had it involved working with middle-class, white-collar colleagues, or an authoritarian foreman who threw his weight around, he'd not have stayed a week. Instead, he found himself working at the local council yard, where the foreman was somebody he knew already. This was Ted Potts, a sharp but very likeable old-timer, whose son, David, used to be a friend of Wilf's at school.

Wilf's first job was working as relief dustman on any of the council dustcarts when somebody was off sick or on holiday. From the start he got on famously with the other dustmen, some of whom were great characters, and all of them had a strong sense of loyalty to the crews they worked with. Each crew seemed to have some individual, usually the driver, with a special nickname. There was a six-foot, one-inch gentle giant nicknamed 'Lofty Goldup'. 'General Stillwell' was a former army man who still wore his regimental badge and beret. 'There was,' says Wilf, 'the lovely Cab Calloway, named after the American bandleader of the 1930s.' But his favourite was 'Chin' Grinham, whose real name was Bill. He came from Oakfield and remembered Wilf as a child.

In fact, Wilf got along with almost everyone and soon felt entirely accepted. From the start he loved the job. He was strong, he enjoyed working in the open air and began to appreciate the beauty of the island, together with other sorts of beauty. For after eighteen months of sex-starvation at the training school at Blyth, Wilf was starting to discover that a surprising number of Ryde's female population had an eye for a young, good-looking council dustman.

As well as being so surprisingly enjoyable, his job also started working wonders for his need for security and self-respect, until a fresh disaster threatened to destroy whatever hopes he'd had of a trouble-free life since leaving Blyth.

The trouble blew up after what was meant to be a fairly harmless practical joke. He and a friend had bought some leftover Chinese firecrackers and had thought it funny to set them off in Lofty Goldup's cab while he was drinking his lunchtime cup of tea. What they hadn't realised was that Lofty couldn't bear the sound of loud explosions after experiences as a soldier in the war and was badly shaken. He was also very angry when Wilf and his friend owned up. Despite their deep apologies, he said he was going to report them to the foreman.

So next morning, when Ted Potts took Wilf aside and said he wanted a serious word with him, he thought it was over Lofty and the fireworks. But as soon as Wilf started to apologise, Ted looked puzzled. What he wished to talk to him about had nothing to do with fireworks. It was about a visit he had had the day before from a policeman in search of information about Wilf Pine. The policeman had asked which wagon he was working on, on certain dates, and whether he appeared to have more money than he earned. When Ted asked the reason for these questions, the reply was that the police were investigating a series of local burglaries, and because Wilf had only just arrived from an approved school it was possible he was the culprit.

At this point Ted asked point-blank if the policeman intended to arrest Wilf. 'Not yet,' he said. 'So far we haven't any proof. That's why I'm asking you.'

'Well, officer, if you haven't any proof,' said Ted, 'I intend to tell young Wilf every word of our conversation. And now good day to you.'

Ted was as good as his word. Wilf angrily denied the accusations and asked Ted if he believed him.

'Of course I do,' said Ted. 'If I didn't you'd be out of this yard and walking up the road right now.'

Wilf thanked him and returned to work. But all that day he was fuming to himself, and the more he thought about it all the angrier he became.

Had he been older and wiser, he would have realised that he was in a horribly vulnerable position. As an approved school boy recently released on licence, any trouble with the law would guarantee a swift return to Blyth. But since, for once, he was completely innocent, and Ted and his workmates would have supported him, the best course would have been to have said nothing until the police came up with some definite evidence against him – which he knew they never could.

But when angry, Wilf Pine wasn't wise, and the character created by those years of rejection and abuse was not easily placated. The strongest influence on his behaviour now came from the very lessons he had had at Blyth. The grudge fights had taught him that the surest answer to injustice 'in a world where dog eats dog' lay in fighting back rather than passively accepting. And he had meant it when he vowed that in future he would not let anybody harm him without retaliating even stronger in return.

So all that he could think about that day was getting even with the policeman who had been spreading totally unfounded accusations against him. Ted had told him who he was, and it turned out that Wilf already knew him. He was the local bobby in the nearby village of Binstead, and after work Wilf went straight to the police house where he lived. He says that he had no idea in advance how to play it, nor does he know what prompted him to walk around the back of the house instead of knocking on the front door.

Since it was summertime, the back door of the house was open, and who should be sitting at a table in the garden with his sleeves rolled up, drinking an off-duty glass of beer, but the man he wanted.

'At the sight of him I completely lost it,' says Wilf. ' can remember asking him if he'd been round to the yard questioning the foreman about me and showing people my photograph. When he said, yes, he had, the smug arrogance of the man got to me. I suppose he was counting on me saying: "Yes, officer. No, officer. Three bags full, officer." Instead, I pulled him out of his chair and dragged him into the garden, screaming every four-letter word I knew at him. He started shouting back that he was only doing his job, at which I said he could have made me lose *my* job, so what the fuck was he on about? God alone knows how I stopped myself from chinning him, but somehow I did. Then I let him go and stood there, expecting him to say: "I'm arresting you for assaulting a police officer." When he didn't, I just turned around and walked away.

'I was feeling pretty cocky, I suppose. All I could think of was that he knew that if he tried to treat me like a dog again I'd behave like a dog and bite him back. At the time I really didn't give a shit for whatever happened to me next. But the odd thing was that nothing did. No summons from the law. Not even a complaint to my probation officer. Nothing. So I suppose I must have been feeling pretty pleased with myself when Christmas 1962 arrived. I was still in my job, and as an extra Christmas present I received official confirmation that I no longer had to report to my probation officer. My sentence was officially over.'

Wilf remembers 1962 for the way the 'big freeze' hit the island. But despite the cold and the discomfort of clinging to a dustcart on a frosty morning, he was enjoying life. As a cheery dustman, he discovered that he had a way with women, and he also had a regular girlfriend, a pretty girl from Cowes called Jill. They were going steady. She would generally come over to see him twice a week on the bus from Cowes, but this didn't stop him enjoying himself for the rest of the week. If his evenings often ended with a row and a punch-up in a local pub, Wilf was better trained than most to defend himself.

It was this that set him on the next stage in his life of violence after a night out drinking in a pub at Sandown. With his quick temper and his ready fists, eighteen-year-old Wilf was not the man to choose for an argument and the two would-be tough guys who picked on him that night should have known better.

He had been developing his skills as a bar fighter since leaving Blyth, and was not averse to a good old-fashioned brawl. The fact that he was taking on two opponents didn't worry him, and he was just starting to enjoy the fight when suddenly he felt himself being grabbed from behind and lifted off his feet.

Had he been more careful over where he drank, he would have known that, although this particular pub had always had a reputation for the occasional roughhouse in the past, the management had had enough of paying for the damage and had recently engaged the services of a full-time minder. His name was Arnold Olive – 'Big Arnie' to his intimates. Not only was he a massive hunk of high-grade muscle, but he was also a surprisingly genial, all-round sportsman, famous on the island as a footballer, athlete and amateur boxer.

On this occasion he grabbed Wilf by the scruff of his neck and forcibly ejected him from the bar. Before Wilf could even splutter out a word, Big Arnie was berating him for his filthy temper, which he said he should learn to control.

For once in his life Wilf knew better than to argue back. 'If I had, I realised he could have killed me.' He was only too relieved when he saw Big Arnie's face break into a smile. He asked Wilf his name, then made a quick decision. 'Until you lost your temper you were doing pretty well,' he said. 'So why don't you come and join me working the doors as a bouncer? As long as you're able to control your temper, I need somebody like you who knows how to fight and can deal with unruly punters.'

During the early 1960s the Isle of Wight was changing rapidly from the sleepy island with its memories of Queen Victoria and beginning to appeal to a new generation of holiday-makers. These were younger, drank more and were out for a spot of action in the evening, unlike the staid, largely middle-class family holiday-makers who had been the stand-by of the island in the past. Islands always seem to have a liberating influence on visitors, and this influx of the pleasure-seeking young who flocked from the mainland for a few days' fun brought money to the island – and also problems. Sometimes the old-fashioned police force couldn't cope with them, and Arnie's pub was not the only one that had turned to freelance bouncers to stop trouble getting out of hand.

Wilf liked the idea of becoming a bouncer, and Big Arnie trained him well. He showed him that the bouncer's real task was not to fight but to stop others from fighting. This might have been difficult for Wilf, who was only five feet, nine inches tall and turned the scales at ten stone, seven pounds, and he sometimes found himself with no alternative but to counter violence with violence. But he also discovered that his real strength lay more in convincing a potential troublemaker that he meant business than in fighting for the fun of it. This proved to be a useful lesson for the future. But there were times when this didn't work. 'Sometimes someone, usually a holiday-maker, would have had a drink or two too many, and when I told him to pack it in or he'd be out on his ear, I'd always get the same reply: "OK, big boy, you and whose army?" When this happened, as a former pupil of "the approved school of charm", I knew better than to wait for the next line,' says Wilf. 'Instead, I'd let my fists do the talking, and they seemed to get the message over.'

By the end of that summer of 1962 Wilf was thoroughly enjoying life. During the day he was still working as a dustman, which he loved, but after work he washed and changed out of his dustman's clothes into something smart for the evening. With two jobs, he could afford to dress the part, and after the compulsory close haircuts that had been rigidly enforced at Blyth, he could now indulge in the Beatles-style sideboards and long hair that were all the fashion as the Swinging Sixties started swinging, even in the Isle of Wight.

All this coincided with a fresh discovery. As a young dustman with a quick smile for a pretty woman, he had already had the odd fling with several girls as well as Jill. But once he became a bouncer the amorous potential of the job amazed him. For certain girls there seemed to be an instant switch-on in his pugilistic role. He was still seeing Jill, and usually taking her to wherever he was working on the two nights when she came over on the bus to Ryde. But since she was living with her parents, and they insisted on her being in by midnight, she had to leave before the evening ended to catch the last bus home. This left Wilf on his own among a club full of holiday-makers just as the fun was starting, and for him the fun would often end with a more-than-willing female in an after-hours club, or in bed together in some holiday chalet where she was staying.

He regarded his behaviour philosophically, telling himself that, in spite of the fact that he believed he was in love with Jill, what he did when she was back in Cowes was his own business. As long as she didn't know, she didn't suffer, and certainly it didn't worry him. As he says, 'It was summertime, the 1960s had just started, and I was eighteen. What did any of it matter?' What *did* matter was a different sort of fun that Wilf was also starting to enjoy.

'I must emphasise,' he says, 'that Big Arnie was one hundred per cent straight and in no way was it thanks to him that I started picking up the occasional bonus on top of the legitimate money I was earning on the doors. What happened was that, with the name I was getting as a bouncer and the fact that I was known to be an ex-approved school boy, several lively lads who needed help over some dodgy deal or other began to turn to me. And not just them. You'd be surprised how, even in a place as sleepy as the Isle of Wight, so many people seemed to need a spot of muscle to sort out their problems – and this included several well-known so-called "straight" businessmen on the island.'

For a while Wilf operated as a freelance enforcer in the grey area between what was lawful and what was not. Then that autumn, largely for the hell of it, he saw no reason not to turn properly to crime. Through the clubs where he was working, he had met several small-time criminals from London who were beginning to frequent the island. He found that he could talk their language, and they told him about the rackets they were up to, which included what they called 'the jump-up game'. This turned out to be hijacking lorries, when they had stopped for the drivers to have a break or to rest up for the night.

The hijackers relied on tip-offs, not only on the nature of the lorries' goods and whether they'd be easy to dispose of, but also on the route and regular stopping places. But besides accurate information, the hijackers had to have some 'well-trained muscle' at the ready, just in case anything went wrong, and this was where Wilf came in. On the few occasions when he participated in a jump-up, his services weren't needed. But although he liked the money, what really turned him on was the excitement of the game.

It was much the same as with the secret sex-life he was now enjoying with the girls from the clubs he minded. Then suddenly all the excitement of the charmed life he was leading seemed to vanish in the face of uncomfortable reality.

Early that September he had been feeling particularly flush with the extra pounds that he was earning in his pocket and had promised Jill that he'd take her out to dinner. But when he met her off the bus her face hadn't got its usual smile. When he enquired what was wrong, she told him she was six weeks late with her period and was certain she was pregnant. Today it's easy to forget what a nightmare situation this could be for an innocent young couple in the early 1960s, particularly in a gossipy, small community like the then Isle of Wight. Contraception was erratic, abortion unthinkable, and unmarried motherhood regarded as a fearful stigma.

All Wilf remembers of that dreadful evening was that dinner was forgotten, and the more the two of them tried working out what to do the more it seemed that there was only one solution – marriage. But even this was a hopeless decision from the start. They had no money, no experience of life, and they were little more than children. What made things worse was that they didn't dare confess to their parents what really lay behind their desperate eagerness to marry.

Since both were under twenty-one they were required by law to get their parents' permission to marry. This led to several stormy sessions, at the end of which both sets of parents grudgingly signed the consent forms, but all of them firmly refused to attend the wedding. But although this left the child bride and the young bridegroom feeling anxious and isolated, they put their best face on the situation, and while Jill was buying herself a wedding outfit Wilf found a cheap two-room flat in Ryde, and booked an appointment with the registrar for 12 October.

Wilf was always grateful to his brother Bernie, who not only brought in several friends to help redecorate the flat, but also did his best to cheer everybody up. Where Bernie might have been more careful was when he decided it was also his duty, as his brother's best man, to organise a lively stag night on the evening before the wedding.

Many bridegrooms have been known to greet their wedding morning with a hangover, as did Wilf, but not many bridegrooms open their eyes on their wedding morning to a prison cell, being woken up not by his mother with a loving cup of tea but by the duty constable with a shout of 'rise and shine'.

As Wilf tried gathering his wits about him, he started to remember what had happened. As neither set of parents was attending the wedding, the young couple, rather daringly for the Isle of Wight in the early 1960s, had already started living together in their tiny flat. Because of this, Wilf had decided that he couldn't possibly leave his bride alone there on the night before the wedding, so he took her along to the dance hall where Bernie had arranged the stag night with several of their closest friends.

As far as Wilf could remember, the evening was a great success. The drink flowed freely. There were the customary silly jokes, most of them at Wilf's expense, and everyone was happy until the time arrived to leave. It was a freezing-cold night, and Wilf remembered having to wait outside the hall with Bernie and his friends while Jill collected her coat from the cloakroom. This took her longer than it should have done, and suddenly she came flying down the steps and landed on the pavement in a heap. Luckily she wasn't hurt, but when she had been helped to her feet, and Wilf asked her what on earth had happened, she replied that she'd been jostled by several loud-mouthed idiots who were trying to chat her up, and made her lose her balance.

For Wilf there could be only one answer. Bernie was already halfway up the steps to where several boys of Wilf's age who'd clearly drunk too much were pointing down at Jill and creasing up with laughter. Wilf insists that all he and his friends did then was to 'wipe the smiles off their silly faces. The scuffle – for that's all it was – was over in a matter of minutes, and the only medical treatment any of them would have needed next morning would have been an aspirin for their hangover.'

But for Wilf the trouble wasn't over. While he and his friends were walking back along Ryde High Street, a police car pulled up alongside them and a posse of police leaped out and started questioning them about 'an incident' outside the dance hall. 'Incident, officer?' said Bernie. 'What incident?' But the police meant business. When they started questioning Wilf, he tried explaining that he was getting married in the morning. This cut no ice, and out came the notebooks as the policemen started writing down names and addresses. When they reached Wilf, they seemed to recognise him, and one of them said he would be needed back at the station for further questioning. The rest of them could be dealt with later. Bernie began arguing on his brother's behalf, but Wilf stopped him, asking him to see Jill back to the flat, and adding that he'd follow on as soon as possible. But he didn't.

At the police station he tried explaining what had happened, including the fact that he was getting married in the morning, but none of this made the slightest difference. He was to be the guest of the police for the night, while they pursued their enquiries, and as the cop was showing him his cell, he quietly remarked, 'Wilf, this is just the start. Remember our guy in Binstead? We don't forget a thing like that.'

Next morning he was let out just in time to get to the register office by eleven, and the wedding was followed by a very small reception at the flat. Wilf was still there with Jill and their guests when the police turned up again, this time to arrest him on a charge of 'assault occasioning actual bodily harm'. Thus ended Wilf Pine's first – but not his last – wedding breakfast, with him being led off in handcuffs by the law.

At the station he was formally charged, then granted bail and told he would be appearing at Ryde magistrates' court at a later date. It was not the best start for a marriage, but there was worse to come.

*

Once again, it's easy to forget how innocent and unsophisticated young couples were in the early 1960s, and for nineteen-year-old Wilf, growing up in an approved school had added to his immaturity. Neither he nor his young bride had the remotest notion of what marriage meant and their relationship wasn't helped when, a week later, she had her period and resumed her monthly cycle. They had both been so naive that they had taken her pregnancy for granted, but when she saw a doctor he assured her that she definitely wasn't. Their shotgun marriage had been totally unnecessary, and it says a lot for their mutual good nature that they had no recriminations. But now that the real reason for marrying had gone, so did the purpose of the marriage.

Wilf had just one stroke of unexpected luck. When his case came up in court, his solicitor discovered that, thanks to the incompetence of the police, his charge had been incorrectly worded, and the lawyer was able to persuade the judge to dismiss the case against him. As he walked from the court a free man, he was just nineteen and more determined than ever to fight whatever battles came his way.

4

The Burying of Scots Billy

IT HAD BEEN another fine hot August Saturday on the island and Wilf was feeling weary, as he often did now at the end of long hot Saturdays. It was 1966, and three years had passed since his marriage and his close shave with the police. Miraculously he had steered clear of trouble ever since and had discovered that he possessed an unsuspected talent – a flair for business and a natural taste for organising other people.

Sensing a need for responsible and properly organised bouncers on the doors of the drinking clubs and dance halls and concert halls springing up across the island, he had recruited twenty or so tough individuals who could look after themselves and be relied on. Wilf could guarantee their competence and their discretion, and their presence would ensure that any trouble was averted long before the police were necessary. He called them the 'crew'; he organised the deals with the club managers and owners and they shared their wages equally. Wilf was also emerging as a considerable control freak, and he ran his 'crew' with a few associates he trusted and who remain close friends today. The first was Dave Farley, a tall good-looking Canadian whom he described as 'every married woman's dream and every husband's nightmare'. There was Clive Jenkins, aka Jinxie, a former merchant seaman, and there was stocky Colin Marden, three times southern counties boxing champion. By the summer of 1966 Wilf and the crew had long had the major venues on the island, as he put it, 'sewn up'.

Since six o'clock on that August evening Wilf himself had been in charge of the door at the Manor House Ballroom between Ryde and Shanklin, one of the most popular dance halls on the island. As its name suggests, the ballroom started life to cater for sedate pre-war holiday-makers seeking an evening's ballroom dancing. But the Saturday-night crowd the ballroom was attracting now was not sedate, nor was the dancing strictly ballroom. Most were young weekenders over from the mainland, and the island had a strange effect on some of them. Once across that strip of water between Ryde and Southampton and after a drink of two, a sort of unexpected madness came over them, and if they ended up in the Manor House, something about the atmosphere seemed to make them throw their weight about. Sometimes that wasn't all they threw — hence Wilf nicknamed the Manor House 'the Bucket of Blood'. This didn't suit the management and was certainly not the image they desired.

To a point, of course, the ballroom's popularity with the younger generation was good for business, but there was always a risk of the disorder getting out of hand, and if this started to become a habit the police might urge the authorities to revoke its licence. The crew had been signed on for the season to stop this happening.

This wasn't always easy once the mainlanders arrived and the action started. For Wilf it meant another heavy evening with various would-be tough guys eager for a spot of action to impress their girlfriends, and some of them would probably be hyped up with something more than alcohol. By now the drug culture of the 1960s had hit the island, and while marijuana didn't bring Wilf and the crew any serious problems, something called black bombers did. The black bomber, a powerful form of amphetamine, otherwise known as 'speed', is one of those forgotten features of the 1960s which have gone the way of vinyl records, teeny-boppers and flower power, but in this period they were highly popular. Wilf himself had tried a couple, just to see what all the fuss was about, and they had scared the daylights out of him, making him so crazy that until the effects wore off he felt all-powerful and that nobody on earth could harm him. All that was needed was for two or three young idiots to turn up fuelled with booze and a handful of black bombers, and the task of keeping any sort of order in the clubs became a nightmare.

By now Wilf had learned to recognise the signs of anyone on

amphetamines, and experience had taught him that the only way to deal with them was to do something he normally would not indulge in – hit fast and hit to hurt. But he found job satisfaction in this sort of work distinctly minimal, and when practised night after night it was also very tiring. That evening had been worse than usual, and it was well past midnight with the club about to close, when the phone rang.

'Call for you, Wilf,' said the manager. 'It's Clive Meddick. Says he needs to speak to you.'

Clive Meddick, who ran the Disco Blue Club in Ryde, was one of the crew's important clients and Wilf had put Colin Marden on the door.

'Wilf, I need you here at once,' said Clive.

'Won't it keep until tomorrow?' Wilf replied.

'Wilf it's urgent. U-R-G-E-N-T. We've got trouble.'

Normally Clive was so laid back that if he'd been telling him his trousers were on fire he'd still have sounded cool, but tonight he wasn't sounding cool.

'What sort of trouble?' Wilf said wearily.

'It's Scots Billy. He and your man Colin had a disagreement earlier this evening. You know Scots Billy, Wilf.'

Wilf did know Billy. At six feet two and weighing over sixteen stone, Scots Billy was hard to miss, especially on so small an island, and although he had only recently come down from Scotland he had already made his presence felt by kicking the shit out of anyone he didn't like. Wilf had seen him performing several times in public and, as something of an expert in that sort of thing himself, had frankly been impressed.

'So what's happened with Billy?'

'I think he's dead,' said Clive.

'I'd best get over right away,' said Wilf.

As the owner and manager of the Disco Blue, Clive Meddick was an important figure in the transformation of the island that was occurring in the 1960s. The club, which he began in Star Street, Ryde, next door to the island's first casino, was the island's first authentic disco. It also had a stage for live concerts, and during the holiday season the Disco Blue was currently packing in several hundred young tourists every evening. Clive himself was tall, good looking and something of a playboy. But behind the playboy image lurked a shrewd businessman who had made the club a smooth, successful operation. Thanks largely to Wilf and the crew, he had been equally successful at avoiding trouble.

The Disco Blue was seven miles away from the Manor House, and since there was virtually no traffic after midnight on the island in those far-off, car-free days and Wilf was beginning to see himself as something of a demon driver, it can't have taken long before he was screeching up outside the club's blue, neon-lit exterior. Clive was waiting in the road outside.

'What the hell's going on?' asked Wilf.

'It's Colin, bloody lunatic. He's in the foyer right now. He lost it, Wilf, and you know what Colin's like when he loses it. Billy's been bugging him for weeks, and tonight he turned up as the club was closing, pissed to kingdom come and out for trouble. When Colin informed him it was closing time, Billy went for him and started shouting.'

'So?'

'Colin flipped.'

'Where's Billy now?'

'He's behind the counter in the reception area. He's out cold and he hasn't moved for the last half-hour. Thank God two of the boys came in to help from the casino when they heard the noise. They're with Colin now, and somehow they managed to drag Scots Billy out of sight behind the counter.'

'Some feat,' thought Wilf, remembering Billy's sixteen stone. 'And what am I supposed to do?'

'We could have a murder on our hands,' said Clive. 'If the law gets wind of it, it'll be curtains for the club – and Colin could be facing life. Colin's your friend. For Christ's sake, Wilf, do something – fast.'

Wilf followed Clive into the club and found Colin waiting for them. Far from looking like a man who'd probably just topped somebody, he was as cool as the proverbial cucumber. 'Scots Billy asked for it,' he said. 'The bugger was always looking for a fight, and when he got going on me I let him have it. First in, first served, Wilf. That's always been my motto. What else did he expect?'

If Wilf had been around, he would have warned Scots Billy in advance exactly what he could expect from Colin Marden, and that if he picked a fight with him he'd be taking on a human wrecking machine. 'Once Colin got going, to put it mildly, you were fucked. Unless there was someone there to pull him off, he'd just keep on like a machine – which was more or less what had happened with Billy.'

When he saw Scots Billy stretched out on the floor behind the bar, Wilf knew they had a crisis on their hands; and since Colin was his colleague and his friend, he also knew that it was up to him to deal with it. After thanking the boys from the casino and bidding them goodnight, requesting that they kept their mouths shut, his first priority was to check on Billy – but even that was easier said than done. The way he was lying, wedged behind the counter, was blocking the door, and Wilf had to heave himself across the top to reach him.

'Since Billy was lying face down and I couldn't feel a pulse in his wrist, I lugged him over to see if there was any sign of breath coming from his mouth. But his head was black and blue and covered with what looked like claret and so swollen that I couldn't find his mouth. I had to know if he was dead or not, so there was only one thing for it – kick him in the ribs as hard as possible and see if there was a reaction. I did. There wasn't. "He's dead all right," I told them.

'Colin took this calmly, as he took most things in life. But the look on Clive's face said what he and I were thinking. Luckily he didn't say it out loud, for two coppers chose that very moment to shove their ugly mugs around the door.

'In fact, they were on their regular nightly rounds, checking on the clubs, but there was I, stuck behind the counter with a body at my feet, facing two real-life coppers on the far side of the foyer, who hadn't the faintest notion of what was going on. On top of this I was worried stiff about Colin, for if there was anything Colin hated in those days it was cops. A month or two before he'd gone to court when his brother was up before the beak, and when he saw him being manhandled in the dock by a pair of coppers Colin hopped down from the public gallery and knocked one of the policemen spark out before the magistrate. I was half-expecting a repeat performance, but luckily the police weren't interested in Colin.'

All that seemed to interest them was what Wilf was doing at the Disco Blue when he should have been working at the Manor House. 'I just dropped in for a drink with my friends before they closed,' he said. This seemed to satisfy them, and after telling Clive to be sure to lock up, and wishing everyone good night, they left.

But this didn't solve the problem – what to do with a sixteen-stone body before its owner was reported missing. One suggestion was dumping it in the sea, but, as Wilf said, it would almost certainly be washed up later and traced back to the club. Another suggestion was to bury it in the woods, but again Wilf pointed out that this would take a lot of time, and freshly turned earth was certain to attract attention.

But talk of burying the body had given him an idea.

'You know that kid who comes here every Saturday? Tall, dark-haired fellow who works as a grave-digger in the cemetery. Any idea where he lives?'

'Sure,' said Clive. 'I know the guy you mean. He lives quite close, but he'll be tucked up in bed by now.'

'No matter. Do as I ask, Clive. Drive round to his house straight away and fetch him. Tell him we need him.'

When the need arose, Clive moved fast, and it seemed that barely ten minutes later he was back with the grave-digger in tow. Hardly surprisingly, he was looking distinctly nervous, and Wilf did his best to calm him down.

'Listen,' he said, 'we have a little problem. I won't go into it, but we promise that in no way will you be involved. You've our solemn word on it. But we need to know if there are any funerals scheduled for tomorrow.'

The kid nodded. 'There's one for the afternoon,' he said.

'And you've dug the grave?'

Again he nodded.

'Good. Now, all we want you to do is to drive round to the cemetery, then wait until we come and then unlock the gates for us. Oh, and can you tell us where to find a pair of shovels?'

When Clive also gave his promise that this was all they wanted, he agreed and said that there were shovels under a tarpaulin by the open grave. He added that the cemetery gates were secured with a chain and padlock.

'Fine,' said Wilf. 'Give us twenty minutes. That'll give you time to go home and collect the keys, then meet us at the cemetery, unlock the gates and show us the grave. Then you can pack off home to bed. We'll snap the padlock shut behind us when we leave, and no one will be any the wiser that you've ever been there.'

When the grave-digger departed, Wilf explained his plan. As Clive had pointed out, they couldn't just heave the body into an open grave and leave it there, but Wilf's idea was for two of them to get down into the grave, dig down far enough to take the body, then cover it with earth and smooth it over, so that when the burial took place that afternoon, no one would be the wiser.

But first they had to get the body to the cemetery, and even that wasn't easy. Getting Billy out was quite a struggle in itself for three strong men, and it was obvious that in no way would Billy fit in the boot of Clive's car as they'd hoped. So Wilf said he'd sit in the back seat with the body lying on his lap, and Clive produced some black drapes from the club with which to cover it, so that if anyone happened to look in, all he would see would be three men sitting in the car.

They were lucky. Star Street was empty as Clive and Colin dragged Scots Billy from the club into the car; and when they started driving down the High Street, they found it empty too. Wilf remembers passing the Catholic church when he heard a muffled noise coming from the bundle on his lap. Clive heard it too and stopped the car. 'What the fuck's that?' he said

'Take no notice,' Colin said. 'It's gas escaping from the stomach. Drive on before someone sees us.'

Then they heard a retching noise like someone trying to be sick, and the bundle moved.

'Christ!' said Wilf. 'He's still alive.'

'So what the fuck do we do now?' asked Clive.

'Bury him as planned, 'said Colin, who had not forgiven Scots Billy for all the aggravation he had caused him.

'We can't do that,' said Wilf.

'So what can we do?' said Clive.

'Take him home,' said Wilf. 'He lives near here. I know his wife. She's the understanding kind and she's used to him getting into fights when he's been drinking. We'll tell her that we found him lying in the road.'

Since this seemed the most sensible solution, even Colin finally agreed.

Although he had moved, and was definitely alive, Scots Billy was still out cold, and the three friends had an even greater struggle carrying him up two flights of stairs to his flat than they'd had dragging him down the stairs from the disco. It also took a while before anyone answered when they rang the bell. But at last Billy's wife appeared, and when Wilf had spun his story she seemed genuinely grateful, thanking them for being so extremely kind, and when Wilf asked her to forget the whole affair, she said of course she would.

And that was that. Instead of some very hard work in the cemetery burying Scots Billy, the three prospective grave-diggers went off to celebrate their happy release from involvement in a murder, and ended up as drunk as lords in one of the island's late-night drinking clubs. Scots Billy was so strong that he recovered in a day or two and appeared to have forgotten what had happened. As for the grave-digger, he never did discover why the owner of the Disco Blue had been so anxious for him to unlock the gates of the cemetery and then never came.

Curiously, that mad night's work marked something of a turning point in Wilf Pine's strange career. To understand why, one must know a little more of what had happened to that angry, crime-loving, heavily tattooed character since he stepped out of Ryde magistrates' court three years earlier.

Surprisingly, his marriage had survived the false alarm about Jill's pregnancy and, making the best of things, the couple had moved into a slightly more comfortable flat in a slightly better part of Ryde and had been there ever since. But although Wilf did his best to stay a faithful husband, he soon found himself involved in a double life. This time it was not with other women but with crime.

It all started at the end of the summer of 1963, when he lost his job with the borough council. Until then he had been spending every morning working happily away as a dustman and thoroughly enjoying it. The work was in the open air and humping several hundred heavy galvanised iron dustbins into the council dustcart every day kept him in trim and developed his arm and shoulder muscles. His job was to go ahead of the dustcart, bringing out the dustbins from the houses in advance so that by the time the cart drew up they were standing neatly by the roadside ready to be emptied. Thanks to Wilf's efficiency, his dustcart always finished long before the others. But as so often in his life, his temper was finally his undoing.

Trouble started early one September morning as he was carrying an overloaded dustbin from a quiet residential area. As he closed the gate behind him, several dead flowers fell from the dustbin on to the garden path.

'Dustman, pick those flowers up,' he heard someone shouting from an upstairs window.

'Anything wrong?' said Wilf.

'Yes. I told you to pick those flowers up.' The voice belonged to an angry-looking man with a moustache. Wilf did not take kindly to orders from irascible householders, so he told the man exactly what to do with his flowers and left them where they were, along with the entire contents of the dustbin. Then Wilf turned and walked away, closing the gate behind him and leaving the furious householder lost for words.

Next morning he arrived for work to find a message summoning him to the office of Mr Rowbotham, the borough surveyor, who had just received a furious complaint from the man with the moustache.

'Unfortunately, Pine,' said the borough surveyor, 'you picked on one of the Ryde town councillors, so I have no alternative but to sack you here and now.'

Something about the way he said this made Wilf think that he might not have been entirely unsympathetic, and a few days later he received a letter in the post. It was a glowing testimonial to the conscientiousness, hard work and cheerfulness which Wilf Pine had shown during his time working for the borough council. It was signed 'William Rowbotham, Borough Surveyor'.

This is the one favourable testimonial Wilf Pine has ever had from anyone, and at the time he proudly showed it to his mother. Later, he sometimes wished he hadn't. For it so impressed her that in years to come, particularly at moments of success, Millie would look at him and say: 'All this is all very well, Wilf, but if you'd only kept that job with the council, you'd have been driving the dustcart by now, *and* you'd have had a pension.'

After working for the council, Wilf found work hard to come by on the island once the holiday season ended and bouncers were no longer needed.

Mr Rowbotham's letter got him a job digging trenches for the electricity board, but he didn't like it and soon took another job painting and decorating houses, but didn't like that either. Colin Marden found him work demolishing part of Ryde sea wall with a pneumatic drill to make room for a heliport. But none of this was Wilf.

'The truth was that me and manual work just didn't get along together,' he says. Instead, he preferred relying on his talent as a freelance fighter, and when Big Arnie told him he was off to London Wilf went with him. During the day he worked as one of Arnie's labourers on building sites, and in the evening they worked as bouncers in various East End pubs and clubs. They shared a down-at-heel bedsit in Leytonstone and usually returned to the island at weekends.

While Wilf was doing this, he also started making what he called 'some useful contacts on the villainy front', but he kept all this from Arnie. Big Arnie was essentially straight. He was a gambler, not a criminal. Left to his own devices he would have made his money from the horses, and when the bouncers' work in London ended he was happy to return to the island and his trade as a bricklayer. But Wilf was not interested in laying bricks and stayed on in Leytonstone, 'ducking and diving' for a living from anybody who could use his services. For a while he did some strong-arm debt collecting and some petty thieving, along with anything that needed someone who could get into a fight without worrying too much about his looks.

This suited Wilf. The years of bullying from his father and the brutal lessons driven into him at Blyth had left him with an attitude to life which, like the tattooing on his hands, was also there for good. Deep down he saw himself as a lifelong rebel against the straight world around him. He had little time for honest toil any more than he had for 'respectable' society. What he did have was a deep distrust of all authority and the forces of law and order. Nor had anything changed his view of the world as a place where ultimately dog ate dog. The one trade at which he knew that he excelled was fighting, and he was perfectly prepared to take on anyone and, if necessary, accept any amount of punishment in return. It would be many years before he could resist the lure of violence – the adrenalin rush at the beginning of a brawl, the excitement of a fight with no holds barred, and the chance to prove himself wickeder, stronger and more vicious than anybody he encountered.

Throughout that winter he was usually back on the island with Jill at weekends; by the following spring he was home for good, and looking forward to once more working as a bouncer when the season started. On the island he was becoming something of a character, warm-hearted, always very charming and popular. He was also smart and beginning to develop a natural talent as an organiser, with an eye for detail and an even sharper feeling for a deal.

Wilf had already started building up the 'crew' by the time the first of that year's holiday-makers were stepping off the Isle of Wight ferry. There was no effective competition. As he says, he and his friends were offering the dance halls and the clubs a service that most of them were happy to accept. Then, when the season ended, it was back to London.

Wilf loved London. He felt at home in the rich Dickensian world of villainy, with the excitement and the thrills and gossip of the underworld. Criminals were non-judgemental people, and he really did enjoy their company.

He also loved the island, not least for the advantages it offered an ambitious would-be gangster like himself. In those days nobody at Scotland Yard would ever have imagined a violent criminal emerging from a gentle backwater like the Isle of Wight. Nor for that matter would other criminals, and the island was a perfect base from which to operate, not just in London but throughout the country if he got the opportunity.

Once off the ferry at Portsmouth, even on the notorious old A3, London could be reached in less than two hours, in spite of which most Londoners still saw the island as a foreign country. As for the islanders themselves, the less any of them knew of his activities, the better – and that included Jill. But among certain people on the mainland Wilf was beginning to acquire a reputation as a boy who was both tough and hungry – so hungry that he would take on almost anything to get a living.

The early 1960s were a good time for hungry tough young men. 1964 not only saw the end of the death penalty for murder but also the passing of the Gaming Act, which was meant to decriminalise gambling but which did the opposite. More than anything, it was the profits from gambling that turned organised crime into a high-growth industry. Gangland was growing, rackets were flourishing and new outlets for criminal activity were rapidly increasing. Beneath its glossy surface, 'Swinging London' was remarkably corrupt and had suddenly become the most lucrative criminal capital in Europe.

The Wellesley Nautical School at Blyth had fitted Wilf to take his place in it by giving him the criminal equivalent to an old school tie. Not merely had it turned him into a lethal fighter, more fitted to pursue a life of crime than any comparable career, but through its old boys he had access to a network of invaluable contacts in the criminal underworld throughout the country. To get ahead, ambitious villains like Wilf knew about networking long before the yuppies discovered it ten years later; and it was thanks to people he had known or heard about at Blyth that quite a number of riskier but more exciting propositions came his way. He was a conscientious worker, and he made a point of accepting any feasible proposal and always delivering on anything he'd promised. But the most important thing about Wilf Pine was that he was a natural at the game.

In many ways he was not unlike countless youngsters in the early 1960s, eager to grab their share of the country's growing prosperity and trying to build a reputation and a lucrative career – except that his chosen field was crime. At the end of 1964 he stumbled on an unexpected line of business which offered him the opportunities he wanted.

Again his contact was someone he had known at Blyth, who had recommended him to certain 'friends' in Manchester as a likely candidate for what was known in the business as 'heavy work'. 'Heavy work' was criminal parlance for a willingness to carry and if necessary use a gun, and the 'friends' were a syndicate of some big-time Manchester club owners who were coining vast amounts of money out of gambling. They were being threatened by an upstart local gang, trying to muscle in on their territory by shooting up their clubs, and there was a danger of a gang war breaking out. This would lose the 'friends' a lot of money, and to stop this happening they needed the two leading tearaways involved given a lesson they would not forget. Not the sort of lesson that would bring in the police and they certainly didn't want them murdered. All they wanted was that they were hurt sufficiently to convey the message that behaviour like theirs would not be tolerated.

Wilf met his former schoolmate in an all-night café in the Edgware Road to discuss the situation with an employee of the 'friends' from Manchester. He was an old-time villain and a typical Mancunian himself in the way he didn't beat about the bush as he told Wilf exactly what was needed.

'D'you think you're up to it, lad?' he asked. Wilf nodded confidently.

'And you're used to heavy work?' Again Wilf nodded, though in fact he wasn't. But this seemed to satisfy the old villain, who went on to point out that there was, of course, a risk of Wilf getting hurt himself, and he wanted it clearly understood that if anything went wrong Wilf was on his own.

'Suits me, 'said Wilf, and they shook hands on it.

'Of course,' says Wilf today, 'it was a crappy deal, and in fact it was my very first experience of this sort of thing. But you must start somewhere, and when you're trying hard to make a reputation in our world, you start off with the crap, do as good a job as possible and hope to earn the respect of your peers. Then, with luck, the next time round you might be offered something better.'

Fortunately for him, the arrangements had been put together by professionals and nothing had been left to chance. His instructions were to take the main road up to Manchester and arrive at 11.30 p.m. at an address they gave. He'd find a grey Ford Cortina parked outside the house, with someone sitting at the wheel. He was to draw up alongside, wind down his window so that he could give the other driver a prearranged password, then swap cars with him. Inside the glove compartment of the Ford he'd find two things: a black knitted balaclava and a .38 Smith and Wesson. From then on it was up to him, and he knew already what he had to do. It shouldn't take him long – a quarter of an hour at most from start to finish. As soon as he'd done the job, he should replace the gun and the balaclava in the glove compartment, drive back slowly, to avoid arousing the suspicions of any police car in the neighbourhood, and pick up his own car from where he'd left it. The man would be sitting in it with his wages. End of story.

On the night everything went smoothly. Wilf had had no difficulty in acquiring a .38 automatic from friends in London, and practised firing it against a tree stump in an unfrequented part of the island until he felt confident about using it. Then, a day or two before going into action, he had driven up to Manchester for a dummy run in daylight, driving around until he knew his route by heart, together with the street and his victim's house. He wasn't worried in the least that he'd be on his own. It avoided any rumours getting out, and if anything did go wrong he'd have only himself to blame. Nor did he feel the slightest pity or concern for the man he had to hit. 'It wasn't as if he was a civilian. He was a villain, like me. We were both in the same racket, and as I didn't know him it was strictly business, not personal. I might have felt different if they'd wanted me to kill him, but they didn't. As they kept telling me, this was not to be a murder but a warning.'

Which is exactly what it turned out to be. Everything went like clockwork, and on arriving at the house he smashed his way in through the flimsy front door, and everything was over in seconds. 'The guy was sitting by the fire, watching television, and I remember the stupid look on his face when I burst in on him. I used two shots, one into the wall behind him and one that caught him in the leg. Then I was out through that front door before he'd even started yelling. I'd left the car outside with its engine running, and I was off at once. Into the glove compartment with the balaclava and the shooter, then back at a steady thirty miles an hour to where I'd left my car. From start to finish it had taken me twelve minutes, not fifteen. I was surprised how cool I was, and I remember sitting with the guy beside me on the front seat of the car, checking my money.'

The journey down the long road back to London passed without incident, and Wilf and his dark red Humber were aboard the first Ryde ferry of the day as dawn was breaking. Apart from Jill, no one so much as realised he'd ever been away.

A few days later there was a repeat performance, following more or less the same pattern, except that this time Wilf varied things slightly by shooting the guy in the buttock. But 'heavy work' like this was rare. Wilf's 'warning' proved so effective that the 'friends' weren't anxious to continue. Enough was enough, and Wilf himself was anxious to preserve his precious anonymity. For a while there seemed little sign of any really lucrative work emerging on the criminal front and he returned to the island for Christmas. 1965 arrived, and Wilf celebrated his twenty-first birthday at the end of February. Then a fortnight later, on 7 March, Jill presented him with a delayed birthday present – a son. Wilf always remembers 7 March as 'the greatest day of my life'.

From the start he was determined to make up for his failings as a husband by becoming a devoted parent and never to forget how much he had suffered from his own father. Had he needed a reminder, it came sooner than expected. After visiting Jill and the baby in hospital, his first thought was to walk round to his parents' house to tell them the good news and take them out to the local pub to 'wet the baby's head'. Millie, of course, was thrilled to be a grandmother, but his father went on watching television.

'So what are you calling him?' asked Millie.

'Sean,' said Wilf.

At this his father did react. 'You can't call my grandson that,' he shouted. 'It's a fucking Paddy name.'

At first Wilf thought that he was joking, then realised he wasn't. So instead of the newborn bringing happiness and reconciliation to the house of Pine, the day ended with yet another bitter argument.

A few months later, still very much the proud father, Wilf was pushing baby Sean out in his pram, when he passed his old head-mistress, Sister Paula. Caught by an unexpected feeling of goodwill, and anxious to let bygones be bygones, he thought that this would be a good occasion to make peace with his old enemy, not to mention the Church that he grew up in, and, who knows, even with God himself.

'Sister, this is my son, Sean,' he said. 'In a few years' time, when he's grown up a bit, I hope that you'll be teaching him.'

But Sister Paula hadn't changed, and without so much as looking at the baby she replied: 'Wilf Pine, there's no way I would ever teach a child of yours.' Then she abruptly turned her back and walked away.

'That finished me with the Roman Catholic Church for ever. I still believe in God, but since that very day I've never entered a church except to light candles for those I love.'

Money was tight and with a wife and a new baby to support Wilf realised that as a villain he could no longer stay a loner. He needed backup and support and had in fact already chosen the man he wanted. This was one of the leading members of the crew, the quiet Canadian, Dave Farley, who had already proved himself a natural fighter in the bar fights and the scuffles of the summer. There was something else about Dave Farley that appealed to Wilf. 'He was the one member of the crew who was even more secretive than me.'

Once they began to work together their joint reputation rapidly got round the criminal fraternity. In London, more work began to come their way and no reasonable proposition was refused. Together they soon became more organised, and throughout the spring of 1965 they were busy building up more contacts for their sort of work, most of which involved violence or the threat of violence.

Soon, even the Isle of Wight police force got wind of them and often tried to catch them out. For a period, Wilf was their favourite suspect and was regularly pulled in for questioning. If there'd been a robbery or somebody was hurt and the police needed an arrest, they'd automatically bring in either Wilf or Dave. But it was an unequal battle. Clever Wilf and quiet Dave were too smart to have presented the island's police force with the unlikely accomplishment of arresting them. Besides, by now their pickings were coming from more distant and far richer pastures than the Isle of Wight, and during this period Wilf took a further step into the world of professional villainy as he and Dave became jointly involved in several unexpected episodes of 'heavy work'.

These started when one of their regular London contacts, having heard of Wilf's two successful trips to Manchester, came up with a surprising proposition. He was a big-time figure in the underworld, a well-known 'face' who is still active today, thirty-eight years later. Back in the mid-1960s he was some Mr Big of gambling, making a fortune organising gaming clubs called 'spielers' throughout London. Thanks to the Gaming Act, these were now legal, but although they were no longer vulnerable to the police they were at the mercy of organised criminals who preyed on them, charging heavily for so-called 'protection' in the process.

As Mr Big was also widely known as a powerful gangland figure, this should not have been a problem with his clubs, but this very immunity gave him a very smart idea. Since no other gang in London would risk raiding any of his clubs, why not arrange to raid a few of them himself?

With most of his clubs this would have been impossible. The clientele would be too well known, the police would become involved and the reputation of the clubs would suffer disastrously. But there were just a few small gambling clubs he owned where none of this applied. These were clubs catering for some of the most addictive gamblers in London, many of whom were members of the Turkish and Cypriot communities. Like the Greeks, Turks have always been great gamblers, but there was another reason why these small clubs often dealt in such extremely large amounts of money, and why they were so vulnerable.

In these clubs many of the high-rolling gamblers were criminals or semi-criminals themselves, specialist jewel thieves or con-men and fraudsters, and they often liked to celebrate a coup by betting everything they'd earned in the hope of winning 'the really big one' every criminal dreams of.

If there is such a thing as honour among thieves, there wasn't much of it around as Mr Big explained his bright idea to Wilf. The key to it lay in the fact that since a large part of the stake in these games was criminal money, many of the gamblers would not risk going to the police if they were robbed themselves. So what could be easier than for two unknowns like Wilf and Dave to do it for him? He would provide them with details of the location and layout of one of these clubs of his, and tip them off when he knew that an evening's heavy gambling was in the offing. Then, when the play was at its height and as much cash as possible was on the table, one of his men in the club would dial a prearranged number to a nearby phone box where Wilf and Dave would be waiting. Once they heard the call, all they had to do was don their balaclavas, grasp their guns and make as fearsome an entry into the club as quickly as possible.

Only the most suspicious gambler would ever wonder if the man who owned the club had been behind the heist – and even if he did, so what? But to be on the safe side, one man in the club would have to suffer – his own employee who had arranged the phone call. For his own sake, they would have to rough him up to allay suspicion. 'Make a good job of it and don't feel sorry for him while you're doing it, 'said Mr Big. 'He'll be well paid for his suffering.'

Mr Big was also offering Wilf and Dave a good wage for one night's work, and they took a lot of trouble preparing for their performance – which, of course, was what it was.

'Once we'd heard the call in the phone box, we'd be round the corner like a flash, and through that door like a tornado, balaclavas over our heads, both of us with a piece in our hands, clumping our man's man as hard as possible to make it look right, and screaming and hollering for all we were worth. With his accent, Dave had to be careful not to *say* anything – his accent would've been a dead giveaway and we relied on staying totally unknown. Not that it was likely anybody there could have placed us, but why risk it? Then it was grab the money from the bank, shake down everyone around the table and vanish into the night as fast as we'd appeared. Had any of those punters been a real gangster with a gun, we'd have been in trouble. But apart from letting off a few shots into the wall above their heads, we never fired a shot in anger and nobody was ever hurt.'

Job done, before they'd finished for the night, Wilf and Dave would drive round for a rendezvous with Mr Big and hand him the bag in which they'd shoved the money. They always made a point of paying him every penny they had taken. As Wilf says, it would have been 'inadvisable' to try to cheat him. 'Besides, he said his man would inform him later to within a tenner exactly how much was on the table and how much every player there was worth.' Once they had given Mr. Big the takings, each received an envelope in return which made the whole night's work worth while.

Wilf and Dave did three or four of these heists without a problem. The takings were good, the money was extremely welcome and they were both starting to enjoy what was almost routine when their cosy little racket ended as abruptly as it started. Mr Big was suddenly arrested over an unrelated matter and was subsequently sentenced to a prison term. Wilf and Dave were sad to see him go, and sadder still to see the end of an easy source of income from the world of high-stakes gambling.

But the truth was that they were lucky that their game was over, for they had both become involved in something far more dangerous than they suspected. Big-time gamblers, and particularly big-time criminal gamblers, aren't endlessly gullible, and once these heists became a habit, one of them would finally have put two and two together. As Wilf himself says, all it needed was for another gangster with a gun to have been sitting at the table, and the fun would have started as theirs ended. Opposed armed hold-ups have a nasty way of getting out of hand, and once somebody was killed or seriously wounded the charmed criminal careers of these two young musketeers would almost certainly have ended with two long, unpleasant prison sentences.

So by going to prison, Mr Big may well have saved both Wilf and Dave from a similar fate. Instead, it was soon back to the island, where the true temptations for them both were girls, not guns. Wilf remembers that summer season as the one when, as he puts it, 'I started to play away from home. The truth was that I was a devoted father but a lousy husband, and there wasn't any excuse for my behaviour. I just found it far too easy to pull the birds, and that year there was an abundance, or so it seemed, of unescorted female holiday-makers on the island. I just took advantage of the situation. To me, and I'm sure to them, it was only one-night stands, and I told myself that as long as the wife didn't find out there was no harm done. It's no excuse, I know, but then again it's what everybody says.'

The attempted burying of Scots Billy followed late that August and was only the start of Wilf's involvement with the owner of the Disco Blue, Clive Meddick, and that memorable night became memorable for something more than what happened to Scots Billy. Thanks to Clive Meddick, Wilf was just about to stumble into a new life and a new career.

5

A Reluctant Promoter

FOR WILF, THE aborted burial of Scots Billy didn't end when he woke up the following afternoon with a monumental hangover, but it brought an unexpected bonus by involving him more closely with Clive Meddick and the Disco Blue. What few realised at the time was that Clive Meddick was starting something at the Disco Blue which became part of a movement that would culminate in the Isle of Wight Festival of 1970, when a quarter of a million young pop music fans turned the island into the nearest thing in Europe to the legendary Woodstock Festival.

This all began when an extraordinary range of up-and-coming bands started visiting the island for one-night stands, producing something of a transformation of the island until it became what Alan Jones, saxophonist of Amen Corner, today refers to as 'a place of pilgrimage for anybody interested in pop music'. And much of this was due to Clive Meddick, who, encouraged by the success of the Disco Blue, decided he would seize the day and expand his field of activities.

This was very much on his mind around the time of his trouble with Scots Billy, and by early that November of 1966, going against the accepted notion that entertainment on the island had to stop when the season ended, he started a series of live Saturday-night pop music concerts in the Art Deco ballroom of the Royal York Hotel in Ryde. (It helped that his father, Leslie Meddick, owned and managed the place.) They were a sell-out from the start, and were still packing in the crowds until nearly Christmas. Then, three months later, he reopened in the bigger Seagull Ballroom, now needlessly demolished, at the end of Ryde Pier.

When choosing his performers, Meddick had a knack of picking groups with maximum appeal for an audience of young pop music fans, many of whom came flocking over from the mainland. In fact, what he was doing was tapping into one of the most exciting periods in the pioneering days of pop, when new bands were springing up like mushrooms in the fertile compost created by Elvis and the Beatles. And while all of this was going on, destiny also decreed that the twenty-two-year-old, heavily tattooed and increasingly dangerous young villain, Wilf Pine, should have woken up one morning in the very middle of it all.

In fact, the relationship between Wilf and Meddick started with a flash of mutual recognition between two tough young cookies over the recumbent body of Scots Billy. For despite his looks, Meddick was more than capable of taking care of himself in a spot of trouble, and what he'd seen of Wilf while dealing with the problem of the drunken Scot made him aware of his potential.

To begin with, Wilf's career with Meddick was conducted on a fairly humdrum level. Many painstaking, often tedious tasks were involved in preparations for the live performances, and Meddick, who liked to live a relatively easy life, needed a resourceful helper on to whose sturdy shoulders he could heave the petty cares and problems of concert promotion. Who better than Wilf Pine, whose shoulders were certainly extremely broad and who was already developing a knack for taking on other people's problems? Since he was often on the door at the Disco Blue, it was not a major step for him to move into the office, and before long Meddick had him working on the detailed preparations for the opening performance at the Royal York Hotel. These preparations ranged from answering queries from the media and arranging advertising and flyposting to dealing with agents, making reservations with hotels and looking after individual group members, not to mention coping on the night with the frantic following of excited fans, who could make, or literally break up, a concert.

Wilf not only dealt with these tasks, but found himself actually enjoying them. Perhaps it was not as immediately exciting as a quick spot of heavy work with a .38 Smith and Wesson, but for Wilf it had simpler attractions. 'Before long I was loving every minute of the game, and became utterly obsessed with it,' he says. More important for the future, he seems to have found himself an alternative career to life as a full-time gangster.

Here he was lucky to have Meddick as a teacher. Had Meddick been an authoritarian figure, jealous of his own importance, like so many impresarios, Wilf's temper and suspicious nature would have inevitably produced a violent reaction – as did happen in the end, much to his regret. But having launched his ship, Meddick was more than happy to entrust much of the day-to-day routine to this willing helper, and Wilf, aspiring gunman, natural rebel and instinctive organiser that he was, was more than happy to accept.

Clive Meddick, who according to Wilf possessed 'the Midas touch' when picking his performers, kicked off his concerts at the Royal York Hotel with the Move, the noisiest, wildest, most sensational rock band in the country. And from the first hypnotic blast of their opening number – 'Night of Fear' – Wilf was hooked. For the first time in his life he was hearing a real live concert by a big-time band – and has never forgotten the experience. All the group's five members were great showmen, and their manager, the legendary Tony Secunda, had cleverly helped create their image as the most uninhibited rebels of British rock'n'roll. After their opening number they continued with their current No. 1 UK hit, appropriately entitled 'Fire Brigade', and the evening climaxed with the group's lead singer, the wild young man of pop, Carl Wayne, smashing a TV set on stage before an all but hysterical, largely teenage audience. For possibly cathartic reasons, the youngsters loved it. So did Wilf. With the Move that night, heavy rock exploded like a landmine in the middle of the Royal York Hotel, and Queen Victoria's favourite island was never quite the same again. Nor was Wilf.

The following week it was time for a very different group, the soul and blues band Amen Corner, leading with their latest hit, 'Gin House Blues'. Before long, the Corner's lead singer, Andy Fairweather-Low, the sweet-voiced Welshman from the valleys, would be thrilling his teenybopper audience with one of the 1960s still-remembered hits, '(If Paradise Is) Half as Nice'. Other famous acts followed, including the Tremeloes, Dave, Dee, Dozy, Beaky, Mick and Titch, and a group called Traffic Jam which became better

71

known when it changed its name to Status Quo. But the big band that proved to be the biggest draw of all featured the three Schulman brothers in a group mysteriously entitled Simon Dupree and the Big Sound.

The following April, when the Saturday-night shows began again in the Seagull Ballroom, Wilf found himself more involved than ever in management and preparations. Week after week on the Isle of Wight, pop music fans were enjoying something that would be virtually impossible to find anywhere today – regular appearances by top commercial bands in a competing range of local venues. For these were still the pioneering days of pop, when almost anything seemed possible.

Still barely twenty-two, Wilf was of an age with most of the performers, and as Meddick's representative he was in constant contact with them all. With really successful bands like the Move and Amen Corner being regularly invited back by popular demand, he got to know many of the performers in the excited atmosphere following the shows, and some of them became close friends. He was good looking in a rough-and-ready way, he could always make them laugh, and he began to feel very much at one with them. But there was more to it than that, and already his credentials as a villain and man of violence were making him extremely useful to members of the groups if the need arose.

It sometimes happened that, following a show, there was a party for the stars to meet their fans. In the context of such parties, there would always be a chance of trouble from a very corny situation – famous young pop star, doe-eyed female groupie fawning all over him, and jealous boyfriend somewhere in the background waiting for the chance to punch a pop star's face in. 'It could happen so easily,' says Wilf, 'and often did, if I didn't step in fast and stop the trouble before somebody was hurt. But usually a word or two sufficed to calm things down.' If it didn't, Wilf was always ready with a neat right-hander.

While Wilf's combined virtues as youthful member of the management and tough guy in residence were adding to his prestige among performers, he soon discovered that there was another service he could offer them. As Wilf explains:

In the mid-1960s the music business was a tough old game. The acts, the good ones, would often find themselves performing in a different town almost every night of the week, and even the less good acts were usually kept busy. In those days even the smallest town had somewhere where live music could be played, and it was by continually moving and performing that groups became established, getting noticed by the record companies, who would sign them up on the strength of their pulling power with the kids. If the kids who came to their concerts bought enough of their records, even groups that hadn't made it on to radio or television could still make it into the Top Twenty list of the week's best sellers.

At the time, apart from the most famous stars, all performers lived on their weekly earnings and treated performing as a job of work. Even performers in the most successful bands were on wages ranging from £15 a night to a princely £25 if the group had one or two hit records to its credit. Today, such wages sound a touch pathetic, but thirty years ago young popular performers didn't do badly – provided that they got their money. But as I soon discovered, all too often they just didn't. As with anything bringing in ready cash each night, the pop music business also brought along its share of 'knockers'.

These were rogue 'promoters' who would hire a ballroom for, say, ten successive Saturday nights and then approach the agent of a successful group to arrange a booking. To ensure the group was paid, the agent would automatically ask the 'promoter' for a cheque payable at least seven days before the concert. No problem. The cheque would be forthcoming, the group would happily perform and the cheques would continue to arrive for several weeks before the next concert. Then when everyone was happy, the moment came when the 'promoter' asked the agent if he could pay in cash on the night of the performance or, better still, with the promise of a cheque within seven days. If the agent agreed to a delayed cheque there would be no problem; it would arrive as promised in the post and everyone would still be happy.

It was usually now that the 'promoter' would make what

seemed like an irresistible proposal to the band. As they had been so successful, he would tell their agent that he'd like to book them for at least three more consecutive dates, say a Thursday, Friday and Saturday, with each night aiming for the maximum possible audience by bringing in an extra act or two, and if necessary some further support to give the show the greatest possible impact. By now the members of the group would be so excited at the prospect that when the 'promoter' mentioned paying them by cheque within seven days, 'as usual', no one was likely to object.

The 'promoter' would ensure that these final performances were held in the largest venue available, holding if possible an audience of 1,500, with the chance of packing in an extra 200 at the last minute. He would also engage in as much advance publicity as possible, ensuring that all three nights became a sell-out. The shows would go ahead and everybody would be happy until the promised cheque failed to appear. The nightly earnings from three successful big performances are considerable, and having pocketed the lot the 'promoter' would either disappear or simply, in criminal parlance, 'knock' the group by telling them to whistle for their money. As Wilf discovered, 'Nine times out of ten, trying to get your money through the courts gets you nowhere. And since the 'promoter' knew this from the start, he would brazen things out, and the members of the group would never get their wages.' End of story – except that with Wilf around it wasn't.

By now he and several of the crew, who had spent the summer in close contact with a succession of performers, had also got to know many of their managers and agents. From time to time they would complain to him about these rogue 'promoters', and as something of a last resort some of them had even asked if he could help them.

Sometimes, when trying to extract money owing to his group, an agent would end up being threatened by what Wilf calls 'the broken-nosed brigade' of hired thugs, who would order the agent to back off – or else. At other times the so-called 'promoter' would have simply vanished without trace.

After hearing a succession of such stories, Wilf decided that the time had come for him and the crew to get themselves involved in something more useful than manning doors and dealing with drunks and troublemakers. 'Which was how I got into the debt-collecting business on behalf of the music industry,' he explains.

'By now,' he says, 'the crew had been working together for so long that with Dave and Jinxie in their midst they were quite simply the best outfit of the sort I've ever seen.' Backed up by a few selected members of the crew, Wilf didn't find the London 'broken-nosed brigade' a problem. 'If they fancied their luck against us, a few whacks with a pickaxe handle here and there soon changed their minds – and after that my friends would always get their money.'

What could have been more difficult were cases of 'promoters' who had simply disappeared, but here Wilf's network of contacts dating back to his earliest days at Blyth paid off again. 'Say, for instance, that the "promoter" was known to have been working in the Birmingham area, all it needed was a phone call to one of my oldest friends, Big Albert Chapman, doorman-in-chief at Birmingham's famous club, the Rum Runner in Broad Street. Albert had been a kingpin in Birmingham's nightlife scene for years and what he didn't know about anybody in the city he'd soon find out. So all I had to do was telephone him and mention the name of the "promoter". As a good turn from one old friend to another, Albert would soon be on the phone telling me where to find him and who, if anyone, was looking after him. Once I knew this it would rarely take more than two or three more calls for me to arrange that the vanishing "promoter" had a visit, as a result of which the money owing would swiftly be forthcoming. If it wasn't, I and a few members of the crew would personally go up ourselves and make sure it was.'

Word soon got around that Wilf Pine had a way with vanishing 'promoters', and before long his telephone was ringing with more requests for help collecting money owing. As he had friends like Big Albert throughout the country, it wasn't hard to do similar favours for other groups. As he says, 'everybody loves the guy who gets results', and he and the crew had found themselves an extra role as debt collectors to the music industry.

As his reputation grew, he also started to become increasingly involved in the social life that was such a part of the whole pop music scene, and he makes no bones about the effect this had on his marriage. As part of the entourage of almost all performing pop groups at the time, hordes of young female fans were only too available, and Wilf, as usual, found himself unable to resist temptation.

'By now,' he says, 'I was becoming a serial cheat to Jill', but he had been an absent and unfaithful husband for so long that he felt little guilt and didn't really care. 'Even now, after all these years, I feel no shame for my behaviour then. It was unforgivable, I know, but there it is.'

But while he continued to be 'the worst kind of husband any girl could have', he was also a devoted father, and although he says that 'home had simply become a place I went to when I needed to sleep, have a meal and be with baby Sean', he still found time to make Jill pregnant. On 26 July 1967 she gave birth to a second son, called Scott. Wilf loved babies and was once again besotted, but new babies rarely turn erring husbands into faithful spouses and Wilf's extra-marital pleasures continued to the point where, late that summer, for the first time in his life, he fell in love.

For him the experience was as strange as it was unexpected, and it left him overwhelmed. Love like this was something he had never known before and was the last thing he had thought would hit anyone as ruthless and cynical as him. The very thought of Wilf Pine, tough guy, control freak and serial seducer, in the role of a romantic lover was hard to credit.

Her name was Lesley Wheeler. She was just sixteen, blonde-haired and very pretty, but then all Wilf's girls were pretty, and perhaps what really made the difference was simply that she made it clear from the start that she had no intention of going to bed with him – not immediately, at any rate.

As far as he was concerned, this gave Lesley irresistible allure. He remembers being tongue-tied in her presence, which again for him was most unusual. Even today when talking about her he admits, 'she completely blew me away'.

And since this girl would come in and out of his life for many years to come, she is an important part of his story.

*

Shortly after their first meeting, he had plucked up his courage and invited her to be his guest at the following Saturday's performance at the Royal York. He had asked her to come half an hour before the performance started for a drink so that he could introduce her to a few close friends.

But when Saturday arrived, she kept him waiting anxiously in the bar of the Royal York Hotel, suddenly fearing that she might not come. Jinxie and Dave Farley made things worse by ribbing him about the aftershave he had put on for the occasion. 'If she does turn up and gets a nose-full of that, she'll be off in a flash,' said Jinxie.

To make things worse, an acquaintance chose this very moment to come over to their table with a story of how he'd just been drinking in the Bow Bars around the corner and had overheard a conversation between four or five dubious characters who had been working as bouncers at a rival club. 'Some of them were drinking heavily, and two of them were tooled up and seemed to be looking for a fight.' He told Wilf he had heard them boasting that later on that evening, 'they intend to come over here and sort us out'.

Wilf being Wilf knew who they were. They were south Londoners and had only recently arrived on the island, but already he'd been hearing of the threats that they'd been making against him and the crew behind their backs. Normally Wilf would not have taken any notice, but in the nervous state that he was in that evening he decided he would get his blow in first.

Normally, whenever Wilf was contemplating any act of violence in a public place, he and Dave would plan things very carefully beforehand to minimise the risk of being recognised. Now there was no time for that, but luck was on their side. As it was November, it was already dark, and rain was pouring down outside; also, purely by chance, Wilf and another member of the crew happened to be 'well tooled up' themselves. He was carrying his favourite weapon, an old-fashioned plumber's hammer which he had carefully adapted for this sort of work. It was very heavy. The head was cast iron, and each end consisted of a rounded piece of solid copper, all of which he had carefully bound over with black insulation tape. He had also shortened the handle to fit neatly into his hand. 'In the half-light, if you were in a row and had to use it, nobody would see what had hit them. And believe you me, that hammer equalled all men, no matter how big or tough they may have been.

'By now,' he says, 'I knew that to succeed in this sort of an attack you need two things – surprise and speed – and within minutes the four of us were crammed into a car being driven by a friend and on our way to the Bow Bars. It was raining heavier than ever now, and nobody was in the street to witness our arrival. As we knew our targets in advance, our plan was simple. While the driver kept the car parked by the kerbside with the motor running, we'd be in through the door, do as much damage as we could in as short a time as possible, then it would be into the car and back to the Royal York as quickly as we came.

'This is exactly what happened. Our loud-mouthed friends were still standing together at the far end of the bar with their backs to us, and we steamed straight into them. They never saw us and they didn't stand a chance. Everything was over before they knew what or who had hit them. Then we were off into the night. The whole episode had taken us less than ten minutes, and we had five minutes to spare before the doors opened for the concert. This just gave us time to clean up and remove any bloodstains from our hands and clothing and we were ready slap on time to take the tickets at the door and welcome the punters to another fun-filled night of rhythm and excitement at the Royal York.

'It was nearly twenty minutes after the doors were opened, and at least a hundred members of the audience had already passed through, when six policemen stormed into the foyer and insisted on closing all the doors behind them, leaving a long queue outside in the rain. They wanted us to stand in the empty foyer while they questioned us, but they'd not counted on the Royal York's general manager, Clive Meddick's father, Leslie. "Sergeant," he bellowed at the policeman in charge. "Would you be kind enough to tell me on what authority you think you are entitled to close the doors of my premises and totally disrupt this evening's entertainment?"'

The sergeant wasn't used to being spoken to like this, but he did his best to explain his business and why it was imperative to question Pine and the three members of the crew as soon as possible.

'Absolute nonsense,' Les replied, 'unless, that is, my four

employees here are supermen, with the ability to be in two separate places simultaneously. All of them without exception were here at the front of the house taking tickets at the time you mentioned. I'll swear to that effect on oath if you want me to. So, I'm sure, will my cashier, together with any member of the audience you care to ask.'

This gave the six policemen pause for thought, and for a minute or two they stood huddled together by the door, discussing their next move. They made all four suspects show their hands, which they examined in minute detail, front and back, but discovered nothing. They then examined their clothing and finally their shoes, again without success. After another brief discussion among themselves, the sergeant said that they'd be making further enquiries and would be in touch with them later. For the time being they could continue with their work.

Later, Wilf was told that when the police returned to the Bow Bars and tried to interview the original witnesses, no one could now be sure of the identity of their attackers. So no statements were ever made to the police implicating Wilf and any members of the crew in the attack, and in the end they dropped the whole matter from lack of evidence.

As for the Londoners, three of them needed hospital treatment and, bashed and beaten with Wilf's hammer, all of them soon returned to London. As for Lesley, she arrived just as the show was starting.

Wilf worked for two years with Clive Meddick, by the end of which he was virtually running the show and beginning to know the daily business of concert promotion inside out. He had also formed close friendships with many of the leading pop stars who visited the island. These included the teenybopper idol Alan Jones from Amen Corner, and Carl Wayne, the wild man of pop, from the Move, who in normal life was a gentle, rather clever boy from Birmingham. But by another of those tricks of fate that had a habit of abruptly altering the course of Wilf Pine's life completely, his most important friendship in the business suddenly proved to be with three young brothers from Portsmouth, Phil, Ray and Derek Schulman.

During the late 1960s and early 1970s the Schulman brothers were one of the most continually successful groups in British pop music. They had called their band Simon Dupree and the Big Sound, thinking that the name 'Dupree' had more appeal than Schulman. The original Simon Dupree had once been Lord Mayor of Portsmouth. At any rate, the Big Sound had an almost magical impact on any audience, and their current records were invariably near the top of the charts. As their home in Portsmouth was only a ferry-ride away from Wilf's in Ryde, the two families saw a lot of one another.

By the time the season started in 1968, Clive Meddick had closed down the Disco Blue, and as he also felt that Saturday Night at the York had run its course he was looking for a brand-new venue and picked on a ballroom called the Hunter's Den in the plush Ryde Castle Hotel. This generated much excitement on the island, especially when he chose the Big Sound to perform on the opening night. Since this band virtually guaranteed a sell-out, Wilf was not surprised by the decision. Nor was he any less surprised when the next he heard from the boys' agent was that they were already booked for that night – as were all the other popular bands. Since the opening night was particularly important, Meddick asked Wilf if he could try to persuade his friends the Schulman brothers, as a personal favour, to change their minds. 'Don't just telephone,' he told him. 'Take the ferry over to Portsmouth first thing tomorrow morning and use every argument you know to get them.'

Somewhat reluctantly Wilf agreed. He took the morning ferry, unaware of the effect the trip would have on his career.

All three Schulman brothers were at home, and after the usual civilities Wilf got down to business, explained the problem and asked them if, as friends, there was anything they could do to help.

Phil Schulman, who was the funny one in the trio, looked at both his brothers, then at Wilf before replying.

'In the words of the great Joe Louis,' he began, 'a friend in need is—' he paused '—a pest,' he said. At which all of them burst out laughing, assuring Wilf that in spite of the famous boxer's warning they would try their best to help him. They added that they didn't actually know where they were supposed to be performing on that night, so they'd ring their manager immediately and see what could be done. As their manager, John King, also happened to be their brother-in-law, this wasn't difficult and he promised that he'd talk to the promoter straight away and try his best to rearrange the date. Wilf had an anxious lunch with the brothers, but before it ended King was back on the telephone with good news. The promoter had taken a while to convince but had finally agreed to reschedule the band, leaving them free to play on the opening night in the Hunter's Den. He named a fee, which Wilf thought extremely reasonable and promised to put a contract in the post.

Later that afternoon, when an elated Wilf Pine returned to the island, Clive Meddick was not around to hear the news and it was not until the following day when he arrived at Meddick's flat for lunch that he finally had a chance to tell him. He was expecting thanks and warm congratulations for having pulled off something of a coup. Instead of which Meddick made a face and calmly told him he had changed his mind about the Big Sound. Instead of them he'd just booked another band for that evening.

'Then you'd better think about unbooking them,' said Wilf. 'These were personal friends of mine, and they were doing me a very special favour. If we go back on it now, they'll be up shit creek, and I'll be left looking a right prat.'

This was the beginning of what rapidly became a stand-up row between them. Wilf describes it as 'an altercation', which denoted a fight which, while not carried to the limit, included harsh words, lost tempers, blows and the termination of a friendship.

'I entered Clive's flat with a spring in my step,' says Wilf, 'and left it with my heart in my boots.'

The truth is that he terribly regretted what had happened and still believes that, given time, relations with Meddick could have been restored. But time was something that he didn't have. The first thing he had to do was obviously to ring the Schulman brothers. He dreaded doing this, but instead of the furious reaction he expected, Phil Schulman couldn't have been more understanding. So was their manager, when he rang him next; his chief concern appeared to be for Wilf, and he said how sorry he was that he had presumably lost his job with Meddick.

'But I've an idea,' he said. 'Give me an hour or so and I'll ring you back.'

True to his word, he rang back twenty minutes later. He'd been talking to the band and had a proposition.

'Since it's thanks to you that the band has lost a night's work, we'd like you to find a suitable new venue on the island for that evening and you can promote the show yourself. Your deal would be with them. They'd meet all the expenses, and at the end of the evening we'd all have equal shares of what was left in the pot.'

By now the level-headed Dave Farley was in on the discussions and outlined the consequences if Wilf and the crew accepted. The chief objection was that by promoting a rival show on Clive Meddick's opening night, Wilf would be burning all his bridges with him for ever. But if he refused he'd be letting down his friends, the Schulman brothers. Having weighed the pros and cons, Wilf decided to accept.

The biggest problem was finding somewhere big enough for the band and the sell-out audience they expected. Wilf's preference was for almost anywhere apart from Ryde, as he didn't wish to give the impression of acting out of spite against Clive Meddick. But every hall was booked, except one – the old Seagull Ballroom, where he and Meddick had promoted so many successful shows the year before.

As luck would have it, the lease on the ballroom had recently been taken over by another of Wilf's friends, the promoter, Peter van Buren. He was happy to rent it to him for the night, and Wilf was delighted.

There were some stressful weeks before the concert, but on the night itself everything worked perfectly. All the arrangements were in order, and Wilf remembers to this day the band giving their performance of a lifetime. Perhaps they really did. Certainly everyone was very happy, and to cap it all van Buren asked Wilf if he would be able to promote full-scale Saturday-night shows at the Seagull for the whole season.

'I'd love to but I haven't any money,' Wilf replied.

'That's not a problem,' said van Buren. 'I'm perfectly prepared to back you for as long as necessary.'

Wilf agreed. Almost overnight, Wilf Pine, formerly of Blyth Wellesley Nautical School, discharged dustman, bouncer and occasional ruthless gangster, found himself a fully fledged promoter in the music business.

Once this was settled, his next task was to find a sufficiently exciting group to fill the ballroom the following Saturday. The Big Sound was a hard act to follow, and he needed something equally impressive that would pull the crowds and maintain momentum. His first thought was his favourite band, the Move, who were still as firmly in the charts as when he'd heard them two years earlier in that never-to-be-forgotten concert at the Royal York. He'd heard rumours recently that they were resting, and as it was a Sunday morning he couldn't ring their agent. But he had the home number of his friend, Carl Wayne, the band's lead singer; and since time was of the essence he took his courage in both hands and rang him.

'Don't you know it's Sunday?' a voice answered that he didn't recognise.

'I'm sorry to trouble you,' said Wilf, 'but I need to speak to Carl Wayne urgently.'

'And who wants him?'

Wilf gave his name, and heard someone laughing. 'Wilf, you old fucker. What the hell are you up to, ringing me on a Sunday morning?'

Wilf suddenly remembered that Carl was a merciless mimic and spent the next ten minutes explaining what had happened. Suddenly Carl couldn't have been more helpful. Of course he and the boys would love to perform for him, but as they'd been resting he'd have to clear things with their manager, Tony Secunda, and also with their all-important agent, Sue Rose at Galaxy Entertainment. He'd speak to both of them first thing on Monday morning and if Wilf called him at eleven he'd have an answer.

Sure enough, at eleven sharp Wilf rang and found that he was still in luck. Tony Secunda had agreed, the band had agreed and even their agent had agreed. The Move were ready and willing to appear at the Seagull Ballroom, Ryde, that very Saturday. All Wilf had to do was contact Sue at Galaxy and sort out the details and a contract.

Sue was an important agent in the business, and like everybody else that morning she seemed to be on his side. Not only did she rapidly sort out the preliminary details of that Saturday's show, agree a fee and arrange to put a contract in that night's post, but she also enquired if there was anything else that she could do to help him. When he replied that, just for starters, he desperately needed four top bands to fill the Seagull for the coming month, she said she'd think about it.

Now that everything was settled for that Saturday, Wilf's next task was to arrange for the advance publicity. After placing large ads in the local papers, posters were urgently required and he rang another of his friends, a local jobbing printer, explaining what he wanted.

'How soon d'you need them, Wilf?' he asked.

'Half an hour ago,' Wilf answered. To which the printer's reply was that provided Wilf came straight away to sort out the artwork, and was happy with simple black and white, he could have a run of a hundred posters by early evening. Which he did, and by nine o'clock that evening, with their hundred posters barely dry, Wilf and Dave, armed with brushes and buckets full of paste, started working through the night 'slapping posters all over the island'.

Next morning, in almost every corner of the Isle of Wight, people awoke to the news that on Saturday evening Carl Wayne and the Move would be appearing at the Seagull Ballroom. And later that morning Wilf received his first, but not his last, warning from the local council about a crime he'd never previously committed – flyposting.

But all the work paid off, and Wilf's apparently charmed first season as a full-time promoter happily continued. Carl and the Move were great, and Wilf's new friend, Sue Rose at Galaxy, found him a succession of top bands to please the weekly punters at the Seagull. There were some great names from the 1960s, many of which have earned their places in the early history of pop music – bands like the Tremeloes, who, with three major hits already, were back in the charts with 'Silence Is Golden' and 'My Little Lady', the Marmalade, who had made their name with 'Lovin' Things', and once again the teenagers' favourite, Amen Corner, who were once more in the charts with 'High in the Sky'.

This meant that thanks to Wilf's 'slight altercation' with Clive Meddick, that golden summer of 1968 turned out as something of a vintage year, with only one thing to mar his happiness. Almost overnight, the girl he was in love with vanished from his life, as unexpectedly as she had entered it.

By now they had been meeting almost every day and were apparently inseparable. Certainly Wilf was totally besotted, and when she failed to turn up for a date he nearly rang her parents' home. Then thinking better of it, he made his own enquiries, as a result of which he discovered that she'd abruptly left the island. But it wasn't until some time later that he found out why. From the start, he had never told Lesley that he was married. Since she'd never asked him, he'd always kept off the subject. But without realising it, Wilf had a hidden enemy – a girl with a grudge against him for banning her from one of the clubs that he looked after. To get her revenge, she had written an anonymous letter to Lesley's parents, informing them that Wilf was a married man with two small children. They had acted very swiftly, and their daughter's departure from the island followed almost instantly. She had been so upset to hear that Wilf already had a family that she had agreed to go and never write or contact him again.

Wilf took this badly, but life had to go on, and by now, he says, 'life seemed to be whizzing past me at a hundred miles an hour'.

The season at the Seagull Ballroom had concluded with something of a triumph. Sue Rose at Galaxy had arranged for Procol Harum, one of the biggest international groups of the day, to appear at the ballroom on that last Saturday. With such a draw, the show could have been sold out many times over. It was when they were performing a final encore of their greatest hit, 'A Whiter Shade of Pale', that Wilf was summoned to the telephone. Someone called David Arden was on the line and wished to speak to him. As Wilf knew exactly who he was, he immediately took the call. 'My father needs to speak to you as soon as possible,' David Arden said. 'Can you manage Monday afternoon at his office in Denmark Street?'

'Yes,' said Wilf without hesitating. 'Tell your father I'll be there.'

6

Meeting Mr Rock'n'Roll

'DON ARDEN? WHAT do you need to know about him?' said Bunny warily.

'Anything you can tell me,' Wilf replied.

Bunny was a well-known London agent who was staying on the Isle of Wight with a friend of Wilf's at Seaview, and Wilf had rung him late that Sunday evening. The call was Dave's idea. When Wilf had told him he was seeing Don Arden on Monday, Dave, shrewd as usual, said that before the meeting Wilf should talk to somebody who really knew him. Wilf tried several contacts who knew Arden, but either, like Carl Wayne, they weren't answering the phone, or if they did they made it clear they didn't want to talk. Bunny was the only one who would; even then he was wary.

'I'll talk to you on one condition: if Don Arden ever asks you where or how you got your information, my name will not be mentioned.'

'Understood,' said Wilf.

During the guarded conversation that ensued, Wilf received his first real lesson on the subject of the larger-than-life character who was to dominate his life for the next eighteen months.

'Don started with ambitions as an actor,' said Bunny. 'He's a born performer, but he made his name as a singer and a stand-up comic. It was only when he ceased to tread the boards that he discovered that his true talents lay as a promoter, making serious money from bringing top American acts on tour to Britain and Europe – performers such as Little Richard, Gene Vincent, Jerry Lee Lewis and the Everly Brothers, and many others. Then he moved into management and the agency side of the business. Don's a star-maker

Wilf's wedding. Left to right: Trish Pagano (bridesmaid),
Theresa Pagano (matron of honour), Lesley, Sammi Pine (bridesmaid).
Top left: Joe Pagano (best man), top right: Wilf Pine.

Ros and Wilf. Wedding 26 July 1980.

Above: Receiving Gold Disc for the Stray LP. Mudanzas Back row, left to right: Steve Gadd, Richie Cole, Del Bromham, Gary Giles, Clive (Jinxie) Jenkins, Ken Mewes. Seated: Wilf Pine.

Black Sabbath. Taken *circa* 1990. Tony Iommi (lead guitarist), Wilf Pine.

Left: Wilf's life long friend, Big Albert Chapman.

Below: Don Arden.

Billy O'Brien (Joe Pagano's bodyguard) and Wilf Pine.

Rare photo of the Pagano brothers together.
Pasquale (Pat) Pagano and Joseph Pagano.

Alphonse (Funzi) Tierie boss of the Genovese. First boss to be convicted by the RICO Act. Died of natural causes.

Rare photo of Pasquale (Pat) Pagano.

Left: Anthony (Fat Tony) Salerno. Boss of the Genovese family 1970–80s. Sentenced to 100 years in the Commission Trial. Died in prison.

Below: Anthony (Fat Tony) Salerno. Last photo taken by cops.

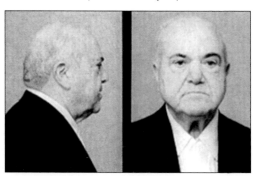

John Gotti, boss of the Gambino family.
Died of cancer in prison.

Left: Angelo Bruno.

Below: Angelo Bruno dead
by shotgun blast, 1980.

Arnold (Zeke) Squitteri, Wilf's friend,
on the death of John Gotti. Newspapers and the FBI
claim he is the new boss of the Gambino Family.

Alphonse (Funzi) Cisca, Wilf's friend and drinking
partner, at Danny Pagano's going away party.

Wilf's wedding. Left to right: Trish Pagano (bridesmaid),
Theresa Pagano (matron of honour), Lesley, Sammi Pine (bridesmaid).
Top left: Joe Pagano (best man), top right: Wilf Pine.

Ros and Wilf. Wedding 26 July 1980.

Above: Receiving Gold Disc for the Stray LP. Mudanzas Back row, left to right: Steve Gadd, Richie Cole, Del Bromham, Gary Giles, Clive (Jinxie) Jenkins, Ken Mewes. Seated: Wilf Pine.

Black Sabbath. Taken *circa* 1990. Tony Iommi (lead guitarist), Wilf Pine.

Left: Wilf's life long friend, Big Albert Chapman.

Below: Don Arden.

Billy O'Brien (Joe Pagano's bodyguard) and Wilf Pine.

Rare photo of the Pagano brothers together.
Pasquale (Pat) Pagano and Joseph Pagano.

Alphonse (Funzi) Tierie boss of the Genovese. First boss to be convicted by the RICO Act. Died of natural causes.

Rare photo of Pasquale (Pat) Pagano.

Left: Anthony (Fat Tony) Salerno. Boss of the Genovese family 1970–80s. Sentenced to 100 years in the Commission Trial. Died in prison.

Below: Anthony (Fat Tony) Salerno. Last photo taken by cops.

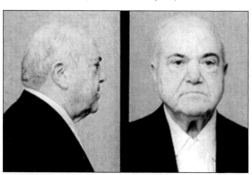

John Gotti, boss of the Gambino family.
Died of cancer in prison.

Left: Angelo Bruno.

Below: Angelo Bruno dead
by shotgun blast, 1980.

Arnold (Zeke) Squitteri, Wilf's friend,
on the death of John Gotti. Newspapers and the FBI
claim he is the new boss of the Gambino Family.

Alphonse (Funzi) Cisca, Wilf's friend and drinking
partner, at Danny Pagano's going away party.

with a touch of genius who single-handedly created groups like the Nashville Teens and the Small Faces'.

Bunny paused, as if uncertain whether to continue. When he did, he sounded quieter, as if about to let Wilf into an appalling secret.

'If you meet Don, there's one further thing you must remember. He can be dangerous, particularly to anyone who tries to muscle in on his territory, and he's not averse to using heavies to scare off any opposition. You've probably heard what happened to his rival promoter, Robert Stigwood.'

'No,' said Wilf. 'Tell me.'

'From all I've heard, Stigwood was showing too much interest in a group Don managed who were growing dissatisfied. Don's way of dealing with this was to go straight to Stigwood's office with his heavy friends, drag him personally from his desk out on to the balcony, and then dangle him looking down at the pavement four storeys below. Legend has it that he asked his friends if he should drop him or forgive him. All of them shouted, "Drop him", but Don forgave him. There was no further trouble.

'It's probably true,' said Bunny. 'Stigwood himself has never denied it, nor has Don. And certainly after that no other manager or agent in the business has dared to tangle with Don Arden. So never forget: he's not a man to mess around with.'

Don Arden had recently bought up Galaxy Entertainment, the agency where Wilf's friend Sue Rose worked, and had moved into their offices in Denmark Street, above the old Tin Pan Alley Club. In those days Denmark Street was still a decaying mix of showbiz and seediness off Charing Cross Road, and in its time the Tin Pan Alley Club had been the favourite haunt of many phoney – and a few genuine – underworld figures. Both 'Mad' Frankie Fraser and Charlie Richardson's younger brother, Eddie, were rumoured to have had a share of the action.

On entering the office just before midday on Monday morning, the first person Wilf saw was Sue Rose. Although they'd never actually met before, they'd talked so often on the telephone that they were friends already. Sue said that Don had an appointment in the City but would soon be back. In the meantime she introduced Wilf to another of his telephone acquaintances, Don Arden's son David. He was of an age with Wilf, and Wilf sensed that they would get on well together. By now the office was humming with activity, and Wilf was feeling quite at home when Don Arden entered.

Wilf had never met a big-time pop group manager before, and in spite of himself was most impressed. Don was a stocky man in his early forties, immaculately dressed in a pale grey suit, his beautifully coiffured hair slightly greying at the sides, and with one of the most engaging smiles Wilf had ever seen. But there was something else about Don Arden. Although not quite as tall as Wilf, 'he had a chest and pair of shoulders that wouldn't have looked out of place on an England rugby forward'. And despite the regulation showbiz smile of welcome, Wilf still remembers feeling 'as if those gimlet eyes of his were boring straight through me'. Over one thing, at any rate, Bunny had been right. This was clearly not a man to mess around with.

Surprisingly for such a forceful character, it took Arden quite a while to get to the point of why he'd invited Wilf to see him. 'It's rather a delicate matter, and as it concerns a mutual friend of ours I must ask you to promise that anything I say remains strictly confidential.'

First Bunny, now Don Arden, pledging Wilf to secrecy – what was going on? And had Don Arden known Wilf a little better, he'd have known that this was not the way to win his confidence. Wilf has many faults, but he has always been uncomfortably loyal to his friends.

'Who is this friend of mine?' he asked.

'It's Alan Jones from Amen Corner.'

It was then that Wilf decided that the time had come to go, and he started rising from his seat.

'If what you want involves anything physical happening to Alan, I think we'd better end this conversation here and now,' he said.

Don Arden could not have been more apologetic.

'Wilf,' he said. 'Calm down. Forgive me. I put things badly. If I wished a friend of yours the slightest harm, I'd not be so stupid as to talk to you about it. You have my solemn word that Alan Jones is not in the slightest danger – not from me, at any rate. And as you've already come a long way to see me, let's go and have a spot of lunch and I'll do my best to explain what's going on.'

As Wilf discovered, Don Arden enjoyed his food. Sue had booked a table at Bianchi's, an old-fashioned Italian restaurant around the corner, where they could talk in peace. Over a steaming plateful of osso buco, Don explained that when he purchased Galaxy Entertainment from the impresario Ron King, who had emigrated to Australia, the deal included a management company along with all the current artistes they had under contract. These included Amen Corner, but suddenly there was a problem. It turned out that long before he'd thought of selling his agency, King used to joke with members of the group, saying that if they misbehaved he'd sell their contracts to Don Arden. As he said this, Arden laughed, but Wilf had the feeling that he didn't really find it funny, particularly when he went on to explain that on account of this the situation had suddenly turned serious.

'As you know, the boys in Amen Corner are young Welsh lads from the valleys, and when they heard that along with the agency their contracts had passed on to me, they were not unnaturally upset and said they wanted out. From all I hear they still do, without even giving me a chance to show what I could do for them and their careers.'

Arden paused to sip his wine before continuing.

'If that was all, I'm sure that we could work things out, but it isn't all – not by a long chalk. During these last few days I've been hearing rumours that, on top of this, the boys have been approached by someone acting on behalf of one of my rivals, and that he's also urging them to break their contracts. I don't have to tell you that with a group as valuable as Amen Corner, a lot of money is involved and these bastards seem determined to take them over.'

He paused and looked at Wilf with those piercing eyes of his.

'Don Arden has no intention of allowing that to happen.'

'So where do I come in?' asked Wilf, who was beginning to feel slightly out of his depth.

'Good question, Wilf. Now I happen to know that Alan Jones is a friend of yours and that he recently spent a few days with you and your family on the Isle of Wight.'

'Sue must have told you that,' said Wilf.

Once more Don Arden laughed, but this time more spontaneously than before.

'You could be right. But as I'm in the dark about the group's real feelings, and as I also know you're close to Alan, I wanted to ask you if he's ever talked to you about this. If he has, you could possibly provide me with a clue as to what is really going on.'

'Sorry, Don,' said Wilf. 'If I could help, I would, but honestly I can't. Alan's a very private person, and he didn't mention any of this while he was with us. To tell the truth, Don, he didn't even mention you.'

If Don Arden was disappointed, he didn't show it, and he showed such charm as he apologised for wasting Wilf's time that, in spite of himself, Wilf felt he'd like to help him. Since he was already in London, he said that he would pay the group a visit and do his best to find out what was happening. Alan had said that they were living in Harrow-on-the-Hill, so he'd drive there straight away, and if he did discover anything, he'd ring Don later.

As Wilf tells the story, he makes it sound as if the house at Harrow-on-the-Hill was in a state of siege from teenage groupies desperately seeking contact with their idols – which was why, when Clive Taylor, the group's bass player, answered the front door, he quickly pulled Wilf in and bolted it behind him.

'Sorry, Wilf, but those three females have been trying to force their way in here all day.'

'Such is the price of fame,' said Wilf, trying to sound sarcastic and hoping his envy didn't show. Then Alan Jones appeared, and when Wilf had had a chance to talk to him about Don Arden, and why he'd come, Alan said that he should talk to all the group – so once more Wilf related his story to them all in the kitchen over a cup of tea. He explained about the conversation he had had with Arden, adding that if he was in their shoes, he'd be feeling worried to have a powerful third party involved in a fight with Don Arden over their contracts. But as he said this, Wilf tried to make it clear that he was speaking purely as their friend.

This kitchen conference was the start of an endless discussion that continued almost all that night. In the end Andy Fairweather-Low, the group's willowy lead singer and the country's number-one teeny-bopper idol, showed that he was very much the leader of the band by taking charge of the discussion. What concerned him was the band's future and the welfare of its members, and Wilf was left to answer questions and offer his opinion. Andy admitted then that a rival impresario, with powerful financial backing, had been pursuing them for quite some time with very tempting offers – but so far no decisions had been taken.

On hearing this, Wilf replied that in his position he'd want to be a hundred per cent sure of anyone he was going to entrust with the group's future. Andy agreed. All the uncertainty was bad for everybody, and he'd come to the conclusion that, since Don Arden's reputation as a working manager was well known, the boys should follow Wilf's advice and give him a chance. When the group agreed, Andy said to Wilf: 'Tell Don Arden that we'll give it a go.'

Dawn was breaking, and Wilf said that he would like to snatch a few hours' sleep before going to Denmark Street to break the news to Don in person.

'Fine,' said Andy. 'All of us should see him too. So tell him we'll come to his office at around 11.30.'

Wilf arrived at Denmark Street early, hoping to be the bearer of good tidings, but when he saw Don Arden and told him of the group's decision, Don was sceptical.

'I'm still not absolutely sure I trust them, Wilf, and we'll just have to see what happens. But however things turn out, I'm grateful to you for trying.'

'You shouldn't have to wait long for an answer,' Wilf replied. 'The whole group will be turning up here in a few minutes, and I think they're keen to get things settled.'

Barely had he spoken than Sue put her head around the door to announce the arrival of Amen Corner. And within a few minutes, Don Arden and the group were chatting away like old friends, as if nothing had ever come between them. As for Wilf, he felt he'd done everything he could. He also felt in need of a good night's sleep and suddenly couldn't wait to get back to his precious island.

Courteous as ever, Don Arden saw him out, and as he shook his hand asked him what he owed him.

And Wilf had the sense to answer, 'Nothing, Don. I'm just delighted everything worked out.'

'It was thanks to you it did,' said Don. 'We'll be in touch.'

Sure enough, a week later Wilf received another call from Arden asking him to come to see him. Rather than face another nightmare journey up the old A3, Wilf decided he would go by train. He arrived at Denmark Street in time for his midday appointment to find no one in the office. It was almost an hour before Sue turned up, with effusive apologies for having kept him waiting. David Arden arrived next, apparently exhausted after an all-night session taking care of a group he was managing; and then it was Don Arden's turn to enter the office like a human whirlwind, trailing his assistant, Pat Meehan, in his wake.

He apologised to Wilf for having kept him waiting and said he'd be with him in a moment. But this was time for action stations and the office started buzzing like a power station. Wilf had never seen anything like it before and sat patiently for the next two hours feeling utterly useless. He was beginning to wish he'd never come and was on the point of leaving when Don turned to him with a smile on his face.

'It's all go, isn't it, Wilf? Let's go out and find ourselves a sandwich and a good strong cup of coffee.'

Walking several paces in front, he charged his way up Charing Cross Road, to a little café opposite Tottenham Court Road tube station, where everybody seemed to know him. Not for nothing had he started his career as a stand-up comic; even before he'd ordered the sandwiches he had the staff in fits of laughter. As an excuse to Wilf for keeping him waiting so long, he started explaining how he'd been caught up in some complicated deal, then stopped and laughed and looked Wilf in the eye. 'The truth is, Wilf, I just forgot that you were there.' And they both started laughing.

This was the point when Wilf decided that he liked Don Arden, which was just as well as the next thing Arden said to him was: 'Because of the way you handled things with Amen Corner, I'd like to offer you a job.'

'Doing what?' asked Wilf.

'To be honest, I'm not absolutely sure, but I'll think of something. How's about it?'

Wilf remained cautious, saying that he needed time to decide.

'Well, take your time, but not too long. I'll pay you well and you can use the flat above the office – no rent and slap in the middle of the West End. Can't be bad. Anyhow, Wilf, give me a ring when you've decided. Now I must rush. Another meeting. Late already. No peace for the wicked. Wilf, I hope you'll join us.'

Throughout the journey back to the island, Wilf sat in his third–class carriage trying to work out what a job with Arden would entail – and whether he really wanted it. As he had only limited experience as a promoter, and since his hands were covered with tattoos, he couldn't see himself sitting in the office as one of Don's personal assistants. And since Don couldn't be wanting him for his brains, that left only one other reason – muscle – and he wasn't sure he wanted to be taken on for that.

On arriving home, he told Jill of the offer and asked her how she felt about it, as it would mean his being away in London all week.

'As far as I'm concerned, I can't see it'll make much difference. As it is, we only see you when you feel like coming home.' With this she turned away, and Wilf knew that what she said was true. He felt much the same. His marriage had reached the point where neither of them really cared what happened.

So he spent that evening out drinking with the crew and afterwards took the opportunity to discuss Don Arden's offer with the man who had become his personal adviser – Dave Farley. For the winter, Dave had found himself a job for which he was highly qualified – not in crime, but as a specialist marine engineer, which is what he was by training. At first he seemed put out that Wilf hadn't even told him he was seeing Don.

'I rang you, you bastard,' Wilf replied, 'but as far as I remember you were far too busy trying to get that blonde I saw you with to bed. How was she, incidentally?'

'Too good for the likes of you, my friend. Anyhow, I'll forgive you for not telling me you had a job in the offing. How do you feel about it?'

Wilf explained his doubts, and with his usual caution Dave said he couldn't make his mind up for him. But the truth was that with the winter coming Wilf was beginning to find life on the island difficult. He'd had plans of following his summertime success with a similar winter season, but it was hard to find a suitable location. As usual in this situation, he could always turn to crime, but there was precious little on offer, and the police had been taking a more serious interest in his activities lately. Until now, he'd been lucky, but he felt his luck was running out and, as he puts it, 'that I was long overdue a taste of prison food'.

Indeed, the very day after his discussion with Dave Farley, the police arrived at his house accusing him of receiving a consignment of stolen booze. 'They knew it was a load of bollocks, but it was their charming way of letting me know they'd not forgotten me.'

So Wilf took the hint and that very morning rang Don Arden to accept his offer.

'That's great,' he said. 'We need you around. Things are happening. Can you start today?'

Wilf thought he sounded agitated.

'Just give me time to pack a case and I'll be with you,' he replied.

Wilf reached Denmark Street soon after lunch to find Don Arden wreathed in cigar smoke, in the middle of his customary symphony of phone calls. When finally there was a lull, he welcomed Wilf and told him what was going on.

'More trouble with our friends in Amen Corner, I'm afraid. Nothing obvious, but I'm not happy. Call it a sixth sense, if you like, but I know there's something in the wind.'

Wilf tried to say that it was less than ten days since they'd seen the group and perhaps they should give them a chance. But Arden shook his head.

'Take it from me, Wilf. I've had a lot of experience with groups, and I know this lot are definitely up to something. Anyhow, I'm flying to Italy on business first thing tomorrow morning, and by the time I return tomorrow night I expect to have some news. Here are the keys of the flat. Make yourself comfortable, and why don't you give your pal Alan Jones a call to let him know you're working for me? Ask him out tonight and see if you can learn anything. Oh, and by the way, my wife Paddy would like you to come for dinner with us all tomorrow night. See you then.'

After Don had left the office and Wilf had had a chance to think over what he'd said, none of his suspicions over Amen Corner seemed to make much sense. One minute everything was fine, the next Don was imagining something going on behind his back. On top of this, Wilf still didn't really have a clue as to what his role in the Arden setup would be. What the hell was going on and what, he wondered, was he doing there at all?

Later that afternoon Wilf rang Alan Jones, as Don suggested, but there was no reply, so he went up to inspect his flat. It was small but comfortable, and that evening, since unable to contact Alan, he ate a solitary meal, watched television for a while and turned in early. Next morning, when he reached the office, Sue told him why he hadn't been able to reach Alan the previous evening. It was due to nothing more sinister than the fact that Amen Corner had been out of town, performing at a gig in Bristol. At the same time, David told Wilf that his mother was definitely expecting him for dinner. It would be strictly family, and he gave him an address in Mayfair, suggesting he arrived around 7.30.

The Arden apartment was in a street off Berkeley Square, and from the moment Wilf stepped into that marbled lobby and was respectfully greeted by the uniformed porter he found himself in a world that he never realised existed. The porter took him up to the apartment in the lift, and when David Arden answered the bell Wilf was greeted by a sight that he had seen only in films and magazines.

Pop music had made Don Arden rich, and the Ardens lived in style – thick-pile carpets, gilt mirrors, oil paintings on the walls and, as a centrepiece to the apartment, an enormous crystal chandelier.

'Everything in that room was class,' says Wilf, 'and the classiest thing of all was the lady who greeted me, David's mother Paddy.' He was particularly impressed by how immaculately she was dressed. Like Don, not a hair was out of place, and although he later learned that she was nearing fifty and was slightly older than her husband, 'she was oh so stunningly beautiful. She asked me to sit down, and offered me a drink, and within a few minutes I was talking to her as if I'd known her all my life.'

Then another member of the family arrived, David's younger sister Sharon. Wilf had no way of knowing that one day she would become one of the most successful managers in the music business and the dynamic wife of the superstar of heavy rock, Ozzy Osbourne. His only memories of Sharon at this first meeting are of a lively sixteen-year-old, 'who most definitely took after her mother in the looks department'.

If it hadn't been for Paddy, Wilf would have found the dinner that ensued a nightmare. 'To me the table looked sensational, but there was far more cutlery in front of me than I knew what to do with. But when Paddy had served us all soup, she could see that I had no idea which spoon to use, so she gave a discreet cough to catch my attention, then lifted her soup spoon with a look that said, "Just do as I do" – and I did, throughout the rest of the meal. It was typical of her to have understood my problem, and thanks to her I actually ended up enjoying that evening with the Arden family. She really was a very special lady.'

According to Wilf, during dinner the four of them never stopped talking, and it was after ten before Don got back from Italy and Wilf had a chance to see Don Arden the family man in action. Although he had been absent for only a day, he and the family greeted one another with such kisses and hugs that he might have been away for weeks. Never before in his life had Wilf witnessed such a show of love and family affection. When it ended, Don excused himself in order, as he put it, mimicking a woman, 'to slip into something more comfortable'. ('As I'd already discovered, Don really was a funny guy,' says Wilf.) But when he returned in a smoking jacket and settled into a comfortable armchair with a good cigar and a glass of his favourite malt whisky, the serious side of him was back, and he started quizzing David on what had been happening throughout the day.

Wilf asked if he should leave the room.

'Certainly not. You're part of the team now,' said Don. Then he turned his attention to Wilf and asked how his evening with Alan Jones had gone. Wilf told him what had happened, then made the mistake of adding that he thought that Don might possibly be reading something into the Amen Corner situation that simply wasn't there.

Whisky forgotten, Don was out of his chair in an instant and started lecturing Wilf on how cunning and two-faced bands could be, and how years of experience had taught him always to stay two steps ahead of them by picking up the vibes when groups were up to something.

'I know you're fond of the guys in Amen Corner, Wilf, but I'm fairly sure that they're in contact with a certain person who is doing his damnedest to make them break our contract. I also know that I can deal with them. Tomorrow morning Andy Fairweather-Low is coming to see me in the office, and, as it happens, while I was in Italy today I was offered a song that, unless I'm very much mistaken, could give the group their very first number-one hit. The lyric's still in Italian at the moment, but I'll be getting my friend, the writer Jack Fishman, to put it into English. Tomorrow, when Andy comes to see me at the office, I want him to hear it as it is in Italian. I've an idea that if nothing else this song will keep that whole group loyal.'

Wilf asked if he should cancel his evening out with Alan.

'No, don't. Alan's your friend and – who knows? – something might slip out in the conversation that could be useful.'

After this, the talk turned to less important matters, as if everyone was genuinely anxious to make Wilf feel one of the family. It was long past midnight before he thanked Paddy for a wonderful evening, said good night to his new-found friends and walked back to his little flat in Denmark Street.

That evening shows something fascinating about Wilf Pine. Barely two years earlier, he had been sacked as a council dustman. He had indulged in villainy, physical brutality and armed extortion. And at this point in his own career, Don Arden clearly needed somebody like Wilf to use as a heavy, whose very presence would strike terror into the hearts of his opponents in the music business.

But for the Arden family to have taken anyone as rough as Wilf into their family on the very first evening of his new employment says something else about him. Even then, what was unusual about Wilf Pine was that, along with the aggressive, ruthless, highly dangerous side of his divided nature, went an exceptional warmth and sensitivity that some found irresistible. Certainly that first evening he brought out the motherly instincts in Paddy Arden, who from then on showed him real affection and took a personal interest in his career, while from Wilf she would always inspire his absolute devotion. Simultaneously, the Arden family became for him the image of the perfect family he'd dreamed of and that in his own strange, baffled way was always seeking.

Next morning Wilf was already in the office when Andy Fairweather-Low arrived, and much to his surprise he was closely followed by another of his old friends from the music world, Carl Wayne. Wilf hadn't realised until now that Don also had the Move under contract, and Carl was equally surprised to find Wilf sitting in his office. Carl was there to collect a cheque and sign contracts for some future gigs before leaving for the West Country, where the Move was appearing the following week.

That morning, as usual, Don was in a tearing hurry, and as he had to rush off for another meeting when he'd finished seeing Andy, Wilf had a chance to talk to Andy on his own. Naturally he didn't mention any of Don's suspicions, but Andy said that Alan had mentioned that he and Wilf were going to a gig that evening. Since he was going too, he'd see him later. As he was leaving, Wilf managed to ask him what he'd thought of Don's Italian number.

'Far better than anything I expected. Great melody line. Can't wait to hear the words translated into English.'

'What's it called?'

'According to Don, in English it translates as "If Paradise Is Half as Nice".'

That evening was another first for Wilf, when Alan Jones picked him up from the flat in his gleaming sports car. Wilf had decided to ignore Don's request to try pumping him over what was going on behind the scenes in Amen Corner. As he told himself, 'my friendship with Alan Jones dated back to long before I started working for Don Arden, and all I was interested in that evening was enjoying myself with my friend'. At first it was not that easy. Even getting to the venue was an ordeal, as every groupie in England seemed to be packing the roads for miles around, and when they recognised Alan in the car they almost ripped his clothes off his back. According to Wilf, the group performed superbly and afterwards the fans were wilder still, with some of them even lying in the road trying to stop Alan's car so that they could reach him.

'For the first time in my life I found myself being grateful to the police for the way they escorted us on to the main road in safety.' From there Alan took him on to the Revolution club in Bruton Place, where Wilf was introduced to Maurice Gibb of the Bee Gees. In those days Alan was a formidable drinker, but Maurice Gibb was better. Wilf could also knock it back himself, and after one of the most riotous evenings of his life all three of them went home considerably the worse for wear. So Wilf was nursing the hangover of all hangovers when, next morning, he dragged himself into the office and awaited Don's arrival. He wasn't kept waiting long before Don came bouncing in.

'What did I tell you, Wilf? 'I knew those boys in the Corner were up to something. Now I can prove it. I've been promised that before lunchtime someone will ring me with the names of all the people who are behind this plot to make them break their contracts. And once I know, certain people would be well advised to watch out.'

But the morning dragged by without anyone phoning with the promised information, and Wilf had briefly retired upstairs to lie down with a monumental headache when Sue was knocking on the door saying that Don needed him in the office straight away. Wilf entered to find Don on the phone, making notes on a pad in front of him. When he'd finished, he looked up.

'I'm sorry to have to tell you this, Wilf, but I was right about Andy. According to my information, yesterday morning, after seeing me, Andy Fairweather-Low went straight to a meeting with a shady character known as the Weasel, who turns out to have been conducting negotiations with the Corner on behalf of my enemy.'

Wilf had never met the Weasel, but he'd heard about him more than once as a known con-man who specialised in promoting phoney companies and dodgy business deals. He was a fairly smooth operator, with a good lifestyle and a mews house in west London, who'd made and spent a lot of money. According to Don Arden, the people who were trying to steal the Move were using him as a front man for their shady business. But the Weasel was also anticipating trouble, since he was rumoured to have hired what Wilf describes as 'a right tasty crew from west London to look after him in the muscle department'.

Far from being worried by the possibility of violence, the idea of it instantly aroused the combative instincts in Don Arden's strongly theatrical personality. As a born actor, there were few roles in life he enjoyed more than playing the smooth, fast-talking tough guy. On a later occasion he would describe himself in a newspaper article as 'the Al Capone of pop', and it was very much as an Al Capone faced with the prospect of serious gang warfare that he now addressed his words to Wilf.

Wilf had asked him about their next move, and Don fixed him with those curiously hypnotic eyes of his and very calmly and deliberately announced: 'Wilf, when people want to fight the champ, they had better be prepared to go the full fifteen rounds, because, believe me, nobody, and I mean nobody, is going to fuck with me. If it's war they want, they've picked on the right guy. How soon can you have some members of the crew here?'

'It will take me two telephone calls,' said Wilf. 'I'll let you know the form by midday at the latest.'

Don had several appointments out of the office that day that he couldn't break, but he said he wanted definite news about the crew by the time he returned at five o'clock.

'How much can I offer them?' asked Wilf.

'Don't worry about that. Just get them here, and we'll sort the money out after they arrive,' he said.

In fact, it wasn't all that easy for Wilf to persuade his minions to drop everything and steam straight up to London at a moment's notice – even for him.

'You know I'd do it like a flash if it was just for you, Wilf,' said Dave Farley, 'but I'm none too keen to put myself in the firing line for Don Arden without knowing how long he'll want us, and what the pay will be. I fancy that Jinxie'll feel much the same.'

At this Wilf blew his top and started pointing out some of the past favours he had done him, the jobs they'd done together and the way he'd always looked on him and Jinxie as three musketeers — 'all for one and one for all'. 'But I was obviously mistaken; now that I need you both, all you can talk about is money.'

'Point taken, Wilf. Of course I'm with you, and I'm sure that you can count on Jinxie. Anybody else we're going to need while we're about it?'

'I'd like to have someone we could count on in a fight, who'd scare the opposition shitless from the start.'

'How about the Big Guy? I'll ring him right away and let you know. As for Jinxie, he's currently romancing some bird of his in a place called Tipton in Staffordshire. I'll give you her number. It'd be best if you spoke to him direct.'

A woman's voice answered the telephone, and when Wilf said he'd like to speak to Jinxie, the voice said that Jinxie was sleeping.

'Then wake him, please. It's urgent. Tell him Wilf wants to speak to him.'

It took five minutes before a sleepy-sounding Jinxie answered.

'What's up, mate?' he said.

Wilf didn't want a repetition of the trouble that he'd had with Dave, so rather than go into details he simply said: 'Jinxie, I'm in trouble. I'm in London and I need you here as soon as possible.'

'Give me the address. I'll be on the next train up to London and will be with you just as soon as possible.'

Five minutes later, Dave was on the line again.

'I'm with the Big Guy now,' he said. 'He's on. Give us time to pack our bags, and we'll be on the next ferry. Expect us at around five o'clock in Arden's office'.

'Thanks, Dave,' said Wilf. 'And thank the Big Guy for me. Oh, and by the way, Dave, when you're packing don't forget to put in two of those things we keep in the onion box.'

According to Wilf, 'just in case anyone was listening in, the "onion box" was the word we used on the telephone for the place we kept the guns. We never knew when we were going to need them, and I've learned that in our sort of life there's just one golden rule — always prepare for the worst.'

Jinxie turned up first. Wilf took him up to the flat, and when he apologised for pulling him away from his bird, Jinxie told Wilf to say no more about it.

'Tell you the truth, Wilf, I was just about to do a runner, anyway. You know me – a couple of days with any bird and I start getting bored.'

Then, just before five, Dave and the Big Guy put in an appearance. The task force was complete, and while they waited for Don Arden to appear they decided how much they wanted for their daily wages, plus a bonus for a successful outcome.

When Wilf heard Don arriving in the office, he went down to tell him that the boys were upstairs, ready and eager to meet him.

He was delighted at the news and started grinning like a happy schoolboy.

'You certainly wasted no time getting them here, Wilf. I like that.'

Wilf replied that before meeting them, he and Don should agree on a figure for their wages and a bonus – which they swiftly did. Having reached what Wilf calls 'an amicable figure which I knew would be acceptable', he summoned them down to meet their new commander, who, seated behind his king-sized desk, proceeded to spell out his plan of battle.

To hear Don talk, he might have been a battle-hardened veteran.

He started by ruling out explicit violence, explaining that if his plan worked as it should it wouldn't be necessary. 'What we're engaged in, gentlemen, is psychological warfare, and what I want from you is simply the threat of violence. Nothing more.'

'It might be hard to get results without a spot of genuine violence,' said Dave, who was always the realist.

'Not necessarily,' said Don. 'Once your presence here is known, it will send a message through the industry that Don Arden means business and is not prepared to mess around. That's where the psychology comes in. Fear is all I need. As I discovered many years ago, fear always seems to bring results.'

He paused and took a long, hard look at his troops before continuing. 'Let me explain something to you that you're probably not aware of. For the most part the music industry is made up of two separate groups – drama queens and wannabe gangsters – and they're always gossiping among themselves. So once the gossip grapevine gets going, and word passes round it that you're with me, you'll discover that your numbers have increased from four to twenty-four men, and all of you armed to the teeth and drinking babies' blood instead of coffee.'

Don had an actor's knack of playing to his audience, and they started laughing.

'Trust me, gentlemen,' he said. 'I know what I'm doing, and I know this strategy of mine will bring results.'

With that, the meeting ended, and he asked if Wilf would stay behind for a few moments.

'Listen, Wilf,' he said. 'We don't want this dragging on too long. During the next few days I'll be finding out all I can about the opposition, and while I'm doing that I want you and the boys to make your presence felt as widely as possible by turning up at all the gigs and clubs where the Corner are likely to appear. You play Mr Nice Guy while you're talking with the group, but the rest of the boys must do their best to look and behave like animals. Real heavies, as threatening as possible, and if anyone talks to them they simply grunt in answer. Do this everywhere you go, and once the Weasel's gang are told about it they'll feel obliged to show their lovely faces, if only to impress the members of the Corner. From then on, Wilf, it's up to you. I know you'll deal with them if they start anything. Don't let me down.'

During the next ten days Wilf and the crew behaved exactly as Don told them to – with remarkable results. So much so that Wilf soon received a worried phone call from his friend Big Albert in Birmingham.

'Wilf, what the fuck's going on?' he asked. 'During the last few days everyone up here's been talking about how you and a load of heavies have been working for Don Arden and making certain people, whose names I won't mention on the telephone, shit their pants in fear.'

'Who's been saying that?' said Wilf.

'Don't be daft, Wilf. You know as well as I do that this club here is something of a showbiz club and that anyone who's anyone in the entertainment industry comes here for his first night out whenever he's fortunate enough to be in Birmingham. Without exception, all of them are suddenly talking about you and Don Arden, my friend. As I've asked you once already, what the fuck is going on?'

Since Albert was an old friend whom Wilf would have trusted with his life, he told him everything – and in return Albert promised to keep his ears wide open and report back anything he heard about the Weasel and his rival gang.

It was only then that Wilf realised what a smart tactician Don Arden really was, and next morning, when he saw him in the office, he said so.

He was clearly flattered. 'Excellent,' he said. 'It looks as if my little plan is working out. I think we're just about to reach the second stage, as the time has come to turn the heat up on our friend the Weasel. I've discovered where he's living and my informant tells me that he'll definitely be there at eight o'clock tonight. Take the address, and I leave it to you entirely how you handle things. Remember, Wilf, I don't want any violence, but I would appreciate it if you'd really put the wind up that creepy little bastard.'

After discussing this with the crew, it was decided that the surest plan was to reach the house at least half an hour before the Weasel was expected, then grab him as he was getting out of his car. 'We'd make sure there were no witnesses about, and we would take him for a ride that he was never going to forget.'

They already knew the number of the Weasel's car and parked their own a discreet distance from the house and lay in wait. Eight o'clock came but no sign of the Weasel. Ten, twenty minutes more, and still no sign. So Wilf decided that the time had come for him and Dave and the Big Guy to walk straight up to the house and hammer on the door. 'If he wasn't in, the neighbours at any rate would hear us, and certainly tell him later that he'd had interesting visitors. At least our trip would not have been entirely wasted.'

The three of them had actually reached the door and were just about to knock when Jinxie, who was sitting in the car, started shouting: 'Look out, boys, he's coming.'

As they spun around, all of them were caught in the Weasel's headlights. Although they rushed to catch him, the Weasel was faster.

Spinning the wheel, he swung the car around, and before they could reach him he was off, his tyres screeching. All four of them jumped into their car in pursuit, but as they left the mews they found the road blocked by a builder's van pulling out of a parking space, and the Weasel was away.

Whether he was fighting, stealing, chasing a woman or promoting a concert, Wilf had always had a deep, almost pathological fear of failing – and he knew that he had failed now. Because of this he secretly dreaded telling Don the news next morning. But when he did force himself to enter the office, Don wasn't there and Sue had no idea when he'd be arriving. So rather than hang around, Wilf went back to his flat upstairs, where, in considerable discomfort, he and the crew had somehow all been sleeping. The morning dragged by. Still no sign of Don, and Jinxie and the Big Guy decided to go out to get some fresh air, leaving Wilf and Dave behind them. To pass the time, they took out the guns and began to clean and oil them. Careful as ever, Dave kept reminding Wilf 'if you look after your tools, your tools will look after you'. They were just finishing when Don appeared in the doorway with a sharply dressed character with a pointed beard and heavily brilliantined jet-black hair

'Wilf, Dave,' said Don, 'I'd like you both to meet a very dear friend of mine, Henry Henroid.' Wilf went to shake the newcomer's right hand without realising that he was holding a pistol in his left. Henry Henroid turned decidedly pale and asked Wilf if he'd mind putting the gun down before shaking hands, 'just in case the thing goes off'.

Don Arden thought the situation funny and began to laugh, but Wilf could see that Henry was serious and did as he requested. Henry had worked with Don for years, first as a road manager with singers like Gene Vincent, then as Don's personal Mr Fixit, and in spite of Wilf's annoying habit in the months ahead of calling him Henry Haemorrhoid, they became great friends. 'Henry was a character,' he says, 'and more your typical cockney than any real cockney I've ever known.' Now it was thanks to him that Wilf was saved the embarrassment of confessing to Don that the Weasel had escaped the night before.

105

'No need to apologise about it, Wilf,' said Don. 'Henry's already been telling me what happened.'

More important, it was also due to Henry Henroid that the war with the Weasel now entered its most dramatic phase and finally reached its legendary conclusion.

As Henry told his story, it appeared that the night before at around nine o'clock he had been out drinking with some friends at the Moscow Arms off Bayswater Road, when they were joined by an acquaintance he had never met before. This was none other than the Weasel. Henry already knew of him by reputation and they were introduced. The poor man was clearly in a state of shock, and swiftly downed a double Scotch. When someone asked him what was wrong, he blurted out the news that he had just barely escaped with his life from three great toughs who worked for Don Arden.

As soon as Don's name was mentioned, Henry stayed silent, grateful for the fact that neither of his friends knew that he worked for him. So he was able to listen quietly as the Weasel went on telling them of his ordeal and mentioned that luckily he had someone looking after him who would deal with any perceived threat.

'So who was that?' Wilf enquired.

At this, Henry looked decidedly uneasy and explained that while Don had been like a father to him in the past, by a wild coincidence the Weasel's minder turned out to be someone whom Henry looked on as a brother. This placed him in an awkward situation, and before he told them he would have to have their solemn promise never to say that he had told them his identity. By now Wilf was getting used to this, and nodded.

'You've my word on it,' he said. 'Who is it?'

'Jimmy Houlihan,' he answered.

Now it was Wilf's turn to be surprised.

'Know him?' said Henry.

'Sure I know him. Nice guy. Lives in a maisonette over a greengrocer's shop in Bayswater, doesn't he? Been there several times myself to have a drink with him. Typical Irishman. Good as gold as long as you don't try any tricks with him.'

'That's Jimmy,' Henry said, then, looking at his watch, suddenly exclaimed that he must hurry. He was already late for an appointment at the BBC with a famous disc jockey he was managing.

'Who's that?' asked Wilf.

'Emperor Rosco,' said Henry, going through the door. 'And don't forget, Wilf. Not a word about Jimmy to anyone – apart, of course, from Don. I've no secrets from him.'

When Wilf saw Don later in the morning and told him about Jimmy Houlihan, he remembered him at once from the days when he was looking after a good friend of his, Philip Solomon, the owner of Major Minor Records. So when Wilf said he thought that this could be an opportunity to settle all the nonsense over the Weasel and Amen Corner once and for all, he agreed.

'I know where Jimmy lives,' said Wilf. 'I'll go round and see him there this evening and just hope that we can talk this over.'

Wilf thought it sensible to take someone with him and picked on Jinxie, who appeared by far the least threatening member of the crew. At six o'clock sharp Wilf, with Jinxie behind him, knocked on Jimmy Houlihan's front door.

At first the big Irishman didn't recognise him, and Wilf had to mention the Isle of Wight and his connection with Amen Corner before he remembered who he was and asked them in. Jimmy hadn't changed; he was as genial as ever and offered them a generous welcome from his well-stocked drinks cupboard before getting down to business.

'Tell me now, Wilf. To what would I be owing the pleasure of your visit?'

Wilf explained. There was no point in hiding anything, so he told him the whole story – apart from the role in it of Henry Henroid. Jimmy seemed amused.

'Silly man, the Weasel. Lucky not to have got hurt the other night with characters like you around. I've known him for years, and he usually means trouble. When he approached me for help in the muscle department, I went along with it but had no intention of ever getting seriously involved.'

'So why did you bother, then?' asked Wilf.

'Wilf, I'll be honest with you, since you obviously know the score.

My thinking was that just suppose, by some miracle or other, this ridiculous character did manage to secure the management of Amen Corner, then of course I'd have been on to him at once for my whack.'

'Not much chance of that,' said Wilf.

'I was coming to much the same conclusion,' said Jimmy. 'In fact, I'm far too busy to get actively involved with the Weasel and all this crap. But tell me something. How far are you and your boys prepared to go for Don Arden?'

'All the way,' said Wilf.

'Are you, now? Then I'll tell you something. As what you might term a professional courtesy to an old friend, in the same line of business as myself, this is what I'll do. As soon as you've gone, I'll ring that Weasel straight away and tell him I'm withdrawing. I'll say that I didn't realise that it was you who was looking after Don Arden, and as the two of us are friends there's no way that I can possibly become involved against you. I'll also tell him that, if he values his skin, he should just be sensible and walk away.'

By now Wilf and the boys were looking forward to returning to the Isle of Wight, but if they thought that Don was finished with them they were much mistaken. When Wilf recounted what had happened with Jimmy Houlihan, Don appeared pleased, but not quite as pleased as Wilf expected. For what seemed like several minutes he said absolutely nothing, but rose from his desk and stared through the window at the street below as if there was still something on his mind.

'Wilf,' he said quietly. 'You and the boys have all done well. I'm grateful. If Jimmy says the Weasel's off the scene, I'm sure he is. I know Jimmy's someone whose word we can trust.' He paused again before continuing.

'But I'll be honest with you, Wilf. Something is still troubling me. It's the band themselves. I'm not happy with the situation. Only a fool would insist on hanging on to somebody who doesn't really want them, and it's the same with a band. Apart from all that nonsense with the Weasel, I get the feeling that the Corner aren't entirely happy and I intend to sort it out one way or the other. As you know, the group's on tour in Ireland at the moment and are flying into Manchester tomorrow morning to appear in the last *Pop North* BBC radio show. When they arrive at the studio, you know what, Wilf? You and I are going to be there to meet them and to sort things out. Be ready to hit the road at eight o'clock sharp tomorrow morning and we'll drive up to Manchester together.'

'And what about the crew?' Wilf asked. 'Now you no longer need them, shall I stand them down?'

'No, don't do that. Something tells me I'm still going to need you all.'

It never stopped raining all the way to Manchester, and with Don in one of his uncommunicative moods the journey seemed to take for ever. The show was being broadcast from the old Playhouse Theatre in Hulme on the outskirts of the city, and Wilf and Don arrived with a quarter of an hour to spare. The commissionaire recognised Don at once and tried to engage in conversation. But Don cut him short and asked where he could find the Corner's dressing room.

Backstage, the theatre was a maze of corridors, but Don, as usual, charged ahead and when he found the Corner's dressing room he didn't knock but barged straight in. The members of the group were so surprised to see Don Arden quite unexpectedly in Manchester, of all places, just before a show that they were lost for words, and without giving them time to think he calmly spoke to them.

'I'd like you all to know that I'm fully aware of what you've all been up to over the last few weeks, and I realise that what you'd really like is to be rid of me. To tell you the truth, I wouldn't mind being rid of you either. But we have a problem. When I purchased R.K. Records I also bought your contracts, in all good faith, for a very large sum of money. And much as I'd like to see the back of you, I have to tell you that you're going nowhere until we've sorted out a deal that's mutually beneficial to us all.

'Agreed?' he asked and went round the group one by one asking each member if he agreed that this was fair. Everyone said yes.

'Right,' said Don. 'That's settled. We'll talk again about this in a day or two.'

And that was that. As quickly as he and Wilf had entered the dressing room, they took their leave. But once they were in the car outside, Don seemed more preoccupied than ever. It was still raining, and after driving in silence for a while he turned into a dingy-looking side street with row upon row of small, dark, terraced houses. He stopped the car, switched off the engine and for a moment sat in silence, staring through the windscreen at the rain.

'You see that house over there?' he said at last. 'The one with the brown front door. That's where I was born and where I grew up. And you see those two big gates at the end of the road? That used to be a scrap yard where I played as a kid. I used to catch rats there and kill them and cut off their tails and take them to the owner of the yard who paid me a penny a time for them. That's how I earned the money to go to the cinema every week. So in a way that's how my interest in show business started. Catching rats in a scrap yard. Life's a funny business, isn't it?'

But Don Arden hadn't finished. He was still gazing at the little house where he was born, and Wilf realised he wasn't talking to him but to himself.

'If anyone or any group that I've invested money in thinks they can screw me so that I and my family end up back in a place like this, it will be over their dead bodies, not mine.'

With that, he started up the car. The rain was beginning to turn to snow, and they drove back, still in virtual silence, down the long white road to London.

Wilf was particularly impressed by Don Arden's philosophy, which was very like his own, after the grudge fights and the daily battle for survival he had endured at the Wellesley Nautical School at Blyth. During the next week or so he heard nothing more on the subject of Amen Corner, and he assumed that relations between Don and the group were working out. Wilf, however, had to face a different problem.

This involved another of Don's groups with which Wilf had close personal connections – Carl Wayne's band, the Move. The Birmingham-based group was going through an awkward period after parting with Tony Secunda, their powerful manager. Without his dominating presence, one of the group, Ace Kefford, was increasingly at odds with the rest of the band, who wished to sack him, but they were frightened by the fact that Ace had two supposedly aggressive brothers who they worried might cause trouble. As Wilf was a friend of Carl's and had connections of his own in Birmingham, Don asked if he would go there as soon as possible and sort matters out.

Although on the face of it it seemed a relatively straightforward operation, Wilf knew that it could also go badly wrong. So not for the first time in his life, he turned for help to his best friend in Birmingham, Big Albert, and once again the influence of the doorman extraordinary of the Rum Runner proved all important. Wilf explained to him how anxious Carl and the whole group were becoming. All they wanted was to get on with their music without the perceived threat, real or imaginary, of Ace and his two brothers.

Albert promised to find out what was happening and see what could be done, and thanks to his connections he soon had an answer. Although Ace's brothers were said to be 'a little lively', they were nothing to worry about. He also had a solution to the problem in the shape of Mickey and Bluey. These were a pair of very tough twins he knew, whom he described as 'an unbelievable fighting force' whenever they worked together, as they sometimes had for him. He promised to speak to them on Wilf's behalf and explain the situation.

The following evening, when Albert saw Wilf at the club, he told him he had had a little chat with the twins and that they promised him they'd help. 'I tell you what,' he said to Wilf, 'give Carl my telephone number and the number of the twins and tell him that if they get any bother from the characters we talked about, all they need to do is call us, and we'll deal with it for you at once.'

Later, when Carl and the members of the band arrived at the club, Wilf was able to set their minds at rest, and he enjoyed a last leisurely drink with them before driving back to London. But before this he was in for something he would never have expected in a thousand years. While he was drinking with the boys, he noticed out of the corner of his eye two attractive girls sitting together on the far side of the room. From where he was sitting he couldn't see them clearly, but something about one of them seemed vaguely familiar. Now, as he went out to reception to pay his bill, he could take a proper look at them and saw that they were looking straight at him. For a moment he stopped dead in his tracks as a glance of recognition passed between them. They were Lesley and her friend Janice from the Isle of Wight. He hesitated for a second, longing to speak to Lesley, but at that moment she turned away, so Wilf did the same and walked on.

All the way back to London he was haunted by Lesley's face, and it went on haunting him for many months to come. But although he knew that he could almost certainly find out from Big Albert what these two pretty girls were doing in his club and where they lived, he never did ask him. The past was the past. Why court further heartbreak? That episode in his life was over – or so he thought.

Next morning, back in Denmark Street, Wilf was in the office early, and as soon as Don arrived he told him of the way he'd dealt with the problems of the Move. Don listened politely and congratulated him for having coped with things so efficiently, but throughout their conversation he seemed preoccupied, and Wilf knew him well enough by now to recognise the signs. Something was making Don Arden worried.

To start with he gave no hint of what was on his mind. He took a few short telephone calls, then rang through to Sue, saying he was not to be disturbed.

'Wilf,' he said. 'Bad news, I'm afraid. We thought that we'd got rid of our friend the Weasel, but it seems we haven't. Last night I had a phone call from an anonymous source informing me that the people behind him have taken out a £3,000 contract on my life.'

'Don, you must be kidding.'

'Do I look as if I am? Whoever was behind that call would be better off killing himself than he would be once I discover who he is. I know what you're thinking, Wilf. This *might* just be a load of bullshit to put the wind up me. It might, but then again it might not, and with my family to think about, it's not a risk I'll take.'

As he said this, Don's appearance had taken on an extraordinary air of menace, but as he continued speaking Wilf was struck by how calm and how controlled he was.

'Here's what I think that we should do,' Don said. 'First, get all the boys up here as soon as possible – and anyone else from the crew that you can trust. And once we're ready, I want you to go after the Weasel. In situations like this, the harder and the quicker you can strike, the better, if only to show the enemy that you're not frightened.'

'What d'you want us to do to the Weasel? Kill him?'

Don shook his head. 'No. I just want you to scare the living shit out of him, so that as well as giving him the message, it will also get back to whoever is behind him.'

'But where is the Weasel? I'm told he moved from his previous address after our last social call.'

'Don't worry. I've found out already. He's taken a small mews house in a very smart part of Kensington. According to my information, he's at home now and will be there all day.'

Wilf took the address and, while he was waiting for Dave and Jinxie and the Big Guy to arrive, decided to jump into a cab and reconnoitre. He was relieved to discover that the mews had an exit at each end, and that no one seemed to be about. He told the cabbie to drive slowly down the mews, saying he was looking for a house but couldn't recall the number. Then he recognised the car at the far end of the terrace. It belonged to the Weasel.

Back in Denmark Street, Don had left his office, but the boys had now arrived and Wilf explained their mission. Following Don's instructions, he emphasised that there was to be no violence, but in order to convince the Weasel yet again that this time they really did mean business, and that he was putting his life in danger by his behaviour, they would be armed. As the coolest driver in the crew, Dave was to drive.

'When do we leave?' he asked.

'No time like the present,' Wilf replied.

Once they reached the mews, Jinxie parked behind the Weasel's car, and he and Dave stayed out of sight as Wilf rang the bell. In fact, there were two bells; the bottom one didn't seem to work, so Wilf pushed the top one and could hear the bell ringing somewhere in the house. Then he heard someone opening an upstairs window. He took a few steps back and beckoned to the boys to join him in a line below, with guns pointing straight towards the window, where he could recognise the Weasel peering out.

'Three grand is not enough!' Wilf shouted, and they cocked their guns as if about to shoot him.

'In my time I've heard women scream their heads off,' says Wilf, 'but I've never in my life heard a scream like the Weasel's. It echoed down the mews, and he was still yelling as we got in the car and drove away.'

Back at the office, Don, who had only just arrived, was expecting to give the crew their final orders for action against the Weasel. When Wilf told him that the Weasel had already been sorted out, he looked serious, and for a moment Wilf thought that he was annoyed.

'You did this in broad daylight? Good God, you've all got quite a nerve,' he said. And then he smiled. 'Well, whatever else you've done, you've well and truly put the cat among the pigeons. Now all we can do is sit back and wait and see what happens. Thanks to you, my friend, I think the activities of the Weasel and any talk about a contract on my life are over.'

He was right – but then came trouble from another quarter.

A few days later a senior police detective invited Don to an appointment at Savile Row police station. Someone – unfortunately he couldn't say who – was alleging that he had been involved in an incident outside a Kensington mews house a few days earlier.

It was obviously a serious allegation, and the policeman, who knew all about Don Arden's reputation, was clearly out for an arrest. Don endured more than two hours of intensive questioning. But Don evidently knew how to deal with this and ended by convincing the policeman that anyone who tried to link his name with some far-fetched incident in a mews that he had never even heard of must be crazy. And that, apparently, was that.

For the next few weeks, peace descended on Don Arden and his activities. But to make absolutely sure there was no further trouble, he kept Wilf by his side everywhere he went. There were no more death threats, no signs whatsoever of the Weasel, and the spirit of goodwill even extended to Don's relations with Amen Corner. It was in this period that this troubled saga was concluded on terms that were highly beneficial to everyone concerned.

Thanks, in part at least, to Wilf and the members of the crew, no more was heard from the Weasel or from his sinister promoter. Nor was there any question now of Amen Corner reneging on their contract. After lengthy negotiations, Don sold his recording rights with the group for a massive sum to Andrew Loog Oldham of Immediate Records, formerly manager of the Rolling Stones, who had nothing to do with the Weasel or his promoter. As well as Don, Immediate Records also did well from the deal, and early in 1969 Wilf remembers being in the office and signing for a telegram on behalf of Don which had been sent to him by Andrew Oldham. It simply said, 'Don, thanks for the snowball', referring to the first new number his company had recorded with Amen Corner. Its name? 'If Paradise Is Half as Nice', which went on to become one of the pop classics of the late 1960s.

7

Don Arden's Ashtray

A S DON ARDEN knew quite well, the way he had seen off the Weasel and the threat to his interests with Amen Corner had done no harm to his reputation. Quite the contrary. During this period, much of the pop music industry was still lawless territory ruled over by those 'drama queens and wannabe gangsters' Don described to Wilf early in their relationship. With them in mind, Don now made sure that news of his behaviour made the rounds of the battle-scarred landscape of the late-1960s pop scene. Relishing his self-proclaimed role as the Al Capone of pop, he was cleverly employing Wilf and the crew as a highly visible bodyguard for himself and his family.

There was, however, just one area where he still needed to tread gently – over relations with the police and Scotland Yard. And if he really thought that the smart way in which he had dealt with the detective inspector at Savile Row marked the end of his troubles with the law, he should have known better. But he was on a winning roll, and even now his luck stayed with him. His next encounter with the law ended as a further triumph, partly thanks to Wilf, partly to himself, but thanks most of all to the sheer ineptness of the boys in blue.

The origin of the trouble was a new progressive rock band with the frisky name of Skip Bifferty who, like several struggling new pop groups at the time, were attracted by Don Arden's notoriety. They joined him in 1968, hoping he would bring them overnight success. Instead, they found the Arden style of management was not for softies or for prima donnas. When he was creating some of his early groups like the Nashville Teens and the Small Faces he had ruled them with a rod of iron, and even with Skip Bifferty the unremitting schedule of one-night performances he imposed on them in the hope of building up their reputation ended instead by sapping their confidence and their morale. Soon they were performing badly, missing engagements and seeming to lack that extra level of necessary dedication. Don Arden was not impressed. As he said about them later, 'Skip Bifferty weren't tough enough to make it. They wanted to become stars, but when we got them up from £10 to £100 a night they went to pieces.'

Simultaneously they began to make it clear that they wanted out from their management agreement, but while Arden would probably have been glad to see the back of them, he had invested so much money in promoting and financing the group by now that he would let them break their contract only on terms of his own making. These terms were not acceptable to the gay, new, pop group manager who was pursuing Skip Bifferty with an enthusiasm Wilf believed might have had more to do with the flowing hair and pretty face of the group's lead singer, Graham Bell, than with any real admiration for their music. In the stalemate that ensued, the grumbling disagreements which developed between themselves and Don Arden seem to have made them genuinely scared, as potential victims of the fearsome gangster king of pop. Rather than face whatever dangers lurked in darkest London, they cancelled their current engagements, fled to the safety of a house in deep suburban Beckenham and contacted the Beckenham police, saying they were frightened for their safety. Here they were visited by Detective Inspector John MacNamara, attached to the Beckenham police, who told them to telephone immediately they received the slightest threat from Don Arden.

In fact, Don Arden had more important things on his plate than attempting to aggravate relations between himself and this relatively minor group. Diplomatic for a change, he asked his son David to take the office car, drive down to Beckenham and, as a member of Skip Bifferty's own generation, try sorting out the trouble. Rather than send David on his own, he asked Wilf to go with him, just in case of trouble. As they were leaving, Dave and Jinxie asked if they could go along as well for the ride, as they had nothing on that evening. David said, 'Fine, as long as you stay outside when we arrive' – which they did, waiting in the car while Wilf and David went in to meet Skip Bifferty.

'As soon as we went through the front door,' says Wilf, 'I could sense that there was something up, and that the group seemed to me to be out to antagonise us by their behaviour. I thought they might even have been recording the conversation, hoping it would give them grounds to break their contract. But David was too smart for them, and after half an hour of getting nowhere he told them there was no point in continuing the discussion, said good night and left. I left with him, having said next to nothing throughout the meeting.'

Dave and Jinxie were still waiting in the car outside, and on reaching London they dropped Wilf and David off outside the Arden flat in Mayfair, saying that they'd take the car on to Denmark Street and would see Wilf in the office later. Wilf stayed talking to Don longer than expected, and Don agreed with him that Skip Bifferty were definitely up to something. However, he was busy and, rather than get involved in discussing the group's behaviour there and then, he told Wilf that they'd talk about it in the morning. As there seemed to be no great rush, Wilf took a leisurely stroll down Piccadilly and Shaftesbury Avenue before heading back to the office.

By then, Skip Bifferty must have talked to Inspector MacNamara, who was taking them at face value and had contacted Don's friends in Savile Row police station, who in turn had thundered into action by the time Wilf arrived.

As he entered Denmark Street, he was puzzled to see no sign of the office car. What he did see was a succession of men emerging from the entrance that the office shared with the Tin Pan Alley Club below them. As these clearly weren't the sort of men who normally resort to Soho drinking clubs in the early evening, Wilf quickly dodged down the basement steps of the coffee bar opposite and watched what was going on through the railings. By now, more than a dozen men had emerged from the doorway and were standing together on the pavement. Then an unmarked dark blue van drew up, all of them clambered in and the van drove off. For this there could be but one explanation – a raid by plain-clothes police on Don Arden's office.

Only when the van was safely out of sight did Wilf emerge from his hiding place and start looking for the car, but it had disappeared. Nor was there any sign of life in the office, so he went up to his flat, found himself a drink and settled by the telephone, waiting for Dave and Jinxie to telephone. When they didn't, he started ringing around everyone he could think of who might have known their whereabouts, but always the answer was the same. Nobody had seen them.

Next morning, when Don Arden arrived at the office, he and Wilf began systematically ringing around all the hospitals and police stations in central London enquiring after Farley and Jenkins – again without result. Then Don had a brainwave. Remembering that the office car was hired in his name, he checked on the hire agreement for its registration number and rang several car pounds just in case it had been towed away. With the third call he struck lucky. The car was in the police car pound at Battersea, and he was told that on production of his driving licence and hire agreement, together with the cash to pay the fine, he could collect it straight away.

'There was no way that either of us was going near that pound until we knew what had happened to Dave and Jinxie. But at least we had learned something – firstly that the boys hadn't crashed the car, and secondly that the Old Bill had to be involved.'

Now, once again, Wilf's criminal contacts came in useful. Seemingly from time immemorial, one of London's most reliable intermediaries between the law and the underworld had been Sulky, the omniscient maître d' at the famous Astor Club in Berkeley Square, whose telephone book contained the names of many of London's most notorious criminals side by side with those of Scotland Yard's most celebrated detectives. Wilf had the rare privilege of having been entrusted with Sulky's home telephone number, and when he rang and explained the situation Sulky told him to call back in an hour and promised that he'd have an answer.

An hour later, on the dot, Wilf rang – and Sulky had news for him. Despite those firm denials by the police, Dave and Jinxie had been arrested as they descended from their car in Denmark Street and taken to Savile Row police station, where they were being held. But when Wilf rang Savile Row, saying he was Jinxie's brother, the duty officer confirmed that the boys had indeed been arrested but were no longer at the station. That very morning they had appeared at Clerkenwell Magistrates' Court and had been remanded in custody in Brixton Prison.

'On what charges?' Wilf asked.

'On various charges, including being part of a protection racket, being found in possession of offensive weapons and of class–B drugs.'

Instead of showing his customary cool Don flew into an almighty rage, swearing dire revenge on the unspeakable bastards who were responsible for Dave's and Jinxie's situation.

Even Wilf was slightly shaken by his reaction, and it was only when he had subsided that Don was calm enough to ring his lawyer, David Jacobs. Jacobs later made his own enquiries, confirming everything that Wilf had learned and adding that, although he was confident that he could get the boys released on bail at their next court appearance in a week's time, until then they'd have to stay in Brixton on remand.

'No way you can get them out?' Don Arden barked.

'None,' was the reply. And that apparently was that. Except that with Don around, it wasn't.

Wilf's first reaction was to say that, since prisoners on remand were entitled to receive visitors without prior application, he would be going to Brixton Jail on his own that afternoon.

'If you go, I go with you,' said Don Arden.

'No, keep out of it,' said Wilf. 'It's our problem, not yours, and with the law gunning for you now the more you keep out of things, the better.'

'You should know by now that Don Arden doesn't walk away from his friends when they're in the shit,' said Don. 'If they're in the shit, all of us are in the shit together.'

Wilf admired him for that, but at three o'clock next afternoon, when the two of them arrived at the visiting room for remand prisoners at Brixton Jail, a new Don Arden had replaced the embattled champion of the oppressed. He had instructed Wilf to wear a dark suit and tie and was wearing the same himself, together with an immaculately brushed homburg hat, and was carrying an official-looking black dispatch case and a neatly rolled umbrella. Don Arden, the celebrated actor, was taking over.

On entering the visiting room, they were asked by the duty warder if they were solicitors.

'Of course,' replied Don Arden. 'What else d'you think we are? This gentleman here is my clerk.'

'And who have you come to visit, sir?' enquired the screw.

'Prisoners Farley and Jenkins, both remanded yesterday morning at Clerkenwell Magistrates' Court.'

Their names were duly written down.

'Thank you, sir. And if you would be so good as to follow me, I will take you to see the prisoners at once.'

With which they were rapidly led past the long queue of ordinary visitors and conducted to the visiting room, where Dave and Jinxie were waiting for them behind a perforated glass partition.

Once Dave had thanked them both for coming and said how glad he was to see them, he warned them that they were taking a considerable risk visiting them like this. 'You should know that the Old Bill want the two of you big time. Neither of us has mentioned you, of course, and it would be best if you let us face the music on our own.'

'Fuck that,' said Wilf.

'Absolutely not,' echoed Don Arden, adding that he would be getting a top QC to represent them both in court. He would apply for bail, which they were sure to get and for which he, Don Arden, would be honoured to stand surety.

This seemed to reassure them, and Wilf asked how they had come to be arrested. They said that after dropping off Wilf and David outside the Arden flat, they had driven to the office, but no sooner had they parked than the car was surrounded by a crowd of police, with batons drawn, and someone started shouting: 'Pine and Arden, get out of the car with your hands up. You're both under arrest.'

They had tried to make it plain that they weren't armed and that they were neither Pine nor Arden, but the police weren't listening. They were swiftly handcuffed, slung into a squad car and rushed with sirens screaming to Savile Row, where they were separated and interviewed for what seemed like half the night. One thing they were able to confirm was that it had indeed been Skip Bifferty who, after their departure, had telephoned Beckenham police station and made an official complaint.

A week later, when they got to court, Wilf and Don Arden discovered that the protection-racket charges had been dropped, and the barrister had little difficulty in establishing that there was no provable connection between the defendants and the small amount of marijuana discovered in the car.

But it was the allegations that Dave and Jinxie had been armed on the trip to Beckenham that gave Don Arden, former actor, the cue for the performance of a lifetime in one of Her Majesty's courts of law. For when it came to it, the charge that Dave and Jinxie were 'discovered in possession of offensive weapons' turned out to relate to a pair of Indian clubs belonging to Don Arden which he had left in the back of the car. Carefully rehearsed by now, the QC made the most of this before the judge, finally calling on his star witness, Mr Don Arden, to demonstrate to the court how he used his Indian clubs for exercise. Playing to the gallery with his Indian clubs before an appreciative audience, Don went to town with such a virtuoso show of his abilities that he ended up being congratulated by the judge. As for Dave and Jinxie, the case against them was summarily dismissed.

So once again, just as with the outcome of the Amen Corner battle, Don Arden's tough behaviour had paid off. Apart from this high-profile demonstration in court that he was not a man to trifle with or who would leave his employees in the lurch, even the financial side of the Skip Bifferty episode ended in his favour, with the group soon moving on to another management on acceptable terms to all involved.

By now, Christmas was approaching, and Wilf's role in Arden Enterprises was changing too. Now that Don no longer needed him and the crew to act as his bodyguard, Wilf began working more like a personal assistant, liaising between Don and the different groups he represented. And yet again he found himself coping with the complexities and problems of his favourite group, the Move, who were staging something of a comeback after their troubles with Tony Secunda and the near nervous breakdown of Ace Kefford.

Don was particularly anxious for a real success with their new single, 'Blackberry Way', and mounted a heavy promotion campaign for the group, including live dates, radio interviews and television appearances up and down the country. Wilf was closely involved in all these live appearances, but although 'Blackberry Way' had swiftly entered the bottom of the Top Twenty, it looked like staying there, despite Don 's efforts to push it higher.

This was the point at which the record needed the boost provided by the group's appearance on BBC TV's *Top of the Pops* show, which usually guaranteed big record sales. But as Wilf discovered, there was an unofficial ban on the the Move's appearance on the show because of their previous wild behaviour, and no amount of pleading or assurances of good behaviour by Don Arden could change things.

It was then, owing to a lucky meeting with Colin Charman, producer of *Top of the Pops*, that Wilf was able to talk him into a change of heart on one condition – that Wilf and at least one other member of the crew stayed with the Move throughout the show to guarantee their good behaviour. Rather to everyone's surprise, this happened and everything went well at the performance. The group behaved perfectly and received a great reception from the studio audience. But in spite of this, the evening ended with some awkward repercussions, for Wilf, for Don Arden and ultimately for the members of the Move.

Trouble started when the show was over and the various performers and managers were relaxing in the bar. With his naturally suspicious nature, Wilf became curious at the way the members of the Move kept going across to talk to a youngish man sitting on his own, and whispered to Jinxie to get near enough to his table to overhear their conversation. Carl Wayne had been followed by Bev Bevan, the group's drummer, then it was the turn of Roy Wood and Trevor Burton. Seeing Bev walk away, Wilf called him over and asked who he'd been talking to. He replied that it was Clifford Davis, manager of Fleetwood Mac, and an associate of Peter Walsh, owner of the big Starlight Artistes agency that currently managed the Tremeloes.

At this Wilf simply nodded, rather than say anything to arouse Bev's suspicions. Then Jinxie returned and told him he had overheard Clifford Davis offering members of the Move his services as manager and those of Peter Walsh as their agent.

'How did the conversation end?' asked Wilf.

'Roy and Trevor were polite to him, saying that they would discuss his offer with the rest of the group' – and that was that.

Wilf had promised Don that after the show he and Jinxie would go and report to him in person at his flat. Wilf instructed Jinxie to say nothing to Don about what he'd overheard from Clifford Davis, as he'd like a chance to talk things over with Carl Wayne before trouble started. But as it turned out, this wasn't possible. No sooner had he seen them than Don sensed at once that something untoward had happened.

'So how did you think the Move performed?' Wilf asked him.

'I think they gave a bloody sight better performance than the two of you are doing now,' he said. 'Do me a favour, Wilf. Just tell me what happened.'

Realising the game was up, he and Jinxie ended up relating word for word what they'd overheard.

Wilf had been expecting trouble when Don heard this, but this was as nothing in comparison with what actually occurred. Don had been sitting quietly in his dressing gown, enjoying his evening malt whisky and cigar, but suddenly he was on his feet, shouting to his wife to fetch his trousers, shirt and shoes, as he was going off to slaughter Clifford Davis.

'But you can't, darling,' said his wife. 'You don't know where he lives.' And gradually she calmed him down as only she could, and he finally agreed to sleep on his problems and to discuss them in the morning.

Next morning, at 10 a.m. on the dot, Don was in the office. Wilf had been dreading his arrival, imagining a sleepless night in which the great man brooded over how to be revenged on Clifford Davis. Instead, he'd rarely seen Don Arden looking more relaxed. He asked Sue for a cup of tea, he read his mail, he made two short phone calls and then, almost as an afterthought, he asked Wilf if he'd be kind enough to summon Jinxie as he'd like to make sure of exactly what he'd overheard.

When Jinxie finished telling him, Don simply nodded, thanked him and asked him to bring the car round to the office straight away.

'Where are you going?' Wilf enquired.

'*We* are going to see Mr Clifford Davis and Mr Peter Walsh at Mr Walsh's office,' he replied.

'Fine by me,' said Wilf.

But once they were in the car and driving through the morning traffic in the direction of the Starlight Artistes' office in Southampton Row in Holborn, Wilf gave Don Arden some unaccustomed words of caution, the gist of which was that, after their recent brushes with the law, it would be virtual suicide if they became involved in any sort of violence – particularly at eleven o'clock in the morning in a crowded office.

Even then, Don seemed to be the model of sweet reasonableness, as he insisted that the very last thing he wanted was a show of violence. Perish the thought. All he intended was to confront Mr Walsh and Mr Davis in person, tell them he knew exactly what was going on and point out to them that, as the Move's agent, he had a legally binding contract with them all.

'That's what really matters,' he explained. 'And by seeing them both in person I can put an end to all this nonsense straight away.'

'And thank God for that!' thought Wilf, who would have had no objection to a spot of action with a group of hard-faced villains but who foresaw a scuffle involving what he called 'a bunch of civilians' as being nothing less than 'a sure-fire recipe for disaster'.

So it was genuinely with the best intentions that Don Arden and Wilf Pine entered the reception area of Starlight Artistes and asked to see Peter Walsh and Clifford Davis. Looking understandably startled, the receptionist enquired if they had a prior appointment. Don replied that they had just been passing and had called in on the off-chance of seeing them. When he told her his name, she said that Peter Walsh was out but Clifford Davis was in his office and she'd enquire if he was free. She took a while to return, long enough for Don to light a large cigar, and when at last she reappeared it was to tell them that Mr Davis would see them straight away in Mr Walsh's office.

On entering the office, Wilf came face to face with one of the biggest desks he'd ever seen. Seated behind it in an equally impressive large black-leather chair was a diminutive and nervous-looking individual in a smart grey suit, whom Wilf recognised as Clifford Davis. Don didn't waste time on introductions and spoke to him softly and very clearly.

'Clifford Davis, I would like to ask you what you're up to, trying to persuade the Move to break their contract with me in favour of yourself and Peter Walsh.'

Instead of answering, the character behind the desk stayed absolutely silent, as if rooted to where he sat in Peter Walsh's large black-leather chair.

'I'm waiting for an explanation,' said Don Arden, his voice quieter than ever, but even then he didn't get an answer.

At this point Wilf decided to intervene in this one-sided conversation by observing that Mr Davis had had a lot to say on the subject the night before when talking to members of the group, so perhaps he should try answering Don's question now.

Then the floodgates opened, and once Davis started there appeared to be no stopping him, as he rambled on about the Move being free agents ever since they broke with their old manager, Tony Secunda.

Don listened with surprising patience.

'That may be so,' he said at last, 'but I think you miss the point. I'm not here because you put yourself forward to manage the band, but because you were inciting them to break the legal contract which they have with me as their agent, by signing up with Peter Walsh's agency instead.'

When Clifford Davis started to deny this, Wilf once more interrupted, this time calling him a liar. At which point he once again fell silent.

It was now that Don leaned across the desk and with a faint smile on his face tweaked his cheek, as Wilf describes it, 'rather as you might do with a child when making a point'.

As he did this, Don said that he had nothing more to add except that if anything like this ever happened again, Clifford Davis would not be so lucky.

With that, he turned on his heel, and Wilf had actually started opening the door for him to pass when Davis chose to deliver what proved to be a dangerous parting observation. He said that he wasn't worried by threats and that, anyhow, he knew where Don Arden lived.

'Within a heartbeat, Don had spun around, and if I hadn't stopped him he would have dragged him bodily across the desk. What might have happened then I dread to think.'

For as Wilf had learned by now, the one area which was absolutely sacred to Don Arden was his family, and the faintest hint of any threat against them instantly enraged him. As Wilf struggled to restrain him, Don managed to retain the one weapon he was holding in his hand – his large cigar. And now, with a gesture of contempt, he stubbed it out on Clifford Davis's forehead before Wilf could drag him out of the office and into the car below.

Don was still fuming all the way back to Denmark Street, and it was only when he saw Paddy and Sharon descending from a taxi that he remembered having promised to take them out to lunch and instantly calmed down.

'Wilf, not a word to them of what happened,' he whispered. 'I promised Paddy not to lose my temper.'

After greeting them, Don asked if they would wait with David for a few minutes in the outer office, as he had to have an urgent discussion on his own with Wilf. By now, Don was getting slightly worried by possible recriminations from the Starlight agency to the police over his choice of an ashtray for his cigar.

As he said to Wilf: 'It's not as if we need any further trouble from the law.'

Wilf nodded, trying hard to sound reassuring.

'We can only see what happens, but frankly, Don, I'd not have thought that Clifford Davis would be wanting the publicity he'd get from prosecuting you just now, when he's deeply involved in trying to take one of our best-known groups. Besides, he'd look an idiot in court.'

'I hope you're right,' said Don. 'As you say, we'll have to wait and see how he and Peter Walsh react.'

They didn't have to wait for long. For slap on cue, Don's telephone rang. Having listened for a moment, he placed his hand over the mouthpiece and signalled to Wilf to pick up the extension on the other desk.

'Thank you, Sue,' Wilf heard him say. 'Would you put Peter Walsh through to me? I'll take his call at once.'

Wilf listened to the conversation, which he remembers going as follows:

Don: 'Yes, Peter, what can I do for you?'

Peter: 'Don, you've burned a hole in my chair.'

Don: 'I've done what?'

Peter: 'You've burned a hole in the leather of my chair. I'm most upset. My boys, the Tremeloes, bought it for me. Now it's ruined. Don, how could you do a thing like that?'

Wilf never heard the rest of the conversation, for he was unable to control his mirth and had to leave the room. Peter Walsh was a very down-to-earth Yorkshireman, and to hear him with his flat Yorkshire accent placing the damage Don had done to his office chair before whatever injury he'd inflicted on his partner's forehead struck him as the funniest example he'd ever heard of genuine black Yorkshire humour. To make it even funnier, it seems to have brought to an abrupt close this whole extraordinary episode. Don took Paddy and Sharon out to lunch, and although Wilf sat loyally in the office for the rest of the afternoon, waiting for a call from Savile Row, it never materialised.

But the real conclusion of the affair was still to come, for, as in some real-life fairy tale, everyone involved in the saga of Don Arden's ashtray ended with a prize. Just before Christmas Wilf was happy to see 'Blackberry Way' go to number one in the charts. As consolation for the hole he'd burned in Peter Walsh's chair, Don duly sold him his agent's contract for the Move – in return, of course, for a further very large sum of money. And shortly afterwards lucky Don himself received a double jackpot when the Move, although dispensing with his services as their agent, chose him as their manager in preference to Clifford Davis.

But since this is a real-life fairy story, the apparent victim of these events, the unfortunate Clifford Davis, finally received the biggest prize of all when his group Fleetwood Mac, became one of the most popular and most successful pop groups of the early 1970s on both sides of the Atlantic.

The sense of success accompanied Wilf through most of 1969 as life in the straight lane beckoned. During this period there were no more lively punch-ups, no armed confrontations with shady front men like the Weasel, no further threats against Don Arden's life or the safety of his family, and the contents of Wilf's famous onion box remained unused and undisturbed. Growing slightly bored with this, Jinxie finally decided to go back to sea, and Dave, for a while at least, returned to marine engineering on the Isle of Wight.

But as far as Don Arden was concerned, the impresario's carefully created image as the gangster king of pop was paying off. Like the shrewd Mancunian businessman he was, he was ensuring that his groups made steady money while he was steadily expanding his interests in the record business and exploiting not only Europe but the lucrative American market. Having consolidated his reputation 'as someone emphatically not to mess around with', no one risked doing so any longer. Wilf's life also changed accordingly. Now that he was rarely needed as Don Arden's 'muscle', Wilf became a sort of student in the Don Arden private academy of the music business. He was just turned twenty-five and proved himself as keen a learner as Don Arden was a first-rate teacher.

'It was while I was working with him that he taught me almost everything I know about the business,' says Wilf, adding that what he didn't learn from Don he picked up later from his son, David.

What seems remarkable today is the amount of responsibility the Ardens gave him. Shortly after the Clifford Davis episode, he was thrown feet first into the nightmare job of a top pop group tour manager when he and Dave Farley had to hit the road with Moby Grape, the hottest – and wildest and craziest – underground group from San Francisco, during their European tour. This was followed by another American success, which Don had also brought to Britain 'Johnny Johnson and the Bandwagon, who had just topped the US and the UK charts with 'Breaking Down the Walls of Heartache'. These tours and the endless headaches, as well as heartaches, they brought with them meant that Wilf's experience was steadily expanding. So was the range of new friendships he was making in show business. As far as the future was concerned, one of the most important was to be the friendship that he now struck up with the son of one of Don's associates, Pat Meehan. This was Patrick Meehan Jr, whom Wilf actually got to know when his father left the Arden agency and joined Patrick to begin his own independent record production and management company. Another close friend he made now was Roger Daltry, the very young lead singer of the Who, who supported him through difficult days to come. And one of his staunchest friends of all he acquired in this period was Laurie O'Leary, celebrated East End raconteur and friend of almost everyone, who was running one of the trendiest nightclubs in London's West End – the Speakeasy in St Margaret Street. Wilf began to use the club as something of an after-hours office and second home from home. Wilf enjoyed meeting celebrities in the club, but, as he says, 'when you'd been dealing all day with people living in a dream world of their own, Laurie had a wonderful way of bringing you back to reality'.

Not all the meetings Wilf made in the course of his social life were 'unreal' and unimportant. For instance, it was early that autumn, during an evening out clubbing with his old friends Alan Jones and Mike Smith, fellow members of Amen Corner, that Wilf learned that the group's record label, Immediate Records, was on the edge of bankruptcy and that Amen Corner, who were still the biggest teenybopper group in the land, were also breaking up.

'Any plans for the future?' Wilf enquired.

'Both of us are open to suggestions. Any offers?' Alan answered.

'I'll think about it,' said Wilf, and as the evening floated by, and his brain responded to whatever he was drinking, he remembered that another famous teenybopper band, the Herd, had just broken up as well and that the group's young drummer, Henry Spinetti – despite his name, another Welshman – was a friend of Alan's.

'Why don't I talk to Don about assembling a new teenybopper supergroup,' he said. 'There's you two, and you can ask if your friend Henry from the Herd is interested. If he is, then that makes three already.'

Mike's and Alan's first reaction was uneasy laughter. But after Wilf had gone in search of something more to drink, he returned to find that they were no longer laughing.

'Were you serious, Wilf, or was that another of your jokes?' asked Alan.

'As serious as I'm sitting here, but I'll have to put the idea up to Don. He's the boss.'

'Do just that,' said Mike. 'And say that if he's interested, Alan and I are up for it.'

130

Next morning, back at Denmark Street, Wilf learned that Don *was* interested – to a point. After delivering Wilf a lecture on the fearful expenditure involved in launching any major group like this – retainers for members of the band, equipment, transportation, publicity, rehearsal rooms, recording studios, photographers, the list was endless – he said that in spite of this, he'd like to discuss the idea with Alan and Mike as soon as possible.

This was only the beginning. Don guardedly expressed further interest. More meetings followed, and more names were mentioned: a songwriting guitarist friend of Alan's called Trevor Williams, Andy Bown, the former keyboard player with the Herd, and Adrian Williams, yet another Welshman from the valleys, as lead vocalist. When Charlie Harrison, currently playing bass with the Mindbenders, was recruited, the new group was clearly taking shape.

After several days of agonised discussion, they even managed to agree a name for it – Judas Jump.

Throughout this time, Judas Jump remained very much Wilf's responsibility, and when Don ordered him to lick it into shape it seemed a good excuse for a few weeks back in his beloved Isle of Wight. Warner's Holiday Camp at Bembridge out of season is not everyone's idea of luxury, but it gave the boys a chance to work together as a group in peace and quiet, and to write and practise their material. Henry Spinetti called the camp Stalag Wilf, a reference to Wilf's commandant-like control of the group and its members, but it was largely thanks to this that by the end of October Wilf could report to Don that Judas Jump was ready for the recording studio.

During this short stay on the island, Wilf also learned a bitter little lesson over what can happen when promoting celebrities and things go wrong. What is odd about this somewhat silly episode is that, during his short misguided life, Wilf Pine had done almost everything he should not have done. He had robbed, shot, wounded and beaten people up. He had hijacked lorries, demanded money with menaces, and committed adultery more times than he could remember, and yet a genuine attempt that he now made to help some old friends out is one of the few things held against him by his enemies, and still crops up in the legendary history of pop whenever Wilf's name is mentioned.

To make what happened more ironic still, it involved an ageing rock star Wilf had never met before and was not particularly interested in – the one-time idol of the 1950s rock'n'rollers, Gene Vincent. During his long-past prime, Vincent had been internationally famous for such more or less forgotten hits as 'Be-Bob-A- Lula', 'Blue Jean Bop' and 'Pistol Packin' Mama'. But since those golden days, drugs and alcohol had done what drugs and alcohol tend to do, particularly to old rock stars, and Gene had lost his looks, his money and much of his one-time magic. That autumn, as resolutely on the juice as ever, he had gamely tried reviving his fortunes and his reputation with an extensive tour of Europe – which hadn't really worked.

Somehow he managed to re-create the old routines, for audiences largely composed of one-time rock fans, most of them ageing like himself. But the drink caused problems; so did his desperate desire for money, and in France his appearances at Lille and Dijon ended with Vincent yelling at the promoters for payment – which, to be fair to him, was not forthcoming.

This was the situation at the end of that October when he arrived in London for the start of the grand finale of his European tour. To manage his appearances, he was relying on Wilf's old friend, Henry Henroid, who had acted for Gene as road manager in years gone by when he was still employing Arden as his agent. This relationship with Don had ended badly, but Henry was still hanging in for old times' sake. Finding it hard to fix bookings for Gene's British tour, Henry had turned to Don Arden for advice, and Don, again for old times' sake, had suggested an initial performance on the Isle of Wight. Henry had consulted Wilf, and Wilf had put him on to some more old friends of his, the island's favourite native group, the Cherokees, who, for the autumn, had taken over the ballroom at Wilf's old haunt, the Royal York Hotel at Ryde, and agreed to include Gene Vincent in their Saturday-night show.

Wilf gave the project his blessing – but nothing more. And early on the evening of 9 November he turned up at the Royal York before the performance to meet his old friend Henry Henroid to see how things were going. The answer was, they weren't.

Gene was already fairly well away when Henry had met him off the train at Portsmouth, and when they were crossing on the ferry there was a heated argument with Gene over his terms of payment. After his experience in France, Gene was demanding his money before he performed and wouldn't listen when Henry tried explaining that the usual deal was a cheque within seven days of the performance. But there was another, more serious problem. Gene had brought along with him a BBC TV film crew who were making an hour-long television documentary on his British tour with the help of an old friend and fan of his called Adrian Owlett.

This was the situation that Wilf, perfectly innocent for once, wandered into at the Royal York half an hour before the show was due to start. He was hoping for a drink with his old friend Henry. What he found instead was chaos. Henry was getting frantic, while his star was staying in his room, loudly refusing to appear on stage without money on the nail; and Wilf's other friends, the Cherokees were also in a state, trying to scrape around to raise the cash. (Finally they found half the sum in notes and the other half in an instantly payable cheque, which Gene accepted.)

'For Christ's sake, Wilf,' said Henry when he saw him. 'D'you think that you could go and talk some sense to Gene and get him to go on stage and tell him no one's going to cheat him.'

'I'll do my best,' said Wilf, who knocked on the door, and in he went.

As Wilf points out, apart from his friendship with Henry Henroid and the Cherokees, whether Gene appeared or not that night was no big deal for him. He had no financial interest in the show, no connection with the Royal York Hotel and no particular concern about Gene Vincent. As he entered the room, what he saw was Gene standing by the washbasin staring at him with a glazed expression on his face.

'I think I said, "Come on, Gene, it's show-time", or words to that effect,' says Wilf. 'He mumbled a reply I didn't catch, and the next thing I knew someone was training a film camera on me, and a big, furry outside broadcaster's microphone was being shoved in my face.'

What appears to have happened was that the film crew had been on hand in the dressing room hoping for a dramatic confrontation between Gene and his manager, Henry Henroid, over the disputed subject of the fee. What they got instead was Wilf angrily thrusting away the microphone.

'I've never been a member of the diplomatic corps,' he says, 'and, taking this as an invasion of my privacy, lashed out instinctively.'

What followed next is described by Britt Hagarty, quoting from Owlett in his biography of Gene Vincent. 'At first the club owner, Wilfie [sic] Pine, seemed very nice. But it became apparent . . . that Wilfie didn't have Gene's best interests at heart. At one point he tried to stop the BBC from filming, and said to one of the crew, "Stop or I'll smash yer fuckin' head in".'

This sounds like the Wilf one knows, as does the description of the way he 'then knocked the sound recording machine to the ground'. But apart from the fact that no one in his life has ever dared call Wilf Pine 'Wilfie', Wilf still hotly denies it.

First, Hagarty mentions the claim by Adrian Owlett that before the show Wilf had come up to Gene's room with Mickey Finns, 'trying to get Gene so drunk that he'd lash his own show so that legitimately Gene wouldn't have to be paid'. This didn't work because Owlett bravely poured the drinks down the sink, telling Vincent, 'Gene, these are not nice drinks'.

Apart from the fact that the idea of Wilf Pine doctoring anybody's drink is out of character, this 'incident' is not plausible to me for the simple reason that Wilf first became involved with Vincent on behalf of his friends the Cherokees and Henry Henroid in order to persuade him to appear on stage, and not to stop him from doing so.

Anyhow, it didn't need help from Wilf to get Gene Vincent drunk, but somehow he did stagger on to the stage, and Wilf remembers 'watching the opening numbers by that ageing, bloated old rocker, and, yes, he did give a good performance, as drunk as he was, and that's a fact'.

But the troubles of the camera crew and Adrian Owlett were far from over. Despite the fact that Wilf was not in any way responsible for paying Gene, and that the Cherokees, who were, did find the money, Owlett claims that after the show he became involved in a scuffle with 'Wilfie' because Gene had not been paid, and 'when Wilfie tried to get heavy' he 'thought he might be killed'.

In spite of this, Gene, Owlett and the BBC film crew pulled

themselves together and went on to an after-hours drinking club, which was 'just like a Chicago gangster club in the 1930s with guys running around in striped suits, black shirts and white ties'. But even here they could not escape the dreaded 'Wilfie Pine', who had not only turned up among these striped-suited, black-shirted Chicago-style gangsters but who they now 'discovered' to their horror actually owned the club. On learning this, they all fled back to their hotel, but even in the safety of the Royal York their tribulations were not over.

Next morning, after breakfast, 'Wilfie' and the boys, presumably intent on revenge, were still in hot pursuit as Gene Vincent, Adrian Owlett and the BBC film crew scurried from the island. Wisely they 'took a different route back to the ferry', but despite this they were 'actually chased to the ferry landing by another car and just got on in time'. Phew!

Wilf says most of this is nonsense. In any even, the simple facts are that Wilf has never owned an out-of-hours drinking club on the island, that there has never been such a club where the waiters dressed as Chicago-style gangsters, and that Wilf and presumably the crew have never chased anybody, let alone a film crew and an ageing rock star with a bad hangover, on to the Isle of Wight ferry.

But while many of the tales that went the rounds about that famous evening when Wilf Pine met Gene Vincent seem to me to be a bit ridiculous, they are also interesting for a single reason: they offer us some indication of the sort of fear that Wilf could undoubtedly strike into the hearts of impressionable 'civilians' when his temper was up, and also of the reputation he commanded in the music industry.

As far as Wilf himself was concerned, by the time the trouble broke he had more important things to think about. Throughout his time at Bembridge with Judas Jump, Jill was just a few miles away and in the final stages of her third pregnancy. This meant that he had being seeing more than usual of his family, and he was particularly excited by the way the two boys, Sean and Scott, were growing up. Whatever his failings as a husband, he was as devoted as ever to his sons, and in that last week of November he was offered something else on which to lavish his fatherly affections, when Jill gave birth to a very healthy baby girl. They called her Sammi and, at Wilf's insistence, to this was added the second name of Hope. Hope was the given name of Don's wife, Paddy.

For a few days following the birth, Wilf did his best to make himself useful around the home, but it didn't really work. However much he loved his children, by now nothing could revive his marriage. His life was in London with the new band and his new friends – and enemies – in the music business.

By now, Don Arden had grown rich enough to realise his dream of moving on from Mayfair to Wimbledon Parkside, facing Wimbledon Common. His new abode was more a mansion than a house, his neighbours were film stars and millionaires, and the All-England Tennis Courts were nearby. After the little terraced house in Manchester with the scrap yard at the end of the road, 'the Al Capone of pop' had really made it.

So, it seemed, had Wilf, who more than ever now appeared to be sharing in Don Arden's success. It was as if the Arden family had decided to take him under their wing. Don was his teacher, David his personal friend, and Paddy Arden was a steadying figure, giving him advice about his private life, encouraging his ambitions, and opening his eyes to a more sophisticated world around him. After that first uncomfortable dinner with the family, he was beginning to enjoy the pleasures of the rich and feel at ease among them. 'It was thanks to Paddy that I learned that there are better things in life than egg and chips,' he says. She also taught him how to dress and sent him to Don's tailor. She even suggested a new barber. And now, with the move to Wimbledon, his involvement with the family almost overnight became closer still.

With the flat in Mayfair standing empty, Don had decided he would use it for his agency, selling the Denmark Street office in the process. As this meant selling the flat as well, Wilf had to find somewhere else to live, so he asked Don how long he had to find himself fresh accommodation. Don looked puzzled.

'But Paddy and I are expecting you to move in with us and the family, Wilf. God knows the place is big enough,' he said.

Gratefully – but also rather warily – Wilf thanked him and agreed, and at the beginning of 1970, he found himself living in this great house in Wimbledon. His twenty-sixth birthday came and went, and it seemed as if his life was suddenly mapped out for him. He had what looked like the rosiest of futures in the music business. He had a wife he didn't love and three children he adored. And now he also had Don Arden's family offering him a life of unaccustomed luxury and treating him as one of their own.

But was this what he really wanted? For that matter, what *did* he want? The truth was that he really didn't know. Then, early in 1970, two separate events occurred that changed his life and helped to shape his future. As Wilf says:

Around February 1970 Don was approached by Black Sabbath asking him to manage them. Even then they were on the lookout for somebody to steal them from their existing manager, Jim Simpson, and I remember going with Don to the Marquee Club in Wardour Street, Soho, to see them performing. It was the first time I'd heard them in action, and they totally blew me away. I thought they were terrific, but I'm pretty sure Don didn't really understand them. However, Don being Don, he didn't let on what he thought about them. I remember that we laughed a lot together during the per- formance – to tell the truth, we were enjoying ourselves and I always seemed to laugh a lot when Don was around – and as he had an important appointment, we didn't hang around for long when the show was over.

Tony Hall, the head of Tony Hall Enterprises who recorded Sabbath, was there that night along with their publisher, David Platz of Essex Music, and as we were leaving we met Ozzy Osbourne, and I remember Ozzy saying that he'd be in touch with Don. But he never did get in touch, nor did Don get back to them.

Later I learned that either Hall or Platz had told Ozzy that Don had regarded Sabbath as such a joke that he couldn't stop laughing throughout the show. Which of course, was totally wrong. If Don had been laughing at anyone, it had been at me.'

Wilf thought no more about this at the time and went on working – and also living now – with the Ardens. During the early spring of 1970 he was kept busy preparing for the launch of Judas Jump, which Don now thought had great potential for the lucrative teenybopper market. That April Wilf was very much involved in the group's first full-scale concert before a youthful audience. To anticipate the possibility of a hostile reception from the British music press, which would have thrown them badly, Don suggested trying out Judas Jump abroad, and Wilf was more than satisfied with the enthusiasm of the youthful audience at Liège in Belgium when they made their debut.

But although Wilf was working harder than ever for Don, he was growing uneasy over the direction of his life when something happened that made his mind up for him. He had just wrapped up the detailed preparations for the next stage in Judas Jump's career when out of the blue Dave Farley rang, saying that he needed help. He explained that he'd been offered what he called 'a piece of work', which they both knew meant something more or less illegal. Even as he listened, Wilf felt an unaccustomed rush of adrenalin, and when Dave went on to say that it involved going to the West Midlands and would probably last a week, Wilf's instant reply was: 'Count me in.'

Dave was in fact in London already, and when they met that evening, he outlined the plan. He'd been approached by an old villain Wilf remembered from the past who wanted a lorry-load of stolen TV sets recovered. The thief he had paid to steal them in the first place had not delivered on the deal, and had disappeared with the lorry, TV sets and all. Dave was being paid to do whatever was required to get them back.

It wasn't that difficult for Wilf to make up an excuse to cover his absence from the office, and next morning he and Dave were hot on the trail to the West Midlands and the twice-stolen lorry-load of television sets. It took a lot of time to trace the disappearing thief, and the end of the whole adventure proved an anticlimax. When they finally got their man, it turned out that ever since stealing his already stolen lorry he had been so terrified of the guy who'd paid him that he'd hidden the lorry with its load intact in a warehouse on an industrial estate and left it there. All he wanted was to forget it and make whatever peace he could with the villain who employed him. In the end Wilf, in his favourite role of go-between, was able to arrange this, the villain got his two hundred stolen television sets, Dave got his fee, and nobody was hurt. End of rather silly story.

But for Wilf it wasn't silly, and those few days on the loose with Dave had been like the sudden taste of alcohol to a reformed alcoholic. After ensuring the safe delivery of the stolen lorry and driving back to London with Dave beside him, he knew for certain that for all the kindness of the Ardens, their sort of world was not for him. He missed his old life, and he missed the people. No amount of rich living could compensate for that. He had come from the streets, and back to the streets he had to go. But he took his time.

He spent a few days on the Isle of Wight. He had missed his family, and now he was back again he smelled the unaccustomed air of freedom. And as luck would have it, Jinxie was back as well. His ship had docked the day before at Southampton and he was home on twenty-four hours' shore leave. So to make an evening of it, Wilf rang around all of the old members of the crew to join him for a drink. They had a great party at their favourite club, La Babalu, and during the evening Wilf got talking to the club manager, Clive Martin, who told him that the company he worked for owned the lease on another nearby club, the Music Box, and were thinking of renting it out for Saturday-night music promotions during the forthcoming summer season.

On the spur of the moment Wilf asked him to put his name forward, which he did, and the following day he agreed a deal for the summer with the owner. He returned to London having firmly made his mind up to tell Don in person that he was leaving. But it wasn't that easy. On arriving at the office that Monday morning, David told him that his parents had gone off for a week in America, leaving Wilf a list of tasks to be performed in their absence. These included what turned out to be a fruitless trip to Paris chasing up some long-overdue royalties. As Gene Vincent had learned the hard way, the French were notoriously bad payers – particularly to foreigners. For a moment Wilf did think of making trouble but thought better of it, realising that the guys in the agency had no great love for the English, 'and that if I did I might well have found myself in the Bastille'.

139

By the end of the week he had tidied his office, done everything that Don had put on the list and was once more returning to the island.

'I had still not mentioned leaving to David or to Don, and rather than risk letting Don talk me out of going. I opted for the coward's way out by ringing him after the weekend. But even on Monday morning when he called, Don had not returned, so Wilf plucked up all his courage and broke the news to David Arden. After a lengthy chat, David did understand the reasons why I felt the time had come for me to go, and he wished me well and promised to explain everything to his father when he did return.'

But although Wilf did talk on the telephone to Don during the months to come, he could tell at once that he had hurt him and that things would never be the same again. Wilf felt bad about this. He had enjoyed his time with him and was grateful to him as a friend and as a mentor. As he says, 'for me Don Arden will always be my Mr Rock'n'Roll', and some years later, in another country and in very different circumstances, he would be able to repay the debt he felt he owed him.

8

Here Come the Sabbath

UNTIL NOW, MOST of Wilf's experience with Don Arden had involved him in stopping people from stealing acts. But early in the autumn of 1970, for the first time but not the last, he stole an act himself, and in so doing changed his life.

When he baled out from the good life with the Ardens, he had imagined he would be returning to a less demanding world of casual crime and small-time promotion in the Music Box in Ryde. But by bringing his talents as a thief directly to the music industry, within the next two years he would be running his affairs from an office in Mayfair, driving a Rolls-Royce and playing a crucial part in the early career of one of the most explosive and enduring bands in the world of popular entertainment. And throughout all this, Wilf would be acquiring more groups as he perfected his extraordinary role as the most successful thief in show business.

All this began by chance. Back on the island, as he began promoting for the summer season at the Music Box, he realised that the acts that had drawn the audiences in the past no longer seemed to work. Popular music was changing. Soul and pop were not the draw they used to be, but he was puzzled over what, if anything, would take their place. Then he had a stroke of luck.

Don Arden's former personal assistant, Pat Meehan, who had left Arden Enterprises six months or so before him, rang out of the blue to ask how he was getting on. He said that while he wasn't losing any money he wasn't making much either, and Pat Meehan brought the subject around to his own affairs. Since leaving Don, he'd gone into management himself, in partnership with his son, young Patrick

Meehan, and they'd been doing rather well. They had been particularly successful managing a way-out group called Black Widow who were really making money. Why didn't Wilf book the group for the Music Box?

Wilf had heard about Black Widow from the media interest they had been attracting recently. By all accounts they were an oddball, cult group, who were cashing in on the current craze for the occult, with dramatic stage lighting, whippings on stage, 'devil worshipping and Christ knows what'. But whatever Black Widow were or weren't, everywhere they played sold out.

So there and then Wilf fixed an evening for the group with Pat for a few weeks later; and when Black Widow played at the Music Box, the fans went wild. More to the point, he made a profit and began to feel a lot happier than he had for weeks.

As it happened, Pat Meehan himself accompanied the group, and after the show, while he and Wilf enjoyed a drink together, the talk soon turned, as it often did, to the subject of Don Arden. Pat asked him what went wrong that evening at the Marquee Club between Don and Black Sabbath. Wilf's reply, which happened to be true, was that he hadn't the faintest idea. At that time all he knew for certain was that Don had been expecting a call after the show from Ozzy Osbourne, but that it never came, and six months later Sabbath were still being managed from Birmingham by their original manager, Jim Simpson.

'Listen, Wilf,' said Pat. 'There's a lot of talk going on at present in the record industry about Black Sabbath. Take it from me, they're going places, and although we all know that Jim Simpson's a lovely human being, who managed the group from the day they started, he's also very much a Birmingham-based character and Sabbath won't stay with him for ever. That evening when Sabbath played at the Marquee they were all set to leave him for Don Arden, but something happened and they didn't. Why not do yourself a favour, Wilf, and have a go at managing them yourself?'

Wilf laughed at that. 'Be realistic, Pat. What the fuck do I know about management?'

'Well, you didn't do so badly with Judas Jump and keeping things together there. Why not give it a whirl? Whatever happens, you can't lose.'

Wilf shook his head.

'It's not for me,' he said.

'Pity,' said Pat. 'All the same, if I were you I'd think about it. Oh, and by the way, my son, young Patrick, wants to come to see you.'

'Fine,' said Wilf, who remembered Patrick as a personable teenager studying at Redhill College. 'Tell him to give me a call some time.'

His call came sooner than expected. And after telephoning Wilf first thing next morning and fixing an appointment, Patrick turned up at his home in time for lunch.

Wilf realised at once that since the last time he'd seen him Patrick had become a very self-possessed, confident young man with all the charm of his father. He also struck Wilf as remarkably determined.

'As soon as he arrived, I congratulated him on the success Black Widow had been having and told him how good they'd been at the Music Box.

But Patrick had no time for compliments, nor was he all that interested in talking about Black Widow.

'Yeah,' he said, 'but there's another group that's going to be huge, and far, far bigger internationally.'

'Who?'

'Black Sabbath.'

'So we're getting back to that again. First your father, now you.'

They laughed at that, and then they talked a lot, and Patrick stayed over and they began to get to know each other. Little more was said about Black Sabbath, except that, before he left, Patrick asked if the group was now under new management. Wilf replied that he had no idea. All that he did know was that after his success at the club with Black Widow, he'd booked Black Sabbath for a gig at the Music Box and was getting a great advance reaction from the fans. And that was that. Wilf insists that 'for whatever reason, I still had no intention of getting involved in any shape or form with Black Sabbath. But all this changed after their performance at the Music Box.'

Wilf never forgot that evening. Since their appearance at the Marquee, the band had grown in confidence and power, and the overwhelming noise and rage within this heavy-metal band touched something deep within him. 'It was raw, it was exciting, it was like, you know, you get a twinge and a tickle as you listen to them. With me it went from my arsehole to my earhole. It overwhelmed me. It was magnificent.'

After the show, while they were all drinking together at the Babalu, Wilf had his chance to ask Ozzy why the group changed their minds about moving to Don Arden after that evening at the Marquee. Ozzy replied that, after the show, someone – either Tony Hall, who owned the record deal with Sabbath, or David Platz of Essex Music – told them that while they were performing 'Don was laughing at us and taking the piss'. There and then they all decided to have nothing more to do with him.

Wilf did his best to put them straight over what had really happened, saying that he and Don may have shared a joke or two that evening but that Tony and David had misunderstood that they had definitely not been making fun of them. He personally had enormously enjoyed the evening.

The boys apparently accepted this, and Wilf had his chance to ask them if Sabbath had changed management or were still looking.

'Why, are you up for it?' asked Ozzy.

'Could be,' said Wilf. 'Listen, give me your home number, Ozzy, and we'll talk about it.'

'Fine. We'll listen.'

And that was that. After a few more drinks, Black Sabbath said good night and left to catch the late-night ferry for the mainland.

Although the next day was Sunday, Wilf woke early with a call from Patrick.

'Wilf, how was Sabbath?'

'Fucking marvellous. They went down a storm, *and* I made money. The kids went berserk.'

'I told you they're a winner. And did you discover if they're still with Jim Simpson or are they still looking?'

When Wilf repeated Ozzy's conversation, the effect on Patrick was electric.

'Wilf, I'm on my way. I've got to see you.'

This time, when Patrick arrived there was no more beating about the bush. 'Wilf, we've got to have that band.'

'What d'you mean *we*?'

'You and me. We're in this together. They're going to be world-beaters, and we've got to have them.'

After lunch they continued drinking and talking, and finally Patrick said: 'Wilf, make that call to Sabbath now and see if you can interest them.'

'I got through to Ozzy straight away, and he said that if I caught a train to Birmingham the following day he'd get the guys together and we'd all have a serious discussion.'

Wilf arrived at New Street Station in the middle of the afternoon to be met by Sabbath's lead guitarist, Tony Iommi, who drove him across the city to where Ozzy was living at the time with his girlfriend, Thelma.

The rest of the group were there, and once they started talking Wilf got on so well with them that he grew keener than ever on acquiring the group. He sensed that all four of them, not just Ozzy, but also Tony Iommi, Geezer Butler, the bass player, and Billie Ward, the drummer, were natural superstars already. But at the same time they were all so natural and so unassuming that Wilf had never felt so much at ease with members of a group before.

It was also obvious to Wilf that Ozzy was the leader, and in the end it was he who asked Wilf outright if he was genuinely interested in managing them.

'Of course I am,' he said, 'but there's really two of us.' And he explained about Patrick – how he was also managing Black Widow and how it was largely thanks to him that he was there at all. He also explained that the legal side of the business was Patrick's department. When he said this, Thelma, who was clearly very smart, raised the question of legal indemnities for the group. If Wilf and Patrick became joint managers of Black Sabbath, would they be prepared to indemnify the group against any legal actions that ensued? These could include court costs, legal bills and any damages that followed if Jim Simpson sued for breach of contract, as he almost certainly would.

At this point Wilf clearly had to talk to Patrick, so he asked Ozzy if he could use his telephone and rang his office. Patrick was there, waiting by the phone for news, and after telling him of his success,

Wilf asked if they could agree to guarantee the group legal indemnity. Patrick was, as ever, reassuring.

'Absolutely no problem, Wilf. That's something I'll take care of. All that matters is to get the group here to talk as soon as possible.'

With the problem of indemnity settled, there were no further queries, and Wilf and the boys shook hands on the deal. When he asked how soon they could manage a further talk with him and Patrick, the reply was instant. They'd be on a train to London first thing next morning.

For Wilf, this meant getting back to London before them, so that he would have a chance of telling Patrick what was happening. So he caught an overnight train, which seemed to stop at every station en route to London. Eventually it got into Euston Station at three in the morning. It was freezing cold, and so was Wilf, but Patrick, who was waiting on the platform, took him for an early breakfast at the station café. Warm at last, Wilf told him all about the trip, and they toasted the poaching of Black Sabbath over a cup of railway coffee.

True to their word, Black Sabbath arrived in London just before lunch, and Wilf took them to meet Patrick in the office in Leicester Street which he shared with his father. Everyone was most relaxed, and there was an amicable but businesslike discussion over the details of the contract. This would take the form of a personal management contract between Wilf, Patrick and Black Sabbath, with the indemnities taken care of and the standard management fee of twenty per cent of the group's earnings, to be shared equally between Wilf and Patrick.

When lunch was over and Sabbath were on their way back to Birmingham, Patrick wanted his lawyer to start drawing up the contract straight away. He had already made an appointment with one of the top show-business lawyers in London, David Offenbach of Offenbach and Co, in their Bond Street offices for that afternoon.

Offenbach agreed to prepare the contracts for the group to sign as soon as possible, but, equally important, Wilf and Patrick had to be prepared for an ex parte injunction from Jim Simpson's lawyers which, as Thelma had predicted, would be certain to arrive. This injunction would hold up the contract with Black Sabbath, and to get it lifted Wilf and Patrick needed to swear affidavits before yet another lawyer, which would then be heard before a High Court judge, when Jim Simpson's case could also be considered.

This was the first time in his life that Wilf had used a lawyer, and as they came out of Offenbach's office it was freezing cold and he remembers saying: 'Patrick, are you really sure about this carry-on?'

And Patrick, who was in his element, replied: 'Wilf, you should know that in this game we use the law to beat the law. So don't worry. That's how these things are done.'

But Wilf was a worrier. 'Remember that I was an ex-approved school boy and a thief who'd spent most of my life trying to steer clear of the law, and here I was, suddenly relying on lawyers and the civil courts, which I knew fuck all about – and all to protect the fruits of the biggest theft I'd ever done. Who says there isn't one law for the rich and another for the poor? Still, who was I to grumble? Since Patrick seemed one hundred per cent confident, so was I.'

Two days later Sabbath made a second trip to London and put their signatures to the contracts, which transferred all rights and duties of their management from Jim Simpson to Wilf Pine and Patrick Meehan. When this was done, later that same afternoon David Offenbach took them to the office of another famous West End solicitor before whom, with their hands held firmly on the Bible, they swore affidavits, which gave legal confirmation to their contracts – and to the most profitable act of larceny in Wilf's career. Once this was done they were ready for any legal comeback from the victim of their heist – Jim Simpson.

As expected, two days later they were hit by the injunction from Jim Simpson's lawyers. And now was the moment when everything depended on David Offenbach. Within forty-eight hours Wilf and Patrick were actually sitting in the High Court in the Strand, while the lawyers argued learnedly before the judge on their behalf. On the strength of their affidavits, their evidence was ruled admissible, so that while the judge upheld the legality of Jim Simpson's contract, he also upheld the legality of theirs.

As far as Sabbath were concerned, the change of management brought little in the way of instant change. One of Jim Simpson's stipulations that the lawyers had agreed to was that Sabbath had to honour all existing contracts he had made on their behalf. As these included personal appearances, record and publishing deals and an extremely crowded European tour, both the group and their new managers were kept very busy.

But before even this could happen, Patrick and Wilf found themselves confronted by a more formidable obstacle than Jim Simpson's lawyers – the all-powerful record industry.

Almost the first appointment they had made was with Tony Hall and David Platz of Essex Music. There was a certain irony in the situation. Had these two gentlemen not previously seemingly told Black Sabbath that Don Arden had been laughing at them during their show at the Marquee, it would have been Don, not Wilf and Patrick, who would have been managing the band by now. So Wilf owed them both a debt of gratitude, and he began by explaining what had happened as reasonably as he could. But Hall and Platz weren't having any. They had been more than happy dealing with Jim Simpson and refused to talk to them.

But Wilf and Patrick could both be obstinate as well, and they refused to be dismissed. On one of the rare occasions in his life, Wilf carefully controlled his temper, and they stayed and argued on throughout the afternoon. After several hours, Platz and Hall started to see reason. Not only were Wilf and Patrick still not moving, but they had copies of what looked like legal contracts with the band, along with further documents stating that the contracts had been legally upheld by a High Court judge in a civil court of law. This was hard to argue with and finally, if reluctantly, Tony Hall and David Platz agreed that they had no alternative but to make the best of things and work with Black Sabbath's new management.

With Essex Music in the bag, Wilf and Patrick now presumed that their troubles were over. In fact, they were still only just beginning. Before they left, Tony Hall had told them that they would still have to square things with Sabbath's main recording company, Phonogram, which was issuing the group's forthcoming records under the Vertigo label. Vertigo's manager was a well-known figure in the music business called Olav Wyper, and he was Wilf's and Patrick's next port of call.

But Olav Wyper proved a different proposition from the managers of Essex Music. Not merely did he question their authority: he refused to have anything to do with them at all. 'I don't have to talk to you. I don't even have to recognise you. So we have nothing to discuss. Good day to you, gentlemen,' he said, and shut the door in their faces.

Once again, but with even greater difficulty, Wilf controlled his temper. And as there was clearly nothing further to be done, he and Patrick walked away, returning to the office where they were once more lunching and discussing progress with Black Sabbath. Over lunch they told them of their success with the lawyers and with Essex Music, but that they had drawn a total blank with Olav Wyper.

'Who's Olav Wyper?' someone asked.

'I know his brother,' said Ozzy.

'Who's he, Oz?'

'Arsehole Wyper,' he replied, at which, of course, everybody laughed, making it hard to take any threat from Olav Wyper too seriously.

'In years to come,' says Wilf, 'when millions had come to know Ozzy Osbourne through his appearances on television as the wildest man alive, they probably thought he hadn't all that much savvy about business – but they couldn't have been more wrong. Through all this business, from start to finish, the guy who was speaking for the group and asking the most relevant questions and forcing things on us that we could have done without was Ozzy. So no one should under-estimate him, even now. As far as I'm concerned, I'll always think of Ozzy as a wonderful, beautiful human being, but there's a brain there too, believe you me – and a sharp one.'

Just how sharp, Ozzy now demonstrated in the way he dealt with Olav Wyper. When the laughter died away, he asked: 'Wilf, d'you figure he's in his office now?'

'Fucked if I know,' said Wilf.

'That's fine,' says Ozzy, with a wicked look. 'We'll go and we'll find out. We'll all turn up at the Vertigo office. After all, we are his fucking act, and you two are our managers. Let's see what he has to say about it'

'So next thing, bang, we've piled into a couple of taxis and are on

149

our way back to Vertigo. Only this time we don't wait for reception to ask us who we are. We go straight up the stairs and through that door and who's sitting behind the desk but Olav Wyper.'

'I'll never forget his face when he sees Black Sabbath looking like a group from hell,' says Wilf.

'What's going on? Who are these people? Get out of my office, all of you! Out! Out!' he shouts.

'At the time I can't believe my ears, although now it all seems very funny. I say to him: "You mean you don't know who these people are?"

And he shouts back: "I don't care who they are. I'm not interested in who they are. I want the lot of you out of here right now, or I'm calling the police."

'At this I say: "But Mr Wyper, *this* happens to be your act, Black Sabbath."

'The look on that guy's face had to be seen to be believed, and he went several shades paler than the paper on the desk before him. I've never seen such a rapid change in anyone.

'"Well . . . after all . . . you know," he stuttered, "you shouldn't just barge in here unannounced like that. Now would you please sit down, all of you."'

He did his best to laugh but it didn't really work, and it was Ozzy who then said: 'Look here, Mr Wyper, you've got to understand. We've changed managers. We're not with Jim Simpson any more. We're with Wilf Pine and Patrick Meehan.'

Olav Wyper nodded, and after a short conversation, which was fairly amicable by now, turned to Wilf and Patrick and said: 'Very well. I accept that you two are the band's new management. From now on we'll do business together.'

'All of us shook hands, he saw us to the door, and it was not until we were standing outside in the street that it struck me what had really happened. It had really all been thanks to Ozzy that the worst of our headaches was behind us. As for Olav Wyper, during the next two months this group that he hadn't even recognised became the biggest success he'd ever had.'

Even now Wilf and Patrick had little real idea of what was coming.

When Vertigo released their album five weeks later, it would soon reach number one, and 'Paranoid', the single taken from the album, was to shoot immediately to the top of the pops and stay there for weeks.

'All of this,' says Wilf, 'was really handed to us on a plate, and we simply went along with it. Did I feel sorry for Jim Simpson? Not in the least. It's a world where dog eats dog, and if I hadn't pinched Sabbath when I did, there were ten other bastards out there waiting for the chance to do the same. But did I respect Jim Simpson? That's a different question. The answer is that, yes I did. He was a fine manager and he'd done wonders for the group, but they'd outgrown him. He was based in Birmingham, and their eyes were on London and the world beyond. They were all itching for a change, and that's the only reason I could steal them.'

But before the success of Sabbath really started, Wilf and Patrick, as managers of the band, had work to do. Among Jim Simpson's deals the band had to honour were a number of tough one-night stands in England, followed by a two-week tour of Germany and Belgium where, as Wilf remembers:

Jim had got them booked in here, there and everywhere. So not only did we have to promote the group ourselves, but we were also duty bound to honour those gigs and honour them we did. Patrick stayed in the office, taking care of the business side of things, while I went on the road with the boys. And to tell the truth, I had myself a ball.

It was then I really got to know and love each and every one of them. They were all individual characters in their own right. They weren't the total head-bangers they became later, but straight, earthy Birmingham guys who knew where they were going. As I sat there watching them perform, they were like no other group I'd ever seen. Success was written all over them, and I realised that no matter who their manager was, from now on they were on their way.

Even before the tour, we were working our socks off, finishing those English gigs before leaving for Germany. We began with Düsseldorf, where we found a comfortable little hotel which we made our base. I roomed with Tony Iommi, and every evening we were off working the nearby towns, Essen, Duisburg, Wuppertal, places like that, and coming back each night to Düsseldorf.

To this day, Black Sabbath's music goes down big in Germany, and the German audiences then were already way ahead of those in England. During the next ten days, Black Sabbath journeyed up the Rhine, playing non-stop, every night, then crossed over into Belgium, where an equally gruelling programme awaited them.

This Belgian tour had only just begun, and Wilf, Ozzy and one of the roadies were driving in the truck carrying all the group's equipment for that night's gig when they got lost. The others had gone on ahead, and Wilf realised that they had the itinerary with details of where they were performing. Neither he nor Ozzy nor the roadie could remember where it was. Finally they arrived in Liège, and in total desperation Wilf put a call through to Patrick back in London, asking where they ought to be.

Patrick sounded unusually excited.

'Great that you called, Wilf,' he exclaimed. 'I've got news for you and for the boys. Tell them their album's gone straight to number one. Give them my congratulations. There's not been anything quite like it since the Beatles.'

In his excitement, Wilf nearly forgot to ask where they ought to be.

'Ghent,' said Patrick.

'That's a pity. We're in Liège,' said Wilf. 'We'd best get moving.'

It took them two hours to reach Ghent, but luckily they had time to spare and were driving in a state of near euphoria. Patrick had said that they were performing in a school, and when they eventually found the place the other members of the group were there already. Ozzy told them the good news, and in the midst of the excitement Wilf asked someone where they were due to spend the night. He was told that it was arranged that after the show they'd all sleep on judo mats on the floor of the school gymnasium.

'Fuck that,' said the lads when they heard the news. 'With an album at number one, no judo mats for us! We're off back home.' As soon as they'd finished the performance, they loaded up the truck, drove straight to Ostend to catch the overnight ferry, and were back in London in the early morning.

What happened then was unlike anything Wilf had ever experienced – before or since. Black Sabbath literally took off. But although they returned to find themselves instant celebrities, they were still required to soldier on for a while, honouring their existing bookings before they could really enjoy their new success. With the 'Paranoid' single already picking up airplay and entering the lower part of the charts, Wilf had no difficulty in securing them a place on *Top of the Pops*, along with performers like Cliff Richard and Engelbert Humperdinck. This was the beginning as everything started shooting past at a hundred mph, leading up to their appearance soon after at the Royal Festival Hall in London. This appearance has always stood out in Wilf's memory as the climax of one of the most extraordinary periods in his life. The very night before, he was with Sabbath as they completed the very last of Jim Simpson's gigs at a scruffy pub in Islington with the band using the gents as their changing room, and all for the princely sum of £50.

'The following evening, just before the Festival Hall concert, when we were testing the sound balance of the band, we realised that the drum riser, which kept the drums in place, was missing. So Bill Ward, the drummer, who was known for hitting the drums with a force like no one else, produced some three-inch nails and started hammering them into the beautifully polished floor of the stage before somebody did produce a riser just in time.'

That night there were two separate shows. They began excitingly enough with the first full-scale public appearance of the celebrated group, Emerson, Lake and Palmer. That was a sell-out, but so was Sabbath, and as Wilf walked his band out on to the stage that night and saw the audience go wild as they struck up the first chords he knew then that this really was a monster ready to rear its head.

During the following weeks, Wilf found himself booking other gigs for Sabbath for more money than the band itself had ever seen before, and in the midst of this excitement and success a tremendous sense of camaraderie grew up between him and Patrick. But there still remained one all-important booking for Sabbath to complete – a tentative tour of America, which Simpson had already set in place for them.

But buoyed up with their success, everyone involved was regarding this no longer as a hardship but as an enormous challenge. Patrick flew out ahead to arrange the details of the tour and to meet the band's American record company, Warner Brothers, who were underwriting the tour. Wilf, who kept in daily contact with him by telephone, found Patrick more and more elated at the response and sheer enthusiasm for the group that he encountered – particularly from the then president of Warner Brothers, the all-powerful Joe Smith.

With all the arrangements completed, Wilf and the band finally took their first eventful plane journey together to America. And flying with them to New York. was the already massively successful group, Traffic. Wilf remembers talking to Traffic's drummer, Jim Capaldi, and asking him how he thought Sabbath would go down in America. He replied that, given the chance, he'd bet all his wages from his own forthcoming tour that Sabbath would simply conquer America.

As it turned out, Capaldi's prophecy summed up what happened in the next few weeks. As Wilf puts it: 'They went, they played, they conquered. By the end of that first phenomenal tour they had already been booked back for a repeat performance at every venue where they had previously appeared. And the rest is rock music history.'

9

A Hoodlum in Mayfair

BLACK SABBATH'S FIRST whirlwind tour of America was such an overnight success that it turned the group into seriously big business. As their joint managers, Wilf and Patrick were very much part of this, responsible for organising the group's tours, appearances, promotion and marketing, together with their worldwide record sales. It was an increasingly demanding – and profitable – operation, and Patrick's company, Worldwide Artistes Management, was at the centre of it and prospered accordingly. So did Wilf. During that first year co-managing Black Sabbath, his existence changed dramatically. For the first time in his life he found himself OK for money and started renting a comfortable but not over-luxurious apartment on West Hill, Wandsworth, not far from the two houses Don Arden owned on Wimbledon Common. (Arden had recently acquired the house next door and used it as an office.) Wilf still wore his hair long, but had not copied Sabbath's wild man image, and continued following Paddy Arden's advice and had his suits hand made by a West End tailor. Now that he could afford almost anything he wanted, one of the first things he bought with his newly acquired wealth was a gleaming Aston Martin DB5.

With ever-increasing revenues rolling in from Sabbath, Wilf's and Patrick's friendship flourished too. Then, early in November 1971, thirteen months after taking over Sabbath, to everyone's surprise, Wilf went to Patrick and calmly informed him that he wanted out from his involvement with the group.

He had several reasons for doing this. The most compelling, as he tried explaining to Patrick, was that 'just as you can't have two captains of a ship, so you can't have two managers of a group like Sabbath. Co-managership never really works.'

Patrick disagreed. 'Wilf, we're doing fine. Forget it. There's no problem.'

But for Wilf there was a problem. 'Most of my work with the group was really over once I'd nicked Sabbath, and I found myself doing less and less with them by now. They were becoming such big business that it needed a business brain like Patrick's, and the youth of Patrick and his sort of go, to see it through.'

Patrick still tried talking Wilf out of his decision. 'Wilf, you're crazy doing this. With the sort of success that Sabbath's having, you'll go on making money for ever. Do yourself a favour. Think again.'

But Wilf had thought a lot already and had made up his mind – which with Wilf is notoriously hard to change.

So, as he says, 'We parleyed around a bit, and in the end Patrick agreed to buy out my percentage of Sabbath on just one condition – that we continued working together. I agreed to join the management of his company, Worldwide Artistes, as a salaried associate. In return, Patrick looked after me handsomely.'

When the deal was done, Patrick turned to Wilf and said: 'Whatever you want to do in the future, I'll back you.'

This sounded reassuring, but what *did* Wilf want to do?

His answer showed that money hadn't changed him in the least, and that he was still a hoodlum at heart.

'Patrick,' he said, 'I'm pretty sure that there are still a lot of acts out there that I can get hold of if I set my mind to it. If I can, and if we can then still work together, I've an idea that we could build up a tremendous rock stable – and a very powerful one. But I must be free to go out first and poach them.'

'I've said I'll back you. Go ahead,' said Patrick, or words to that effect. And this was how the golden years of Wilf Pine's life of crime in the music business started. Once a thief, always a thief.

During his year as joint manager of Black Sabbath, Wilf had enjoyed the reputation that had grown up around him. This dated back to his days with Don Arden, when he became a legend as someone you tangle with only at your peril, and deep down he was as violent and rebellious as ever. But there was nothing violent about his first acquisition for his new 'stable'. It came about entirely by chance and proved so easy that it barely rated as a poach at all.

He was driving home for a weekend on the Isle of Wight in his Aston Martin. Finding himself in Portsmouth waiting for the ferry, he decided to pay a call on his old friends, the Schulman brothers. He had known them originally as the group Simon Dupree and the Big Sound, since when they had progressed, becoming what Wilf describes as 'a very polished, sophisticated act' called Gentle Giant. As in the old days, Wilf stayed longer than intended, enjoying a laugh and a cup of tea with the boys in Phil's front room, and he was soon telling them all about the current situation between himself and Sabbath.

He could see at once that they were impressed, for as he was perfectly aware 'once you have a world headline act like Sabbath, other acts want to join them. Success attracts success the whole world over.'

When Wilf enquired who was managing Gentle Giant, they replied that they were now managing themselves.

'Then I wouldn't have to steal you. You're your own bosses,' he joked, adding that if they ever felt like joining him and Patrick, they should let him know. After another cup of tea, they said they'd think things over, and Wilf went off to catch his ferry, nursing a copy of the new Gentle Giant album which they'd just recorded.

'To tell the truth,' he says, 'I was really pleased to see them all again, but once I was back on the island I honestly didn't give too much thought to them or to their album.' He had more important things to think about. During his busiest times with Sabbath, even when on tour, Wilf had always made a point of telephoning the children every day. 'It was my one way of keeping in touch with them, and they had come to expect that daily call. But for me nothing could take the place of seeing them, and it was great being back with them, even for a weekend; but the gap between me and their mother had become unbridgeable by now. We didn't argue any more. We'd simply reached the point where we had nothing left to say to one another. After the initial excitement of seeing the kids and tucking them up in bed, I found myself sitting there on my own, playing the new Gentle Giant album – and I just loved it. It wasn't heavy rock. It was very polished, sophisticated music. The band's famous "big sound" was still there, but the group had changed and had become, well, "a gentle giant".'

Back in London after the weekend, he told Patrick all about the group and played him their album. His father, Pat Meehan, was in the office at the time, and while everyone enjoyed it the old man was particularly enthusiastic. When he'd listened to the album for the second time that afternoon, Patrick said: 'Wilf, I think you'd better go and nick them.'

'Whoa!' said Wilf. 'These happen to be my friends and they're also artistes. I'd ask you to respect their feelings.'

Patrick was contrite and said he'd like to meet the group in person and talk things over.

'Fine,' said Wilf. 'Give them a call.'

Next morning the Schulmans were, of course, delighted to hear Patrick on the phone. And Patrick was so anxious to acquire the group that he insisted on Wilf driving down to Portsmouth with him straight away to see them. (Another reason for this eagerness may have been the fact that he had just taken delivery of his own new Aston Martin V8 Volante and longed to try it out.)

Wilf was not so keen to accompany him. The smell of new leather always made him feel queasy, the Volante was a powerful motorcar, and he knew that Patrick was a very fast driver. But nothing had prepared him for the nightmare journey that ensued. Not only was Patrick driving like a lunatic but soon he seemed to be missing things by inches. As Wilf recalls:

I said to myself, keep calm. Perhaps he's just nervous about meeting Gentle Giant. So I talked away to him, hoping to take his mind off things, but once we'd reached Portsmouth I couldn't get out of that fucking car fast enough. In fact, the meeting with the Schulmans went like a dream. We all hit it off, and after an hour or so they had agreed that, subject to contracts and the usual carry-on, they'd like to join Worldwide Artistes Management.

So when we left Portsmouth, Patrick really was elated, and I thought to myself, thank God! Now that we've got the group, perhaps he'll calm down and the journey back will be a little easier. Not a bit of it. By now it was getting dark, but Patrick was driving worse than ever. Whereas before he seemed to be missing things by inches, now he was missing them by millimetres.

Somehow I kept my nerve, and just before reaching the Kingston bypass Patrick says to me: 'If Gentle Giant sign with us, you know who'd really go to town with them?'

'Who?'

'My father. Didn't you see they way he weighed that music up when he was listening to the album? He really loves it, and I'd like to involve him in managing the group, if only to keep him out of mischief and get him off my back.'

'Fine, Patrick,' I replied. 'Anything you say. But would you mind getting off *my* back and just pull over before we hit something? You nearly killed us going down, and you're ten times worse coming back. What's going on? If you don't object, I think I'd better drive.'

Patrick said nothing but he did pull over, and when I was safely at the wheel he said: 'Wilf, I should have told you. A week ago I had contact lenses fitted, and this afternoon I forgot them. Without them I'm as blind as a bat.'

'And so,' says Wilf, 'by the end of that afternoon, I'd risked my neck, I'd driven my first Aston Martin Volante, and although I hadn't had to nick them from anyone, I'd acquired the first new group for that stable I had promised Patrick, so I felt quite happy.'

There was something else that Wilf felt happy about over this deal. Apart from acquiring the Schulman brothers, whom he loved, the final contract stated that Pat Meehan Sr would be managing them, 'which meant that, whatever happened, nothing would come between me and my friendship with the Schulman brothers in the future'.

But as so often in his life, it was the acquisition of Gentle Giant that led Wilf to commit a real theft, which brought a second, more important band into the powerful 'stable' of rock bands that he was rapidly acquiring.

*

It was by sheer coincidence that, as with Sabbath, Gentle Giant's first appearance was on London's South Bank. This time, however, it was not at the Festival Hall but in the smaller Queen Elizabeth Hall, where they were supporting a more famous band, the Groundhogs. Since Wilf hadn't seen the Schulmans performing live since they formed Gentle Giant, he went along with Pat Meehan specially to hear them.

'They were sensational,' he says. 'Pure class. Every member of the band was a trained musician, and they were brilliant to watch. When they'd finished, Pat Meehan had to get back to the office, but as I'd never heard the Groundhogs perform before I decided to stay on and hear them too.'

At the time the Groundhogs were United Artists' best-selling group of the year, and their current album was a top seller. 'But although musically they were wonderful, they were not so exciting to watch as Sabbath, and they struck me as a very odd collection of individuals,' says Wilf. One of the oddest looking was their lead singer, Tony McPhee. 'He just stood there in the middle of the stage, in a pair of old tatty jeans, with long hair hanging down, and a Zapata-style moustache. But he had a great blues voice, and what he could do to a guitar was incredible. On top of which, everything he sang was his own original material.'

No sooner had he seen him than Wilf knew at once that he'd spotted the next candidate for his stable. 'I just couldn't get over that voice of his, and I knew that one day I was going to steal the Groundhogs. As things turned out, that day came sooner than expected.

Following the South Bank concert, Wilf had to attend two major European pop festivals, the first in Vienna, the second in Frankfurt. At both, Sabbath were topping the bill, and although he was no longer their manager he was as keen as ever to hear them perform. But he had another reason for attending. With Sabbath in first place on the bill at both these festivals, he wanted to use the clout this gave to Worldwide Artistes to ensure that Gentle Giant weren't left out.

'A lot of that sort of arm-twisting goes on in the business. You use the power of a major act like Sabbath to get a lesser-known act included. And now that Giant was Pat Meehan's baby, he had made me promise to see that this would happen.'

Wilf flew with Gentle Giant from Gatwick to Vienna, in an elderly propeller-driven chartered Douglas DC3 belonging to the now-defunct airline Dan Air. Two other famous bands, Fleetwood Mac, and the Groundhogs, who were performing second and third on the bill, were also on the plane, and as Wilf took his seat he found that, of all people, he had been placed next to the one-time victim of Don Arden's cigar, Clifford Davis, who was still very much Fleetwood Mac's manager.

He began talking to Wilf immediately. 'And this time around,' says Wilf, 'I must say he was absolutely charming. Instead of the arrogant character I remembered, he was a genuinely nice guy who even seemed to see the funny side of what occurred with Don – which in the circumstances was very nice of him.'

During the concert at Vienna, Sabbath had their usual wild effect on the audience, and later in the programme Gentle Giant did extremely well. But just as at the South Bank gig, at that concert in Frankfurt the one performer who gripped Wilf's attention was the Groundhogs lead singer, Tony McPhee. When the show was over Wilf got his chance to meet him in the bar, for McPhee, like Wilf, enjoyed a drink. Instead of taking drugs, he smoked a pipe, which struck Wilf as original for a rock musician.

'The two of us got talking, and he really was great fun, and although he could talk about absolutely anything, at heart he was a natural musician, who incidentally remains a close friend to the present day.'

But early next morning, when the Dan Air DC3 took off from the runway at Vienna bound for Frankfurt, it was obvious that something was very wrong. No sooner was it airborne than for whatever reason the pilot decided to return to the airport, and the passengers were ordered to disembark.

Hardly surprisingly, this left everyone feeling distinctly nervous, particularly the six-foot six-inch-tall Mick Fleetwood, who had a natural fear of flying. An hour or so later, when it was announced that whatever had been wrong with the aircraft had been rectified, and that it was now ready to depart for Frankfurt, no one was particularly keen to take the risk. 'But since this was our only way to reach Frankfurt in time, we'd no alternative.'

McPhee also hated flying, and noticing that he seemed nervous, Wilf talked to him and tried to calm him down. After arriving in Frankfurt, he called him up at his hotel to enquire how he was. Apparently he was fine, but as he told Wilf, he and the group were having trouble over arrangements for the concert which Wilf felt their management should have organised before the trip. Wilf helped to sort them out, but when he learned that the trouble appeared to stem from the way the group was being run by two separate managers, and that this clearly wasn't working, Wilf saw his opportunity.

The Groundhogs had been placed third on the bill that night, and to impress them Wilf persuaded someone to change their place on the bill with Fleetwood Mac, who now became number three, letting the Groundhogs play in second place. Apart from providing a useful boost to Wilf's standing with the Groundhogs, this was no big deal, and although it might have annoyed Clifford Davis or even Mick Fleetwood himself, no one felt like objecting except for tough little John McVie, one of the band members who, backed by a couple of the group's roadies, tried cutting up rough with Wilf. This was a dangerous thing to do, but it was the sort of situation Wilf enjoyed. When things turned nasty, so could he, and success had in no way softened his intimidating presence. The pale blue eyes would turn to steel, and in a moment that apparently warm-hearted character would transform itself into a lethal adversary. No one in his right mind would pick a fight with an enemy like Wilf, and just in time McVie and the roadies all backed off. The Groundhogs duly performed in second place.

According to Wilf, that night they were 'a knockout'. More to the point, they were grateful to Wilf Pine and unanimously wanted him to be their manager. With their support, he had even less trouble seeing off their existing managers than he had with John McVie.

'The managers were nice guys, but nice guys never win,' says Wilf. And the Groundhogs duly took their places in his stable.

For Wilf, poaching groups was fun, but managing them afterwards could be intensely hard work. With the Groundhogs he took this very seriously. Once he had settled the legalities and made his number with the record companies, he decided it was time to improve the group's overall image by organising an extensive nation-wide concert tour. Here his workaholic side emerged, and by the beginning of 1972 he had arranged no fewer than thirty-four separate venues where the band would perform throughout the length and breadth of Britain. The boys responded, his confidence in the pulling power of the band was not misplaced, and each and every per-formance by the Groundhogs, from Edinburgh to Land's End, was a sell-out.

As Wilf's reputation as a highly energetic manager took its place beside his legend as a dangerous villain and a thief, it became easier for him to pick and choose the acts he needed for his stable. Groups were not slow to see the advantages of having a workaholic villain running their business and, if the need arose, fighting their battles for them in the rough, tough world of the music industry.

This lay behind the almost suspiciously peaceable acquisition of his next group, the highly successful and profitable Edgar Broughton Band. They were swiftly followed by a very different band called Stray. These were a young, enthusiastic band who acted as support group during the Groundhogs tour, and Wilf had a soft spot for them from the start. In those days every young group tried playing heavy rock either like Black Sabbath or Led Zeppelin, but Stray were somehow different, not for what they played but for how they played it. Even when performing really heavy rock, there always seemed to be a melody line that people could remember and even whistle afterwards. The more Wilf listened to the group, the keener he became, until he knew he had to have them.

'Here we go again,' I thought, 'and this time I really didn't have to steal them. All I had to do was ask them "Are you happy with your management, or do you fancy changing it?"'

Unanimously they replied: 'We want to change.'

'Right, you're in,' said Wilf. 'When the tour's over, come and see me in my office.'

Once more it was the same old story. When we start talking, what do I find? That they too have co-managers, which as usual never works. So I go and pay their managers a visit and tell them Stray want to come to me. And just like the others, they don't choose to argue. There was no question of any money changing hands, and as their contract with the group was coming to an end, shall we say they acted in their own best interests. No payment, no lawyers, everyone agrees. Bye-bye.'

By the spring of 1972 Wilf's ill-gotten gains in the rich and riotous world of rock were mounting up, and if one includes the increasingly popular Gentle Giant, which was still being managed by Pat Meehan, he had now brought four groups into his precious stable. As some indication of his growing prosperity, it was now that he traded in the Aston Martin for a Bentley S2.

Now that he had bought this splendid motorcar, he had to drive it to the Isle of Wight and park it right outside his parents' house. But instead of the proud mother Wilf expected, when Millie first spotted it through her front-room window she was horrified and started waving him away. Puzzled, Wilf sat where he was and his mother hurried out, seeming more agitated than ever.

'For God's sake, Wilf, take this thing around to the car park and leave it there at once. The law are always driving up and down the road in their police cars, and they'll know you've pinched it.'

Wilf tried to tell her that he'd actually just bought it, but she wouldn't listen, and to calm her down he did as he was told and drove his precious Bentley to the car park. Afterwards he showed her the bill of sale for the car and thought he'd convinced her that he was legally employed and really making money.

In fact, he still had his old happy-go-lucky attitude to money and wasn't remotely interested in his future. Which makes it all the stranger that a few weeks later, without any further effort on his part, he suddenly found himself at the head of his own flourishing small company with a staff of ten and offices in Mayfair.

He clearly remembers how it all began. One morning he woke early and, looking out of the bedroom window, saw something stuck on the windscreen of his car. At first he thought it was a parking ticket, but on second thoughts he realised it couldn't be, so he wandered down in his dressing gown to find it was a note from Patrick.

'Need to see you urgently. Please contact me at once.'

There had apparently been some fault with his telephone, so after he'd fixed himself some breakfast he drove across town to the little office of Worldwide Artistes above a café in Leicester Street, off Shaftesbury Avenue. Both Meehans were there already, and they had news for him. Patrick, as usual, did the talking.

'Wilf, I've negotiated a deal which I signed yesterday with the Hemdale Leisure Corporation, and we're now part and parcel of the Hemdale Group of Companies.' Wilf remembered that since it was founded a few years before by the actor David Hemmings and a producer called John Daly, Hemdale had become the biggest and richest independent group in the British entertainment industry, producing successful films like *Women in Love* and later blockbuster movies like *The Terminator*, starring Arnold Schwarzenegger. They also managed a band called Yes, which was one of the most profitable British rock groups in the business.

'Congratulations,' Wilf replied. 'I hope everything has turned out well for you.'

'It has,' said Patrick, 'splendidly.'

'And where does that leave the two of us?' Wilf asked.

'Exactly as we were before.'

'That's fine by me,' said Wilf, 'I'm very happy for you both.'

In fact, he felt they might have let him know what was going on, but since Worldwide Artistes was their company it really hadn't anything to do with him, and he genuinely thought that that was that. It wasn't, as he discovered three days later when he tried to telephone the office. This time it was their phone that was out of order, and when he went around to Leicester Street the office was no longer there. When Wilf finally reached Patrick, he asked him to come to see him straight away. Wilf enquired where he was, and Pat gave him an address in Park Street, Mayfair. 'What's that?' Wilf asked. 'Our new offices,' Pat Meehan answered.

When Wilf took a taxi to the address, he found himself facing a very grand eighteenth-century building with an embassy next door and, as far as he remembered, Stirling Moss's house across the road.

The front door stood open, and when he entered he found the whole place still in chaos. A pretty receptionist he'd never seen before was sitting behind a lovely desk. 'Can I help you?' she enquired.

'I'm looking for Pat Meehan, but I'll find him for myself,' he said.

Wilf's surprise continued. The first room he peered into along the corridor was a boardroom, complete with heavily upholstered chairs and a highly polished boardroom table. In the next door office he found Patrick, sitting behind an even more highly polished, mammoth walnut desk.

'What's going on, Pat?' he asked. 'Is this the way things are going to go?'

'Absolutely, Wilf,' said Pat. 'It's all enormously exciting. You've no idea of the money that's available and what we can do with it. Hemdale is a publicly quoted company with a tremendous amount behind it.'

Wilf said: 'Fine, but where does that put my acts like Broughton and the Groundhogs and Stray?'

'As I told you, exactly where they were before. What I intend to do, Wilf, is offer you a deal.'

Wilf said: 'We've got a deal already.'

But Patrick said: 'No, I want to set you up in an autonomous company of your own under the Worldwide Artistes umbrella, which in turn would be responsible to Hemdale. Wilf,' he went on, 'when you left Sabbath you told me you never wanted to manage anything again. But since then you've been managing every group you pinched and doing very well. So I know you've got the know-how and the energy to make this work.'

Then he offered me a serious amount of money, since there was so much of it around from Hemdale. When I told him I'd think about it, he said: 'Wilf, don't think about it. Take it. You'll be running your own show.'

'Yes,' I said. 'But responsible to the board of Hemdale.'

'No,' he said. 'Responsible to me. Our relationship isn't going to change.'

'And the Groundhogs, Broughton, Stray? Who'll manage them?'

'You will, Wilf. You'll be managing the whole show. Here,' he said, 'let's go and grab ourselves a pint.' Which we did, and when we'd had a second I agreed.

Wilf was none too pleased when Patrick told him that he'd have to meet his company's accountant, appointed by Hemdale. 'But he turned out to be one hell of a nice guy, called Peter Parkinson. Six foot two with a grin to match, fabulous character.'

He told Wilf: 'First off, we've got to find you offices. And not too far away from Park Street.'

'If you say so, Peter. Here's my number.'

Within a couple of days he called me. 'Wilf,' he said. 'I've got you an office with an entire floor in the middle of Mayfair. No. 27 Dover Street.' So I went along and saw it, and found I'd got a desk as big as Patrick's. There were telephones and secretaries and typists, but the most important thing of all, I now had a base for all my acts. Peter even produced a name for the company, which he purchased off the shelf. For whatever reason it was called the Gladglen Group, and I was its managing director.

In its way this whole new setup suited Wilf, who was turning out to be a natural organiser. He liked Mayfair and enjoyed the office, which, as Patrick pointed out, made it much easier to deal with the complicated business always going on around the groups. And now that he had his own show, Wilf decided to exercise his managerial power by signing up the two people he always knew he could trust, the two old faithfuls from the crew, Jinxie and Dave Farley, who acted as his very personal assistants. Both of them were ideal characters to be involved with the individual members of the groups, and soon Jinxie formed a specially close relationship with the members of the Groundhogs to whom he acted as a friend and coordinator.

At the same time Wilf's neighbours in up-market Dover Street seemed particularly welcoming, the occupants of the business down below especially. This was the London headquarters of the small Bank of Bangladesh, and its manager was particularly amiable. No sooner had Wilf arrived than he sent him up a bottle of Johnnie Walker with his compliments, and he later came in person to tell Wilf that should he ever need an overdraft he'd be more than happy to oblige.

By now, an overdraft was one thing that Wilf didn't need, and during that summer he acquired a smart seaside property of his own. Surprisingly this was not some happy haven on his beloved Isle of Wight but a five-bedroomed modern villa on a residential development at Minnis Bay in Kent, which had once belonged to Don Arden.

Although this house had happy memories for Wilf dating back to times he'd spent there with the Ardens, he found that this meant little to him now, for, as he says, by now he was 'breathing, thinking, talking nothing but the music business and the groups he was managing'. Which makes it all the more surprising that in the late summer of 1972 he suddenly decided to make contact with the only person he had ever really been in love with – Lesley. Since catching sight of her that time at Big Albert's club in Birmingham, he had rigidly blanked out any memories and longings that he may have had for her, and his romantic life, if one could call it that, had been confined to nothing but casual affairs that didn't interfere with anything that mattered.

But during a brief visit to the island he rang Lesley's parents to enquire how she was getting on. Soon after this they met, but both were wary of each other and, although they started going out together and realised their love continued, neither was prepared to make a deep commitment to the other.

That September Wilf returned from a brief visit to New York with his mind made up to ask Jill for a divorce. As the marriage had effectively been dead for years, she raised no objection, and with the help of a local lawyer the marriage ended as swiftly as it had started. By late 1973 Jill was awarded custody of the children, and Wilf had access to them whenever he wanted. As for the children, it was only gradually that they realised that anything had happened.

Nor did the divorce make much real difference to Wilf and Lesley. By now, they were living together in their own distinctly independent fashion. 'Of course, I'd always loved her, but she was a free spirit,' says Wilf. Since his divorce, Wilf was also free, but he insists that there was no talk of marriage. In spite of this, in their own strange way they were always tied to one another, and one day they would marry in extraordinary circumstances and most unlikely surroundings. But by then it would have taken something more powerful than love to make this happen.

In the meantime Wilf was increasingly enjoying life. The Bentley was succeeded by a white Rolls-Royce Silver Cloud, along with an E-type Jaguar and a Corvette Sting Ray, while on the home front that November he and Lesley moved from West Hill, Wandsworth, back to happy Wimbledon and a luxurious apartment overlooking the All-England Tennis Club. The apartment belonged to Rupert Perry, future vice-president of Capital Records and later still the European chief executive of EMI.

But during this period the one thing Wilf remembers with unaffected pride is what he did with his group called Stray.

'Once I'd pinched them, the first thing I decided was to take them off the road. After the time they'd spent as a supporting group with the Groundhogs they were overworked and overexposed, and I talked things over with the band's leader, young Del Brougham. I told him he would have to face it that they were never going to be a Sabbath or a Led Zeppelin. I also said that what endeared me to them was, one, their image and, two, those marvellous melody lines of theirs. So I asked him if he could write a powerful rock album with the sort of melodic music people could remember. He replied that he and Steve Gadd, the group's lead singer, had worked out lots of tunes and songs together but that they had had neither the money nor the time to develop them.'

Luckily for them, Wilf now had money at his disposal, so he arranged for every member of the group and the roadies to be paid a weekly retainer. But what Wilf had set his heart on was to get actively involved with the group himself, and he started going to the rehearsal rooms and listening to their new material. As he listened, he remembers hearing strings, brass, backing singers in his imagination, 'all the things that, properly put together, would have made a very different Stray with a brand-new interpretation of their songs. Hey,

I thought, why not have a go at producing this fucking band yourself? And even as I said it, I knew that I was going to do it.'

But he faced a problem. In the first place he had no idea himself how to arrange music. And, secondly, he had no legal say over their music, since the group were assigned to the powerful Transatlantic Records. So he had absolutely no right to do what he intended doing. But being Wilf, he said: 'Fuck that. I've lived my life disregarding every rule in the book, and it's too late now for me to change.'

So he spoke to all the members of the group and told them: 'This is what I want you all to do. Tell nobody, but I'm going to take you to the Olympic Studios in Barnes, and we're going to make an album like you've never done before. All I can say is trust me and you'll see some real changes.'

As the managing director of Gladglen, he had no problem booking the studio. Nor was there any problem with the actual music, which Del and Steve had written. Wilf hired the technicians, and by the end of the recording session he had all the basic tracks required – drums, bass, guitar and vocals – from which the sound engineer created what were known as 'rough mixes'. By now, Wilf was thoroughly excited, as he knew he had exactly the raw material he needed.

What he wanted next was an arranger. He remembered having been impressed by the work of a young professional musician called Andrew Powell, and when he spoke to him he was more than interested and agreed to help.

'I have to hand it to that kid, he was a fucking genius,' says Wilf. 'We sat in the Olympic Studios with Del and Steve, who were becoming really excited as we played the tracks through, and Andrew suggested putting some cellos here and strings there and brass after that. You know, in those days I really did love music, and it was one of the most exciting moments in my life. By the end of an eight-hour session, by working together Andrew Powell had everything he needed.'

When Andrew had completed his arrangements, it would be time to bring in hired professional musicians to play together and complete the full performance of the album. So far, Wilf had been operating on his own authority, but now, with expenses mounting, he had to come clean with Patrick over what was going on. When he explained the situation, and that studio and technical costs could reach £10,000, Patrick said: 'Easy, Wilf. I thought we were going to be respectable, and that's an awful lot of money.'

Then he thought a while and said: 'Wilf, you really rate this?'

When Wilf told him, 'Yes I do', he gave him permission to continue, which was all he needed. And as usual Wilf was lucky. Andrew Powell had turned up trumps, his completed score was wonderful, and at the full recording session with the professional musicians everything fell perfectly into place.

Then it was time to mix the album, with Wilf in the role of producer working in the studio with Andrew and Alan O'Duffy, the sound engineer. It took two more days to get it right, at the end of which he called the members of the group together to hear the result. Wilf had purposely kept them away from the sessions with the extra musicians, so they had no idea of what was coming, and when Wilf played the opening track they were so excited that to start with none of them could really understand what had happened. As Wilf had promised them, things had changed, and it was now that someone had the bright idea of calling the new album *Mudanzas*, the Spanish word for 'changes'.

Now that he had his record, Wilf had to face his most awkward moment – owning up to Transatlantic Records that he had just broken every rule in the book and recorded their artists quite illegally. By now, Wilf was sufficiently notorious in the music business to be able to get straight through to Nat Joseph, Transatlantic's managing director and ask if he could come to see him.

As soon as I heard his voice on the telephone, I knew I was going to get on with him. When I see him he already knows, of course, that I'm managing Stray, so he asks: 'Nothing wrong with them, I hope.'

'No, the boys are fine,' I say. 'But I've something that I need you to listen to.'

Without any further explanation, I just put the finished tapes of *Mudanzas* on the reel-to-reel tape machine and start playing it, giving him no hint of what it is. He listens carefully, then suddenly I see that he recognises the distinctive voice of Steve Gadd.

'Hey,' he says, 'it's Stray.' And I say: 'Yes, it is.' And he says nothing but just goes on listening to the end. By the time it finishes, I'm thinking, 'Wilf, you've well and truly landed in the shit.'

But all he says is: 'Well, what do you want me to say about it?'

I reply: 'I suppose you're going to sue me?'

To which he replies: 'I think you've done an incredible job. It's highly unorthodox, but that whole album is fantastic. What do you want to do with it?'

In the end Wilf got around to suggesting that they might share the costs and have a joint production deal on the album with Transatlantic Records.

'By now,' says Wilf, 'I was really loving Nat Joseph, especially when he agreed, and he was as good as his word. Somehow he straightened out the lawyers, and when the time came to release *Mudanzas* everybody seemed to love it, especially the boys in Stray. It was the first album I produced, and, when it went gold, to celebrate I held a party for the group at my house in Kent. Nat Joseph came as guest of honour and presented every one of us with a gold disc of *Mudanzas*.'

During the recording of Stray's album, *Mudanzas*, Wilf was struggling to get the right note for the brass section on a track called 'Gambler'. Some of the notes Andrew Powell had written were hard for the trumpet players to reach. After six or seven unsuccessful takes, Wilf was starting to lose patience when, out of nowhere, he and Alan O'Duffy heard a voice singing exactly the right note, showing the trumpet players what was required. Looking to see who was responsible, Wilf saw that the voice belonged to a good-looking black guy who Alan told him was called Jimmy Helms. Wilf pressed the TALK button to the studio to congratulate him and tell him that he'd like to see him before he left. Thanks to Jimmy, the players now had no problem reaching the note that had eluded them, and within ten minutes or so their part of the score was finished.

Later, when they talked, Jimmy told Wilf that, although he had been playing flugelhorn during the session, he was first and foremost a singer, so Wilf asked him to come to see him the next morning in his office, as he would like to, as he put it, 'make him an offer he couldn't refuse'. At this Jimmy burst out laughing and Wilf asked him what was so funny, at which Jimmy told him that he had just finished recording a song by John Worth with the same title. For Wilf, that settled it and he knew he just had to sign up Jimmy Helms come what may.

Next day, over drinks in the office, they agreed that, provided Jimmy could obtain a release from Jimmy's current agent, Robert Patterson, he would enter into a management agreement with Wilf. Once again lawyers were summoned and, when a financial settlement had been reached with Patterson, Jimmy joined Wilf in what, as time would show, would be yet another highly successful musical partnership.

As for Wilf, the year ended with a unique tribute to his role as a thief in the music industry. After a long period of restoration, Alexandra Palace was reopening. The first event held there turned out to be a pop concert with, top of the bill, Black Sabbath. Second on the bill was the Groundhogs, and third was Stray, airing their new album, *Mudanzas*. Opening the show was another group that Wilf had newly acquired called Jonesy. In one way or another all these acts had been stolen by Wilf Pine.

Not bad for a natural hoodlum who, eleven years earlier, was released from an approved school with no prospects and not a penny to his name.

10

New York, 1973: 'Talk to me like you've known me thirty years'

ALTHOUGH HE CONTINUED to reject the Catholicism of his childhood, Wilf remained convinced that somehow his life was mysteriously mapped out, and during 1973 his whole existence changed in ways that only an exceptionally imaginative fiction writer could have invented.

Already his life had been directed by a series of events that brought the most unlikely consequences – the spell in the approved school which turned him out a violent criminal, the chance encounter with Don Arden which showed him a side of life that he had barely dreamed of, and the poaching of Black Sabbath, which took him to the very top of the pop music industry.

'If it hadn't been for Sabbath, I'd have ended up with a twenty-five-year stretch inside, like my friend Charlie Richardson,' he says.

But what is fascinating about the life now building up around him is that through all these transformations, his essential character stayed virtually unchanged.

He was still, as he says, 'a street guy', foul-mouthed, hard-drinking, rebellious, promiscuous. He loved a fight as much as ever, and given the chance would still belt anybody who offended him. And despite his success as a group manager, he never really felt at home in what still struck him as the essentially phoney world of show business. Like all true criminals, he saw something degrading in the thought of saving and, although he loved money, no sooner had he got his hands on it than he spent, lent, wasted or simply gave the stuff away to his friends, to whom he was as loyal as ever. In spirit he remained an unregenerate hoodlum and a thief, and it was largely thanks to this that, at the end of 1973, in the last year of his twenties, he was able to effect his own unique entrée into the very heart of an organised crime family in New York.

Although Wilf says that by the start of 1973 he was already 'wondering what the hell I was doing', the truth is that he thoroughly enjoyed running his independent company with its office around the corner from the Ritz. He genuinely loved music and had a natural flair for organising people – which showed in the way he ran the different acts he managed. He was very much the boss. He wouldn't delegate, and the workload of managing four increasingly successful groups fell firmly on his sturdy shoulders. Fortunately he was in his prime. Not yet thirty, he had the stamina and energy to cope with the pace of his existence. But the workload was increasing, particularly with his hands-on style of management, and apart from taking care of the day-to-day business of his groups – arranging tours, sorting out recording sessions, taking care of their publicity – he was always going somewhere on a plane, and as often as not that somewhere was Los Angeles.

For most European groups like his, the perpetual problem lay in finding record outlets in America, and, since this was where the real money lay, one of the most important tasks for any pop group manager was to sell his act to a major US record company. As most of these companies had their headquarters on the west coast of America, Wilf began to know Los Angeles like the tattoos on the back of his hands.

In many ways he loved Los Angeles, just as he loved America, and there were times when he was practically a resident at the Beverly Hills Hotel. 'Of course, I'd seen hotels like that in the movies, but I never thought that one day I'd actually be staying there as a guest.' He had a few close friends in LA too, such as the owner of his flat in England, Rupert Perry, who was now in Hollywood with Capitol Records and doing very nicely. 'Whenever I arrived in Los Angeles, I always tried to have Rupert and his wife for dinner in the Polo

Lounge. Rupert was a breath of fresh air, unlike so many of the west coast record company executives I did business with, who struck me as little more than laid-back poseurs. With them everything was slow, slow, slow, and come midday it was time for cocktails, then it was time for lunch and then forget about the rest of the day' . . . which wasn't how Wilf Pine liked doing business.

Not that things were entirely to Wilf's liking back in London either, where his friend and partner, Patrick Meehan, had embarked on a bout of empire-building. Backed by the money and resources of the Hemdale Leisure Group, he had just acquired the Beatles' old company, Nems, started by their former manager, Brian Epstein, and moved his base from Park Street to Nemperor House on the corner of Berkeley Square. Wilf remembers Ozzy saying that 'the older Patrick gets, the more interested he seems to become in the size of his desk – and sure enough his desk in Nemperor House was even bigger than the one he had in Park Street. But then, that was Patrick.'

In fact, more things were forcing the old friends apart than the size of their desks. 'I was still the normal Joe on the street,' says Wilf, 'and my real pals still hadn't changed, but when I started seeing articles in the Hickey column of the *Daily Express* about Patrick and his Rolls Corniche, I realised that to me, he was becoming a bit of a socialite. I don't think that music or anything else came into it any longer. He wanted to be a big-shot businessman and, believe me, Patrick was a big-shot businessman by now. No sooner had he moved to Nems than he decided to create his own Worldwide Artistes record label, WWA Records, and asked me if I'd anyone in mind that he could feature under his own label.'

Without the faintest inkling of where this would lead to, Wilf was just about to make another of those apparently innocuous decisions that would decisively change the rest of his life.

As he says, 'When Patrick asked me to suggest someone, I remembered a young singer I'd bumped into on the Isle of Wight called Derry Ryan. Like many bright young pop musicians, he actually hailed from Birmingham, and he had a unique voice, which sounded like someone moving in a gravel pit. When I mentioned him to

Patrick, he said fine, and asked if I had in anyone in mind who could produce him.

'I thought at once of Andrew Loog Oldham, who created the Rolling Stones. Andrew also happened to be a good friend of mine, but he was living at the time in Bridgeport, Connecticut. However, I'd heard he was in London, so I rang him and got hold of him for lunch. As usual he was great company, and afterwards, when I told him about Derry and played him a tape of his voice, he said at once that he'd produce him. He also thought he had the perfect song for him, an Italian number called "Vado Via". The only problem was that I'd have to bring him to America to record it.'

When he broke the news to Derry, he was naturally delighted. So was Wilf, who fixed an appointment with Andrew Oldham at the Syncrom Sound Studios in Wallingford, Connecticut, for a few weeks later. Without realising it, Wilf had made a date with destiny for perhaps the most important episode in his life to date.

Not that he had much time to think about it. 'That summer things were running like a bastard for me. Jimmy Helms had just released, "I'm Going to Make You an Offer You Can't Refuse". I had secured him *Top of the Pops*, and I was even luckier to get him his own TV series on BBC2, called *Colour My Soul*. This instantly made him in demand for countless TV appearances all over Europe, and since I couldn't handle all of them myself I made Dave Farley Jimmy's personal road manager.'

Although so much was going on around him, Wilf got hold of Derry, booked himself a flight, and ended up in Wallingford, Connecticut, where Andrew tried 'Vado Via' out on Derry. As he didn't speak any Italian, Andrew found him a voice tutor who taught him to sing it beautifully, and when it was finally recorded it proved to be a considerable success.

While I was at the studio with all this going on, I got stuck with a guy who seemed to be always hanging around the place. He was sort of unavoidable, as he was six foot four or five, weighed around three hundred and fifty pounds and looked like Al

Capone. He said he came from New York and gave his name as
Irwin Schiff.

Something about Irwin Schiff made Wilf dislike him from the start.

'One of his biggest problems was that he couldn't stop talking, and
when I asked him what he was doing there he explained in detail. He
said he came there most days, as he was looking for a studio for a
protégé of his, a singer called Jimmy Price.'

To get Schiff off his back, Wilf promised that if he left him a tape
he'd listen to it and give him his truthful opinion. Schiff produced a
tape at once, and that evening Wilf listened to it. It consisted of
ballads, which were not quite Wilf's sort of music, but he could tell
at once that Jimmy had a lovely voice.

Next morning, no sooner had Wilf entered the studio than he saw
that Schiff was waiting for him, and the first thing he asked was what
he'd thought about the tape.

Wilf told him the truth but added that he thought the boy had a
great voice.

'Do you think you could help me to promote him?'

'I'd like to, but I'm working here flat out, so it would have to wait
a while,' he said.

But Irwin Schiff didn't give up easily.

'Wilf,' he said. 'You look like a regular guy, so I'll let you into a
secret about this boy. This is in absolute confidence, of course, but
Price isn't Jimmy's real name. He is actually the son of Joe Pagano,
who is a capo in the Genovese crime family.'

'Why does that have to be a secret? What's the problem?'

'Because Jimmy hasn't told his father anything about his singing. If
he did, he knows he'd disapprove.'

'And would that matter all that much?'

'Would it matter? My friend, do you know anything about Joe
Pagano?'

Wilf said he'd heard of him.

'Have you read a book called *The Valachi Papers*?'

Wilf said, yes, he had, some time ago, but he couldn't remember
the exact details.

'Perhaps you should take a fresh look at the book,' he said. 'It'll tell you a lot you ought to know about Joe Pagano. I've a copy in my car. I'll let you have it. Listen Wilf,' he went on, 'if you can do anything to help me over Jimmy, I'd be really grateful. You must tell me if there's anything that I can do to help you in return'.

By now, Wilf was getting bored with Schiff and to shut him up he gave him what was meant to be a silly answer. 'OK, Irwin, since you ask, there is something you might be able to help me over. I'm interested in buying a company called Worldwide Artistes.'

'How much d'you need?' asked Schiff at once.

Since Wilf was not entirely serious, he threw a silly figure at him. 'I was thinking of around six million dollars,' he said.

'At this stage all I was really doing was humouring him, and I thought that the mention of six million dollars would be the end of it,' says Wilf.

Wilf's trip to Connecticut was drawing to a close and, apart from a surfeit of Irwin Schiff, he had thoroughly enjoyed his brief stay at Wallingford. The recording sessions with Andrew and Derry had been a great success, and Wilf loved the acoustics of the studio. The studios were owned by a former New York dentist called Doc Cavalier, and remembering that he would soon be faced with producing Stray's next album for the Transatlantic label he thought that it might be a good idea to make it there. The acoustics in the Syncrom Studios were so different from anything the British studios could offer that they would give Stray's next album a completely new sound.

When he suggested this to Del Bromham, he liked the idea and said he'd got most of the songs for the album already written. Things seemed to be falling into place, and when he mentioned using the Syncrom Studios to Andrew, he told him he'd already arranged to record Donovan there in two weeks' time during the day, and suggested that Wilf could use the studios in the evening. Wilf discussed this with Doc, who was perfectly happy with this arrangement and everything was settled.

But once again the pace of life caught up with Wilf, and at the last minute he was forced to change his plans. Suddenly he had to get to Los Angeles for the release of Jimmy Helms's latest record by MGM and, as this was followed by unexpected business in New York, he had to arrange with Lesley to bring Stray over to the studio in Conneticut. Wilf got there the day after, and no sooner had he started working in the studio than who should turn up but his *bête noire*, fat Irwin Schiff, still trying to get him interested in his protégé.

By now Wilf had in fact become intrigued by this boy who was the son of Joe Pagano, for while in England he had been re-reading the copy of *The Valachi Papers* Schiff had lent him.

The author of *The Valachi Papers*, Peter Maas, related the true story of a middle-ranking Mafia killer, Joe 'Cago' Valachi, who turned police informer and in September and October 1963 produced something of a sensation on American TV when he was shown testifying before the Senate Investigations Subcommittee on organised crime in America. It was by far the most dramatic occasion on which any member of the American Mafia had openly betrayed the Mafia's rigidly enforced code of silence, and what particularly interested Wilf was Valachi's account of the killing, back in 1952, of a member of the Lucchese crime family, who had become an informer to the US Bureau of Narcotics. His name was Eugene Giannini.

The order for the killing had reached Valachi from one of the still-powerful founders of the modern Mafia, Charlie 'Lucky' Luciano, who by then was in exile in Italy; and in accordance with standard Mafia practice, Valachi passed the order on to what he described as 'three young hoodlums from East Harlem' who were keen to make their names within the Genovese crime family. One of them was Valachi's nephew, Fiore 'Fury' Siano, and the others were two brothers, Joseph and Pasquale 'Pat' Pagano. The killing, which was meticulously set up by Valachi, was performed by the trio with clinical precision in the small hours of the night of 20 September. Gianini was neatly dispatched with several well-aimed shots to the head as he stood outside a gambling club on the corner of Second Avenue and East 112th Street. Until Valachi named them, the identity of the killers had always been a mystery.

Valachi's testimony on the Paganos did not end there. According to him, some months after the killing of Giannini, young Pat Pagano was involved in a more personal operation on behalf of Vito Genovese himself. Here the victim was the diminutive Steve Franse, a former associate of Genovese, whose death he had decreed for little more than failing to keep proper supervision of the erratic Mrs Genovese, who had caused her husband serious loss of face by daring to sue him for divorce. According to Valachi's testimony, Pat and an accomplice grabbed Franse while he was preparing them drinks in his apartment, and after roughing him up finished him off by strangling him with a chain as he lay on the floor. Valachi described how, when Franse started moving, 'Pat put his foot on his neck to keep him there' until he died.

Having read this, Wilf was so fascinated by the Paganos that, when Schiff suggested taking Wilf and Lesley on their next free day to a restaurant he knew in New York State to meet Jimmy, he didn't instantly refuse, as he almost certainly would have done before he'd read *The Valachi Papers*.

'I'm sure you'll like Jimmy, Wilf,' said Schiff. 'And I'd also like you to meet his father, Joe Pagano.'

Wilf said, 'Joe Pagano? You must be kidding.'

'Would I kid you, Wilf, about a man like that? I've already told him about you, and he says he'd like to meet you too. But whatever you do, say nothing to him about Jimmy being Jimmy Price. What I did tell Joe about was that company you said you'd like to buy. He seemed interested, and believe me, Wilf, Joe Pagano could be a very useful man to have around with a project like that.'

'Easy, Irwin, easy! Not so fast,' said Wilf.

'You know what?' said Schiff. 'You worry too much. What's your problem? Money can always be put together for a deal like this. Aren't you interested in money?'

Wilf said that of course he was interested in money – to a point. But the truth was that since reading *The Valachi Papers*, he was far more interested in Joe Pagano.

It took two hours to drive from Connecticut to the restaurant in Rockland County in upstate New York, where they were meeting the Paganos. When they arrived the place was empty apart from a group of five men sitting at a table. They seemed to be expecting them, and Schiff made the introductions.

First came his 'protégé' the so-called 'Jimmy Price', who was actually James Pagano. He turned out to be an exceptionally good-looking, dark-haired boy in his early twenties with the sort of gentle, easy manner that made him seem as if he meant it when he shook Wilf warmly by the hand and said: 'I'm really pleased to meet you, Wilf.' Next came his brother, Danny, who although sharing his brother's dark film-star looks seemed an altogether tougher proposition. Then he shook hands with the brothers' friends, all three of them young Italian–Americans, who would also become close friends of Wilf's and remain so for many years to come. These were Arnold 'Zeke' Squitieri, Alfonse 'Funzi' Cisca and a fair-haired, blue-eyed Sicilian called Joe Pata. When he got to know him, Wilf learned that Joe was particularly proud of his fair colouring, which he claimed came from the Norman aristocracy who had once ruled Sicily.

But to Wilf, meeting them for the first time, they simply appeared like friendly, sociable guys who obviously enjoyed each others' company. The one exception was the enormous Irwin Schiff, who from the start seemed nervous in this close-knit company. He asked anxiously what everyone was drinking, and while he was ordering the drinks Joe Pata went and made a phone call from a telephone on the far side of the room. Wilf heard him saying, 'The English guy? He's here now', and on returning to the table, he said: 'OK. He's on his way.'

Ten minutes later a rugged, thick-set character entered the restaurant and was introduced to Wilf as Billy O'Brien. He soon learned that he was Joe Pagano's private bodyguard. Shortly afterwards O'Brien was followed by someone requiring no introduction – Joe himself.

Joe Pagano could not have been more different from the tough-guy gangster Wilf had been expecting. He was of medium height, dressed stylishly but casually and wore expensively cut, dark blue trousers, Gucci loafers and a yellow cashmere sweater.

'Like all the Paganos, Joe was a good-looking guy,' says Wilf. 'Something about him reminded me of Charles Aznavour.' He had a deep voice and the quietly commanding presence of somebody who rarely had to raise it. To begin with he said little to Wilf beyond 'I'm pleased to meet you' 'and 'How are you?' but, as Wilf remembers: 'There was something about the way he spoke that told me at once that, in contrast with a guy like Irwin Schiff, Joe Pagano was a

Joe Pagano on his mustang at his farm in the Catskills.

Dominick (Quiet Dom) Cirrilo and Joe Pagano, 1957.

Joe Pagano, Joe's father Daniel Pagano and Dominick (Quiet Dom) Cirrilo.

Friends on East 115th Street. Left to right: Robert Milano, Wilf, Danny Pagano, Charlie Salzano and Joey Cusumano.

Wilf with Charlie Kray and Lesley.

Wilf's close friends. Left to right: Vincent De Salvio – a relative by marriage to Joe P, Carmine De Noia, Mike Miaone and Joe Pagano.

The Krays.

Boy's Night Out. Left to right: Wilf, Charlie Richardson, Joseph Pagano, Joe Pyle Jnr, Joe Pyle, Dave Courtney. Kneeling: Tony Lambrianou.

Charlie Kray four days before he died, after his emotional meeting with F.F. left to right: Wilf, Diane Buffini, Charlie Kray and Freddie Foreman. April 2000.

Charlie Kray's funeral service.

Raising Charlie Kray's headstone. Left to right: Tony Lambrianou,
Freddie Foreman, Joe Pyle, Wilf, Roy (Pretty Boy) Shaw, Johnny Nash.

gentleman.'

More drinks arrived. Soon everyone was talking, then Joe abruptly turned to Wilf and said: 'I'd like a word or two alone with you for a moment. There are certain things I'd like to ask you.'

He rose and led Wilf over to a table in a quiet corner. 'So,' he said, 'Irwin tells me that it looks as if you'll soon be doing business with him.'

'Possibly,' said Wilf, 'but it's still early days.'

'Early days or not, if there's anything I can do to help, just know that you can always talk to me about it.'

Something about the way he said this made Wilf answer: 'But Joe, I've just been reading *The Valachi Papers*. How the fuck do I talk to somebody like you?'

'When I said that,' says Wilf, 'Joe just smiled at me and said: "Hey, listen, Wilf. Talk to me like you've known me thirty years".'

And the strange thing was that, as they went on talking, Wilf found himself doing exactly that.

" It was really odd, but from the beginning I felt I had no secrets from him. Certainly I had no difficulty explaining that I'd really been just kidding Irwin for the hell of it, and that the whole idea of buying out part of Worldwide Artistes was something that I dreamed up on the spur of the moment. But on second thoughts maybe it wouldn't be a bad idea.'

Joe clearly understood this, but when Wilf had finished he paused a while and said: 'Wilf, there's something about this guy that you should know. Whatever else he is or isn't, Irwin Schiff's a money-getter, with access to serious amounts of capital, so why not give it a whirl? You've nothing to lose, and if it works out – and who knows? It may – I'll be very happy for him, but I'll be even happier for you. So think about it.'

While Joe was talking, Wilf saw Schiff rising from the table and coming across to talk to them. Joe had seen him too, but before Schiff could reach them or even say a word, he had turned towards him and raised one finger in his direction. Nothing was said, but Irwin Schiff backed off at once and returned to his table.

'That was the first time I saw just a little of the power of Joe Pagano,' says Wilf. 'We went on talking, and by now it really *was* as if I'd known him thirty years. He had that way of seeming genuinely interested in everything about me. He asked about my life, my parents, where I had grown up, and when he noticed my hands he asked about my tattoos. When I told him that I got them in reform school, he gave that smile of his again. "I could tell from the first moment I saw you that you were no lightweight. I knew at once that you were one of us," he said.'

Wilf thanked him for the compliment, then once again Joe abruptly changed the subject. 'Just now you mentioned *The Valachi Papers*.'

Wilf nodded.

'And you seriously believe that shit?'

Wilf said: 'Well, to tell you the truth, Joe, yes I do.' And at that Joe Pagano really started laughing. 'Wilf, there is one thing I will say about you. You've got balls. If I asked that question to anybody else, they'd back off right away and say: "No, of course not".'

But Wilf pursued the subject. 'Joe, I know you all call Valachi a rat, and anyone who betrays his friends like that has to be a rat. But rat or not, surely he can't have made all of that stuff up.'

Joe shrugged at this but said nothing, and Wilf asked how he really felt about the book himself.

'Listen to me,' he said. 'We had it good here. We had it *real* good until Joe Cago opened that big mouth of his, but you should know that none of the people fingered by Valachi was arrested, and certainly not a single conviction followed. No, Wilf, what caused us real trouble was all the ensuing publicity. After that, nothing has ever been quite the same again.'

Then Joe asked Wilf if he had any plans for that evening. Wilf replied that he had to get back to Wallingford for an important business meeting.

'Why not forget it, Wilf, and bring that beautiful young lady of yours along to a dinner I'm hosting tonight at a golf club in Westchester?'

When Wilf said he couldn't, as he was meeting several people he just had to see before returning to England two days later, Joe took his telephone number.

'Whatever happens we must stay in touch,' he said.

Later in the day, when Irwin Schiff was driving them back to Connecticut, he made it clear that he couldn't get over the way that Joe Pagano had taken to Wilf. 'Most people are lucky to be given ten minutes of his time. Do you realise you sat talking to him for over an hour and a half?'

Once back in London, Wilf settled down to business as usual, and a few days after his trip to the States he had a phone call from New York. It was so unexpected that he didn't recognise the voice at once.

'It's Joe Pagano here. How are you? Look, I've been talking to Irwin Schiff about your business project, and he'd like to come to London to see you and check out the situation. In fact, he's here with me now, Wilf. Have a word with him.'

He put Schiff on the phone, who said he had already booked his flight for the following day. Could he please get him a hotel reservation and arrange for someone to pick him up at the airport. 'Fine,' said Wilf. 'No problem. See you tomorrow, Irwin.'

Wilf booked him a room at the Intercontinental Hotel, and after meeting him next day took him for dinner at a favourite haunt of his, the dining room at the Mayfair Hotel.

Over dinner, Wilf realised once more that he really couldn't stand Irwin Schiff, but he did his best to be polite. He also warned him that Worldwide Artistes was owned by his friend Patrick Meehan, who may well not wish to sell.

But it was not until the following day, when Schiff visited his Mayfair office, that Wilf finally lost his temper with him. Schiff told him that he'd been doing some investigating on his own behalf and had discovered that Worldwide Artistes was owned by Hemdale.

'I see you've been doing your homework,' said Wilf.

'And Hemdale is a big leisure corporation,' Schiff went on. 'They own betting offices, record companies, and are also into films. It's the sort of thing my friends are really interested in. While we're about it, maybe we could even buy into Hemdale.'

According to Wilf, Schiff had an irritating habit of saying 'we' as if implying he was firmly in this deal with Joe Pagano. But having talked to Joe himself, he knew this wasn't really true. However, Schiff was so thick-skinned that he went on doing it, without realising he was getting on Wilf's nerves. Finally, when he said in his patronising way, 'Wilf, maybe you should speak to this Patrick guy', Wilf had had enough.

'Irwin,' he said, 'you've got an attitude which doesn't go down well with me. You're big and you're loud, and to be quite honest I've got better things to do than put up with you.'

Schiff looked surprised. 'Hey, I don't need this, buddy. I've travelled all these miles to see you, and what do I get?'

Wilf replied: 'You travelled all these miles on your own volition, not mine. So do it your way but leave me out. I'm a busy man and I've got other things to do.'

Wilf showed Schiff the door, but no sooner was he back at his hotel than he was on the phone.

'Hey, buddy. It was stupid of me. I didn't realise I offended you. I'm real sorry.'

By now, even Wilf was feeling slightly guilty, and made a half-hearted apology. 'It's just the way I am,' he said, and arranged that they'd meet again for lunch next day.

This time, over lunch they agreed to go ahead. Wilf would find out if there was anything that he could do, and Schiff promised to look around to raise sufficient capital to buy out Worldwide Artistes. Nothing more was said about Hemdale.

A few days later Wilf got another call from Joe Pagano.

'I hope you're not ringing me to tell me off about my attitude to Irwin Schiff. The fact is, Joe, I just don't trust the guy.' said Wilf.

'Maybe you're not such a bad judge of character,' said Joe. 'But as I told you before, he's close to those with money, and if anything comes of this you could do very nicely for yourself, and I'll take a backhander off him too. So let's see how it goes. Anyhow, I'll leave it all to you. Any chance of you coming over soon?'

'Not for a while, Joe, I'm afraid.'

'That's a pity. You remember my son, Danny? He's getting married on 24 November and I'd have liked to have seen you at that wedding.'

Even as he said this, Wilf knew it was impossible, as once again he was all but overwhelmed with work in the studio, and there was no way he could cancel his arrangements to go to a wedding in New York, much as he'd have liked to.

Three or four days later, Wilf had another call from Joe Pagano. He was surprised to hear him, and after the initial courtesies asked him how the wedding went.

'Oh, the wedding went well. Real well. Nothing wrong with the wedding. The trouble was what happened afterwards. You could say that it ended in tragedy.'

'A tragedy, Joe? I'm sorry to hear that. What happened?'

Joe said that Irwin Schiff was at the wedding, and after the ceremony Jimmy had borrowed his car, telling him he needed to go somewhere or other in a hurry and would soon return – but he didn't return. Instead, late that evening several state troopers burst in on the wedding party asking for Irwin Schiff.

'They could have been a little more discreet,' said Joe. 'After all, they obviously knew who we all were, as they have us under surveillance all the time, so I wasn't exactly low profile and they knew that it was my son Danny's wedding. But as the car was registered in Irwin's name, the trooper insisted on telling him that his car had been found parked at the side of Route 207 at the intersection with Route 45. Then he told him that Jimmy was discovered lying behind the wheel with a bullet in his head, and a gun beside him. They said the gun had fired just a single shot. Right now, we still don't know for sure if it was an accident, a suicide or whether it was – shall we say? – something else.'

Wilf did his best to tell him how very sorry he was to hear such dreadful news, 'but what else could I say? I'd only met Jimmy once, but the news of his death really got to me. He was such a good-looking guy, and seemed so full of life. Perhaps it was just because I couldn't express this to his father that I found myself saying: "Look, Joe. I want to come over to see you. I can wrap things up here in the studio in a day or two, and if it's any help I'll be with you before the weekend."'

All that Joe replied to this was: 'Wilf, that'll be just great. I'd appreciate it. And before you leave, make sure you call and let me know your flight. I'd like to send a car to meet you.'

In those days Wilf's favourite New York hotel was the Park-Sheraton on 7th Avenue, and when he arrived at Kennedy Airport, Joe's driver, Charlie, was already there to drive him to the hotel in Joe's own car, a highly polished black stretched limo. Wilf remembers thinking: 'Even at a time like this, you can count on Joe Pagano to put on a first-class act.'

By the time Charlie had got Wilf's luggage into the hotel, Joe himself had arrived, together with fair-haired Joe Pata and his bodyguard, Billy O'Brien. Wilf automatically found himself giving Joe a hug and a kiss.

He asked him how he was.

'Well, Wilf, things have been—' Instead of finishing the sentence, Joe gave a shrug. 'He was a very private guy who was not in the habit of talking to anyone about his feelings. All he said was: "D'you want to wash up first, or will you come straight to the bar and get a drink?"'

After the long flight, Wilf felt badly in need of a drink and they went to the bar. As Wilf knew, the front part of the bar at the Sheraton had once been the famous barber shop where in 1957 the notorious Gallo brothers, acting on orders from Vito Genovese, reputedly gunned down Albert Anastasia while he was reclining in the barber's chair with his face covered in hot towels. The actual barber's chair remained there as a gruesome souvenir for ever.

After a while Wilf enquired about Jimmy.

'Well, it looks as though we must accept the fact that he killed himself.'

'How is his mother coping?' Wilf asked.

'Real bad,' said Joe. 'The two of them were very close.'

By now Billy O'Brien and Joe Pata had made themselves scarce, leaving Joe and Wilf to talk together. Wilf felt that somehow he and Joe had formed an instant affinity and understood each other. He felt that the best thing he could do now was just to sit and listen to him.

'It's a tough time, Wilf,' he said. 'A real tough time, and the toughest thing about it is that it had to happen on Danny's wedding day. And to make it even worse we know that Danny has to go off to jail early in the new year.'

He told Wilf how earlier in the year Danny had been arrested in a hold-up that had gone wrong and where he had been shot in the back. Danny's life had been in the balance for some time, and although he was later given a zero-to-nine-year sentence, he was granted bail while he recovered from his injuries. In a few weeks' time his bail would expire and, having just had one son kill himself, Joe would soon be seeing his second son be taken off to prison.

Even as Joe told Wilf this, his voice remained as expressionless as ever, and his face betrayed no flicker of emotion either. 'Joe Pagano had the darkest and the most piercing eyes I'd ever seen, but even those eyes of his gave nothing away.'

'I tell you what, Wilf,' he said finally. 'If you've a little time to spare, how about coming to my home to meet my wife, Theresa?'

'Joe, are you sure? I'd feel I was imposing.'

'No, you wouldn't be imposing. You're my friend.'

With this, he said he'd make arrangements for Wilf to come and visit later in the afternoon and said goodbye.

Wilf ate lunch alone, only to discover that Joe had asked Irwin Schiff, of all people, to drive him to his house. Schiff seemed as nervous as ever and explained that since Jimmy had been found dead in his car, he had been getting constant aggravation from the local district attorney.

'I hope you won't take it amiss, Wilf, but there's just one piece of advice I'd like to give you. When you get to Joe's house, do be careful with your language in front of Theresa. People like Joe Pagano tend to be very protective of their wives.'

Schiff added that the Paganos had a comfortable but fairly modest detached house in a place called Monsey, not that far from the restaurant in Rockland County where they first met, and when they entered the little town Wilf was surprised to see that most of the men in the street were strict Hassidic Jews wearing traditional black hats and ringlets.

'Irwin, are you sure we've come to the right place?'

'Sure. It's a strictly Jewish community, and Joe lives right in the middle of them all. As the only Italian in the neighbourhood he gets along real good with them.'

They drew up outside No. 6 Jill Lane. Wilf could see that the house had a raised deck with a pool and verandah at the back and that Joe was sitting there alone. But as soon as they arrived he came out to meet them, and led them into the house to meet his wife, Theresa. 'Although she was in her mid-forties, Theresa was still a beautiful, dark-haired Italian-looking woman. Her face showed all the signs of grief, but despite her sorrow she kept her dignity. In front of others, she knew how she was expected to conduct herself.'

But when Wilf showed his sympathy and told her that although he'd only met Jimmy once he could understand what a wonderful son he must have been, she broke down crying. 'I didn't know if it was proper to hold her or not, but anyway I put my arms around her.' Then Joe appeared and comforted her as best he could, and at this point a girlfriend of hers arrived at the house and the two of them went off to talk together.

Wilf and Joe went and sat by the pool. 'Wilf, I'm glad you came. It's been very hard, you know. Theresa sometimes goes to the cemetery several times a day, and I feel there's nothing I can do to help her. She gets upset with me because I don't show my feelings. What she doesn't understand is that I'm suffering as much as she does, but I've learned in life never to let my feelings show. But inside, you know, I'm really broken up.'

At this moment Irwin Schiff appeared, looking as if he wished to join them, but Joe waved him away. 'Not today, Irwin, not now. Can't you see I'm with my friend?'

So Wilf stayed where he was and went on talking about this and that. Then suddenly he had a bright idea. 'Do you have any recent photographs of Jimmy? I'd like to show them to a friend of mine in England.'

'I'm sure we have. I'll ask Theresa', Joe replied, and seeing that his wife was now on her own he called her over and said: 'Theresa, Wilf wants to see some up-to-date pictures of Jimmy.'

She found three or four recent photographs of her son, and Wilf asked if he could borrow them. He promised to take good care of them, saying he would bring them back when he returned to New York in three weeks' time.

Back in England, Wilf had an artist friend called Henry, living in his village, who specialised in painting portraits. He showed him Jimmy's photographs and asked if he could paint a portrait from them within two weeks. Henry said he could, and when Wilf returned to New York three weeks later he was carrying an oil painting of Jimmy Pagano in a fine gold frame. He went to Monsey straight away, and when he saw Theresa the first thing he did was give her back her photographs.

Then he handed her the parcel.

Henry had done his work so well that when she opened it she couldn't believe her eyes – the likeness was uncanny. She was overcome with gratitude, and so was Joe.

'This portrait of Jimmy will always hang in our house,' he said. And the portrait of Jimmy Pagano hangs in its place of honour in his brother Danny's house to this very day.

Joe must have called his brother, Pat, to tell him all about the portrait, for it was shortly after this that Wilf remembers what looked like a bigger, more rugged version of Joe Pagano coming into the living room. He had the same good looks as Joe and the same resonant, deep voice, but he was easily six feet tall, and at less serious moments, was rarely seen without a smile. The word Wilf still uses to describe him is 'awesome', and one can understand something of his feelings when he walked straight up to where he was sitting, looked him straight in the eyes and said: 'Stand up a moment.'

Wilf felt he might have somehow offended him, but if he had there was nothing he could do about it now except obey him, so he did as he was told. The next thing he knew was that he was being given a massive bear hug and a kiss on either cheek.

'You'll do for me,' said Pat Pagano. 'What you did for my brother and Theresa was wonderful. Theresa's just shown me that portrait of Jimmy that you gave them. For doing that you're here in my heart for ever.'

Six months earlier Wilf's father had died at the age of fifty-six in a hospital in Ryde. By then Wilf had made his peace with him, and although he had been working in Switzerland had flown back on hearing he was dying and saw him a quarter of an hour before he went. Hardly surprisingly, in spite of this, following his death he found he hadn't missed him. But after this latest trip to New York, and his visit to the Paganos, things had changed. In Joe Pagano Wilf had found at last the father figure he had always wanted.

11

'One of the Family'

THE TRANSFORMING OF Wilf's life happened quickly. No sooner was he back in England than Christmas was upon him. It was the first Christmas he had spent as a divorced man, but luckily there were no problems over his access to the children; and if anything all three of them, Sean, Scott and Sammi, were more important to him now than ever. But the finality of divorce can be nothing but a break, and for Wilf it marked the end of ten years of his life. But even as his marriage ended, a very different set of family loyalties and affections was about to take its place.

For him it seemed only natural to have rung Joe Pagano to wish him and his family a happy Christmas and to convey his hopes for a happier 1974. Joe was obviously pleased to hear him, and on the surface at any rate he seemed to be coping with his grief over Jimmy. When Wilf said he hoped to see him soon, he responded by asking if Wilf could make it over to New York during the next fortnight.

'As I told you, Wilf, my son Danny has to go away to jail on 9 January and over here we have a custom that we hold a party the night before he goes and gives himself up to the authorities.'

'In England if you get sent to prison, you don't get no party. You go to fucking jail straight away,' said Wilf.

'Is that true, Wilf? 'I'm sorry to hear that. That's a rough country you live in.'

Wilf laughed, and then, without a moment's hesitation, said that of course he'd come. In fact, by now he had finally started delegating in the office and had recently appointed Ken Mewes, formerly Andrew Loog Oldham's label manager, as his personal assistant and office manager. This relieved him of many of the day-to-day chores in

Dover Street, as did the work of Jinxie looking after the Groundhogs and Dave Farley doing much the same for Jimmy Helms. Lesley was in theory 'looking after' Stray.

On the afternoon of 7 January 1974, when Wilf arrived at the house in Jill Lane, Monsey, the first person he clapped eyes on was Joe Pagano. But this was a Joe Pagano he had never seen before, a Joe Pagano dressed in overalls, covered in paint and with a paintbrush in his hand. Several of Joe's friends that Wilf had met before, including Joe Pata, were with him and similarly attired as they worked busily away in the basement area of the house.

'What gives?' Wilf asked.

'It's for Danny's party,' Joe replied. 'We've invited a lot of people. This will be the place for tables for the guests, and over there against the wall we'll have a bar. I know that as of now it looks like a tip in here, but tomorrow night you'll see the difference. When Danny's party starts it'll be more like a nightclub than a basement.'

'If you say so, I'll believe you, Joe,' said Wilf.

But when he had driven back from Monsey to Manhattan and was having an evening drink at the Park-Sheraton, the thought of transforming that empty basement of the Pagano residence into a nightclub in twenty-four hours struck Wilf as ridiculous.

The following evening Joe had as usual insisted on laying on transportation, but Wilf's spirits sank when he realised that once again his driver had to be the inescapable and intolerable fat man, Irwin Schiff. As Schiff told Wilf, it had been Joe's idea to send him, 'as Joe is getting real keen on the Worldwide Artistes project and thought we should have a chance to talk things over during the journey.'

In fact, as far as Wilf remembers, 'all that Irwin came up with was the same old bullshit as before, and I'm sure that I was pretty noncommittal'.

By the time we arrived in Monsey it was dark already. The house and garden were lit up, the road outside was jammed with cars, and the noise coming from the basement sounded like a dozen nightclubs. Inside the house the atmosphere was quite unreal, for believe me this really was some party. The house was already full of guests of the family, and downstairs the whole basement was crammed with people. In the short time since I'd seen it, Joe and the boys had made a bar, and what a bar it was. The whole far wall of the basement had been bricked over, and in front of it there was now an illuminated waterfall, with live fish swimming in a pool below. There were barmen in white jackets, serving every fucking drink beneath the sun, and gilt tables and chairs for the guests, and carpets on the floor. From the atmosphere you'd have thought we were celebrating Danny's birthday, not his final night of freedom before he went off to prison.

'All Joe's friends that I'd seen in overalls the previous afternoon were there, of course, but now they were all impeccably dressed, as were the other male guests. Most of them I'd never met before, but I recognised them at once for what they were. In my world, you know your own.

Almost the first person I saw was Danny and I sat at his table together with Arnold Squitieri, and Funzi Cisca. In those days, with his dark good looks Arnold could have been an all-Italian film star, and Funzi was one of the funniest men I've ever met, with a wicked sense of humour. They were great company, and we really made it a night to remember, despite the fact that Arnold and Funzi were both of them out on bail, Arnold on a charge of manslaughter and Funzi for something I forget. I remember remarking that I couldn't believe my eyes. 'Only yesterday all this was just a basement area, and now look at it.' To which Arnold said: 'You gotta understand that with Joe Pagano, if things happen, they happen real quick.'

But it was Danny who most impressed me. Here's this guy who's going away to prison next morning and he's having a ball. He's laughing. We're all laughing. So is his new wife Sarah, for that matter. The wives who'd been cooking for the party all that afternoon soon started bringing in platefuls of great Italian food – meatballs cooked to some old Italian family recipe, and all kinds of delicious pasta. And throughout the evening I noticed people giving Danny envelopes. When I asked Joe about this, he explained: 'When someone goes away to jail, we Italians like to give a present of cash to help the wives meet bills and suchlike in their absence.

Later in the evening, it was Arnold who got me going with some serious drinking, by saying: 'I guess you guys in England can't drink as good as us.' To which, of course, I had to answer: 'Arnold, I've an idea that I can drink enough to stick with you lot.'

'We'll see,' he said, and the drinking started. During the rest of that night we must have tried almost every alcoholic concoction known to man, but my downfall came when Funzi introduced me to something he called 'Black Russian', made up of vodka, cream and some mysterious liqueur or other. In the end I'd no idea where I was. All I did know was that I'd had a night I'd not forget in a hurry.

It must have been around this time that Irwin Schiff reappeared. Until then he'd spent most of his time near the kitchen, not drinking – Irwin never drank alcohol, only diet cola – but eating and eating, as I suppose he had to, seeing the size he was. For believe me, when it came to eating, Irwin Schiff was in a class apart.

By now the time had come for me to head for home, and Joe must have arranged for Schiff to take me back to the hotel, but when I tried to stagger up the stairs my legs gave way. I've been pretty drunk on many occasions in my time, but never quite like that, before or since. I was poleaxed. God knows how they got me into Schiff's car, and then, to cap it all, just before we reached New York it began to snow. When a blizzard hits New York, it's as if the Arctic's come to town. I'd never have believed it if I hadn't seen it.

Throughout the journey I kept the rear window open so I could get some air, and Schiff kept complaining that he was freezing. Ice was soon forming around the car, and once I started throwing up I must have left a trail of frozen vomit all the way from Rockland County to Manhattan.

Somehow fat Irwin got me back to the hotel, but like the idiot he was he dropped me off at a side entry instead of the main entrance. Not that this meant anything to me; I was so drunk that I hadn't the faintest notion where I was. I was bouncing off the walls, and someone must have called the security man saying: 'We've a drunk here.' Two of the security staff arrived to throw me out, but somehow I convinced them that I was a guest at the hotel, and in the end I found my key. At this they told me I was in the wrong part of the hotel, and they took me up in the lift to the twentieth floor. There they simply opened the door of my room, pushed me in and left me to get on with it.

The room was stifling. With the cold spell, the heating had been turned right up and I was so drunk I couldn't find the regulator to turn it down. I was really desperate. I thought I was suffocating with the heat, but I was still so drunk that all I could do was stagger to the windows and open them as wide as possible to get some air. When I crashed out on the bed, I was so far gone that I couldn't even take my shoes off.

Next morning I was woken by someone banging on the door. I thought to myself, 'What the hell's going on?' I was still in my clothes and shoes from the night before, and when I looked across the room there was deep snow all the way from the windows to the bed. At first I thought that someone must have made a snowman in the corner of the room. In fact, it was the TV set fixed to its stand, which had become covered in thick snow.

The blizzard must have raged all night, and by now, with the central heating, the snow in the room had started melting and was leaking through the floor to the room below. In the end two of the hotel staff came and opened my door with their key and were horrified by what they saw. Later, when I'd pulled myself sufficiently together to face the day, I was presented with a bill for $1,500 to cover the damage, and asked to leave the hotel immediately. Then the phone started ringing It was Joe Pagano, and when I told him what had happened he thought that it was really funny. When I mentioned the 1,500 bucks and said that Funzi and Arnold ought to pay the bill, since they were the ones who got me drunk in the first place, his mirth was almost uncontrollable. It was only when I told him that the hotel was also throwing me out that he took my situation seriously.

'Just don't worry, Wilf,' he said. 'You'll come up here to stay. I'll send a car at once, and book you into the local motel.'

'Thanks, Joe,' I said. 'But for God's sake don't send Irwin Schiff.'

Around noon, after packing my bags and settling the bill, I made my way to the bar for a badly needed hair of the dog. I asked the front desk to let me know when my driver arrived. When he did, I saw that mercifully it wasn't Schiff this time, but Joe's personal driver, Charlie. Almost the first thing Charlie did was ask me what had happened.

'Charlie, you don't need to know,' I said as I made myself as comfortable as possible in the back of Joe's stretched limo for the journey back upstate. An hour later we arrived at the Westgate Motor Lodge, which was situated in a town called Nyack, and Charlie departed, saying he was off to get Joe. In the fragile state that I was in, I was grateful for a chance to sort myself out and, sure enough, in half an hour or so Joe arrived, accompanied as usual by his bodyguard, Billy O'Brien and Joe Pata.

By now all three of them had heard about Wilf and his snowman in the Park-Sheraton and treated it as one enormous joke. Wilf, who was still suffering from a splitting headache, didn't see the funny side of it, but as is often the way with funny stories it didn't do his reputation any harm. On the contrary, the story rapidly became an important part of the process of Wilf's introduction to Joe's followers, proving that, unlike the usual image of the effete and snooty Englishman, Wilf Pine wasn't scared of liquor and, despite his nationality, was probably a regular guy.

When Joe and his companions stopped laughing at Wilf's misfortunes, there was a reminder that his new friends' interest in him wasn't purely social. Joe told Billy and Joe Pata to make themselves scarce for a while, as he and Wilf had something they needed to discuss, and they'd all meet later in the bar.

Once they were alone, Joe came straight to the point. The fat man, as he referred to him, had been driving him mad about the

Worldwide Artistes deal, and it had to be sorted out as soon as possible. What really was the situation back in London?

Wilf told him that he'd mentioned it to Patrick, but only briefly as he didn't know if Schiff had been for real or was full of bullshit. 'If you'd like me to pursue it further, Joe, I will,' he said.

Joe said he'd be grateful if he spoke to Patrick Meehan about the deal as soon as possible. 'There's a phone here, Wilf, and now would be as good a time as any.'

Wilf was lucky to find Patrick in the office. When he said he was calling from New York about the Worldwide Artistes deal, Patrick said he hadn't thought that Schiff was serious, as he'd never mentioned a figure. But as soon as Wilf said that Schiff was talking about six million dollars, Patrick was all attention.

'Six million sounds pretty good to me. But is this friend of yours good for that sort of money?'

'I'm told he is, and he's so eager for a deal that he's driving me fucking nuts. It's your business, Patrick, not mine, but it might be a good idea to let him know whether you're interested or not.'

Patrick quickly answered that he definitely was interested.

'As you're coming back to London in a day or two, try and bring this Schiff character with you. If you can, and if he's as gung ho as you say he is, I'll make it my business to meet him immediately and sort this whole thing out.'

When Wilf reported this to Joe he seemed satisfied.

'Now, that wasn't so painful was it, Wilf? And it's not such a bad idea if you take the fat man back to London with you. If nothing else it'll get him out of my hair, and I really want this whole thing settled.'

'Is it that important to you, Joe?'

Joe nodded. 'Wilf, to me it is. The fat man's in with certain friends of mine, who are not the sort you mess around with, and Schiff has got them very interested in this deal. That means that I'm involved as well. You understand?'

Wilf said he did, and although he could think of few things more unpleasant than flying back to London in the company of Irwin Schiff, if that was what Joe Pagano wanted, that was what he'd do. Joe thanked him and rang Schiff, telling him where they were and that they had to see him straight away.

'And now I guess we need a drink,' he said to Wilf, leading him to the bar where Billy O'Brien and Joe Pata were already waiting.

As in corporate America, so in the world of Joe Pagano, an ability to hold one's liquor was important, and according to Wilf 'Joe could drink for America, without ever once becoming a fall-down drunk. Alcohol seemed hardly to affect him', and while they were waiting for Schiff the drinking started.

At the mere mention of Irwin Schiff, Billy O'Brien made no attempt to hide the fact that he disliked him even more than Wilf did, so that when the fat man bulked his way into the bar, Wilf saw Billy's expression darken ominously. 'At this Joe gave his bodyguard a look as if to say: "Billy, behave." And Billy O'Brien did behave.'

Joe himself was cool but perfectly polite with Schiff, and after offering him a diet cola they got down to business. He explained that Wilf had just spoken to the guy in charge of Worldwide Artistes, who was keen to meet him.

'Wilf here is flying back to London in a few days' time, so I want you to have a suitcase packed, as you're going with him. From now on, Irwin, the deal's up to you. I've done my part. OK?'

While Joe was calling for another round of drinks, Wilf noticed Billy O'Brien staring at the fat man with a look of loathing on his face. Joe must have seen it too, as he said: 'I think you should do yourself a favour, Irwin, now, and leave us.' He added that Wilf would be in touch regarding times of flights, and Schiff departed.

When the door closed behind him, Joe turned to Wilf with an expression of relief and said: 'Well, that's it. End of business for the day. Now you will meet some friends of mine. My brother Pat's on his way to join us here, and the three of us will make a day of it.'

When Pat arrived, he greeted Wilf as warmly as he had before, and after one for the road, Wilf's outing with the two Paganos started. But instead of 'making a day of it', as Joe had promised, they ended up making three, with sleep becoming largely incidental.

The first stop turned out to be lunch at that gastronomic bastion of old New York, the famous Oak Room Restaurant at the Plaza Hotel on Central Park. This gave Wilf his first, but not his last, lesson on the social clout of Joe Pagano. The entrance to the restaurant was, as usual, crowded with the hungry rich, waiting for their tables, but although the Paganos hadn't made a reservation, it was apparent that for them this wasn't necessary. No sooner were they spotted by the maître d', than he came bustling towards them and treated them like royalty, almost falling over himself in his eagerness to find them a table. It was much the same with the waiters; once the three of them were seated, nothing was too much trouble for the staff.

In London, Wilf had seen celebrities throw their weight around in restaurants, but the Paganos didn't have to throw their weight around. 'This was power of a sort I'd never really seen before,' he says.

Their guest arrived soon after. He was a distinguished-looking man in his late fifties, white-haired and immaculately attired in a pale grey suit. He was simply introduced to Wilf as 'Raymond', with no hint of who he was or how he was involved with the Paganos. Wilf guessed he might have been a banker or possibly a politician, but whatever he was or wasn't Raymond treated the Paganos with unfeigned respect. At the end of the meal, Joe turned to Wilf and asked if he'd mind leaving them for a few minutes as there was something they needed to discuss in private. Wilf gave them twenty minutes. When he returned, Raymond had disappeared as unexpectedly as he arrived. During his time with the Paganos, Wilf would often meet characters like Raymond, who floated in and out of Joe Pagano's world without a word of explanation.

Lunch over, Wilf's outing with the two Paganos rapidly took on a very different character. For the truth was that Joe and Pat were engaged in considerably more than just a drinking spree, and during these three days Wilf was receiving what amounted to an intro-duction to the way these two new friends of his conducted their business. This was totally different from any business, criminal or otherwise, that he had ever been mixed up in in England.

Back in the Pagano limo, with Charlie at the wheel, the first stop was a run-down district of New York which Wilf had never seen before. This was East Harlem, once home to the poorest immigrant Italian families and still the traditional heartland of the Mafia.

'Wilf, we're taking you to what we call a social club,' said Joe. 'Italians have them all over the old neighbourhoods, here in Harlem, in the Bronx, and in Queens – you'll find them everywhere there are Italians. They're called social clubs because that's what they are – places where the men still meet as they always have done in the past, to play cards, place a bet on the horses, have a drink and talk about the old country. They're also where we do a lot of our business, for they're mostly run by friends of ours, and it's in places like these we meet our sort of people. There's someone here I want you to meet called Vincent Mauro. He's a very old and very special friend of ours, and I'm hoping that you get to know him in the future. I don't need to tell you to treat him with respect.'

The interior of the social club came as a surprise after the Oak Room at the Plaza. It was small and subdued, with two or three card games in progress, a little bar, and beyond it was a kitchen where an elderly gentleman was making coffee. But as they entered they were greeted by a striking-looking man Wilf realised at once was Vincent Mauro. He was tall, with thick, greyish hair, and even if Joe hadn't told him in advance he would have known that he was someone special from the way they treated him. Even Joe and Pat seemed fairly anxious to agree with anything he said. To Wilf, he was extra-ordinarily polite. Wilf makes the point that he was not exactly charming; more what Italians call *simpatico*. 'He made me feel comfortable,' he says, and soon he had Wilf talking about London, which he appeared to know.

Joe butted into their conversation. 'Dom around?' he asked.

'I told him you were coming and he's on his way,' said Vincent.

'Then, as usual, I got the feeling that he and the Paganos had something they needed to discuss among themselves very quietly, so I went to get myself a cup of coffee when this guy arrives. What followed next was like an old school reunion, but with people like Joe and Pat it happened every day of their lives. Whenever they met one of their own it was always the same, a warm embrace, a kiss on the cheek and an enquiry of "How are you?", which they invariably made as if they really wished to know the answer. This new friend was another striking-looking guy, not so big as Vincent, but very bronzed and muscular, and I put him in his mid-forties. He was dressed casually but immaculately: freshly laundered, short-sleeved shirt, beautifully cut trousers, and highly polished loafers.' He had dark hair and was what Wilf describes as 'a real good-looking guy with that genuine old-fashioned Italian look about him'.

His name was Dominic Cirillo, but they called him 'Quiet Dom' because he spoke so softly and you had to be attentive to listen to him. During the years to come, he became increasingly important in the world of Joe Pagano.

It took a while for Wilf to start to understand that what he was observing was nothing less than the day-to-day working of an Italian-American organised crime family. For Joe Pagano, work involved this constant social round with all that it involved – drinks, meals, the exchange of scandal and always the enquiries about the other person's family. Their 'business' depended on this sort of personal contact and networking, for along with the gossip and the expressions of goodwill and respect this round of endless meetings was their time-honoured way of transmitting orders and information, together with passing on messages, making alliances and deals and settling disagreements.

This 'business' continued until late that night, when Charlie finally drove them back to Rockland Country, depositing Wilf at his motel, before taking Joe Pagano home. Next day Joe called him after breakfast with the news that Pat was otherwise engaged but that there were more friends and neighbourhoods that Joe would like to show him. More clubs, more guarded phone calls, more intricate conversations over glasses of Scotch and water, and yet more bottles of good red wine with more delicious meals.

By the third day Wilf was just beginning to get the gist of what was happening, and while drinking and eating his way through the length and breadth of the five boroughs of New York he had picked up something else – a love of Italian food that continues to the present day.

The second night, when Joe dropped Wilf back at his motel, there were inevitably more drinks, and the two of them got talking. It was the first time they had had a chance to talk together freely and learn something of each other's lives. Joe made little reference now to what he called 'business', but he talked a lot about his family, and particularly about his other brother, Johnny, who, like Pat, had started his working life as a bricklayer and later became a union delegate. He also talked about his three sisters, Lena, Mary and Rose, making it fairly clear that his favourite was Rose, who was married to a welder and had four sons.

'You'll have to meet them all,' said Joe.

Then he talked of Danny, and how much he missed him since he'd been 'away'. He said this was different from the way he felt after losing Jimmy. 'Like Jimmy, Danny is my son, but he also happens to be my best friend.' When Wilf said how much he wished he could have had that sort of relationship with his own father, Joe replied: 'As far as Danny was concerned, I guess I just got lucky.'

Then Joe began questioning Wilf about his family, in a way that nobody had done to him before. 'No one had ever been that interested, but Joe was interested. He was interested in everything. Having been brought up a Catholic himself, he could understand what I'd been through when I told him about Sister Paula. And he couldn't hear enough about the Wellesley Nautical School at Blyth, and the grudge fights and how I got the tattoos on my hands. He said: "Well, you didn't have it very easy, did you?" And I said: "Well, it all seemed pretty normal at the time, and I thought that that's what life is like."

'"Perhaps it is," said Joe.'

It was late on the third afternoon of fairly non-stop drinking and eating and driving around New York, that Joe stopped to make a phone call and afterwards said: 'Sorry, Wilf. We got to go back into Manhattan. Something's just cropped up.' When Joe told his faithful driver, Charlie, the address, Charlie swung the limo back in the direction of Manhattan.

'By now, I must admit to feeling pretty drunk. Not drunk like I'd been the night of Danny's party, but drunk enough for Joe to notice. Joe, on the other hand, who'd had far more than me, seemed totally unaffected, with not a hair out of place.'

'Wilf,' if you want to call it a day I'll understand, but I have to see this guy, and if you can just last out I think that he might interest you.'

Wilf said of course he could last out, and they ended up outside a small bar restaurant on the smart upper east side of Manhattan. The early 1970s were the heyday of the plush look in New York restaurants – red carpets on the floors, black leather chairs, subdued lighting, but this was *plush de luxe*, with a hushed atmosphere and lowered lighting even in the afternoon. And even here the owner greeted Joe Pagano like a respected, long-lost friend.

'Mr Pagano, your guest has just arrived. He's waiting for you in the VIP booth.'

After all that he had drunk, Wilf found the atmosphere a relief, but he was not at his most perceptive in the dark interior of the restaurant and took little in about Joe Pagano's guest, apart from the fact that he was black.

'Sammy, I'd like you to meet my pal Wilf. Wilf, this is Sammy.'

Once again drinks were served, and, realising that Joe had something serious to discuss, Wilf turned tactfully away. He heard Joe talking softly to his guest, as he almost always did, but from his tone of voice Wilf realised that, for the first time since he had met him, Joe was angry.

'Sammy, you fucked up on our friends,' he heard him say. 'That wasn't clever of you, Sammy. I'm your friend, but there's only so much I can do to help you. Now just you listen to me, Sammy. You're going to give those guys some fresh dates, and this time you're going to keep them. I need to come away from this meeting with you knowing for certain that you'll stick to those dates and will perform.'

'Sure, Joey, sure. No question about it. I apologise. I'll do just as you say. And Joey, promise to sort this whole thing out for me. You've always looked after me, Joey, from the days when I was just a kid playing in the street.'

'I'll do my best, but there's one thing I must tell you, Sammy. If you let me down this time, you'll lose that other fucking eye of yours.'

Joe was actually sounding quite jovial as he said this, and when the two of them suddenly began laughing I wondered what the fuck was up. Joe must have seen that I was puzzled, for he turned the table-light up, and as his guest rose to go to the toilet, I caught sight of him.

'Joe, isn't that Sammy Davis Junior?'

205

'Who did you think it was. Of course it's Sammy Davis Junior.' And when Sammy returned, the two of us started talking. When I said I lived near London and worked in the music business, he said, as New Yorkers always seem to, that of course he just loved London.

'You know, I've done a royal command performance for your Queen at the London Palladium. And since what happened afterwards concerns Joey here, I must tell you all about it.'

'No, Sammy, no. Not now,' said Joe.

'But, Joey,' said Sammy,' the guy's an Englishman and this is about his Queen. I have to tell him.'

Wilf says that he is still not sure whether the story Sammy told is true or not, but from what he said it seems that, after the performance, Sammy was invited back to the palace to have supper with the Queen and various friends and members of the Royal Family. Someone had already told him how to behave in the presence of royalty, but once she arrived and everyone was seated, they quickly put him at his ease and were very charming.

'I couldn't believe that I was really there, me a black kid out of Harlem, sitting talking to the Queen of England. And suddenly I thought, I've got to call my friend Joe Pagano. I have to tell him where I am. So when there was a pause in the conversation, I asked if I could be excused a moment. A footman showed me to the men's room, and I asked him if I could make an important phone call to America. "Certainly, sir," he said, and showed me a telephone in the corridor. I was put through to an operator, and I gave her Joe's number in New York.'

Here Joe interrupted. 'Sammy, enough. That's quite enough.' But Sammy paid no heed.

'The next thing I know I'm talking loud and clear to Joe Pagano and saying to him: "Joey, guess where I am?"'

'I know where you are, Sammy. You're in England,' Joe replied.

'No, no. Listen, Joey, you don't know where I am. I am in Buckingham Palace with the Queen of England. I'm having supper with her. And then, instead of being pleased to hear me, all Joey said was: "Sammy, get off that phone. I'm telling you to get off the phone." Then he hung up on me.

'I felt terrible. All I'd wanted was to share that moment with my friend Joey, but I'd forgotten that his phone was tapped from time to time, and as soon as I was back in America I had all kinds of people calling from the FBI, and God knows who else, questioning me about what I was doing making a call from Buckingham Palace to Joe Pagano.'

Joe was smiling now in spite of himself, 'Sammy,' he said. 'That's enough of your bullshit. It's getting late. Just one more drink, then me and Wilf have got to go.'

When they were in the limo and heading back once more towards the Bronx, Wilf asked a question that had puzzled him.

'During these last three days, while we've been going around New York, everyone we meet seems to know either you or your brother, Pat. How come?'

'I'd not say everyone,' said Joe, 'but I do know a lot of people like Sammy in the entertainment business. It started several years back with the Copacabana Club. You know the Copacabana?'

Wilf said he understood that it was New York's premier nightspot, the equivalent of London's Talk of the Town.

'Yeah, maybe I heard about that place,' he said. 'Anyway you've heard of somebody called Frank Costello?'

'I said of course I have, Joe. I've read most of the books about the Mafia. Frank Costello used to be the boss of the crime family started by Lucky Luciano.'

'That's what they say. Then you probably read about how Frank had a little problem with a friend of mine called Vito Genovese. Shall we say the two of them fell out and Frank got the worst of the argument and took early retirement at his place on Long Island. Well, you see, Wilf, Frank Costello used to have a sizeable piece of the action at the Copacabana Club. And since Vito Genovese is my friend, he presented it to me. As you said, the Copacabana is the premier nightspot in New York, and we've had most of the big entertainers there in our time. That's how I got to know them all.'

Including Frank Sinatra?

'Yeah, including Frank Sinatra.'

★

Early next morning Charlie picked Wilf up from his motel to drive him to the airport. The only person in the world for whom he would have endured crossing the Atlantic with Irwin Schiff was Joe Pagano – just as it was for Joe that he had invited Schiff to stay for the weekend at Minnis Bay, so that Patrick could meet him. It sounds like a thoroughly uncomfortable weekend, since Lesley was also there with her parents, and if there was anyone Lesley disliked more than Irwin Schiff it was Patrick Meehan. To make things worse, none of this discomfort really carried negotiations over Worldwide Artistes much further forward.

During a predictably uncomfortable weekend, Wilf learned little that he hadn't known already. Schiff still refused to reveal the identity of his backers beyond confirming that one of them was an important figure in the American organised crime scene who was hoping ultimately to take over WWA and so gain an all-important foothold in the lucrative British entertainment business.

At the same time, Schiff went out of his way to emphasise to Patrick that the six million dollars was a firm offer, with the possibility of more if necessary.

'The one thing neither I nor my associates have to worry about is money,' he said grandly, and as he said this Wilf recognised a glint in Patrick's eye that lasted throughout their subsequent discussion. Wilf was, as he puts it, 'led to believe' that, as a director of Hemdale, Patrick could not only recommend a deal like the one Schiff was proposing to Hemdale's other board members, but that he also had a legal right to buy back his old assets in Worldwide Artistes, then sell them on his own account.

In short, provided Schiff could come up with the six million, the Worldwide Artistes deal remained very much in play. This was precisely the assurance Schiff had travelled to London to get, and it was a happy fat man whom Wilf gratefully packed off back to New York on an early flight that Monday morning.

Wilf was even happier to be rid of Schiff so quickly, since once back in Dover Street, he found a formidable backlog of work awaiting him. Since he was ultimately responsible for five headline acts, most of this consisted of decisions only he could take, and the workload was formidable – personal matters, work schedules, tour schedules, and at the same time looking after budgets. He had developed quite a knack for coping with this sort of thing, even if it did mean often working sixteen hours a day. It also meant that as a driven workaholic he had little spare time to devote to his relationship with Lesley.

'Of course I loved her. We loved each other, but I just hadn't much time to play Romeo to her Juliet,' says Wilf.

One thing he did find time for was coping with the potentially immensely successful and profitable Edgar Broughton Band, which had been showing signs of going off the boil. Once again the band had been overexposed, and he decided the time had come to take them off the road. To give them time to recharge their batteries, he put them into an old manor house in about twenty acres of grounds in Barnstaple, north Devon. With the band in residence, and with an album due for EMI, Wilf got them rehearsing new material, as he had with Stray at the time of 'Mudanzas'.

In the midst of this the last thing he needed was more involvement with Irwin Schiff, but to a point this was inevitable, as the deal appeared to be proceeding. Patrick confirmed that six million dollars for Worldwide Artistes was a very tempting offer, but that he would insist that any deal included a proviso that he kept his position at the head of the company.

At the same time, Joe Pagano called him, thanking him for having dealt with Schiff and telling him that his friends in New York were becoming keener than ever on the deal.

'Great,' said Wilf.

'It might be great for you,' said Joe. 'But I've got the fat man in the room next door, and he's driving me nuts.'

'Joe, for Christ's sake don't put him on the phone to me,' said Wilf.

'No need for that, I just want you to know that we appreciate what you've done, and are going to need you here to help complete it. When will we see you?' Wilf said that hopefully there'd be a slot in which to fly over to New York in three weeks' time, and Joe said they'd talk before then and that, whenever he arrived, Charlie would be there to pick him up.

With the Edgar Broughton Band at Barnstaple preparing for their next album, Wilf had two further problems to absorb his time and energy – getting Stray out of its current record deal with Transatlantic, and Jimmy Helms away from Cube Records. He felt that after Stray's success with 'Mudanzas' and Jimmy's with 'Make Me an Offer', the magic wasn't working any longer, and it was during this frantic period that Wilf personally arranged with Walter Wyoda, the dynamic head of Pye Records, for both acts to issue their next albums under the Pye label.

This all took time and the three-week deadline for Wilf's next trip to New York was rapidly approaching, yet somehow he found time for an overnight stay in Barnstaple with the Broughtons and their band, which convinced him he'd been right to take them off the road.

'When I heard the music for their new album, I realised once more that the sound they made was phenomenal and the writing ability of the two brothers, Edgar and Steve Broughton, was as great as ever.' Knowing that the band would be on time with their new album in the recording studios, with a good chance of another big-time hit, he drove back to London, rang Joe Pagano to say that he was coming, and the following day flew to New York.

When Wilf arrived, it was already dark and he was expecting to see Charlie with the limo, but there was no sign of him. Instead, Joe's bodyguard, the saturnine Billy O'Brien, was there to meet him, along with a silent guy he had never met before called Nicky. Normally Wilf would have asked why they had come instead of Charlie, but for some reason he thought better of it.

When Billy went to fetch the car there was no sign of the stretched limo. Instead, Billy had brought his own blue Cadillac, and as Wilf climbed in the back he was looking forward to arriving soon and having a shower and a drink at the Park-Sheraton, where prompt payment of the fifteen hundred dollars had done the trick, and he had once again been treated as a valued guest when he rang from London to arrange a reservation.

But when Wilf informed Billy that he was staying at the Sheraton, Billy told him he would have to go there later. When Wilf asked what he meant by 'later', Billy didn't answer.

It was a miserable night, pitch black and raining hard, and Wilf said: 'Well, Billy, if we're going somewhere or other for a drink, I'd still rather get cleaned up first and change at the hotel.'

'We're not goin' nowhere for no drinks,' said Billy. 'We're goin' upstate and you're comin' with us.'

'Your mind can play you strange tricks after a long air journey, especially when you've had a few stiffeners on the plane, it's pissing down with rain, you're 3,000 miles away from home, and you haven't the faintest notion where the fuck you're going. All I knew for certain was that these two guys looking after me weren't choirboys. So there was nothing for it but to sit back, keep my mouth shut and accept the fact that, whatever they were up to, there was nothing I could do about it.'

We seemed to drive for hours, and I knew we'd gone way past Rockland County and had to be on the New York State throughway heading for the Catskill Mountains. I also knew that something must have happened. Soon we were in the foothills of the Catskills, driving through dead-looking little townships with the rain still pouring down. Then suddenly there was one almighty bang. At first I thought somebody was shooting at us. Then Billy started cursing and I realised we'd got a puncture. Cursing worse than ever, he got the spare wheel out of the trunk, and Nicky helped him by holding a torch as he changed the wheel. Despite the rain, Billy took his jacket off, and I noticed that he had a pistol shoved in the back of his belt.

Then we were off again, and in the end we did slow down and in the headlights I made out what looked like an abandoned church with a 'for sale' notice on the graveyard. 'Bloody hell', I thought, 'they even sell graveyards here.' And then twenty yards or so further on we took a right, and with the windscreen wipers going back and forth we started climbing up an unmade dirt track following the side of the mountain.

I don't frighten easy, but this was the one time in my life I really felt afraid, and as we left the track and went bumping off across a field I remember thinking: 'This is it ! It's not just the road that's come to an end.'

Then, on the far side of the field, Wilf saw the headlights lighting up a silver object. As they approached, 'I saw it was one of those aluminium-bodied mobile homes Americans are so keen on. Some building work was going on beside it, and at the noise of our car the door of the trailer opened, and in the headlights I could see somebody standing in the entrance.'

It was Joe Pagano, but all I could think was what the fuck was Joe doing at this time of night in the middle of these godforsaken surroundings? We pulled up by the trailer, and Joe came to meet us holding an umbrella.

'How are you, Wilf? Good flight?' says Joe and gives me a kiss. But it shows the state that I was in that, as the car reversed and backed away, I just stood there and in all seriousness said to Joe: 'Hey, listen. If you want to bump me off, OK. There's not much I can do about it anyway. But if you're also thinking of having me buried up here, please don't. There's a couple of thousand dollars in my pocket, which would be enough to send my body home to my mother on the Isle of Wight.'

When Joe burst out laughing, I soon joined in, and the two of us stood there in this field in the rain under the umbrella shaking with fucking laughter.

'Wilf,' he said. 'You know what you are? You're a sick guy. You are really sick.'

When we'd calmed down, I asked where Billy and the other guy were going.

He said that they've got some business to take care of but that we're staying here for the night. 'In the morning Billy will pick us up, but before that I want to show you the new house I'm building here. Now just sit down. I've cooked us some meatballs. We'll eat, and while we eat we'll talk. There's a lot for us to talk about.'

Along with a lot of other things, Joe was one hell of a good cook and after he'd explained that he'd bought this bit of land and was building himelf a ranch house, I asked him what he'd call it. He said: 'Daniel's Acres.'

'Why d'you want to call it that?' I said.

'It's named after my father, as is every first-born male in our family,' he replied. 'It's an Italian tradition.'

And then, as it always seemed that the conversation got around to Irwin Schiff, Joe explained that, as he put it, a friend of ours called Jimmy Nap [Napoli] wanted to meet me together with Schiff to discuss the WWA deal.

Joe was at pains to stress that although he would obviously be earning something from this deal, he, like myself, was only acting as an intermediary, and Jimmy Nap was the one primarily responsible for seeing it through. I asked him about this Jimmy Nap and how I should treat him.

'With total respect,' was the reply, 'because he's a wise guy like me. I take it even you can understand what that means.'

'Sure,' I said. 'Just as long as I know.'

Joe then said, 'D'you fancy going out for a couple of hours? There's someone on the way to pick us up?'

I tried telling him that I needed a change of clothes, which I hadn't got, and a shower, which I badly needed, but he didn't seem very worried.

'Well, the clothes I can't do anything about. And the shower I can't do much about either, as the plumbing's not been fixed. But you're very welcome to a hand-wash if you need it.'

'I'll settle for that, Joe. Thanks,' I said.

Soon a car pulled up and before saying anything else, the driver, a guy called Louis, started complaining about the state of his car after driving through what he called 'this fucking mud-patch' to fetch us.

Joe just laughed. 'Louis, stop your moaning' was all he said, and we both got in and drove away. The journey took no more than twenty minutes, and we pulled up at a roadside motel and bar of the sort that seemed to be scattered throughout the Catskills. Once inside the place, the first thing I clapped eyes on was this guy with a cigar in the corner of his mouth, five foot six or seven, and I must say somewhat overweight for someone of his build.

Joe introduces him as his good friend Anthony (Fat Tony) Salerno. And although he started talking to me, to be honest I couldn't understand a word of what he said, what with that cigar and his thick New York accent. But in spite of this, he struck me as being very pleasant. It seems he had a ranch or some place in the vicinity, and after the usual pleasantries the same thing happened as it almost always did. Joe asks me if I'd mind making myself scarce for just a while, as he had some things to discuss with Tony.

Louis asked if I played pool. I had to admit I didn't, as the game had yet to reach the UK. 'But I'm willing to give it a go,' I said. And did so, for the next hour or so. But I couldn't get the hang of that fucking game, and still can't really make head or tail of it to the present day.

In the end Joe came over to where we were playing, and mercifully informed us it was time to go. I said good night to Tony, adding that it had really been a pleasure meeting him.

'Likewise,' he replied. 'And I'm sure we'll be seeing a good deal of each other.' Over the ensuing years we certainly did.

Once back at the trailer, Joe showed me to a bunk. Having been up all night on the plane, all I wanted now was sleep, and sleep I did, right through until next morning when I woke to the smell of frying eggs and bacon, which Joe was cooking for us. And sitting there at the breakfast table was Billy O'Brien.

My first thought was that now I could get my suitcase and a change of clothing, which was still in the boot of his car, and once I was properly dressed Joe proudly showed me around his property, which in daylight I could see was vast. Behind the trailer stood a most impressive, nearly completed farmhouse, and he pointed out the full extent of the boundaries of his property. They seemed to stretch for miles, and I realised that Joe had bought himself the top of the mountain, from where the scenery was absolutely breathtaking.

Below the house there were corrals for his horses. I already knew that horses were one of the passions of Joe's life and that he loved to ride. Now he was in the process of acquiring some original American mustangs and hoped to bring them here to breed.

★

Later that morning Billy drove Joe and Wilf back to Monsey to inspect the fine new house that he had recently acquired there as well.

'What was wrong with your old one? I thought it was beautiful,' said Wilf.

'Too many memories,' said Joe and changed the subject.

Wilf says he'll never forget that new house of Joe's, if for no other reason than the fact that it had the biggest bar he'd ever seen 'in any house anywhere at any time. It covered the whole ground floor and would have beaten almost any lounge-bar in all but the grandest grand hotel in England. Little did I know that I'd spend many a night here in the years ahead, sitting there with Joe and putting the world to rights over more than a drink or two.'

After being welcomed by Theresa, who seemed much recovered after the last occasion I had seen her, the inevitable happened. In walked the fat man, Irwin Schiff, who had come to tell us that he'd arranged a meeting with Jimmy Nap for Sunday morning.

Other people soon arrived to speak to Joe, so once I'd got my luggage out of Billy's car I was actually grateful to Irwin Schiff when he offered to drive me back to Manhattan, where I could finally enjoy the shower that I'd been waiting for ever since I arrived in New York.

That night in the hotel, I made some calls to England. I spoke to Lesley and to the children, ordered something to eat from room service, and settled for a quiet night and an early bed, with a lot of sleep to catch up on.

Next morning at around seven, I was woken by the one sound I'd rather not have heard, the voice of Irwin Schiff on the telephone, making sure that I was still alive and telling me to meet him outside the hotel at 8.30 sharp.

When he arrived, he said the meeting with Jimmy Napoli had been arranged for nine o'clock in the buffet at Grand Central Station. Since it was Sunday morning, parking was no problem, and the station buffet was all but deserted. There was no sign of the man they were meeting, so they both sat down and ordered coffee, but before they could drink it someone had approached their table and remarked: 'Good morning, Irwin.'

Wilf put the newcomer in his early fifties. He was a portly man of middle height, and at first sight Wilf would have taken him for a middle-aged, middle-class Italian businessman. Everything about him seemed calculated to make him seem as unremarkable as possible, and Wilf for one would not have guessed that this was the business associate of Joe Pagano, the rich and powerful Jimmy Napoli.

No sooner had Schiff introduced him than he came straight to the point and asked Wilf how he felt about the deal with Worldwide Artistes. In reply, Wilf gave him the truth. 'Jimmy,' he said. 'I don't feel anything about it. At the end of the day the company's not mine to sell, and at this stage all I can do is act as an intermediary.'

This reply was not to Jimmy's liking.

'Irwin,' he said, 'you told me this whole deal was pretty much put to bed.'

'No, Jimmy, no,' Schiff said nervously. 'You don't get it, Jimmy. What I said was that I had a feeling it would be put to bed, real soon.'

'If that's the case then, Irwin, I'd like it understood that soon means even sooner than that.'

'Jimmy, that's what I mean too. Real soon,' said Schiff. But Wilf didn't envy Irwin Schiff the look he got from Jimmy Nap.

'Here we go again,' he thought, 'more trouble,' wishing to God that he had never mentioned Worldwide Artistes in the first place. Until now he'd not enjoyed this meeting with Jimmy Napoli, but now, when Jimmy turned his full attention on to Wilf, asking him how Patrick really felt about the money, Jimmy seemed to change and Wilf found himself starting to like him. Did Wilf think Patrick would accept six million dollars? To which Wilf said that he believed that six million was a tentative figure as far as Patrick was concerned. He might well ask for more.

'Well, money's something that we've got, if the deal's right,' said Jimmy. "The figure of six million is something we'd discuss, but what I still don't get is this guy Patrick's attitude.'

'Well,' said Wilf, 'first and foremost he's a businessman, but there's something else you need to know about him. He's built WWA up from next to nothing, and he doesn't want to sell it and then watch it going down the tubes.'

'Nor do we buy things for six million bucks to watch them go down the tubes. So what would he suggest?'

'I imagine some share in the profits and the right to stay on in a senior position in the company.'

'I'd be comfortable with that. And if the rest of the personnel remained, that would suit us too. If we bought into Worldwide Artistes, only the ownership would change.'

Although they talked on for a while, this effectively ended the discussion as Wilf was keen to return to the hotel. But he remembered he had promised Joe to call as soon as the meeting finished, to tell him how it went. But when he rang from one of the phone booths outside the station, there was a voice on the end of the phone he didn't recognise, and he had to wait a while for Joe to take the call.

When he did, Wilf felt he sounded quieter and flatter than the voice he was accustomed to.

Joe asked him briefly how his meeting went. Wilf said as well as could be expected, at which Joe asked him what he thought of Jimmy Napoli.

'I liked him,' said Wilf. He was someone who came straight to the point. 'Good,' said Joe. 'Now listen, Wilf, I'm coming straight to the point.

Last night my brother, Pat, had an accident.'

'He had what?' said Wilf, unable to believe what he was hearing. For he knew quite well that in Mafia terminology 'having an accident' meant one thing only – getting killed.

'I said he had an accident,' repeated Joe. 'At the moment we're not sure what happened, nor what's going on. But if you've finished your business, grab a cab and come as soon as possible to that place by the river where we went the last time you were here. I'll be waiting for you. Don't tell Schiff or Jimmy. Make some excuse and then make your way up here.'

Wilf did as he was told. In almost any other situation he would have enjoyed the journey as he took the scenic route, following the Hudson River upstream through New Jersey.

He had a friendly cabby, who was in the mood to talk, but Wilf asked him to forgive him and told him he was feeling a little sick.

'Just don't worry,' said the cabby. 'And let me know if you need to stop.'

'I'd rather you didn't stop. Just get me to where I have to go as soon as possible,' he said.

And all this time Wilf was thinking that what Joe had said just had to be impossible. Someone like Pat getting killed like that. There must be some mistake.

When they had driven through Westchester and had reached the point where the Tappanzee Bridge crosses the broad expanse of the Hudson River, he knew he'd reached his destination. This was a restaurant just beyond Main Street, facing out across the river. It was called the Captain's Cove.

When he arrived, there were maybe fifteen cars in the car park, and when he went up the steps to the restaurant it was Nicky who opened the door. Wilf asked after Joe. Joe's fine, he said. He's waiting for you. He'll be glad to see you.

There was a long reception area leading to a bar and restaurant with a lovely view across the river.

Joe was standing in another area with Billy O'Brien behind him.

'Joe, did I get it right?' said Wilf. 'Pat? He had an accident?'

'Yeah, last night. We're still not absolutely sure what happened.'

Just as when Jimmy died, Joe was showing no emotion, beyond saying how surprised he was that so far there had been no mention of what had happened on the news or in the papers, as Pat was not unknown.

'At the moment all of us are in the dark, so we've got some people coming, some of my guys and some of Pat's, and we're going to try and make some sense of it all.'

As he was saying this, through the windows Wilf could see that the car park was filling up with cars, and soon more than fifty men were silently gathered in the bar.

'At a time like this,' said Joe, 'there is something to be done that must be done, then I'll know that my brother can sleep peacefully. Once I know he can, then I'll be fine.'

When he said this, Joe was looking straight at Billy O'Brien.

'That right, Billy?'

'Yes, Joe,' he said.

'And then,' says Wilf, 'Joe turns to me, and looking directly in my eyes he says: "Wilf, I want to ask you something. How do you feel about my brother, Pat? I can see that you're upset, but how do you really feel about what happened to him?"'

Instead of answering the question, all Wilf said was: 'Give me a pistol, Joe, and I'll come with you.'

At this Joe tells Billy to give me a gun. It was a snub-nose pistol; I don't know the make. Billy handed it to me, and I put it in my belt. Joe said nothing and stood staring through the window, watching as more cars arrived in the car park until I could see that it was full.

Joe remained there motionless for ten or possibly fifteen minutes. Then he turned and looked at me again and said: 'Wilf, give Billy back the pistol. Don't ask any questions. Just do as I say.' So I gave the gun to Billy and he put it away.

Then Joe got hold of me and said: 'Listen, Wilf, this is what you're going to do. Billy here will take you to back to the hotel, where you'll pack, check out and then Billy will take you to the airport. From there you'll take the next flight to London.'

Then he gave me a kiss and said he'd be in touch when all of this was over. Billy and I drove back to Manhattan in total silence. At the hotel it took less than twenty minutes to pack and pay the bill. And when we reached the airport all I said to Billy was: 'Look after my friend, Joe.'

'Look after yourself,' he said. There was no difficulty in changing my ticket, and less than two hours later I was on a plane and heading back to England. Once back in London, all I wanted was the life I knew – Lesley, the children and, as always, there was the business to attend to. Life went on.

Not a day passed without me longing to ring Joe and find out what had happened, but he'd told me not to, so I didn't.

It was not until three weeks later that I heard from him. It was a short phone call. No bullshit. No emotion. How was I feeling? Fine, and how was he?

Fine, he said. But I'd never been so relieved to hear anyone's voice before.

'Listen,' he said. 'The weekend's coming up. I've nothing much to do. Any chance of you coming over?'

'Sure,' I said. 'I'll have to let you know.' But of course nothing would have stopped me going. I caught an overnight flight that Friday, and early on Saturday, when I arrived at JFK Airport, I was amazed to see who was there to meet me. Standing next to Charlie was Joe.

We greeted each other. I thanked him for coming, and when we were in the car I told him I hadn't made a hotel reservation but I was sure I could get into the Sheraton.

'Wilf, you don't need a hotel,' he said. 'You're staying at my *home*.'

'Are you sure?' I said. 'I don't want to be any trouble. You've got the whole of your family there.'

'Wilf, as far as I'm concerned, for what you were prepared to do that day at the Captain's Cove, from now on you're one of the family.'

12

'Respect Is Everything'

LIKE EVERYONE IN his line of business, Joe never drove a car himself for fear of getting framed by some overzealous cop on a minor traffic violation, but his driver Charlie made the journey up from JFK to Monsey through the morning traffic in less than an hour, and no sooner had the big black limo purred up the drive of the Pagano property than who was standing by the front door to greet them but Theresa.

The gift of Jimmy's portrait had already earned Wilf a place in Theresa's heart, but during that weekend he would learn what it meant to be part of this prosperous, united, highly traditional Italian-American family.

First, of course, he had to meet the children. Theresa told Wilf he'd be sharing a room for the weekend with their youngest son Joseph, a lively ten-year-old whose passion in life was the New York Yankees. Then he was introduced to the three Pagano daughters, Patricia, known as 'Trish', Francine, called 'Fran,' and Antoinette, who was inevitably 'Toni'.

And as with his ranch in the Catskills, Joe couldn't wait to show Wilf around his home. At the back of the house a big verandahh overlooked a two-acre garden, with flowerbeds, a swimming pool and a rolling lawn, all set against a backcloth of untouched pine woods. There was even the inevitable double garage, over which, before long, Joe would be building his separate guest apartment.

After a fairly hurried lunch, Joe had work to do, and for something to do Wilf volunteered to act as barman, as Joe was expecting visitors. Soon, the first of them arrived and for the rest of that afternoon Wilf watched and listened and poured drinks as a succession of friends, dependants and associates arrived at the house to talk to Joe Pagano. Without fail, all of them paid their respects to him in the time-honoured way of a kiss on the cheek and, but for this, had Wilf not known who he was, he might have taken Joe for a high-powered business executive or an influential political organiser, both of which, in a sense, he was.

Joe received his visitors sitting at a table by the window. As he said, he felt comfortable there. From that position he could see everyone arriving at the house, and every visitor had to cross the length of the room to reach him. As for the visitors, at first sight they appeared a fairly rough, cross section of American male society. 'There was even a black guy Joe told me was a garbage man. I told him I was glad to hear this as I used to be a garbage man myself, which made him laugh.' One thing that did strike Wilf was the preponderance of large, powerful-looking characters, and, as he says, 'I didn't need to be a genius to figure out that most of them were my kind of people'.

No sooner had one visitor departed than another soon arrived, and this never-ending stream continued well into early evening. Wilf viewed them all with growing fascination, wondering how one man like Joe could carry on so many conversations on so many different subjects without going off his head. For even when he had a quiet moment, Joe was still compulsively picking up the telephone and making yet another business call.

When work was over Wilf went upstairs to see Theresa in the kitchen and found her at the sink preparing a mountain of vegetables. He asked her why so many. She replied that they were for tomorrow's Sunday dinner and that since Joe had a habit of inviting all his friends, as well as the members of the family, she was never sure of numbers in advance, so she liked to err on the side of caution.

As far as Wilf could see, Theresa had no help in the house, and when he asked her how she coped. she said: 'Oh, Joe's sisters will turn up tomorrow morning, and we'll all do lunch together.'

Later Wilf asked Joe if he knew how many guests he'd actually invited.

'Who knows? Twenty, maybe thirty. Whoever comes just comes. That's the way we are.'

Soon it was getting dark and, supper over, the protesting children were finally packed off to bed. Then, when she'd finished in the kitchen, Theresa brought in coffee, and for the first time Wilf had a chance to see her warm relationship with Joe, as the two of them sat together on the sofa, joking and kidding one another. Soon Theresa started talking about books. She had a surprising wealth of knowledge, and before she went to bed she asked Wilf if he would do her a favour next time he was in England. Would he please bring her back any books he could find on the kings and queens of England.

'Kings and queens?'

'Yes, kings and queens. They fascinate me. I just love reading history.'

Joe had been smiling indulgently as she said this, but he now joined in the conversation.

'Listen to me,' he said. With Joe it was always 'listen to me'. 'When I go to jail, I go to jail, period. As long as I don't see Theresa, I don't get homesick, and time passes easier that way. As for Theresa, when this happens, she stays home and she reads. She's read hundreds of books while I've been away.'

Later, as he got to know her better, Wilf discovered just how well read Theresa really was, with a wide knowledge of different cultures, famous people and far-off places, all drawn from what she'd read while Joe was in prison. She said she wasn't interested in love stories. What she always wanted was to learn about places and people.

Theresa was softly spoken, like her husband, but whereas she obviously enjoyed talking, Joe made a point of keeping his opinions to himself. On the whole, when Joe Pagano talked, he'd say only what needed to be said – no more, no less. But as Wilf had seen that afternoon, he was a great listener. Listening was a skill he'd taught himself across the years, and throughout those meetings Joe would just sit there and maybe say, 'Well, yeah', or 'That's as maybe', and only if he found anything interesting would he ask a question. On the few occasions when he became really interested, it would be a string of questions.

Wilf felt that he had a sense of instant empathy with the Paganos. 'Without being sentimental, by the end of my first day with them I'd fallen in love with the whole lot of them, and it was wonderful being with this guy that I adored together with his wife and children. Not that the kids were particularly well behaved; they weren't. But I liked the way that even when they were running riot, all Joe had to say was, "Hey, hey! None of that", and they'd behave. I never heard him raise his voice to them: still less would he ever shout at them or hit them as my father always did with me.'

Next morning being Sunday, Wilf woke late, and by the time he had showered and dressed the house was already bustling with activity. There were now four women in the kitchen, and Theresa once more did the introductions, this time to Joe's three sisters, first Lena, then Mary and last of all the one the children always called Aunt Roe. 'From that day to this,' says Wilf, 'she's always been Aunt Roe to me.'

Predictably the family was fascinated by Wilf's accent, as in those days they rarely met anyone from England. 'They kept asking me to repeat myself. "Just say that again, for us," they'd say. "The way you say it is so cute."'

While Wilf was talking to Theresa and her sisters-in-law, downstairs in the bar Joe was becoming impatient. ' What are you doing up there, Wilf? Upstairs is for the women. Come down and get yourself a drink.'

Downstairs there were already several of Joe's friends, some of whom he recognised. These included Billy O'Brien and Joe Pata, but the one who attracted his attention was someone he described as 'a giant of a man.' His name, as he soon discovered, was Carmine de Noia, but he was generally known as 'Wassel'. He was over six feet two, but what really distinguished him was that he was also very funny. Apparently he knew a lot of Englishmen, many of them in the record business. Wilf also met Aunt Roe's husband, John Milano, who worked as a welder – 'a rather quiet, very charming man who seemed to be one of life's observers'.

By now three long folding tables and more than thirty chairs had been brought out from the garage, and once they were put up, they ran the whole length of the room. Then the women started laying the tables, and in a quiet corner two card tables were set up, and several guests immediately started playing cards. 'Whenever I watch people playing cards, I have a habit of always looking for the lucky guy,' says Wilf. 'And who was winning on this occasion? Wassel, closely followed by John Milano. Both of them were very good card players.'

As usual with Joe around, there was a lot of kidding, particularly over Wilf.

'Joe suddenly liked the idea that I was his barman, and this became his private joke. "This is my English barman I've brought over from some fancy place in London," he'd say. Then he'd add, "Barman, would you get us so and so, and make sure my guests always have enough to drink whatever happens."'

While this was going on, more and more people kept arriving, and soon the place was packed. As they began to take their seats it was like a big family dinner party. When the tables were laid, the women came from the kitchen with trays of food the like of which he'd never seen before. 'To me it was unbelievable.' Here were several types of home-made pasta, and polenta, plates of roast game and chicken, veal escalopes, meatballs in tomato and garlic sauce, and all sorts of delicious vegetables and different breads and fruit and cheeses.

Along with this there was also plenty to drink – good Italian red wine in two-litre bottles. Joe was proud of the food he served at his table. 'In this family, we don't fool around with supermarkets. To be worth eating, food must be genuine, which means you have to take trouble finding it. When we buy meat, we make sure we know the butcher and where his meat's come from, and how long it's been hung.'

Then an argument began, not about crime or personalities or threats of violence, but about food. Joe said that every day he had someone go down to a little bakery on the corner of 32nd Street and First Avenue. 'There's a baker there whose father came from Naples, and he bakes prosciutto bread like no one else in New York.' But several people sitting near him disagreed, and for a few minutes a furious argument ensued. For whatever else they were, all Joe Pagano's friends were true New Yorkers who would argue over almost anything – even bread.

While this was going on, Wilf was sitting on Joe's right, listening to the conversation. All that talk, not to mention the smell of so much delicious food, had made him ravenous, so that when the bowl of pasta made the rounds, he helped himself to a particularly generous plateful. By the time he'd eaten it, he realised that he was so full that he had room for almost nothing else.

Noticing what had happened, Joe turned to him and gave him some advice. ' Watch me and follow my example. If you take just small amounts of everything, you can enjoy the lot.'

'From that day on,' says Wilf, 'I learned never again to be a pig.'

Sunday dinner at the Paganos started at two o'clock, and it was not until eight that night that the last of the tables had been cleared and the guests began to drift away. Wilf noticed that as each one left he had a quiet word with Joe.

Wilf gathered that this was a regular Sunday routine and was part of the process thanks to which everyone became a part of this strongly traditional Italian–American family. At the same time, all the male guests treated Wilf with considerable respect, shaking him firmly by the hand before they left.

'"Nice to see you, Wilf. See you again soon," they said as if they really meant it, and I'm sure they did. All of them struck me as real good guys. But to be absolutely honest I'd not like any of them knocking on my front door at ten o'clock at night.'

In the end only one of Joe Pagano's friends remained – Wassel – and for a while he sat chatting on to Wilf about the old days when he and Joey were growing up together in the Italian neighbourhood in east Harlem. He said, 'What a tough little guy Joey was.' He also reminisced about Joe's father, Daniel Pagano, who arrived from Naples in the 1920s as an unemployed builder, and how he worked twelve hours a day as a bricklayer in New York, to support his growing family. One of his first jobs was every bit as dangerous and a good deal harder than anything practised by his sons – working as hod carrier, humping heavy loads of bricks on an outside hoist up to the very top of the Empire State Building during its construction. Wassel also remembered how strict he'd been with his children and how he did his best to bring them up in the old ways. All of them had a strict Catholic upbringing, and he was passionate about their schooling. One further point Wassel made about him was that he never struck his children.

According to Wassel, he hid his disapproval of what Joe and Pat were up to. Since he was their father, he always loved them, and for him what counted most of all was that the family stayed united, 'And as you've seen today, they have,' said Wassel.

When Wassel left, Wilf found himself sitting on his own with Joe.

'The children came down to say good night and gave him a hug and a kiss before going off to bed. Then Theresa came to say good night, saying she was tired and would read a little then turn in early. Was there anything we needed before she went to bed?'

'Nothing at all. See you later, sweetheart,' Joe replied.

What followed was the first of many conversations Joe and Wilf would have in that bar in the house at No. 287, Route 306. For a while they continued drinking Joe's red wine. Then Joe turned to Wilf and said, 'As you're an Englishman, I take it that you've never had the privilege of drinking Galliano?'

'What's Galliano?'

'You see that pointed bottle over there? Bring it over here with a couple of glasses. And be careful how you treat it. This is the drink of drinks. This sorts the men from the boys.'

'Joe,' said Wilf, 'I don't need any sorting out. I'm happy as I am, and I'm ready for bed.'

'Not yet, you're not. You're good for a few hours yet, and you're not leaving before you've tasted Galliano.'

'What else could I do? It was bright yellow, and I took a taste of it. God, it was so sweet! "Don't you add anything to it?" I asked.'

'If you're a girl you can dilute it with water.'

'Joe,' Wilf said, 'for just this once I'm gonna be a girl.'

'There was one thing to be said for Galliano. It certainly made time pass, and soon I was feeling so welcome and at ease that I could have gone on sitting there for ever quaffing the stuff. The last thing in the world I wanted was to bring up the subject of either Pat or Danny. But out of the blue Joe turned to me and asked, looking me straight in the eye: 'Wilf, did you ever regret anything in your life?"

'On the hop, like that, I couldn't think of anything to say, so I quickly switched the question back to him: "I don't know. But what about you, Joe? Is there anything you regret?"'

'He thought a moment, then he looked at me with those extra-ordinary dark eyes of his. "Yeah," he says. "Two things I do regret."

'Like what?'

'"Well, first I had this meat company."

'Sure, I read about it in that book.'

'"Yeah," he said. "The Murray Meat Company. I did a silly thing there. I let that company run down. If I hadn't it would have been worth millions and millions a year by now. And so would I. Yeah, I really do regret that."'

Here Joe was referring to what had happened back in 1960 when the mob took over Murray Meat, a wholesale meat company heavily involved in the mass fresh chicken market, and started selling large quantities of chickens at a discount to Peter Castellano, brother of Gambino boss Paul Castellano, at cost price. By 1961, Joe, by then a made man, had been appointed Murray's president, and the company suddenly began increasing its orders from suppliers, but holding back on paying them, and the chickens were passed on to Peter Castellano. Before the suppliers realised the truth, Joe had allegedly cashed $745,000-worth of company cheques in nine days and the company soon went bust. Later, Castellano got five years' imprisonment. In the same trial Joe got six, for, in the words of one writer, 'apparently insulting the judge's intelligence by claiming he had lost the $745,000 in floating crap games in places he could not recall, with players he could not remember'. In 1970 Joe bought his freedom, paying $75,000 to Murray's creditors in final settlement.

After dwelling on what he evidently now considered the mistakes of his youth, Joe paused.

'You said there were two things, Joe,' said Wilf. 'What was the other?'

Joe looked away, and then he said with real feeling: 'Well, there's the guy who killed my brother Pat. I had to pass on that one. But my brother's dead, and not at peace, but this guy is still walking around and breathing fresh air. That I really do regret.'

'Then he turned around and looked straight at me, and there was something in the look he gave me that made me understand he wasn't saying any more, nor could I ever ask him what had actually happened to his brother. As far as Joe and the family were concerned, the subject was closed, and Joe never referred to it again throughout the time I knew him.'

After another silence, Joe brought the subject around to Danny, and Wilf asked him how he was. 'He's doing fine,' he said. 'I speak with him every day.'

'How do you manage that?' said Wilf.

'Over here,' said Joe, 'we have phones in our prisons. You just drop a dime and make a call.'

Joe then went on to say that following Pat's death, the hardest thing he ever had to do was to break the news to Danny. He didn't want him to hear about it from anybody else, so he had to get over to the jail as quickly as possible to tell him.

'He took it real hard,' he said. 'Danny and Pat were very close. In fact, Danny loved him.'

'Then once again, Joe gave me that look of his as if to say: "Enough's enough. Now don't ask any more."

'Then we had a few more Gallianos, and before I knew it I suddenly felt violently sick. Joe,' I said, 'I must get to the bathroom.'

'So you can't take it, huh? Go upstairs. It's on the right.'

'Then, was I was sick!' When I came back I said: "I'm afraid I must call it a day, Joe. I'm off to bed. I hope you don't mind."

'"No, go along," he said, and he teased me all the way up the stairs, saying: "Go along with you, girlie. Good night, girlie! Good night."'

Next morning, in spite of everything, Wilf was up by six, but even so Joe was up before him and already sitting out on the verandah.

According to Wilf he didn't look too good, but he offered him coffee and scrambled eggs, and after they'd eaten, Joe said: 'Listen, Wilf. I've work to do today. Do you want to come along or would you rather hang around the pool with the kids?'

'I said, I'd come along. He told me he'd be ready in a few moments, so I went downstairs and waited for him in the bar. While I was waiting, the telephone rang. Theresa shouted from upstairs: "Will someone answer that phone, please?"

'I picked up the phone and said: "Joe Pagano's residence."

'A familiar voice at the other end asked: "Is that you, Wilf?"'
'"Danny, is that you? How are you?"'
'"I'm good, but I can't chat. Is my father around?"'

Before I could answer, Joe came in and took the call, knowing that Danny couldn't speak for long.

After Danny's call we left the house and Billy O'Brien drove us into Manhattan, where we spent the day in the usual round of visits to social clubs and hurried drinks and business meetings. As a treat, Joe took me for lunch at his favourite pizzeria, Patsy's Pizzeria, between 117th and 118th on 1st Street, east Harlem.

My flight was booked for early next morning, and no sooner was I back in the house than I felt I simply couldn't bear to leave them. That evening we all sat down together for our evening meal, me and Joe and Theresa and the kids, and never before in my life had I felt so much a part of any family. Paddy and Don Arden had been wonderful to me, but this was something different. For all their hospitality and kindness, I never felt entirely comfortable in their home.

Here it was different. I don't know why, but here with the Paganos I just fitted in. It was as if I had known them all my life, and I felt completely at ease among them. As I sat there with them that evening, I felt so happy that I knew for sure that this was where I belonged.

Next morning, flying back to England, Wilf sat taking stock of his life and dreading getting off the plane, for already he was feeling home-sick for his new-found family. As he says: 'During that weekend surrounded by Joe and his family I had felt at peace with myself as I never had before.' The truth was that with the Paganos he had finally discovered something he'd been seeking all his life. Even Joe's sisters, made a lasting impression on him, especially gentle 'Aunt Roe', who is still one of his closest friends and who, to this day refuses to believe that her brothers were anything but good, kind members of a loving family.

And in Joe Pagano Wilf really had discovered not just the perfect father figure – understanding, wise and, like him, remarkably successful – but also in his wife and children Wilf saw the sort of home life he had only glimpsed, just once before, in the family of that Northumbrian miner whose daughter he befriended after leaving the reformatory at Blyth. In contrast, almost everything he had achieved in London suddenly appeared distinctly pointless.

'No sooner was I back than it was straight to the office and everything started up again.' Immediately he had to start planning the forthcoming tours with the Groundhogs and several of his other groups. More urgently, it was up to him to sort out recording deals with his friend Walter Wyoda at Pye Records for both Stray and Jimmy Helms.

But while this was placing Wilf under so much pressure it was also destroying his relationship with Lesley, and not for the first time they broke up. This time the break lasted four or five weeks until it dawned on Wilf how much he missed her. When this happened, he once again pursued her and once again got her back.

Since returning from America, Wilf had been in touch with Joe Pagano every day by telephone. He had just received a call from him suggesting he came over, and since he now had a week in between recording sessions he decided on the spur of the moment to take Lesley with him to New York, 'hoping to rekindle our romance by spending some time together'.

But this wouldn't be as easy as he'd thought, for no sooner had they arrived at JFK than Charlie was there with the limo to whisk them off to upstate New York. And when they arrived at the Paganos, there was a further problem. The Paganos were strict Catholics, Joe was a good family man, and since Wilf and Lesley weren't married, in those days there could be no question of the two of them spending a night together under the Pagano roof. So it was arranged that after having supper with Joe and Theresa, Wilf and Lesley would be driven off for a two-day visit to some mutual friends out on Long Island who had already invited them to stay.

No sooner were they there than Joe was back on the phone again to Wilf telling him he had to see him.

'Of course,' said Wilf. 'Where do you suggest we meet?'

'It had better be Manhattan,' Joe replied. 'How about the Plaza?' Which is how Wilf came to pay his second visit to the famous Oak

Room – but this time Lesley went with him and, just as Wilf had been, she was greatly impressed by the VIP treatment they received. This time it was just the three of them, and halfway through the meal Joe leaned across the table and said in a low voice to Wilf: 'Wilf, is there any chance of squeezing in a day with you? There's someone I really want you to see. I'm afraid you must be on your own. No disrespect to you, Lesley, but I need a little help.'

Lesley was not a problem. She was only too glad to have some time on her own to go shopping.

The following day their friends drove them into Manhattan, where they met Joe in a bar on First Avenue. He told them it was started by a group of British Airways staff, who called the place Drake's Drum. As soon as Joe arrived, Lesley left them to go shopping on Fifth Avenue, and Wilf and Joe drove off to meet Joe's unnamed friend.

He was reticent about his friend's identity throughout the journey. All he would say was that he was a very good friend of his, that he'd told him a lot about Wilf and he was keen to meet him and say hello.

'So where are we going, then?' said Wilf.

'Brooklyn.'

'Fine. I've never really seen the place,' he said.

'Well, to be honest, a lot of Manhattan guys don't like to go to Brooklyn. It's like another world.'

Once in Brooklyn they ended up in a district called Bensonhurst, where there was yet another Italian bar-cum-restaurant. 'Inside, it was crowded with all kinds of guys, and once again there are the usual greetings. Everybody knows Joe, and I'm warmly introduced to everyone.'

Then Joe asked: 'Is that other guy here yet?'

'Yeah, Joe, he's out at the back, waiting for you.'

'Well, let him know we're here.'

Someone went off to make enquiries and soon returned with a message asking them to go through to the room at the back.

'The room at the back' turned out to be a small bar off the kitchen, with just a table and four chairs. 'Nothing elaborate,' says Wilf. 'I'd have thought it was probably the room where the waiters ate their food.'

Just before they entered the back room, Joe warned Wilf to watch his language and to 'be a little respectful, as my friend is getting on a little bit in years.'

'All right. No problem,' I say, and we go in and we're greeted by this guy who gets up. He's slightly bent and looked . . . well, to me he looked about a hundred, but I suppose he was probably in his late seventies. He wore a brown fedora and was in a very, very dapper suit, silk shirt and expensive-looking tie. He wore beautiful matching cufflinks and had this big pinkie ring on his finger, set with diamonds. But what really struck me were his enormous glasses with the thickest lenses I had ever seen on anybody.

Joey and the old man greet each other very warmly, and he says: 'Funzi, I'd like you to meet my friend Wilf from England.' He had a very gruff voice. He was a very thin-faced guy, but it was those glasses that got me. Those glasses of his were awesome.

He said: 'I'm very pleased to meet you. Sit down. D'you want something to eat? Coffee or something, or would you like something to drink? Knowing you, Joey, you'll want a drink.'

So we all ordered drinks, and the guy with the glasses says: 'Joey's told me a lot about you. He tells me, like, you're one of us. You're a good guy.'

I said: 'Well, I take that as a compliment, Funzi.'

And he says: 'I'm always interested to meet people Joey has a good word for.' Then he asks me about England. He asks me if I've ever been pinched. I suppose I looked puzzled, as I wasn't used to that word 'pinched 'in those days, and he explained he meant had I ever been arrested.

At that he had my full attention.

'Yeah,' I said. 'Many times.'

He said: 'You ever do any time in jail?'

I said: 'Well I done it in what you would call reform school,' and I said they keep trying to put me in jail, I said, but I just keep beating the cases.

With that he says: 'Huh. What for? What were you? A robber, a bank robber? What did you do?'

I said: 'You know, I gotta bad temper. Nine times out of ten what I've been pinched for, as you call it, is for fighting.'

'That's a fool's game. A mug's game. You don't earn no money by hitting anybody, you know'. And he sort of just dug away at me, until by the end Joey and he were just talking about this and him talking about that.

And then he says: 'Well, Wilf, it's been a pleasure meeting you. I hope that some day we'll meet again.' And then once again it was the usual scenario. 'Could you give me a few minutes with Joey on his own. That be OK with you?'

I said: 'Yeah. And it's been a pleasure meeting you, Funzi.'

He says: 'I don't really like the name Funzi. My real name's Alfonse, but Funzi I suppose I can live with it with you.'

I said: 'OK, Mr Alfonse.'

He says: 'Oh no, no, no, no. Not Mr Alfonse. It's Alfonse Tieri. But the nickname is Funzi.'

I didn't know what to say. He got me flustered. Was I saying the right thing or the wrong thing? Then we shake hands and he says: 'Hey, give me a kiss.'

I gave him a kiss on the cheek.

And that was that. I went outside and waited in the bar until Joe was ready to leave.

It was not until much later that Wilf realised the importance of this meeting and who Funzi really was. Since his death in 1981, much has been written about this enigmatic figure, including the assertion that he was the mythical 'boss of bosses' of organised crime in America. What is undisputed is that, even before the demise of the unlamented Carlo Gambino in 1976, Tieri was the nearest thing to a 'boss' the Genovese crime family ever admitted to. Even a prominent federal agent described him as 'a real moneymaker and one of the classiest gangsters in the New York City area'. He was also a multi-millionaire and by the time Wilf met him, those under him were prospering as well. During these last years of his life, he has been described as 'the wisest of the godfathers', and it was said to be largely thanks to him that in this period 'many mobsters defected from other crime families to join his ranks'.

Undoubtedly, Joe Pagano also benefited from his friendship and it is interesting that another of Joe's friends, Irwin Schiff's financial backer, Jimmy 'Nap' Napoli, was by now a close associate of Funzi's.

Joe's private conversation with Funzi must have been important, for he kept Wilf waiting longer than usual. While he was waiting, no one had much time for Wilf, but as soon as Joe appeared, the people in the bar were 'all over him'.

Once we're back in the car and driving back to Drake's Drum, I said to Joey: 'Well, that's a scary guy.'

He says: 'Well, yeah, I suppose you could call him that.'

I said: 'What does he do?'

'What does he do? Who are you? An inquisitor for the FBI or something? What does he do? Mind your business.'

I say: 'OK, Joe. Fine.'

The traffic going from Brooklyn is horrendous. The journey could take you forty or forty-five minutes. For a while we sat in silence, then after a while Joey says to me: 'Listen. You want to do something for my friend?'

I said: 'What d'you mean?'

He said: 'I'm just asking you. You don't ask me, "What do I mean?" Do you want to do something for my friend?'

I said: 'Well, I'll do something for you.' And he says: 'Well, that's good enough. So listen, Wilf. My friend, as you must have figured out by now, is a wise guy. And certain things are causing him a lot of grief. Tell me, have you ever heard of the RICO Act?'

The Racketeer-Influenced and Corrupt Organisation Act of 1970 was in theory a serious threat to organised crime in America. Under its provisions, 'top Mafiosi can get long prison terms if the government can prove their connection with criminal enterprise'. In practice, it was erratic and hard to enforce, but it was taken as a very dangerous potential menace by men like Funzi and Joe Pagano, as is shown by the story Joe now related.

He told me about a good friend of his who happened to be in a restaurant where another friend of his walked in. Neither realised they were under observation by the FBI, and the man who was sitting simply waved to his friend and said hello and the next thing he knew he was being arrested under this RICO Act, on the supposition that they were members of a criminal organisation. 'And you know what, Wilf?' he said. 'That guy who waved at his friend and said hello is now sitting in jail for twenty years.'

I say to Joe: 'Christ, that's rough.' And Joe says: 'It's more than rough.' And he goes on to explain that there were certain things that they could no longer do, because of the Act. He says: 'Telephones are dangerous for us. And just being seen with people can be dangerous for us too. Funzi has friends all over America. And when you get someone like Funzi, who needs to do something really important, or contact someone in a hurry, no matter who he sends, if it's anyone who's known to be associated with us, we can be in heap big trouble.

'But you're an Englishman,' he said. 'And at some time or other I might want you to deliver a letter to some other guy for us. You won't need to know what's in the letter, but I'll tell you this. It won't be anything that'll get you into any trouble. It won't be nothing to do with drugs, nothing to do with this, that or the other. You know what I mean? So how d'you feel about that, Wilf?'

I said: 'Well, Joe, I'll be happy to become your personal postman. You just tell me when and where, and if there's anything that I can do to help in any way I can, I will.'

Nothing happened immediately. My trip was coming to an end and the night before I left I had dinner once again with Joe at the Oak Room, where I renewed my acquaintanceship with a friend of Pat Pagano's called Louis Pacella, but he also had another name, Louis Domes. I said to Joe how many names has this guy got? 'Just the two,' he said. 'But over here we got various names. We call them nicknames.'

Later on that evening, after Louis had left, we were joined

again by Joe Pata, Billy O'Brien and a guy that's my friend to this present day called Bobby Bumps.

Now by this stage Lesley is looking a bit peeved, and I knew that she was thinking, here we are again and we're still sitting here and she was starting to get a little rattled and Joe started to break her chops a bit and he said: 'Are you getting bored with just hanging out with the boys?' She says: 'Well, Joe, I like to be doing something.'

So he says: 'We are doing something. We're going into the Persian Room of the hotel. There's a friend of mine here, an artiste, a girl singer and I'd like you to listen. It'll be a real good show.' That made Lesley put a smile on her face. At least we'll be doing something other than just hanging around a bar or a restaurant.

The Persian Room was where they held the cabaret. It was very plush and intimate. I can't remember who the singer was, but she was very well known on the club circuit. Halfway through her third number, someone whispered something to her and all of a sudden she stops the band and gazes around the room and says: 'Are you here, Joey? Joey, are you here?'

And with this she comes down from the stage and walks around the tables looking for Joe. Then she sees us sitting there, rushes up to Joe, flings her arms around him and gives him the biggest kiss you've ever seen.

'Why didn't you tell me you were coming?' she said.

'I came to hear you sing,' he said, smiling. 'Get back up on the stage and sing for me.'

She did as she was told, picked up the microphone and turned to the band and said: 'We're changing the running order now.' She announced: 'I'd like to sing this song, a very special song, that was written for this guy. He's over there now. My dear friend, Mr Joe Pagano.' She burst into the song. It was called 'To the Guy Who Made It Happen'.

I remember saying: 'Well, I never heard this song before.' But it was a great song. It was telling the story of this wonderful guy. At the end of the show there was this great ovation and before we left Joey took Lesley and myself backstage to say hello and on the way through, everyone was lined up there, just to see Joe Pagano. That's how special he was.

I remember afterwards we had a last drink with Joe before being driven back to Long Island and I said to Joe: 'Everyone respects you, but can you explain one thing to me? This kissing on the cheek, I think it's tremendous, but we don't do that in England.'

He says: 'Listen. With us it's a sign of respect. And you gotta learn that in our life, respect is everything.'

We were back with our friends on Long Island with only two days left before going back to England and Lesley wanted some time for us on our own together. 'All we've been doing is meeting guys in bars, or you talking on the phone.' Believe me, Lesley was a very forthright lady with her views when it came to what she wanted and didn't want. Whether it fell in with my way of life or not, she always seemed to have her way.

I say, fine, no problem at all. And then, lo and behold, we get another call from Joe Pagano. He needs to see me urgently. Now this kicks off a row between me and Lesley, which was very embarrassing, as the people we were staying with were in the room at the time and it really got a little heated, to say the least. Lesley wouldn't back down from anything. If she's got to say it, she's got to say it.

So I simply said, I gotta go.

She said, why have you got to go?

Because I have to. I just know I gotta go and that's all there is to it.

I say, do you want to come or do you want to stay here? She says, oh no, you're not getting away from me. I'm coming with you. Joe had also told me on the phone that he was sending someone I'd met a couple of times called Charlie the Greek to collect us.

When Charlie turned up, Lesley was still giving me a bit of earache, but, you know, no holds barred and the row continued through the beginning of the journey and as we were getting on to the Long Island Expressway Charlie apologised for interrupting but asked if we would mind if we stopped off to meet a friend of his, as there was something personal he had to attend to. Fine, I said, and we stopped at an Italian restaurant near the airport called Don Pepe's.

Charlie said the food there was good. That pleased Lesley because, slim as she is, she does like her food. So as we hadn't eaten, I said, that sounds good, but I hope it won't make us late for Joe. No, we'll have plenty of time, said Charlie.

By then it was early evening and the place was swarming with people.

Charlie orders drinks and we were shown to a table and he looks for his friends. When he sees them he takes Lesley and me over to be introduced. There were six or seven men around the table, and when they saw Lesley all of them got up. There was an Angie something and a Tony something, but there was one guy who stood out from them all, a really good-looking guy with dark wavy hair. The guys were wearing all kinds of polyester suits, which was the fashion in those days, but this guy was different. He was entirely in black. He said: 'I'm John Gotti.' He looks at Lesley straight away and says: 'Can I kiss you? I've never kissed an English girl before.'

So he kissed Lesley on the cheek and in spite of looking rather embarrassed she was still so annoyed with me that she played up to his attention. We talked of this and that for a while and then Charlie said that we were on our way to see Joe Pagano.

He says: 'Joe Pagano? That's a real somebody. Say a big hello to him from me. Not that he really knows me, but just say John Gotti says hello.'

He had this great grin. A really warm guy. We didn't get anything to eat. The order was cancelled and we sat there and we drank and we listened to all his funny stories. I'd been seeing a lot of guys like him here lately, but John really struck me as someone special.

We'd have sat there drinking if Lesley hadn't noticed the time and said we ought to go. As we left, Gotti gave me a number of a bar in Queens. 'If ever you want me, you can usually contact me there most days. The next time you're in, give us a call and leave a message and we can meet – that is, if I'm not in jail.'

Wilf didn't know it then, but John 'the Dapper Don' Gotti was currently running the rackets at Kennedy airport and facing a seven-year sentence for the killing of mobster James McBratney, who had had the temerity to kidnap Carlo Gambino's nephew, Manny. On his release he would become a Gambino capo and undisputed 'boss' of the family until his death in 2002.

As well as being a ruthless killer, the elegant John Gotti had a lively taste in women, as Wilf now discovered to his cost.

'I don't know many English guys,' he said. 'In fact, you're about the first one I've ever met, and what I'm going to say now is not meant with any disrespect to you.' And he turns to Lesley with a real twinkle in his eye. 'Lesley, do you ever fancy fooling around with an American?'

Everyone laughed except Lesley, who adopted a face of thoroughly English disdain. 'That was very cheeky of him,' she said afterwards to Wilf. 'But I must admit he had a way with him – and he was a very good-looking man.'

Once we're back in Rockland County, we meet Joe at the Westgate Motor Lodge and to my utter dismay and despair who's with him but the fat man Irwin Schiff. For he means more trouble as far as Lesley is concerned.

I might be sick of him but Lesley detests him and her hackles are really up.

'You mean we've come all this way for that?'

I say, Now please don't start, Lesley. Anyhow, Joe comes and greets her. She's great with Joe. She loved him. But when Schiff comes over she just turned her back and made an excuse she was off to the ladies' room.

Joe says to Schiff: 'Did you insult her or something early on? What's up with her, Wilf?'

I say: 'I'll be honest. She don't like you, Irwin, simple as that.'

'Oh well,' was all he said. That was his attitude. Oh well.

So I say to Joe: 'What's up?'

He says: 'Well, Irwin says he's close to putting all the money together, but he wants to know if everything's still going to be OK.'

So I gave him the same reply I gave him most of the time. This is between him and Patrick. Joe says: 'NO, no, no. I'm asking you.'

And I say: 'I just don't know.'

'Well, when you get back, will you check it for me?' And I say: 'Of course.'

And Joe dismisses Schiff, saying: 'Irwin, I'll say your goodbyes to her, which I think she will take better from me than from you.'

Joe also asked Wilf to look after Billy O'Brien, whom he was sending to London in a couple of days' time. 'It'll do you no harm. It'll be two or three days. Three at the most. He'll be with a guy called Tony G. Will you look after them? Sort out a car and driver for them and see to their needs.'

'I say it will be my pleasure, Joe. Whatever I can do will be done.'

Wilf would do anything for Joe Pagano.

'Anything I can do to help?' Wilf asked. 'No, no. It's only personal stuff.'

After that, Joe was charm itself, especially to Lesley. He even brought a smile back to her face and when they'd said goodbye Charlie was waiting with the limo to drive them back to Long Island. The following day they flew back to England.

Back in London, most of Wilf's time was taken up with studio rehearsals for Stray's new album, but he still found time to keep his promise to Joe and to look after Billy O'Brien and his friend. Since they were friends of Joe's, he put them up at his favourite London Hotel, the Mayfair, at his expense. He saw this as a small repayment for all the hospitality Joe had given him. Throughout his time with Joe in America, he had never once been allowed to pick up a bill.

He got Louis, who took care of his transportation department for the bands, to drive them around. 'But what they did or didn't do was not my business and I didn't ask.' All in all it wasn't a bad visit, but once again it left Lesley feeling uneasy.

By now Joe was ringing Wilf every day and said that he was very grateful for the way Wilf had looked after his friends. Then he asked Wilf again if he could return to America as soon as possible as there was something he needed him to do. It would take only a couple of days of his time. But he would really appreciate it if he would.

As it happened Wilf had some business with a New York agency, as he was trying to get several of his acts signed up with an American outfit for future tours. This meant he could combine his work with whatever Joe wanted him to do.

As soon as he arrived it was once again straight to Joe and he tells Wilf that his friend, Funzi Tieri, wants a letter delivered for him.

I say: 'Well where? I'm on a tight schedule, Joe.'

'Oh, it's only to Philadelphia. I'll supply you with a car. It's about an hour and a half's drive from New York.' He gave me specific instructions where I was to go. As usual it was yet another Italian bar-cum-restaurant on 8th and Lombard in south Philadelphia. He said that when you go in you won't have to introduce yourself. Someone will introduce himself to you. We've obviously explained you're English. Those tattoos on your hands speak volumes. All I really want you to do is deliver this envelope. It's from my friend to another dear friend of his. Will that be OK with you?

I say: 'No problem at all.'

'When can you leave?'

'Tomorrow morning.'

Next morning a smart two-door car called a Cutlass was waiting for him outside the hotel and he drove himself straight to Philadelphia, where he had no trouble finding the restaurant. He went in, ordered himself a drink at the bar and in no time at all was approached by a tall, well-dressed man who came over and asked him if he was the Englishman from New York.

I said: 'Yes, I am,'

He says: 'A friend of mine would like to meet you.'

I followed the guy to the far right-hand corner of the bar, where a middle-aged man was sitting in one of the private booths. He, too, wore big thick glasses, but these were tortoiseshell.

'How are you? Have you got something for me?' he asked.

'Sure.'

'Just put it on the table,' which I did. And while he was making polite conversation, he picked the envelope up, opened it and while he was still talking about nothing really, he read it. He then got a light, held it over the ashtray and set fire to it. To make sure that there was no trace of it at all, he then rubs the ashes in his hands, then wipes them clean with a napkin so that there's nothing left.

He then started chatting and said he'd been to London a couple of times and said: 'You heard of the Krays?'

I said: 'Yeah, of course I have. In fact, the twins' eldest brother Charlie is living with me in one of my houses in Kent.'

'When you see them, give them all my best, especially Charlie. I'm sorry to hear they got what they got, but I did try and tell them, but when you start putting your own hands in you're going to come out covered with shit. That's a rough sentence they got, but that's life, I suppose. Anyway, say hello to them from me.'

'Of course I will. But who shall I say says hello?'

He says: 'My name's Angelo Bruno.'

With that we said goodbye and I drove back to New York.

My head started spinning when it came to me who Angelo Bruno really was. Jesus Christ. It didn't bother me or worry me, but I was just absolutely fascinated.

For the truth was that in this period, without realising it, Wilf was moving in elevated crime circles. Until a shotgun blast almost blew his head off in 1980, Angelo Bruno, known as 'the Gentle Don', was the highly successful leader of the entire Philadelphia crime family. At the time of his death there was widespread speculation in the press that Alfonse Tieri was probably behind his killing.

'When I got back to Joe's and told him everything had gone according to plan, he thanked me and I said: "You could have told me it was Angelo Bruno."'

He says: "Well, I didn't know it was Angelo Bruno."

'I says: "What?"'

'He repeated: "I didn't know it was Angelo Bruno. I knew exactly what you knew. No more, no less. Do you know who Angelo Bruno is?"'

'I said: "Yes, Joe. I've read that he's the boss of Philadelphia."'

'"Uh-uh," he says. "I've never met the guy myself. Now do yourself a favour and forget you ever met him. End of conversation."'

Wilf's meeting with Charlie Kray occurred earlier that summer thanks to his old friend and host at the Speakeasy Club, Laurie O'Leary. Laurie had grown up with the Krays in London's East End, and one day over lunch mentioned to Wilf that Charlie, who had just come out of prison, was having a problem finding somewhere to live for himself and his girlfriend, Diane Buffini and her two young children.

No landlord seemed very keen to let a place to anyone called Kray, and feeling sorry for him, Wilf immediately said that they could use his house in Minnis Bay. Charlie was grateful and, after meeting the following afternoon for tea at the Dorchester, he took Wilf up on his generous offer.

'Lesley had more or less given up on me by now, so when I told her about Charlie and asked her if she'd mind, she said: "You'll do what you want to do anyway, so why ask me?"'

Over the next two and a half years, I did numerous courier jobs for Joe, travelling all over America. I did Chicago a couple of times. Buffalo, New Orleans, Los Angeles, Las Vegas, to name but a few. But I never met anyone face to face again, after that first meeting with Angelo Bruno. What happened was I'd usually take an internal flight from La Guardia Airport and when I reached my destination, someone would be waiting for me in the arrivals lounge with a board with my name on it. Just PINE. Nothing else. I'd go with him to a coffee bar in the airport where I would slip him the envelope and he would leave with it. And that was it. Then I'd be on the next fucking flight back to New York.

I had learned by then to ask no questions, but I assumed that the envelopes were destined for someone just as important as Angelo Bruno in those areas.

I was delighted to help out Charlie Kray and Diane, but what I hadn't bargained for was that he would talk about me to his brothers when he visited them in prison and soon I was receiving messages and letters from Ronnie in particular asking me to do this and that for him. To be quite honest, this was the last thing I needed, as I had too much on my plate already.

Soon Charlie asked me who Joe Pagano was. When I told him, he couldn't believe it. I wish he hadn't said anything about it to Ron, but he did. One day Charlie asked me if I'd mind doing the twins and him a favour. They'd had a book written about them called *The Profession of Violence*, and according to Charlie the twins were desperate to have it made into a film. 'As you've a lot of contacts in the show business world in America, maybe they could help and would be interested in having the film made.'

'Of course, I will,' I said. I kept my word and in November 1974 I took several copies of the book with me. As I was without Lesley this time, I was able to stay with Joe, and over dinner he asked me about Charlie. 'He sounds a nice guy, but that brother of his, Ronnie. He's a faggot, isn't he?'

I said: 'Well, he's a homosexual.'

And he said: 'Well, we've got a few of them in this outfit here. It ain't too bad a thing, although I wouldn't particularly want them around me. But you know, horses for courses!'

While we were on the subject of the Krays, I told him about the book and what the Kray twins wanted. Straight away he asked me: 'What can we make out of it?' I said: 'I don't know, Joe, but if a film deal can be fixed up you can take your commission.'

He says: 'Well, we'd want more than a commission. Anyway, are you sold on this?'

I replied: 'Well, this book has made the Kray twins as famous in our country as Al Capone is in yours.'

'Yes,' he said. 'We know about them here too. So let me read the book.'

He went off to bed early, taking the book with him. Next morning he said to Wilf: 'Listen, that's some book. Those twins are nuts. I just can't believe how nutty those guys are. But it's one hell of a story. As far as the film's concerned, I'll see what I can do.'

Later he told Wilf that he had some 'friends' in Brooklyn who supposedly knew Dino de Laurentiis socially and he arranged a high-powered meeting. The upshot was, as so often happens in the film world, that nothing came of the project.

Back in London, Stray's new album, *Stand Up and Be Counted*, was ready. Everyone was happy with the end result and this left Wilf a little more time to think about his private life. With so much happening in his life, this hadn't given his relationship with Lesley much chance. 'Me being me, I had abused the hell out of this relationship, so I now figured it was time for me to make a commitment to her.' She had always been the girl he was in love with and he knew that if he didn't he might lose her.

He proposed to her in their favourite restaurant in the Mayfair Hotel and her reply was, as usual, a look, and all she said was: 'Why not?' 'I don't think I actually got a "yes".'

Wilf noticed that, sitting at the next table, was Bernard Levin and he suddenly felt so happy that he turned to him and said: 'I've just proposed to her and she's accepted.' He raised his glass and just said: 'Good luck! Good luck to both of you!'

Next day they went looking for an engagement ring and found a good jeweller a friend had recommended in Hatton Garden. Lesley designed her own ring, chose the stones and they had it made up. All this happened shortly before Christmas and the engaged couple returned as usual to the Isle of Wight. Wilf found it difficult to go to his ex-wife's house to see the children, as she now had a new partner. He delivered all their Christmas presents to the house, but he had to wait until Boxing Day to see them. He and Lesley spent Christmas that year with her parents. It was then, over a meal, that Wilf took the ring out and said: 'Is it all right if I marry your daughter?

'Basically I think the reply was: "If you must." That seemed to be their attitude, but her father was a really good guy and I like to think that he was pleased.'

13

A Mini-Appalachin

THE ATTEMPT TO stage a nationwide conference of leading underworld figures at the mansion of racketeer Joseph Barbara at Appalachin in upstate New York in 1957 is often seen as one of the greatest disasters in the history of the US Mafia. Thanks possibly to chance, or more probably to a tip-off, the house was raided by the New York State Police, and many of the leading gangsters in America took flight or were ignominiously arrested. More seriously, the subsequent publicity convinced the public and the FBI of the existence of organised crime throughout America and marks the beginning of serious attempts to deal with it.

One inevitable result of Wilf's friendship with Joe Pagano was to involve him in a punishing double life. His heart may have been with that family in the house in Rockland County, but his work was firmly anchored back in London. And his work in the music business was showing no sign of easing up. On the contrary, the spring of 1974 saw him working almost around the clock with his different groups.

The more established he became in the music business, the more dedicated he seemed to be, emphasising in its way the opposing sides of his divided nature. The man in the recording studio was not Wilf Pine the gangster but a driven perfectionist deeply involved with all his acts. And although he was working simultaneously with important groups like Stray and the Edgar Broughton Band, it was Jimmy Helms who was now taking up most of his time and energy as he continued to promote his TV career, his European tours and spent seven months in and out of the studios preparing every number that would make up the album entitled, *The Songs I Sing*, which appeared to great acclaim that autumn. With other demands being made on him simultaneously by his new friends in New York, it was not surprising that the pressure of this double life began to show.

That spring there was one small mercy – the Schiff business was concluded. Although Wilf had been convinced that the deal for WWA would never happen, Schiff and his financial backers were still as keen as ever for the deal if it was possible. Then in March, to Wilf's relief, something made it crystal clear that it was not. As the result of happenings with no bearing on this story, the Hemdale group were no longer quoted on the Stock Exchange.

For Wilf, with Hemdale ceasing to be quoted or the stock exchange, it inevitably meant a final split with Patrick. He emphasises that this was completely amicable, but it meant that he had to move his operations from Dover Street to an office in his big rented house in Ewell. As the lease had expired on the flat in Wimbledon, he and Lesley had been living there and using the house at Minnis Bay on the few occasions they found time to enjoy it.

But to his great relief, the break with Hemdale also meant the end of his involvement with the fat man. For once Schiff knew that Hemdale had ceased being a quoted company, so his interest regarding Worldwide Artistes also ceased. Wilf says that 'this convinces me that the WWA bid had always been a ploy to get into Hemdale, since Hemdale had the prestige of being a publicly quoted company with a gambling licence for various bookmaking operations they conducted'. More to the point, the purchase of WWA would have given the powerful elements who backed him an easy entry into the lucrative world of London gambling, with even a chance of running of their own casino.

Soon after, Wilf and Lesley were back in Los Angeles negotiating a deal with the president of MCA, the appropriately named Artie Mogul, on behalf of White Heat, who had just finished their debut album and who were ready and enthusiastic to be touring America.

This gave him and Lesley a chance to make the most of one of their favourite haunts in America, the Beverly Hills Hotel. And while they were there they spent much of the week just relaxing. For Wilf insists that, since their engagement, he was now seriously trying to make the relationship with Lesley work.

But for them the course of true love seemed incapable of running smoothly. No sooner were they back in England than an unexpected bombshell burst on them both. At first Wilf had not been particularly troubled by the news that his ex-wife Jill was in love with someone else even when he learned that the man she was in love with was a policeman. But what did shake him was a call he now received from a worried neighbour on the Isle of Wight.

'Is there some problem?' Wilf asked him.

'Yes, Wilf, a big one. Your ex-wife's left the kids here, given me the keys to the house, told me to call you and gone.'

'What d'you mean, gone?'

'She's pushed off. Vanished. Says she can't cope with the children any more and has apparently moved in with that fellow of hers. We've got the children here.'

On hearing this, says Wilf, I was in a state of near panic. I told Lesley what had happened and to her credit she said: 'Let's get down there right away.''

Which we did and found the kids naturally upset. We went to my old house, opened it up and tried ringing around to find out where Jill had gone, but no one seemed to know a thing. Obviously, I called the cop station, but who among that lot would want to talk to me? Especially over something involving one of their own? Here I must be honest. I was a little abusive on the phone, me being me.

We moved into the house and tried to give the kids as much normality as possible, but it was hard, particularly for Lesley, who was a stranger to them. And bear in mind that my youngest child was barely four and a half years old.

I saw a lawyer. As chance would have it he was the same lawyer who'd got me my divorce and I thought he might not be sure whether to believe me when I told him Jill had simply disappeared and left the children. He was probably thinking. I had something to do with her leaving. Certainly at first he was very sceptical, but in the end he saw I couldn't just hang around like this with nothing settled and my children's future hanging in the balance. So he arranged for us to go as soon as possible before a judge in chambers. For as things stood, as I'd given Jill full custody of the children at the time of the divorce, this meant that even now I had no legal right to be with them without her permission.

It turned out that by then Jill had prepared a statement for the judge herself which, and I can't say any more, was not exactly flattering. It would be obvious to anybody that, on paper at least, I did not look like the model father. People thought I was a villain and, to boot, I spent my life travelling the world. That said, I had a brilliant mother and she was happy to look after the children.

The judge really surprised me. He turned out to be a thoroughly nice guy and was really good with the children. He asked how they felt about things and what they did at school. Then he told them to be good and not to worry and wished us well. The end result was that he awarded me custody of the children and appointed my mother as their guardian. Access to Jill was only to be through the court. All I can say is that, in my circumstances, it was a truly astonishing result. The children have never forgiven their mother for deserting them.

Wilf could only stay long enough on the island to make sure the children were properly settled in with his mother. 'To my relief, they seemed a good deal happier than I'd expected.' But he had to hurry to New York to complete negotiations with an agency to represent Stray during their forthcoming American tour. While there he naturally met Joe and Theresa, 'who were most concerned about what had happened with my children. To be honest, Joe was not amused. He thought a woman's place was with her children and Teresa felt this even more. She said: "I know we're three thousand miles away, but if there's anything we can do to help just let us know."

'At least this meant that at last I was able to pour out my heart to these two people who had become not only my very dearest friends but also the only people in the world who really understood me.'

While Wilf was in New York, he fitted in several trips as Joe Pagano's postman, one of which involved flying to Chicago and another to Atlanta, Georgia. Then, just before he left for England, Joe asked if he could do him one further favour.

'There's a cousin of mine with a problem over a stolen picture. [Here, Joe was using the word 'cousin' to denote a member of another family.] Some time back he sent it to a London dealer to sell on for him. I've no idea who the guy is, but my cousin no longer trusts him and is getting worried that he won't get paid. When you're back in London, could you pay him a visit and suggest it's time the money was forthcoming?'

When Wilf said this would be no problem, Joe was grateful and suggested that the two of them should meet his 'cousin', attached to the Bonnanos, called Gus Minicci.

'Gus turned out to be a good guy and we had a very friendly meeting. He gave me the dealer's address and London telephone number and told me everything he knew about him. From New York it took me only a few calls to check him out. God knows why somebody like Gus ever got himself involved with a guy like that. My sources told me that he wasn't even a bent art dealer. He was a common fraudster and not a very good one. The picture had been stolen in America and this character in London thought that because Gus was in New York he could simply stiff him. That was stupid.'

Wilf had a few more days' hard work with the New York agency, checking through the complicated details inevitably involved in Stray's forthcoming tour. Then he and Lesley flew back to London where the usual pile of work awaited him. Before becoming totally immersed in it, he thought he'd better get the job for Gus Minicci off his plate as soon as possible. Also, to be honest, he says he was rather looking forward to it.

The address that Gus had given him turned out to be a smart flat in Knightsbridge. With so much anger in his heart and pressure in his life, Wilf thought that a good row might be what he needed to relieve the tension. So when he rang the bell, he was more than ready for the prospect of a little trouble.

The man who answered the door was bigger than Wilf had expected. From long experience he sized him up as 'a wannabe gangster'. And from the start the man made the big mistake of acting tough and pretending that he hadn't got the money. This was all Wilf needed. He pushed his way in. He closed the door behind him. 'Then I kicked him all around that fucking room.' Soon he had beaten out of him not only an admission that he had the money but where he kept it – in a small safe beneath the floorboards. Wilf made him open it. It contained two hundred thousand pounds in five- and ten-pound notes.

Wilf insists that he made a point of counting out exactly fifty thousand pounds and left the rest of the money in the safe.

'I could have taken the lot, of course, but that wasn't what it was about. I'd got what I came for and I also felt a great deal better. The truth was that with all the stress I'd been having, my head was starting to go and I was looking for somebody to hurt. The guy just got unlucky.'

Later, when he was back in New York, Wilf told Joe Pagano what had happened. He was not best pleased. Not for the first time he told Wilf that he must learn to control his temper. 'Either you should have kept your hands in your pockets or got someone else to do it for you. If you go on like this that temper of yours will get you into serious trouble. With this business you could have got yourself arrested and ended up in jail for ten years. What good would that have done those poor kids of yours?'

'But he was asking for it, Joe,' said Wilf. 'The guy was spoiling for a fight. He was crazy.'

'OK, then. Listen to me, Wilf,' said Joe. 'Over here we've got a cure for crazy people. It's called a little hole in the head, just above the eyes and all the crazy blood in the brain runs out. And the funny thing is it always seems to work. But it's a cure we use only when it's absolutely necessary. '

Joe's displeasure with Wilf soon vanished, when he took him to pay Gus Minicci his fifty thousand pounds. 'Of course Gus loved me for what I'd done and tried to give me ten thousand pounds for my trouble. But I told him: "Thanks, Gus, but this one's down to friendship."'

Afterwards, Joe told Wilf that he'd been silly to refuse the money. 'We could have both had ourselves a good drink with it.'

But Wilf was smart enough to know that once word got around among Joe's 'cousins', news of his behaviour could only help his reputation. 'In fact, it stood me in good stead in the years to come,' he says. 'Over the next decade I was often asked to sort out similar small problems for Joe's friends. From then on I became their man in London.'

Barely a week after returning from New York, Wilf had another call from Joe Pagano, but this time he wasn't calling from his home. He was on the line from Hackensack County Jail in New Jersey.

He couldn't say much because he was on the prison phone, but he said he was hoping for bail in the next few days. 'So could you shift your backside over here as fast as possible? I need to talk to you.'

The idea of Joe in jail seemed so improbable that Wilf started laughing.

'What are you laughing at?'

'Joey,' he said. 'Just pull the other one.'

'Wilf, it's not a joke. I'm telling you I'm in the fucking jail and I need to see you. Are you deaf or something?' And he banged the phone down.

As Joe rarely swore, Wilf realised then that he was being serious.

'Guess what?' he said to Lesley. 'Joe's in jail.'

'Whatever for?'

'I've no idea. He was calling from prison, so he couldn't talk for long, but he needs me over there. I've got to go.'

As Wilf expected, this produced a major uproar. Lesley was very fond of Joe Pagano, but she was starting to resent Wilf's total devotion to him.

'He calls. You jump. What about me? I'm here as well,' she said.

'Listen,' said Wilf. 'He needs me, so I have to go. Accept it. That's the way it is. End of argument.'

But it wasn't quite the end of the argument and while Wilf booked the tickets, as the price of making up Lesley insisted on going too. Also, as Wilf admits, there was another reason why he wanted to get over to New York. His problems in England were getting on top of him and he was desperate for any excuse to get away.

Two days later they landed at Kennedy Airport. They were met by

Charlie with the limo and the news that Joe was out on bail. He was waiting for them at that very moment at the place where Wilf and Lesley always stayed – the Westgate Motor Lodge. So instead of finding Joe in prison, as Wilf had been expecting, they arrived at the motel to find him sitting calmly by the pool. While Lesley was unpacking, he told Wilf what had happened.

'Do you remember a meeting I had at Captain's Cove with a guy from the construction business?'

'No, I can't offhand.'

'Remember that tall ugly guy with the loud check jacket who was there?' said Joe.

'Can't say I do,' said Wilf.

'Then you'll have to take my word for it, but it turns out he was a cop. And he was wired. We're all on tape and fifteen of us ended up being pinched – thanks to Billy O'Brien.'

It was clear that Joe was angry with his bodyguard.

'Wilf, I know the guy's become a friend of yours,' he said, 'but the way I ended up in jail was really down to him.'

It seemed that Billy was the first to be arrested. This happened not in New York State but in New Jersey, which placed him under New Jersey jurisdiction. Somehow the New Jersey cops persuaded Billy to call Joe in New York, asking him as a favour to come in and talk to them on his behalf. Although Joe knew that this would mean leaving the jurisdiction of New York State, where he was safe, for that of New Jersey, where he wasn't, Billy gave him his personal assurance that there would be no problem. Because it was Billy speaking, Joe believed him. But as soon as Joe turned up, even with his lawyer present, he was immediately arrested.

'So your friend Billy O' Brien had better not come near me. In the long run it'll all blow over, but for a while I'll be putting him out to grass.'

When Wilf enquired where Billy was, Joe said he was still in Hackensack Penitentiary.

'But why, when the rest of you are out on bail?'

'Because I want him to stay there for a while to cool his heels. It'll do him good. So I've instructed the bondsmen not to put up bail for him until I tell them to.'

With that Joe started laughing and Wilf knew he wasn't taking what had happened too seriously, particularly when he went on to say that Billy's wife, Pat O'Brien, wanted a word with him and gave him her number.

Wilf promised to ring her, but asked Joe why it had been so urgent for him and Lesley to rush over to New York when Joe and the others all got bail so quickly.

Joe explained that when he telephoned, the judge was still refusing to grant him bail under any circumstances. 'He didn't want our bondsman, he didn't want our property, he didn't even want cash. He would only accept bail from people with property who weren't connected with us in any way. So I thought of you, an Englishman with straight friends living in a house on Long Island. If things got desperate, we might have tried them. In the end we didn't need to. Besides,' he added, giving Wilf a grin, 'I was missing you. I wanted to see you.'

When Joe had gone, Wilf rang Billy O'Brien's wife Pat to enquire how she was. She was living in a place called Valhalla in West Chester. He and Lesley both liked her, and the first thing she did was invite them over that very evening for dinner. She was so insistent that, tired as they were after their journey, they agreed. Luckily, Valhalla was no great distance from the Westgate Motor Lodge and when they arrived they found Pat in the kitchen busily preparing an enormous meal.

'That looks an awful lot for the three of us,' said Lesley.

'Oh, but we're having it with Billy and his friends,' she said.

'But Billy's in Hackensack Jail,' said Wilf.

'That's right. That's where we're having dinner. Billy's arranged it all. He knows you're coming and he'll be thrilled to see you both.'

Throughout the evening that ensued, Wilf often felt the need to pinch himself to prove that what was happening was real. How different it would have been in England. He remembered the time when he and Don Arden visited Dave and Jinxie when they were awaiting trial in Brixton Prison. Like Billy, they had been refused bail but, although they were in prison only on remand, visiting times were limited, their movements were restricted and there was no question of bringing them in so much as a bar of chocolate. But now he was watching Pat packing what looked like a small banquet she had been preparing for the evening, including glasses, plates and cutlery for what looked like a dozen guests.

What happened next was an extraordinary demonstration of the way the influence of people like Joe Pagano extended even into prison. Hackensack County Jail was a formidable building, looking like an old stone fortress, but when they drove up to the side gate it couldn't have been more welcoming. They were evidently expected.

Pat told Wilf to ring the bell and one of the guards appeared. Following her instructions, Wilf said to him: 'I think we're expected. I'm Wilf from England.'

'Good to see you, Wilf. We've been waiting for you,' said the guard. 'Do you need a hand in with the food? There's someone here to help you.' At this a second guard appeared with a tray and started loading the dishes and several bottles of wine which Pat had also brought. Wilf and the others followed them into the prison, where they were shown to the kitchen area set with chairs and an enormous table. While they were being introduced to several more guards, the cutlery was set out on the table and the food placed in the prison ovens to keep warm.

'Then this guy came down and introduced himself to us as the captain of the guard. He seemed to know who I was and said: "Well, Wilf, d'you want to come up with me and fetch him?"'

'Fetch who?'

'Who do you think? Billy, of course.'

'He led me to a lift and we stepped out on the main cell block landing. There were several prisoners around and who was standing chatting away quite casually to one of the guards but Billy O'Brien. He waved me over and seemed really glad to see me. When we'd shaken hands and he'd introduced me to the guard, he said: "Hey, Wilf, there's someone here who wants to meet you. I've been telling him about you."'

He took him over to a man who was on crutches and introduced him to Wilf as Butch Micelli.

'At that moment my toes nearly curled up,' says Wilf. 'Butch Micelli . . . I'd heard a lot about him in the past as a reputed hit man for the Gambinos, who was also a capo. He was credited by the authorities with forty-nine hits that they knew about, but they'd never been able to convict him.'

When Wilf talked to him with Billy, Billy said: 'You'll have to excuse Butch, Wilf. He's got the disease.'

'He didn't enlarge on it and I didn't like to ask in front of him. He seemed very cheerful and I said I hope your health improves. He said that he was sure it would and he'd soon be out and looked forward to having a drink with me when he was.'

Afterwards Wilf asked Billy what sort of disease Butch suffered from. He said he was supposed to have multiple sclerosis, but actually there was nothing much wrong with him and he later heard that as soon as he was out, Butch Micelli was miraculously cured.

With that Wilf, Billy and the captain took the lift down to the kitchen where Lesley and Pat were waiting. Billy greeted Lesley very warmly but was more offhand with his wife. All he seemed interested in was whether she'd brought various things he'd asked her for. Then everyone sat down for dinner, except that by now the party had grown in numbers. As well as Lesley, Pat, Wilf and Billy, there were also about eight guards and the captain, all sitting there, enjoying Pat's cooking, drinking her wine and everyone seemed to be thoroughly enjoying themselves. 'The captain sat at one end of the table and Billy at the other, looking as if he owned the place, while the guards told us funny stories. After an hour or so, Billy says: "Would you all mind excusing me."

'"Why do you want to be excused?" said Pat, looking thoroughly put out.

'"If you don't mind, there's something I want to see on television."

'Lesley looked at me, I looked at Lesley. "Are we dreaming this?" she asked.

'Then the captain said to Billy: "Hang on, Billy. Just a minute. Let me finish what I'm eating and I'll take you up."

'With that Billy thanked me and Lesley for coming. Said he'd see us soon and off he went, with his wife just sitting there fuming. Then we made our excuses and to tell the truth I was glad to be outside that fucking jail. But if there was one thing I'd learned that evening, it was the sort of power these guys could offer to those who were connected with them, as Billy was. And Billy wasn't even a made guy. He was just a bodyguard.'

Back in England, apart from being with the children, much of Wilf's attention was needed over Jimmy Helms, whose success was steadily increasing. An old friend of Wilf's, John King, who once managed the Schulman brothers, was now a drama producer with BBC TV and Wilf persuaded him to cast Jimmy in the lead role in a popular new production, *Demolition Man*. Simultaneously Wilf received a call from a friend of his, the hit songwriter, Don Black, who wanted Jimmy to audition for a song that he had co-written with Elmer Bernstein. This was to be the theme song for the new Roger Moore film, *Gold*. Jimmy passed the audition with flying colours and Wilf was able to conclude the deal there and then. With this, in addition to Jimmy's current album and his tours, his success seemed guaranteed and Wilf could congratulate himself on the extraordinary career of the singer he had spotted when he was once playing the flugelhorn.

By that August life was looking up. On the home front, Millie was more than coping with the children. After the upsets they had been through, they seemed very happy and Wilf and Lesley felt that they themselves deserved a little holiday. The only trouble was that Wilf insisted on having it in his favourite city of New York. Lesley was not so keen. As she said: 'Every time we get there there's an endless round of late nights and conversation with your friends and we never seem to be alone.'

Wilf promised faithfully that this time would be different and they would do the things that she enjoyed. This time they were doing New York in style. He booked a suite at the Plaza, and he told Joe Pagano that after they arrived they'd need their first few days there on their own. Joe said he fully understood.

The visit turned out even better than expected and on the third day, Wilf rang Joe Pagano. As always, he was delighted to hear him and invited Wilf and Lesley up for what he promised would be a quiet dinner with Theresa and himself. To start with Lesley was wary of accepting, knowing what could happen once Wilf was once again involved with Joe. But she was also genuinely fond of both Joe and Theresa and in fact the evening turned out to be one of the happiest she and Wilf had spent together in America.

It was Theresa who noticed Lesley's engagement ring, which was how she and Joe discovered that they were engaged. Warm congratulations followed, then Joe turned to Wilf. 'Are you two really going to get married?'

'Of course we are,' said Wilf, although in fact neither he nor Lesley had decided when or where or even how.

'Get married here,' said Joe.

'Well, Joe. We haven't got as far as thinking about that yet.'

'Listen,' said Joe. 'I want to be your best man and you know that they won't let me into England. So it's got to be America.'

Wilf looked at Lesley and Lesley looked at Wilf. Until that moment they had barely discussed the actual marriage. But once again Lesley used the two words she'd spoken when Wilf had proposed to her.

'Why not?'

This was all Joe needed, and suddenly he was at his most decisive.

'Listen. I'll take care of everything – guest lists, wedding dress, wedding breakfast, accommodation. I'll even fly Lesley's parents in and Wilf's children. We'll take care of everything. This is going to be my treat for you.'

Naturally Wilf thanked him, but the truth was that, hardly surprisingly, the happy pair were slightly overwhelmed. And by now Joe was more excited by the whole idea of the marriage than they were.

'When would you like to get married?' he asked.

'What about October?' said Wilf without really thinking.

'October will be good, 'said Joe. 'This will take quite a while to arrange. Give us an actual date in October that suits you.'

'Fine,' said Wilf. 'We'll pick a date out of the hat and let you know.'

Then he turned to Lesley. 'Well, it looks as if we're getting married,' he said. At which she gave him what he calls, 'that kind of look,' and said: 'It looks like it.' And that was that.

Back in England there was now more than ever to arrange, but soon everyone involved accepted the fact that Wilf and Lesley would soon be getting married and that the wedding would take place somewhere in America.

In the midst of all the preparations, Wilf suddenly found himself performing an unusual service for his forthcoming best man. Out of interest, he and Lesley had gone to see a new film Joe had told them about called *The Luciano Testament*, which was having an advance screening at a cinema near Victoria Station. The film drew heavily on material in *The Valachi Papers*, including the account of the killing of the informer Eugene Giannini and Wilf remarked to Lesley on the fact that the young actor even looked like Joe.

That same evening Wilf phoned Joe about it, who said that while he obviously wasn't happy to see himself and his brother depicted on the screen, there was nothing he could do about it. Wilf replied that he was fairly sure that under English law the film could be deemed defamatory and it might be possible to injunct it. Which is what happened. Wilf contacted his old legal standby, David Offenbach, in his Bond Street offices and as a result of his submission, on behalf of the Pagano children, the film was hurriedly withdrawn from the cinema at Victoria and was never shown in Britain.

Early that October Wilf and Lesley were back again in New York preparing for the wedding, and Wilf remembers Charlie driving him and Lesley with Joe in the back of the limo taking them to the place where they would marry.

Joe was in a particularly good mood that afternoon. Not only were the plans for the marriage going forward, but he was obviously pleased with Wilf for getting *The Luciano Testament* banned in Britain. He turned to Lesley and asked her what she thought of the film.

'Terrible,' she said.

There was a moment's silence and Wilf has never forgotten the look on Lesley's face as Joe turned to her and said: 'But it was true.'

By then the car was following a winding road up the side of a mountain. They passed a little town called Suffern. Then when the car could go no further they had reached their destination. Perched on the mountaintop, set in the autumnal woodland, it could have been Shangri-La. It was called the Motel on the Mountain.

As they prepared for the wedding, Lesley and Wilf realised that, including Lesley's parents, Wilf's children and their friends from Long Island, their guest list totalled no more than fourteen. It was then that Lesley happened to remark to Joe that she hadn't a matron of honour. 'As you're being Wilf's best man, do you think that I could ask Theresa?'

Joe looked doubtful. 'Ever since that business with our son Jimmy, my wife has not attended any wedding.'

'Oh, sorry, Joe,' she said. 'I should have understood.'

'No,' he said. 'I'm flattered that you think that much of Theresa. And I'm sure she thinks the same. So ask her, but I'm sure she won't accept.'

That evening at dinner, Lesley broached the subject only to get the answer she expected. Theresa was clearly touched to be asked, but said she thought it would be too much for her. But later that evening she changed her mind.

'Lesley,'she said quite suddenly, 'I've had second thoughts. I'd be honoured to be your matron of honour.'

A week before the wedding, Charlie drove Wilf and Lesley to the airport to pick up the three children and Lesley's parents who had flown in from London. Everyone was excited, as it was their first visit to America. But what no one seemed to realise was that Wilf was already getting cold feet about the marriage. He felt that as it was, he and Lesley had worked out a good relationship, however volatile at times it may have been. He really loved her, but he felt he wasn't ready for a full scale marriage and all that it entailed. Also, the children seemed understandably worried about what was happening. Eight-year-old Scott in particular made it clear that he wasn't happy about it.

Soon Wilf realised the truth. He didn't want to go ahead with the wedding.

Wilf had wanted his friend Charlie Kray to come over for the ceremony, but although the Home Office said that they had no objection to his going to America, the American consulate refused him a visa. So his girlfriend, Diane Buffini, came instead. On the very night before the wedding, Wilf had a quiet moment with her and told her of his doubts.

'I love Lesley,' he said, 'but I just can't marry her. I know I can't marry her. I can't make the commitment.'

a mini-appalachin

She said: 'Well, that's it, then. But you'd better do something about it pretty quick.'

He said he must talk to Joe and she said that she'd go with him.

By now it was almost midnight, but they called a cab and went to the Pagano house. Joe answered the door in his dressing gown and was clearly shocked to see them.

'Joe, I've got to talk to you,' Wilf said.

'What, at this time of night? You're getting married in the morning.'

'That's what I want to talk to you about.'

'Well, you'd better come on in.'

They went downstairs to the bar, where they were joined by Theresa.

'Joe, I can't go through with this,' he said.

The look on his face! 'You can't what?'

'I'm telling you I can't go through with it.''

'Excuse me,' said Joe. 'Is this meant to be a joke?'

There was a pause then as Theresa turned to Diane and offered to take her upstairs for a cup of coffee, leaving the men to sort this out among themselves. But Diane stayed where she was, and Theresa left the room with what Wilf felt was a look of absolute disgust at his behaviour.

Then Joe looked at Wilf and said in a tone of voice he'd never heard him use before: 'Listen, there's something you don't understand. You are getting married – tomorrow. You are getting married, my friend.'

'If it's the money, Joe, I'll take care of all the expenses.'

'You don't understand. There are so many people you've got coming.'

'But I've only got about fourteen people coming,' Wilf replied.

He said: 'And I've got nearly two hundred coming. They're all good friends of mine and they've all got permission to come to your wedding. Some of them are on bail. Some are on probation. Whatever. They're coming here from all over the States. So you, my friend, are getting married tomorrow.'

'Joe,' said Wilf.

'Don't Joe me. You listen to me. I don't care if after the wedding you want to kill Lesley and bury her in the woods somewhere. I'll be

263

with you then, buddy. I'll come and help you dig the hole and we'll bury her together. But until that point comes around, *you* are getting married.'

'Then I knew,' says Wilf. 'I apologised to Joe. "You're right. You can always get out of a marriage."'

'That's it, my friend,' he said. 'Come on, Wilf, let's have a drink.'

They had a few drinks, then Joe called a cab to take them back to the hotel.

On the morning of the wedding everyone met at the Motel on the Mountain. Theresa came with her youngest daughter Trish, who was the same age as Wilf's Sammi. They were both going to be bridesmaids. And while Theresa helped Lesley to get dressed and do her hair, Wilf had a chat with Joe in the next room.

He thanked Wilf for agreeing to go ahead with the marriage – and added that he was probably doing Wilf a favour, as he was sure everything would work out in the end.

When everyone was ready, they made their way down to a vast function room, which to Wilf's amazement was absolutely packed. All the guests were elegantly dressed and immaculately turned out, but the men were more interested in talking to each other than with the women who accompanied them. As soon as Wilf went in with Joe, the person to come over to greet him was his old friend Vincent Mauro. Soon he was being introduced to their friends from all over America.

After about forty minutes, Joe pulled Wilf to one side and said: 'Come on, now, we're going to do it.'

Now they met up with Lesley and her parents and the children and they all went down some steps to a courtyard with a beautiful fountain playing in the middle. Then someone called Judge Ryan introduced himself and told them he'd be conducting the service. He asked if there was anything they specially wanted. Lesley, of course, remarked that she didn't know what happened in America, but in England the service often included a promise to obey. She said: 'I hate obeying anybody and least of all Wilf!'

It was a short and simple ceremony, with only Joe, Theresa and Lesley's mother and father present. Joe was the best man, Theresa the matron of honour and Trish and Sammi were the bridesmaids. Upstairs, in a small room, they signed the register and paused for photographs before entering the main reception room, where everyone was sitting at long tables. When they took their places at the top table, everyone applauded and the band struck up 'Here Comes the Bride'. In front of Wilf and Lesley stood a four-tier Italian wedding cake.

Neither Wilf nor Lesley ate a thing, but everyone else appeared to be enjoying the feast. At the end of the meal the wedding photographer came in and started trying to take photographs of the guests. But he didn't get very far. Within seconds several burly men had stopped him.

'No photos,' they shouted.

'But I'm the wedding photographer.'

'I said no photos,' one of them repeated.

At this the photographer went over to Joe Pagano, asking what to do.

He explained that they had already had the wedding pictures when they signed the register and that no one in that room wanted to be in a photo.

Wilf says that it was then he knew one hundred per cent that this was not his wedding party. This was Joe Pagano's.

In spite of everything Wilf felt very proud of Lesley and said she looked absolutely stunning. And the time had come to cut the cake. The caterers had given strict instructions over exactly where they should cut the cake. They did as they were told and within seconds they were covered, like everyone else around them, in cream cake. At the same time, four large white doves flew out. It was all quite unbelievable.

Then the band struck up. Joe said: 'Dance. You two have got to take the floor. The married couple, they go first. You get out there and dance.'

Wilf took Lesley by the hand and led her to the dance floor as in a trance. Then everyone joined in. It turned out that Jimmy Helms had been specially flown in. When the dancing stopped, he took the microphone and sang a song. It was the Stevie Wonder number 'All in Love Is fair'.

Wilf said that, to be honest, in the circumstances he found this 'just a little cheeky'. But he went down great.

For Wilf the rest of the evening passed talking to all Joe's friends from across America. By now he knew exactly who they were. But he was so involved with them that he hardly caught a glimpse of Lesley. So even on his wedding night Wilf spent most of his time drinking with Joe Pagano and his friends while Lesley had finally had enough and retired early with the children.

Wilf said: 'This is not for nothing, Joe, is it? This is one of those meets, isn't it?'

Joe replied that he was sorry he couldn't be honest with him. 'But,' he said, 'you got the wedding. And it cost you nothing.'

With that Vinnie Mauro said he was leaving and Wilf walked out to the door with him and Joe. As Wilf said good night to Vincent, he turned to him and said: 'Listen, Wilf. Don't forget that Joe Pagano's stood for you as your best man today. In our world, the guy who stands beside you on your wedding day becomes your goomba, or your godfather. Listen to what he tells you. Do as you're told and go and speak to him if you're in trouble.'

By now Joe was also ready to leave. 'It's been a long day, Wilf,' he said as he bade him good night.

But for Wilf the night still wasn't over. Back in the reception room he saw an old friend, Teddy Randazo and his wife, Vikki, who had been invited to the wedding by Wilf. They were both highly successful songwriters who had written countless songs for Frank Sinatra. He sat with them for a while, then Teddy said: 'Why not come back to my house? We'll play some music.'

'So my wedding night was spent with the Randazos, playing songs and listening to tunes. My wife Lesley, bless her, had my young daughter Sammi curled up in bed asleep with her.

'I returned early next morning and sat on the bed and talked to Lesley. "Listen," I began, but she cut me short. "I know," she said. "The same goes for me."'

She said at one stage her parents had told her: 'Look, we can call the whole thing off and take a plane home.'

So Wilf said: 'You had the same thoughts as me?'

She said: 'Yes. And basically that sums up our relationship.'

'On the flight back to England we argued a little over nothing and I knew, effectively then, that our marriage was over.'

14

A Debt Repaid

IN 1976 THE world of Wilf Pine fell apart, and afterwards he blamed himself for what had happened. 'It's always easy to blame others, but in the end everything was down to me and to my inability to come to terms with certain situations' is how he puts it.

The first of these 'situations' was his hurried marriage, which he says he simply couldn't come to terms with. It was all very well for Joe Pagano to tell him that if it didn't work out he could always get a divorce. The reality was not so simple. For a control freak like him, he felt trapped in something that he felt he should never have allowed to happen. But worse than this was the realisation that his children were uneasy about the marriage, too and that during the time they spent with him in America they had not been happy either.

This hadn't particularly affected five-year-old Sammi, who was still too young to understand. And whatever his true feelings, Sean, his elder son, was saved by his ability to always make the best of things. But Scott, the middle one of the three, had been badly hit by the way their mother had rejected them, 'and with Scott', says Wilf, 'there was deep resentment from the start'. Wilf is keen to emphasise that this had nothing at all to do with Lesley. 'For Scott, his father's marriage was too sudden and at that time he would have been much the same with anyone I married.'

But for Wilf, concern about his marriage triggered off a personal crisis which rapidly affected his whole existence. He'd always been a heavy drinker, but now he found himself having to rely on drink to get through the day. 'I was in danger of turning from a drinker into a drunk and that's a bad thing. Soon, my head was going in so many directions that I'd become a control freak who couldn't even control his own mind.'

His deep dissatisfaction with himself spread to the music business. 'I really detested it and I realised that I was living in a fool's paradise. In the music world, however successful you are and whatever you've accomplished, you need to be a special kind of person to extract much satisfaction out of it. In the first place, you have to believe in it and I didn't. It also helps if you're a dreamer and I wasn't. Arse-licking always helps, and I wasn't much good at that either. To be quite honest, I can't recall a single occasion when I looked forward to going to a party just because I'd been invited by a particular celebrity. As far as I remember, I always had the same reaction – that I'd much rather have been down at my local, having a pint with *my* friends.'

He always emphasises that, in spite of his success, he never felt part of the music world. 'When I left Don Arden, I had thought that I was leaving it behind me and getting back to the world I knew and where I belonged. But then Patrick Meehan came along and talked me back into it again. This, of course, was over Sabbath and since then I'd been getting more and more involved.'

With my limited education and in spite of being the sort of person I was, I like to think that I did a good job while I was there. Most managers can stand the pressure of two or maybe three years working under the strain that it involves and I was now entering my sixth year of top-flight management.

I did my best, because I always like to win. But now I was asking myself what the fuck do you think you're doing? And that made life difficult. It was as if I had two people inside me, one of them always reminding me about my loyalties to my different acts and the other always telling me that, because of this, I was neglecting my children.

To make things worse, I was in this marriage that I didn't want – any more than Lesley did. But at least she was there with me, thank God – but God knows why, as I abused the hell out of her. And then there were the kids. They hadn't asked to be born, but I had got them involved in a marriage which wasn't going to last.

I'd got my mother there, who was still looking after the children, but her health was getting worse. She suffered from bronchitis and emphysema. And recently she'd been saying that she didn't know how much longer she could continue.

So I talked things over with Lesley and gave her all the assurances in the world that I would try to straighten up. Needless to say, I never did. But even so she said that she'd stay on, to look after the children; and to her credit, she did try. But there was only so much she could do, when I wasn't sticking to my side of the bargain. Like I said, I was drinking more heavily than ever and I was still away a lot of the time. Then, when I was back, the arguments got worse. This wasn't good for us and it was worse for the children. Coping with them was far too much for her, although I knew that I was lucky to have her there at all.

In the end I did what Lesley and her parents and a lot of friends thought unforgivable. I simply walked away from the music business. I'd had enough. I spoke to all the members of my acts and explained to them what I was doing and suggested where they could go for management. I just walked away. None of them left me and nobody ever stole my acts.

Looking back objectively, people might say, what a crazy thing to do! The guy's gone nuts! But the truth was I really had gone nuts. In my confusion I asked myself, what the hell do I do now? And what I did was go on drinking – not at home, not drop-down drunk and not in front of the kids. But I drank an awful lot.

None of this helped what was left of my relationship with Lesley. She'd go. I'd somehow get her back Then I'd start again and she'd go again. By June of that year we'd reached rock bottom. She gave me one last ultimatum: 'Six weeks to straighten up, or I'm leaving you for good.'

Needless to say, I couldn't straighten up and this time she didn't come back.

During that summer, despite the drinking and the dramas, life carried on. As Wilf continued closing down his acts, his trips to America became if anything more frequent than before, which meant that he saw as much of the Pagano family as ever. And by now the Paganos had become his own great standby.

More than once Wilf blamed Joe squarely for the way in which he had made him go through with the marriage, to which Joe always answered that he had warned him that if it didn't work he could always get himself a divorce. But Joe clearly felt at least partially responsible for what had happened. He and Theresa offered Wilf emotional support, but they also angrily chastised him for what they called his outright bad behaviour, as they might have done with one of their own.

Theresa was particularly concerned over what was happening with the children. She had a great sense of family herself and during the days before the wedding she had become involved with all Wilf's children. So in this period she often sat him down and gave him serious advice about the children and their needs.

'Wilf, you must put some substance back into these children's lives,' she told him. 'They've already been through the trauma of their mother leaving them and then suddenly a new mother comes along that they don't know and you, by your own admission, are not helping but antagonising the situation. How do you think they feel? They're bound to be frightened. They've got to be confused. If you were mine, Wilf Pine, I don't know what I wouldn't do to you.'

'The Paganos didn't give me an easy ride,' says Wilf, 'but in spite of that I always felt that they were the one family that really cared.

'In New York by now I was finally closing down all my business affairs. There were certain people who still had to be seen and told what was going on, and there were certain people, like accountants, who needed to be paid. There were agents' fees that were outstanding. When everything was settled, it was like running down everything, my life included and I wanted all of it behind me.'

'While I was in New York, Joe told me that my friend Arnold Squitieri had been moved to Sing Sing, to complete the sentence resulting from the manslaughter charge which was hanging over him at the time of Danny's party before he, too, went off to jail.'

Joe said: 'Well, if you get your feet wet, you just have to wait for them to get dry.' By which he meant that once you were in jail like Arnold, everything depended on the authorities and there was nothing for it except patience.

On the occasions when he'd seen him, Wilf had taken a shine to Arnold and told Joe he'd like to visit him in prison. Joe had passed this message on and Arnold had replied that he'd like to see him in return. Joe made enquiries and found out that the fact that Wilf was an Englishman was no problem. All he needed was his passport with him and he arranged for Billy O'Brien to drive him out to what Wilf calls 'that foreboding fortress on the Hudson River, Sing Sing, with its daunting towers and the horrible green walls around it. And when I arrived there it was just like the movies. Jesus Christ, I said to myself, some pisshole!'

Inside it was even worse and the visiting room had a balcony surrounding it with armed guards continually walking around.

'Then Arnold came in, looking fantastic – smart T-shirt, neatly ironed jeans and brand-new sneakers. It was as if he was out to show that nothing in this place could ever get him down and he was even funnier and better company than I remembered. More to the point, he made me put my own troubles in perspective. If he could smile, so could I, and thanks to him I came away from Sing Sing, of all places, feeling happier than I had for months.'

Wilf had been back in England no more than a week or so when he got a late-night call from Joe Pagano. As they'd got into the habit of speaking most days on the telephone, there was nothing strange in that. What was unusual was that this time he sounded agitated, which was something that he rarely did.

'Do you know a guy called Don Arden? He claims to be something in the music business.'

The sheer dislike with which he said this alerted Wilf immediately.

'Yes,' he said warily, uncertain as to what was coming. 'I was once his bodyguard.'

'A bodyguard? For him? I tell you, Wilf, he's going to need a bodyguard.'

'Easy, Joe. What's up?' said Wilf.

'I'll tell you what's up. This guy has disrespected me. And nobody, but nobody, disrespects me.'

When Wilf tried to say that there was surely some mistake, Joe ignored him.

'What are you doing at this moment?' he asked.

'Not much.'

'That's good. There'll be a ticket for you at the airport and I'll call you back within the hour with details of your flight. I need you here. This guy is in New York at the moment and I intend to see him.'

To be honest, Wilf was puzzled to hear Joe Pagano getting so worked up about his sometime mentor, Don Arden. But he knew better than to argue and after throwing the usual necessary possessions into his overnight bag, he was on an early-morning flight from Heathrow to New York.

Throughout the flight he was trying to work out how on earth Don of all people could have so enraged the normally controlled Joe Pagano. For by now Don had reached the very topmost branches of the music business.

But there was no mistaking the seriousness of the occasion. No sooner had Wilf's plane touched down at Kennedy Airport but who was there to meet him but Charlie with the gleaming black Pagano limo. By now it was more than twenty-four hours since he and Joe had spoken on the phone – time enough, he thought, for Joe's anger to have quietly subsided. But it hadn't.

Joe was waiting outside the house to meet him and after enquiring about the flight, his first question was: 'Now about this Don Arden. What d'you know about him?'

Wilf told him all he knew and made it sound as agreeable as possible, but it made no difference.

'Whatever you say, this guy's a no-good, disrespectful bastard as far as I'm concerned.'

At which Wilf did his best to calm him down and he asked him what he'd done to offend him.

So he tells me a story. His old friend, Wassel, who's in and out of the music business, is close to a powerful figure in the music industry. It seemed that Don had had dealings with this man, but then something had gone wrong between them, and Don being Don, said 'Hell, I'm outta here.'

Now, as I'm given to understand, Joe has a connection here, so he sends Wassel around to talk to Don at the Academy of Music on 40th Street. Wassel sees Don there and as tactfully as he can tries to make it clear to him that he's not doing the right thing. He points out that, in all sincerity, he should honour his agreement with Wassel's friend.

With that, and knowing Don as I do, I can picture exactly what happened, Don starts saying: 'You can't tell me what I should or should not be doing,' and he starts trying to get a little cute with Wassel. Now Wassel isn't someone you want to get cute with. He's a big man, which Don Arden isn't and in no uncertain terms he informs him that he ain't going nowhere if he talks like that and does he realise that the people he's with ain't going to stand for it? At this, Don asks him who he's with and he replies Joe Pagano.

Don, being totally ignorant about any major figures in Joe's field replies: 'From what I hear, Joey Pagano is a faggot!'

Now that is some fucking insult. But that's Don and he just doesn't know what he's saying. Then, to make it worse, he goes on: 'You should know I'm something of a tough guy. Back in England I'm known as the Al Capone of pop, so I don't give a flying fuck for any Joe Paganos or whatever. As far as I'm concerned he's a faggot.'

Wassel says: 'If that's your last word on the subject, I'll pass your message on.'

Now as anybody who knows Joe will tell you, you don't go calling Joe Pagano a faggot. But I did my best to calm Joe down by explaining that Don used to be an act and he still has a way of acting up. 'He used to be quite tough and in his own way he's still a little tough guy. He didn't know who you were, Joe. He wouldn't have realised what an insult it was. And knowing Don, he was just playing a part as he often does, thinking he's back in the theatre. So you shouldn't read any more into it than that.'

Joe replied: 'But I have. I have read more into it than that.

Now this guy is in New York. He's staying at the Essex House Hotel, and you're booked into the Sheraton. As soon as you're back there, I want you to get in touch with him and arrange a meeting for tomorrow morning.'

By now Joe simply wasn't interested in any excuses over Don Arden and he gave me no time to argue.

'You know where he's staying. Get him on the phone. And I want to see you, with him, tomorrow morning at Café Seventy-Two on the corner of 77th and Second Avenue. You know the place. It belongs to my first cousin. I want him there tomorrow and I want him there without fail by eleven o'clock.'

I said: 'Well, that's a busy time in that café, Joe.'

'Just do as I ask,' he said and with that I was dismissed. Charlie was still waiting for me with the car outside and for me it was back to the Sheraton.

When Wilf was in his room he knew that there was nothing for it but to ring Don Arden.

'Look, Don,' he said. 'I'm here in New York and I need to see you.'

He said: 'David's with me.'

Wilf replied: 'That's great, but I do need to see you.' So Don said: 'Well that's great. Let's all meet for dinner.'

Wilf says that, in the circumstances, the least Don could do was buy him dinner and he suggested his favourite haunt – the Oak Room at the Plaza, where they duly met and had a great evening. Rather than put a blight on the proceedings, Wilf waited until the meal was almost over before bringing up the subject of Joe Pagano. And Don was completely unrepentant.

'Joe Pagano? I don't give a fuck about Joe Pagano,' was his attitude. 'I said, "Don, don't be a tough guy. I've been around this guy now three years. He was the best man at my wedding. Believe me, Don. Don't play the tough guy with Joe Pagano."'

'So it's serious.'

'Don, it really is that serious.'

By now Don's son David had got the message and was doing his best to make his father see reason. 'Look, Dad, I think you ought to listen to what Wilf's saying.'

To which Don replied: 'Well, I just won't see him.'

To which Wilf told him that if he didn't see Joe Pagano, Joe would end up seeing him and that would not be funny either. So he ended by suggesting that the best solution was that they should do as Joe wanted and all turn up at Café Seventy-Two at eleven the next morning. Then he promised he would do his best to sort out the situation.

Next morning, just before eleven, Wilf, Don and David met outside the café and Wilf was surprised by what he saw. Normally, at that time on a weekday morning the café would be packed, but now it was completely empty.

They tried the door, but it was locked, so Wilf banged on the door. At this, Joe's cousin (actually a blood cousin, whom Wilf had already met) came and opened the door, greeted Wilf warmly and the three of them walked right across the empty café to the bar, where Wilf ordered all of them a drink.

By now the hands of the clock above the door were dead on eleven, the door opened and in walked Joe followed by a character Wilf knew as Johnny H.

'Now I also knew that Johnny H, as one might say, dispensed with people. And after him came Billy O'Brien and Tony G. Now they all stayed back by the door and Joe walked over. I said: "Joe, I'd like to introduce you to Don Arden."'

He just looked at Don and said nothing.

'And this is his son, David.'

Joe shook David's hand and said: 'I'm pleased to meet you, David.'

Then without a word he motioned Don over to a table and sat down opposite him, leaving Wilf and David at the bar.

'Is this going to be all right, Wilf?' David asked.

'I really don't know, David,' Wilf replied.

'Now normally Joe always spoke so softly that when he raised his voice you heard him. He raised it now.'

'Did you call me a fucking faggot?'

As he said this, Joe had raised himself so that he was right over Don, who couldn't answer and just sat there.

Joe repeated the question, more slowly this time.

'Did you call me a fucking faggot?'

Wilf was watching and out of the corner of his eye he saw Johnny H, walking slowly over from the door towards the table and at that moment he knew he had to do something. As he puts it: 'I've been around situations all my life and I know when somebody's going to get killed. I also knew that Johnny H wasn't there for window-dressing, especially at that time of the morning. So I quickly walked across to Joe and said: "Joe, can a speak to you for a minute, please?"'

'No, you can't,' he said.

'Joe, it's important. I really need to speak to you.'

He said: 'We're not finished with each other, this guy and me.' But he got up and walked towards the bar with Wilf.

'Now, what do you want?' says Joe.

Wild said: 'Joe, I see Johnny H here and Johnny H starting to move. That tells me only one thing. You're going to whack him.'

'Yeah, that's right. You got a problem with that?'

Wilf said: 'Yes, I do, as it happens. One, the guy's my friend. Two, his son is my personal buddy. If Don has to go that means David as well.'

All he does is just look at me and I say: 'Will you listen to me for a moment, Joe?'

'I'm listening' he says, 'but make it short.' And his face just told me everything. Those dead-looking eyes of his were looking even more threatening.

I said: 'Joe, over the years you've taught me a lot and one thing you've taught me above most other things is always respect a big earner.' I realised that with this I'd got his attention.

'Well, what are you trying to say?'

'Joe, I'm going to tell you something. This guy's got the biggest act in the world. Right now, they're just about to make it to the very top. They'll be massive. So instead of killing this guy, why not make him your friend? Once you know him, you'll find you get along with him. He's really a good guy. And like I said, Joe, he's a big earner.'

At this I make a money sign, meaning that if he worked with

this guy he could maybe earn a lot of money.

At this he nods at me and says: 'I hear what you say.' And he walks back to the table. Then I see him give Johnny H a look and Johnny goes and sits back down, and I go to the bar and look at David Arden. Now David may be young, but he's no one's fool and he says: 'Is it going to be all right now, Wilf?' And I say: 'I think so. I really hope so.'

I think that Joe would still have liked to chastise Don a little more. But Don apologised. He really did. In every way he knew. He said: 'Joe, forgive me. I genuinely didn't realise. And suddenly Joe lets it go. I'd seen him do something like this before, suddenly switch over from the menace to the charm. And he says: 'All right, then, Don.' And the two of them, Joe and Don together now, come up to the bar. 'OK,' Don says, 'what're you drinking, Joe?' He tried to sound cool, but he was looking fucking drawn to me. And well he might have done. I still felt queasy myself, knowing what had so nearly happened.

With that Joe takes a drink with us and starts speaking.' You know,' he says to Don, 'Wilf here has explained to me that you're in business. I'm in business too.' Here I thought it best to leave them to it. And I do know that from that day on, Joe and Don Arden became inseparable. And from then until the day that Joe died, Don was always there for Joe.

In the mid-1980s, I heard of something else Don did for Joe. At the time, Don was having problems of his own with the British government which was trying to extradite him from California on kidnapping charges of which he was later found not guilty, and when I visited Joe he told me that he'd just missed seeing Don by a couple of days when he'd been in New York.

I asked Joe how he was doing, and he said: 'Well, he just turned up here at the house and before I could say a word he held up a piece of paper on which he'd written: "The FBI have me wired".'

'Are you serious, Joe?' I said.

'Do I say things for the sake of saying them?' Joe replied. 'Of course I'm serious. The Feds were trying to use him to incriminate me and he went on asking me all the things they

277

wanted me to tell him – about getting him a false passport, about a phoney bank account, about a gun. And thanks to his warning, to all these questions I said nothing. So your friend Don Arden did the right thing by me in the end.'

'I also think,' says Wilf, 'that on that day in Café Seventy-Two, I repaid my debt to Don.'

Wilf saying goodbye to Charlie Kray. Third from left Roberta Kray,
next to her Reg Kray. Hand on coffin, Wilf Pine.

'Firm Friends'. Freddie Foreman and Wilf Pine.

Taken in the FCI Otisville New York, 2002.
Wilf and Danny Pagano.

Rose Milano 'Aunt Roe' and Wilf.

Wilf and Ros' very dear friends Robert and Kathy Milano
and their pet dogs Angel and Deacon.

Wilf's wife Ros.

Wilf's late son. Scott Anthony Pine.
Born 26 July 1967, died 16 February 1991
aged 23 years.

Wilf and his youngest son Alex at the wake for Reg Kray.

Wilf and his son Sean.

Wilf and his daughters Emma
and Sammi.

The Crew at Wilf's home, 29 June 2003. Left to right: Clive (Jinxie) Jenkins, Colin Marden, Wilf and Dave Farley.

15

Dinner with Dean and Bankruptcy for Dessert

WHILE WILF WAS busy saving Don Arden in New York, back on the Isle of Wight, with Lesley gone, he was now the head of a one-parent family and his life was not made any easier by the police. Hardly was he home again than his house in Ryde was being targeted by an armed task force complete with sharpshooters, police dogs and a helicopter. This did little for his peace of mind, or his relations with the neighbours.

After organising tours by top-flight bands around the world, he had not found it too difficult to organise his little family and despite the turmoil in his mind he had soon devised a regular routine for all of them. Luckily, all three children, including five-year-old Sammi, were now at local schools and despite her uncertain health his mother Millie was close enough to help him when she could. When she couldn't, he could rely on his friend, Frank, to collect Sammi from her school. He had worked with Wilf in his days on the dustcarts.

On the afternoon when the trouble started, Wilf had had to keep an appointment in Cowes and, fearing he might be late returning, he had arranged for Frank to pick Sammi up from school and drop her back. As Wilf says, one of the beauties of the Isle of Wight in those days was that you never had to lock your door and he made a point of always leaving the front door unlocked. 'There weren't that many break-ins on the island then and, being sensible, no one in his right mind was going to break into my house.'

It was a very hot summer day. He was driving a Vauxhall Cavalier, and after his appointment he remembered he was short of bread and

279

parked outside the nearby village shop. While inside purchasing a loaf, he noticed two large, well-dressed characters outside peering in at him as if they knew him. He recognised neither of them but, as he says,' 'in my world two men behaving like that could be one of two things – either guys like me, or cops. Either way, I was taking no chances.'

As there were no other customers and knowing that the shopkeeper was a local councillor, he asked him to spare a moment and accompany him outside. Whatever these large men had in mind, he knew he'd be safer with a witness present.

The shopkeeper agreed and, following closely behind him, Wilf grabbed the nearest of the men by the lapels 'and was just about to nut him when the other guy intervened and flashed a card before me. They weren't villains. They were cops.' The shopkeeper, realising what was happening, had wisely retreated into his shop and the first policeman introduced himself as a superintendent. The other was a detective inspector and it was he who told Wilf that they'd picked up his identity from his car registration number. Then he broke the news that they'd just carried out an armed raid on his home.

'You've what? Are you serious?'

'Very serious,' said the cop.

'But why?' asked Wilf.

'We were looking for Skingle.'

'Who the hell's Skingle?'

'Come now, Pine,' said the superintendent. 'You must know Arthur Skingle, the cop killer. He escaped a few hours ago from Parkhurst and is on the run.'

'What's that to do with me?' said Wilf. 'And what the fuck has it got to do with my house?'

Rather than have lengthy explanations in the street, the superintendent suggested that they drove back to the house to talk things over. Fuming quietly to himself, Wilf climbed into his Vauxhall and drove off with the police car following. When he reached home, Frank was standing at the front gate and Wilf noticed several of the neighbours also standing in the street, determined not to miss any fresh developments.

'Wilf, you're not going to believe what's been going on', said

Frank. By now the police car had arrived and, although Frank clearly couldn't wait to tell Wilf what had happened, Wilf thought it best to let him go, thanked him for looking after Sammi and turned his full attention on the cops.

Once they were in the house the superintendent started to explain that they had been acting on information that, after escaping, Skingle would be making contact with Wilf. 'As he's highly dangerous, we had to act immediately, so we targeted your house.'

For once in his life Wilf was almost at a loss for words. 'You must be kidding me,' he said.

The superintendent shook his head. 'I'm afraid that we had no alternative and it didn't help to see your curtains were drawn. It looked as if you might be hiding someone.'

'Hiding someone? Don't be daft. The afternoon sun makes the front room hot, so I pulled them to keep it cool.'

'That's possible, but look at it from our perspective,' said the superintendent.

At this Wilf finally exploded. 'To be honest, I don't give a shit for your perspective. Just do yourselves a favour and fuck off. Get out of my fucking house! Get out of my fucking life! Fuck off!'

'All we are trying to do—' started the inspector.

'You're doing nothing except fucking off right now,' said Wilf, showing them the door.

No sooner had they left than two neighbours turned up.

'Jesus, Wilf. You really missed something all right. '

'Like what?'

'Well, there was a police helicopter right overhead and look what they've done to your fence.' Wilf saw that his back garden fence had been smashed down. 'That's what they did when they stormed the back of your house. At the same time they had marksmen on the other side of the road with guns with telescopic sights trained on the house, while more police got ready to batter down your front door. Luckily for you, someone told them that you never locked it, or your front door would have gone the same way as your fence.'

By now everything had more or less calmed down and, thanks to Frank, Sammi didn't seem at all affected. But when he'd calmed down with a cup of tea, Wilf tried to work out where on earth the police had got their 'information' and why they had picked on him. It didn't take him long to figure out that there had to be a connection between what had happened and a phone call he had received that very morning from Violet Kray, the mother of his friend Charlie and the notorious twins.

Although the Kray twins were still very much in jail as maximum-security prisoners serving the thirty-year sentence awarded them at the Old Bailey back in 1969, Wilf's friendship with their brother Charlie had started to extend to Ronnie Kray. Through Charlie, Ronnie had asked Wilf to visit him in prison, but he had refused on the grounds that, under Home Office regulations, he would have had to answer questions by the police in order to be put on the so-called 'A-List' of permitted visitors. But Wilf and Ronnie Kray continued to communicate through Charlie, and a working relationship had started between them. Wilf was in the habit of doing small favours Ronnie asked of him. At this stage these amounted to little more than seeing and talking to various old friends Ronnie wished to keep in touch with and Wilf remembered that in his telephone conversation with Violet she had mentioned something about Ronnie sending somebody to see him.

It had all been very vague. Violet had been well trained by her sons and made the call, as usual, from a public pay-phone, mentioning nobody by name. But if, for whatever reason, Wilf's telephone was being tapped and his incoming calls recorded, it would not have taken the police long to put two and two together after a break-out by a dangerous murderer, with Ronnie Kray also in maximum security in Parkhurst, less than nine miles up the road.

For Wilf it was worrying to think that even on the Isle of Wight his phone was being regularly tapped, but there seemed no other explanation. So he was hardly in the best of humours with the police when, early that evening, he received what amounted to a relatively friendly call from the superintendent.

'What d'you want now?' Wilf asked.

'Just to let you know that we recaptured Skingle. He was about two hundred yards outside the prison perimeter in Parkhurst Forest.'

'That's very nice of you, letting me know,' said Wilf. 'Now why don't you go and fuck yourself,' he said and slammed down the receiver.

But for the next four or five weeks or so Wilf remained puzzled by the Skingle business and what really lay behind such a full-scale raid on his house. It seemed out of all proportion and although there were ways of discovering if his phone was tapped, when he tried them they all proved negative.

Then one evening he had a visit from a well-connected old friend called Alan, who rang saying that he had to see him.

'Wilf, I hear you had a raid on your house a few weeks back,' he said.

'That's for sure, and I think it was down to a phone call that I had from Violet Kray. Obviously someone was tapping my phone.'

'No, no, Wilf,' said the friend, 'you're wrong. No one was tapping your telephone and what happened had nothing to do with Violet. You remember that nasty little nightclub owner you gave a well-deserved beating a couple of years ago?'

'Of course I do. That fucking hard-on had a charisma-bypass at birth. What's his problem now?'

'Just this. You may not know it, but I'm in partnership with him in another line of business and on the day Skingle escaped I was sitting in the office and heard him in the next room on the phone to the police. Apparently he saw you that morning at Bembridge harbour looking around some boats.'

'Sure I was there. I was thinking of buying one, but I didn't.'

'He didn't know that. But, as you and I know, he's a police informer. Somehow he already knew of your connection with the Krays and that morning, when he heard on the radio that Skingle had done a bunk, he told the law that he'd seen you looking at a boat on their behalf to get him off the island.'

Even then, for Wilf, the Skingle business wasn't over, and shortly after this he was drinking in a bar in Ryde when in walked a local plain-clothes detective sergeant called John Barwick. They knew each other from the past. 'Wilf, can I have a word with you?' he said, but Wilf was still not in the best of humour with the law and gave his customary reply.

'You can go fuck yourself. Only the other day I had you bastards nearly blasting down my house.'

'Wilf, that's what I want to talk to you about.'

'Now I'm all ears, but make it short,' said Wilf.

'The guys who did your house weren't islanders. They were a police Immediate Response Unit rushed over from the mainland and I told them they were wasting their time. I said I knew you and that none of this made sense. But they said they were acting on information and that was that. Luckily for you, I went with them, and they were just about to smash your door down when I remembered that you never locked it so I just opened it and let them in. To be quite honest with you, Wilf, I got quite a kick out of seeing those mainlanders running around the house with their guns and shouting their heads off and finding nobody there.'

In his new role at the head of a one-parent family, Wilf had more important matters on his mind than bungled raids by armed policemen. His chief problem was how to look after and to feed three growing children and not for the first time in his life he was grateful for what he'd learned from the Paganos, and all those meals he'd eaten in their home, not to mention all the wonderful Italian restaurants he'd visited with Joe in every quarter of New York.

He was also grateful for the time he'd spent with Theresa and Aunt Roe in the Pagano kitchen, and above all he thanked God that his children liked Italian cooking since that was all that he could do. 'Of course I could just about fry eggs and bacon, make toast and pour a bowl of cornflakes, but beyond that all that I knew how to cook was minestrone and lasagne and Aunt Roe's famous Neapolitan meatballs. Whenever I was stuck for an idea, I'd ring up Joe and ask him what to cook for supper. And since Joe really was an expert on Italian food, he never failed me.'

Wilf also attended all the school open days and dutifully attended concerts given by the school orchestra, because Sean was playing the drums and Scott played the violin. 'I'd go along and I'd sit listening with all the other parents, trying to look keen and interested, but to me it was an abominable row.'

The one thing Wilf never really got the hang of was ironing. But even here, help was at hand. One night there was a knock on the door and who was there but his old friend Dave Farley. 'He'd been travelling abroad and Wilf hadn't seen him for over a year, but everything about him was the same as ever – including his uncanny knack of knowing what Wilf was thinking.

'Something's up,' he said.

'What?'

'Something tells me something's up. I know you're worried.'

'Well, since you mention it, I am. Can you iron children's clothes?'

'Iron clothes? I'm the best.'

And he was. And what's more, he could sew.

'Within a few days, he'd settled in with us and was perfectly at home. I would cook and Dave would do the sewing and the ironing. We would share the housework, which I also hated.

'So between the two of us, we soon had a comfortable little domestic life going on between us. Two middle-aged guys like us left much to be desired when bringing up a five-year-old like Sammi, but here Dave had a hidden asset. As I soon discovered, he hadn't lost his touch. He was still the Isle of Wight's answer to Casanova and his girlfriends who visited the house all loved little Sammi and helped us look after her.

'So all in all we managed pretty well and that part of my life was working out, but more than anything I now had the chance to bond with my children, having effectively been a stranger to them all until now. Soon we were getting along pretty well together, thanks largely to my elder son Sean, who at ten felt very responsible for the two younger children. He was also very kind to them. If I gave him half a crown he'd give his brother a shilling, his sister a shilling and keep sixpence for himself.'

When Christmas came, everything Wilf did for the children had to be slightly over the top – including the Christmas turkey. Wilf took Sean with him to the local butcher and insisted on choosing the biggest turkey in the shop, only to find it would not fit in the oven. So they had to dismember it and cook it in pieces and for their Christmas dinner they put the pieces together on the table so that it looked like a real bird.

Wilf says that largely thanks to Dave his home life was now pretty much in order. He says his mind was still a mess and he was still drinking heavily, but he still never drank at home. He didn't miss London and certainly he didn't miss the record business. Above all, he was happy to find himself united with his children and that year they all had a great Christmas.

Throughout this period Wilf talked almost every day to Joe Pagano, if not about recipes and food then about the family and friends and life in general. Joe kept asking when he was coming over, but because of his responsibilities Wilf kept postponing a visit. Then early in the new year of 1977, Joe rang Wilf, sounding more insistent and said: 'I really need to see you.'

'Is it that important, Joe?'

'To me it is, and it won't do you any harm. I need you here for a few days and I think it's time you had a little *relaxez-vous* as well. So why don't you see if you can find somebody to look after the kids?'

As luck would have it, Millie's health was going through a good period. 'She was a saint and with Dave's help was fully prepared to take over for me.' So early that February Wilf once again found himself flying to New York.

'I wasn't prepared for the effect it had on me. Once I was back in New York it was like being reborn and somehow a great weight seemed to lift off my shoulders. It was all so wonderfully familiar. There was little old Charlie there waiting to meet me and drive me upstate in Joe's familiar black limo. And as soon as I entered Joe's house, it was just like coming home. All the children were there to greet me and make a fuss of me. They were like my other family and already they were growing up. And Theresa, dear Theresa, wanted news of all the kids – how they were, what they were doing at school and how we were managing at home. Although she lived three thousand miles away, she was more interested and involved in my family than anyone in England.'

It wasn't until that evening, when we were sitting together downstairs in the bar, that I had a chance to ask. 'Joe, why did you want me over?'

He said: 'I think you'll have to be a postman again.'

I said: 'I don't mind, Joe. You know I'll do anything for you, but this is a short visit and I'm not that keen on flying halfway around the States.'

'No need for that,' he said. 'This is more local, and you won't be flying anywhere. I only want you to drive up to New England. You'll enjoy that. Ever been to Boston, Wilf?'

'As I remember, it's a very clean city.'

'In more ways than one. Listen to me, my friend and *your* friend, Funzi Tieri. He often mentions you and would like you to see somebody up there and give him a letter from him.'

I said: 'Sure, Joe, that's no problem.'

Anyway, I agreed and drove to Boston, where I met this guy. It was the same old scenario I'd seen so many times before. I was recognised at once not only because of the tattoos and the English accent, but there was something new about me now – my hip, which had caused me grief throughout my life, was now causing me such pain that I was walking with a more prominent limp.

So all in all there was no problem. I enjoyed the drive, and Boston had to be the cleanest city I had seen in America. My contact offered me a meal and asked if I wanted to stay over. All very hospitable, but I refused and said: 'No, I must get back.'

When I got back to Joe, he asked me how it went.

I told him and said the guy seemed most hospitable.

'Yes, they're nice guys up there and very good friends of ours.' Later he told me that the man I met was a high-ranking capo in the Raymond Patricca family, and that was that.

'Are you sure there's nothing else you want me to do, Joe?

'I'll tell you the truth, Wilf. That trip was really just an excuse to get you over here. I wanted to see how you were and spend some time with you. I tell you what, Wilf. Tomorrow we'll go up the farm.'

By now Wilf was starting to worry about the children and said he couldn't spare more than three or four days away.

'Just phone home,' said Joe, 'and find out how they are.' Wilf did, and his mother answered.

Wilf told her that he had a chance of a few days' rest and recuperation.

'Rest and recuperation,' she replied. 'I'm the one in need of that. These kids of yours are driving me mad.' But luckily she was joking and said: 'No, you stay long as you need. Dave and I will cope.'

Next day Wilf drove Joe up to the farm. Things had changed since his last visit. Now there was a man working there full-time – 'a hillbilly, a really nice guy' – and Joe's passion for horses had at last been realised. In one paddock there was a thoroughbred stallion, the mustangs were there in the corral and, along with a goat and chickens, Joe's farm was turning into a self-contained unit.

He was obviously happy here. This was his private place where he could live the sort of life he'd always dreamed of. An old meaning of the word 'Pagano' is 'countryman', and Joe Pagano was an old-style Italian countryman at heart. He even had his hunting dog called Bugsy, which like all good Italians he adored. And now that the farm was finished, it had everything, including, of course, a poolroom, gun racks and a bar. Then he says: 'Right. We're going to cook. You ever eaten chicken cooked my way, Wilf?'

'No, I've never had your chicken before, Joe.'

'Some guys are coming up here anyway, so I'll cook for them. You want to give me a hand?

I had never seen Joe cook before, but he was a master at it. We had bought several chickens at a supermarket coming up and he showed me how to chop them up and skin them. The pieces were first dipped in beaten egg and floured, and finally dipped into the all-important magic mixture he'd made up beforehand. By the time the guys arrived, there seemed to be an awful lot of chicken. Nicky arrived first, followed by Tony G and Frankie D. The last to arrive was the lethal Johnny H. With them they brought bottles of wine, special loaves of bread, cheese and salami and everything we needed. Everyone brought something. As we were all going hunting early next morning, everyone was staying the night.

Everyone was looking forward to Joe Pagano's special chicken and someone whispered to Wilf: 'If he asks you what you think of it, just say it's almost as good as Colonel Sanders' Kentucky Fried. For Joe there's nothing finer, that's what he'll really want to hear.'

Wilf took this advice seriously, which turned out to be a big mistake. After his first mouthful, Joe asked him what he thought of it.

'It's great, Joe. It tastes just like Colonel Sanders' chicken.' With that he got up and clocked me on the back of the head with the palm of his hand.

'You what? You've seen all the trouble I've been taking, and the best you can say about it is that it's no better than Colonel Sanders.'

While Joe seemed furious, all the others were laughing at the joke, but once they had had a drink Joe's anger soon vanished. The more they drank the more they laughed at one another's jokes, and the evening passed with endless funny stories.

'These guys, I'm telling you,' Wilf says, 'they're the funniest people in the world. Tomorrow they might be dead, so in the meantime they enjoy life and sure as hell they like to laugh.'

'You ever hunt, Wilf?' asked Joe when they got up next morning.

'Can't say I have.'

'Then this will be a new experience for you. Come to the gun rack and let's fit you up with a gun and see which will suit you. For someone like you, you'll need a pump action, so if you miss the first time you have a second chance.'

There was something very odd about this group of men, all of whom were used to firearms, as they tramped across the mountainside looking every inch like real hunters. Wilf himself had little idea of what they were even hunting and soon he noticed that they were happy to blast away at almost anything that moved, including racoons.

As they approached a chasm, Wilf saw an official-looking notice nailed to a tree: 'Beware of Bears.' This stopped him in his tracks. The only bear he'd ever seen was in a zoo and he hadn't liked the look of it. He didn't mind facing any human enemy, but a bear was different. By now they were trudging down a path between rocks and boulders, but none of the others seemed particularly worried.

'Joe, I must tell you something,' said Wilf. 'When it comes to bears I'm no fucking hero.'

They must have walked a mile or so when Tony G turned to Wilf and whispered: 'Quiet, Wilf. Just look over there.' Standing upright on a rocky ledge was the biggest bear that Wilf had ever seen.

Wilf made no excuses for what happened next. 'I took just one look at that animal and that was enough for me. I dropped that gun and ran. I ran all the way back to the ranch and that was that. That was my first big hunt and definitely my last. But a couple of hours later, when Joe and the guys returned, they all saw the funny side of it and like the snowman in the Sheraton what happened between me and the bear became the subject of yet another of their funny stories.'

Later that day, when the hunters left, Joe's sisters, Mary and Roe, arrived, together with Aunt Roe's husband, Johnny. And now for the first time Wilf saw another side of Joe Pagano and the sort of horseplay that still went on between him and his sisters. Theresa had told Wilf that this dated back to their childhood when Joe had always turned them into objects for his sense of mischief.

At the ranch, Joe loved his bantam chickens and was particularly proud of the rooster, which despite its size would attack anyone who got too near the hens. It was so aggressive that Joe used to say: 'That's the only chicken I've ever seen that thinks it's an eagle.' It was this that gave him the idea of yet another practical joke on the ever-unsuspecting sweet Aunt Roe.

Wilf was sitting outside with Joe when he heard him shout: 'Say, Roe, would you do me a favour? I need some eggs I promised to take over to a neighbour. Would you mind collecting some for me?'

'Joey, you shouldn't have done that,' Wilf whispered, guessing what would happen next.

But all Joe did was shrug. 'Let's just wait and see what happens.'

They didn't have to wait for long. Aunt Roe picked up her basket, entered the chicken coop and then all hell broke loose, with Aunt Roe screaming and the bantam squawking. When Wilf rushed over to help her, he found that the bantam had caught her by surprise, made her lose her balance and she was lying on her back with the tiny chicken pecking angrily at her forehead.

'As always, Joe thought the whole thing one enormous joke. And, although Aunt Roe began by seeming angry and upset, as always she soon forgave him.'

Both the sisters, but especially Aunt Roe, had a way of bringing out the carefree side of their brother and the next two days Wilf spent with all of them at the farm were one of the last times when he saw Joe really happy. Later, he could still be the unpredictable, tough, ruthless character he'd always been, but something had gone, and at first Wilf didn't know quite what it was.

As the others left before them, Wilf and Joe drove back together and Joe said: 'Wilf, before you leave for London, I have one more little treat in store for you tonight.'

'What's that, Joe?

'You'll find out soon enough. I only hope that I can share it with you.'

Something about the way he said this made Wilf realise he didn't wish to discuss it, so he said nothing. But all the way back, Joe went on coughing. On and off he'd been caught in these spasms of coughing at the farm. Once he was home again they stopped, but that afternoon in the car was the first hint Wilf got that Joe Pagano's health was going.

Back at the house, Wilf remembers a clear hot sunny afternoon, sitting with Joe and Theresa having coffee outside when one of Joe's old friends, Louis Pacella, arrived. Not realising the situation, he said: 'Joe, you're in luck. I've got the tickets for you, Vinnie and Wilf for tonight.'

'It's no good, Louis, I can't go. I'm feeling rotten, and I think I need an early night. But take Wilf with you, and he can meet up with Vinnie at the theatre.'

Louis said: 'Wilf, you'll enjoy it. I'm promoting a series of shows at the West Chester Theatre.' Wilf asked: 'Who's appearing?' Louis looked at Joe. 'Didn't you tell him, Joe?'

'No,' replied Joe. 'It was meant to be a surprise.'

At this Wilf was all attention and asked who was appearing.

Joe said: 'Frank Sinatra and Dean Martin.'

'That's fantastic. Bless you, Joe.'

Joe said: 'Wilf, I've heard both of them many times before, and you haven't, so go and get yourself ready and go with Louis.'

Inevitably the theatre was packed, but Wilf and Louis found Vinnie Mauro, who was strategically placed at the bar. After greeting each other and Wilf telling Vinnie that Joe wasn't well, with the bell ringing they made their way into the auditorium, and – lo and behold – they had front-row seats. As soon as they sat down, Wilf recognised guys he had met just briefly over the last few years, 'and everyone who was anyone in Joe's circle seemed to be sitting in the front row. The show started with a warm-up comedian who came out with all the usual jokes about Frank's connection with the mob. He told them well, and some of them were really funny, and he soon had the audience in stitches, except for the front row. As I looked along that row of faces, not one of them was laughing. The rest of the audience was, but not those guys. They didn't see the funny side of it, so I didn't laugh either.

'After that I had to rub my eyes, for suddenly, no more than twenty feet away from me, stood Frank Sinatra looking exactly like, well, Frank Sinatra. And he was good. He was no longer like he was at his greatest, but the old magic worked and it was still Sinatra. While he was singing, who should join him on the stage but another living legend, Dean Martin. For some reason he was pushing a drinks trolley stacked with booze and, while Frank Sinatra sang, Dean Martin poured himself a drink. I was intrigued by the trolley, but the best was yet to come. When Dean Martin started singing he was quite sensational and he sang as his finale 'Buddy, Can You Spare a Dime?' I'd always thought it a pretty corny number, but as Dean Martin sang it that night it almost brought the house down, and the evening ended with a standing ovation.'

But for Wilf the evening wasn't over. He had intended getting home to bed, but suddenly Vinnie Mauro slapped him on the back.

'Wilf, wasn't that great?' he said. 'What d'you say the two of us go partying?'

'Where do you suggest?' said Wilf.

'We're going to a restaurant Louis owns on the upper east side of Manhattan. You're going to love it. We're having a little party there.'

When they reached the restaurant, it was after one in the morning. No one else was there, but clearly they were expected and the waiters put the tables together and soon more of the audience from the theatre arrived and they all started drinking and talking. The tables were laid up, food was ordered, then the guest of honour arrived. It was Dean Martin. Everyone in the restaurant seemed to know him, and by chance he was placed opposite where Wilf was sitting. All of them seemed to know him personally.

'And, you know, I couldn't eat a thing. I grew up watching the Dean Martin films with Jerry Lewis. I knew his face, I'd always loved his music and here he is just sitting opposite me there. He was wearing black-rimmed glasses and saying nothing and all of a sudden it occurred to me that I must say something to him. So I said: "Mr Martin, can you excuse me for a minute? There's something I would like to ask you."

He took his glasses off and looked at me.

'"Sure. What d'you want to know, pal?"

'Well,' I said, 'I'm puzzled by that booze trolley you pushed across the stage tonight. Were the drinks that you poured yourself the real thing or just cold tea?

'He looked at me for what felt like a very long time, then in that quiet drawl of his he says: "What do you take me for? A phoney?" He replaced his glasses and went on with his meal. That was the end of my conversation with Dean Martin. It may have been short, but at least I had one.'

Back in England I found myself missing the Paganos, but I was very happy being back with my family and delighted that the kids had missed me. They'd even seemed to grow in the few days I'd been away and Sammi, who had scarcely recognised me before, now ran down the path and jumped into my arms.

Now since we broke up I'd not paid Lesley anything. I figured she was young and able to earn her own living. Then out of the blue I received a letter from her. It was written on toilet paper and to tell the truth I couldn't fault her. Even as wacky as I was at the time, I could appreciate the hurt and the embarrassment I'd caused her. Then this was swiftly followed by a letter from her mother.

Now Lesley's mother was a lovely woman, but a mother is a mother and she quite rightly stated that I'd not done the right thing by her daughter, but added that all of that would be put right when she went for a divorce settlement in the courts. Now at that time I wasn't thinking very clearly, and what happened was that I took umbrage. Straight away.

She was stating the obvious, and there were only two ways I could take this – the right way or the wrong way. And being fucking nuts at the time, I chose the wrong way. I said to myself: 'Right. If that's the way you want it!' I looked at my assets. By now there wasn't too much, so I thought: 'Fuck it, I'll go bankrupt.' So I found out about it. I spoke to a lawyer and in the end I said that I wanted to put myself into voluntary liquidation.

I guess the lawyer thought that I was Charles Clore or something. But I told him I had these debts I wanted out of my hair. On his advice, he said I'd have to present myself to the official receiver's office, which was in Southampton, which I did. All in all, there couldn't have been more than three thousand pounds owing. Even then it was, of course, a joke. I could always have gone and got myself that sort of money. But that was me. I put myself into voluntary liquidation. I became a bankrupt just before 1977 ended.

Did I regret it? Yes, I did, for the sheer embarrassment I caused myself and others, especially my mother. I did everything wrong. There was no need for me to go bankrupt. But that was me, and at the time my head was still firmly lodged up my arse – and that was that.

16

'Thank God for Ros'

FOR A MAN who had spent so much of his adult life treating women badly, there is something touching in the way Wilf Pine now stumbled on salvation through a very pretty girl of twenty-one. The one thing to be said in his favour is that no one could accuse him of trying to deceive her with smart talk or false promises. Instead, their love was tested to the limit from the start, at a time when Wilf was suddenly revealed at his worst – violent, drunk, covered in blood and charged with attempted murder. From this unpromising beginning, true love flourished and it was largely thanks to love that he straightened out his mind, controlled his drinking, started a new life and found a mother for his children.

All this began early in 1978 when he first noticed a quiet, dark-eyed girl from Cowes called Rosalyn. In fact, at around this time women were, for once, the last thing on Wilf's mind. But when he saw her for a second time a few days later at a club in Sandown, 'she took my breath away'.

The old, unredeemed Wilf Pine was soon rearing his ungainly head. 'I said to myself, I must pull this girl and went about it in my usual clumsy way by asking her to dance. Now I can't dance and nor, thank God, could she. So we settled for a drink instead. At the time I was still only thirty-four, but I felt older and I asked her out on an old-fashioned sort of date. We arranged to meet at the highly respectable Ship and Castle Hotel and had dinner together. We had a great time, and as it was 13 February I suddenly realised that the next day was St Valentine's Day, so asked her if I could have a St Valentine's Day date with her.'

She said she'd love to but couldn't because she had an evening job.

Undefeated, Wilf suggested that she came around to his house when she'd finished working, saying that he also had to go out earlier in the evening so might be back a little late himself but that the babysitter would be there.' I'll be back by eleven thirty at the latest and we can sit and talk for a bit,' 'said Wilf. Wilf being Wilf, talking was probably the last thing that he had in mind, but then Ros was not the sort of girl to take liberties with. She said: 'Fine.'

'Next day being St Valentine's Day, I was all keyed up and really looking forward to that evening. But like so many good things in my life, the evening went drastically wrong from the beginning.'

Trouble started around lunchtime, when Wilf was in a bar in Ryde and met some old acquaintance who told him that Ronnie Morris was looking for him and that he hadn't sounded too polite.

'I'd not the faintest idea what this could be about, but like everybody on the island I knew all about Ronnie Morris.' He was the island's bully-in-residence, or as Wilf prefers to call him, 'a rock-solid, hard-hitting, no-holds-barred piece of shit'. But Wilf did not let this deter him.

'If I'm told that somebody's looking for me, I don't give a monkey's who he is. So I asked the guy: "Are you sure about this?" He says: "Absolutely sure. He sounded pretty threatening to me. From what I know of him, sooner or later he's going to have a go at you, so take my advice and watch your back."'

Wilf had more important things on his mind at the time, like fetching the children from school and fixing dinner, so he shrugged the warning off and untypically forgot about it until that evening when he was having a drink with another friend and the same thing happened. This time it was a girl he didn't know but who evidently knew him who came up and told him that Ronnie Morris was getting really steamed up and she heard him threatening what he was going to do to Wilf Pine when he met him.

Now Wilf was getting seriously annoyed, particularly as he had no idea what all the trouble was about. He had no intention of going looking for him, 'but if I did meet him now I wasn't exactly going to kiss him'.

At this point Wilf remembered that he had another appointment with a friend of his called Dave the Rave in a nearby pub in Union

Street called the Redan. But Dave had not arrived when he got there and he had been standing at the bar for barely a minute when in through the door came Ronnie Morris. 'He was a tough, good-looking bastard, about my height but broader and he takes one look at me and says: "I want to see you outside — *now*."'

'Are you sure?' said Wilf.

'As much as I'm sure of anything, you bastard.'

Nothing else was said, but almost from the moment Wilf stepped outside the door the action started.

Afterwards, true to the unspoken code he lived by, Wilf not only refused to say what happened but more important he refused to name his opponent. Had Ronnie Morris stuck by this code and kept what had happened to himself, the police would have had no evidence against Wilf and the case would not have come to court. But even when it did, rather than accuse anyone in a court of law Wilf stuck to his defence that he had been so drunk that he was totally confused and could not remember what had happened. To this day, Wilf still adheres to this. He denies that he had a knife but, pointing the scars on his hands, he said someone must have done, as he cut his hands to pieces dragging it away from whoever held it.

He adds that it sounds as if the fight that evidently followed 'must have ended up very bloody, as they said in court that the other guy needed twenty-six stitches to sew his nose back on to his face'.

Luckily for Wilf, by the time the battle ended, Dave the Rave was on the scene. Someone must have taken care of Ronnie Morris and Dave told Wilf he'd better disappear as well before the cops arrived. 'Somehow he got me down to the seafront, but there was so much blood dripping from the cuts on my hands and from my face that he realised the only thing to do was to get me to his house and try to clean me up.'

Dave the Rave proved quite a hero. First he phoned several contacts in the town, who said that the police had been in and out of all the bars and pubs in Ryde, desperately searching for Wilf Pine. That was bad enough, but the state of Wilf's hands was worse. His right-hand thumb was almost severed from his hand, and as nothing would stop the bleeding Dave the Rave got a needle and thread and did his best to stitch it on. Then he tried more impromptu repair work to cuts on his other fingers.

While he was doing this, Dave also rang Wilf's house, where he got through to Ros, who by now had taken over from the babysitter and was waiting patiently for her Valentine's Day date to arrive. She also told Dave that the house had just been raided by the police, demanding to know Wilf's whereabouts and, of course, she'd told them she had no idea. Later Wilf puzzled over who had named him to the police, since as far as he knew there were no witnesses to the fight. But at the time his chief concern was now about the children and about how Ros was coping.

Over many years, Wilf had learned to be wary of telephones, so he wouldn't risk calling her direct, but through Dave he managed to get a message to her asking her to please look after the children until he'd had a chance to sort things out. Dave also organised a friend to check on the house for him and let them know the moment that the police left. Around two-thirty in the morning the friend finally telephoned to say that they had just gone and the coast was clear. Dave drove Wilf home.

'I'd started the evening looking forward to my second date with the most gorgeous girl in the world and here I was finally turning up looking like Frankenstein or the curse of the mummy's tomb. I was all cut about and still bleeding. I was also, well, a little late.'

But when Dave asked Ros if she'd like him to take over, she said she'd rather stay and see that Wilf was all right. When he added that he was still losing a lot of blood, she said she'd try to do something about it and clean him up and look after the children. When Wilf heard her saying this, he realised that she was someone special. 'Most women seeing anyone in that state would have run a mile. Anyway, she soon ran a bath and got me undressed, and as soon as she got me in the bath it seemed to fill with blood. That didn't seem to worry her and afterwards she cleaned me up and stuck plasters on me here, there and everywhere.' Somehow Wilf staggered off to bed. Ros went next door and slept with Sammi.

Wilf insists that next morning, when he woke, he'd bled so much in the night that the blood had soaked through the sheets to the mattress and congealed so that Ros had to pry him off the bed. Again this didn't seem to worry her unduly and after ringing Wilf's mother to take over the children, she left in time to get home then off to work. Wilf was getting more impressed with her by the minute, but he wasn't given long to dwell on this. His next arrival was his mother, who gave him hell. 'What d'you think you're up to? Won't you ever learn? Who was it with this time?'

'Ronnie Morris.'

'Him? *That* animal!'

But before she could say any more on the subject, there was a loud knocking on the front door. The law had arrived, all six of them, three through the front door and three through the back. Wilf noticed a young PC attached to the CID. 'Christ !' he said, looking at Wilf. 'That must have been some fight. Your friend's in the hospital and by the look of you, you should be there too.'

But Wilf was very much awake by now. 'I don't know what you're talking about,' he said. 'All I know is that I had a few drinks with some friends, and went outside the pub and fell down drunk.'

'That's as maybe,' said the young PC.' 'All I know is that I'm going to put you on a holding charge of causing grievous bodily harm, so it's off to the station with you.' As Wilf was escorted to the police car, he heard his mother shout: 'Don't worry. I'll take care of everything.'

Something else that Wilf had learned from his experience of the police across the years was never to get stuck in a police cell if it could be avoided. 'They're the world's worst: cold, uncomfortable, nothing to do and no one to talk to.'

He was determined not to spend the next few days locked up in one and he had to think up a way to avoid it. Suddenly he remembered the time, several years ago, when Tony Iommi, the lead guitarist with Black Sabbath, hit a note on stage that burst one of his eardrums, causing him to lose his sense of balance. Why not pretend the same was happening to him now?

As they were preparing to lock him in one of the cells, he said: 'Easy on. I don't feel too good.'

'Well, I must say you don't look too good either.'

'You don't understand. I must see a doctor. I have this trouble with my ear.'

299

With that an inspector came in, heard what he said and took one look at him. 'Get him to the hospital,' he said. 'Take him straight to casualty and get him checked out.'

By now Wilf was determined to make the most of the situation and as he walked through the crowded waiting room at the hospital with both wrists cuffed to a policeman, he shouted: 'Look at this, everyone! Police brutality!' At this point one of the coppers started trying to explain that it wasn't their fault.

'Come off it, officer,' said Wilf, chuckling to himself. 'Who else could have done it?'

X-rays showed that no bones were broken, but the doctors noticed that his hands were so badly cut that they needed stitches. As the police needed photographs of his injuries, the next person to turn up was the police photographer.

Once again, Wilf thought quickly and while the photographer was taking photographs of his head and body he remembered the damage to his hands and thought himself: 'How would I have cut my hands to shreds grabbing that blade to save myself, if someone hadn't been holding the knife in the first place?'

So he said to the photographer: 'Have you forgotten my hands?' He would probably still have ignored them, but a doctor was there and said: 'Yes, what about his hands?'

Later, those photographs would prove to be of great importance.

When the doctor started giving him tests, he told them about his perforated eardrum and the doctor thought he might possibly have concussion. He wasn't sure, but to be on the safe side he decided to keep him in hospital for the time being.

'Bingo!' Wilf said to himself. 'Fucking great! As I'm under arrest, this will mean that I have to have a police bed escort, but I don't care. In hospital, unlike a prison cell, I can at least meet people, pass messages out and hear what's going on.

'Now the cop guarding me wasn't that bad. He obviously didn't have a particularly high opinion of Ronnie Morris, and he said, "Wilf, your friend [meaning Ronnie Morris] is in the next ward. He's up to something, so take my advice and say something. If you don't, you're in for a whole load of trouble."'

By telling Wilf to 'say something' the policeman was telling him to make a statement, which was something that he never would have done.

An acquaintance of Wilf's often took the papers around to the patients and Wilf saw him in the next-door ward where he seemed to be taking his time. Then when the policeman by his bedside had popped out for a moment, he nipped in to see Wilf.

He told him he had just been in the other ward, talking to Ronnie Morris, who had asked him to give Wilf a message. He said that if Wilf said nothing to the police about the fight, he would say nothing either. In that way nobody would get nicked.

When the policeman returned, he again attempted to persuade Wilf to make a statement. 'For your own sake, Wilf, you must.' But again Wilf refused, saying that the whole thing had gone quite far enough. 'If you really want to help me, get me a lawyer.'

Wilf asked for Marjorie White, the top criminal solicitor on the island. When she asked him what had happened, he stuck by his story, saying that he'd had a drink or two, fallen over and could remember no more. She then told him that he would have to answer the standard police questionnaire. He agreed and later that afternoon a detective inspector came in with a list of thirty questions covering the incident which he had to answer. When he asked the question 'Do you know Ronnie Morris?', Wilf said: 'Of course I do. Ronnie Morris is my friend. What would I be doing, getting in a fight with him?

'From then on I answered everything like a guy who couldn't remember anything.'

Wilf had wanted to remain in hospital for a few more days so that he could see a few more people, including Dave Farley, who had just arrived back from one of his travels. But suddenly the police arrived and told him to collect his gear. He'd been in hospital for eight days by now and they were taking him to the police cells because he was due in court the following morning.

'Have you informed my lawyer?' 'We don't have to inform anyone. You're up before the beak tomorrow.'

Next morning they took him to the police station, where the sergeant read out the charge to him.

'You are charged with the attempted murder of Lord Ronald

Francis Morris.' (Morris was no lord of the realm. 'Lord' just happened to be one of the names he was christened with.)

'Have you anything to say?' they asked.

Wilf made no comment.

The next thing he knew he was handcuffed and on his way to Newport Magistrates' Court. As soon as he had heard that he was being charged with the attempted murder of Ronnie Morris, Wilf knew that, despite his promise in hospital, Morris must have ratted on him and he was now in serious trouble. What Wilf didn't realise was that Morris was so hated on the island that this would act in his favour. Also, for the time being at any rate, luck was on his side. So, to be fair, were some of the policemen in the court who, being local men, knew that it was a policeman from their station who had gone off with Wilf's former wife, leaving him to cope as a one-parent family.

Another key figure in the trial was the clerk of the court, a trained solicitor called Henry Ireland. In a magistrates' court the clerk is frequently a man of considerable importance, since he has to advise the bench on points of law. He did so now.

In court, Wilf was asked how he pleaded: guilty or not guilty?

'Not guilty.'

At this point his solicitor rose to say that she intended to apply for bail. As Wilf was being charged with attempted murder, this brought a look of incredulity to the faces of most of the people in the courtroom, but not to that of Henry Ireland. He knew Wilf well, as Wilf had been up before him many times. He now intervened.

'Excuse me, but there are some questions I'd like to ask. This Lord Ronald Francis Morris. Is he also known as Ronnie Morris?'

Yes, he is.

The clerk whispered something to the magistrates, then asked the inspector to go back into the dock.

'Now, inspector, would you object to bail?'

'Yes, we would.'

'For what reasons?'

'Because of the severity of the charge.'

'Is that all?'

'That is all.'

'Thank you,' said the clerk, then he went to whisper once again to the members of the bench. Then he rose, turned in Wilf's direction and announced: 'Wilf Pine, you will be held in your own recognisance of £100 on a charge of attempted murder. But there will be certain stipulations. You cannot enter licensed premises. You cannot go near the aforesaid Ronnie Morris and you will observe a curfew. This means that you cannot leave your house before eight o'clock in the morning or after six o'clock in the evening.'

To his amazement, Wilf was free to leave the court.

He returned home and who should be there but Ros, laughing and playing with his children. He couldn't believe his luck. And at that moment he realised the truth. He was in love with the dark-eyed Ros.

He also realised that she had changed his life. Since knowing her, the tension in his life had gone and in spite of all his recent troubles he suddenly felt relaxed and happy. This happiness lasted until six weeks later, when he went before the magistrates again for the committal hearing. This began with what appeared to be good news. As soon as he was in the dock they told him he'd be pleased to know that the charge of attempted murder against him had been dropped. 'Jesus!' thought Wilf. 'I'm off the hook.' But they hadn't finished with him yet.

'You are to be charged instead with malicious wounding with intent to cause grievous bodily harm.'

So this was not such good news after all. It would, in fact, have been difficult to get Wilf for attempted murder, since this would have needed proof of his original intention to murder Ronnie Morris. But now he was facing two charges, the first for malicious wounding and the second for causing grievous bodily harm. As Wilf was well aware, both these crimes carried a maximum penalty of life imprisonment. So it looked as if, whatever happened, Wilf would soon be ending up in jail. There was just some alleviation. Until he went to trial at the Crown Court, his bail was renewed under the usual conditions.

While this was going on, although Wilf continued his regular phone calls to Joe Pagano several times a week, he had so far not dared tell him of his troubles. And whenever Joe asked him when he was coming over next, he'd always put him off, pleading general domestic problems but promising that it would not be long.

But the night after the committal trial, Joe rang again for a chat. Wilf could no longer keep his worries to himself.

'Joe, 'he said, 'there's something I have to tell you.' And Joe listened.

'When I'd finished telling him what had happened, he suddenly got real mad at me. "Perhaps it's as well we're on the phone as what I'd like to say to you doesn't bear thinking about. Are you nuts or something? How many times have I told you? With that goddamned temper of yours, when you're up against this sort of trouble you should always keep your hands firmly in your pockets. There's no percentage in doing what you did. Did you think about those kids of yours?"

'Joe, it just happened. It was one of those things.'

'Wilf, there is no excuse and you know it.'

With that he concluded. 'Listen, Wilf. I'm a little disgusted with you so I really can't talk to you any more right now.' And he put the phone down.

'Jesus Christ,' Wilf thought. 'What have I gone and done now?'

An hour or so later Joe rang back.

'Listen,' he said. 'What's done is done. What can we do to help? Do you need me to send someone over?' (By this Wilf knew that if Ronnie Morris suddenly disappeared he would have no case to answer.)

'That's kind of you, Joe, but I don't think that's necessary.'

'Well,' he said, 'I won't ask you again, but you know the offer's always there if you should need it. Now, look. Do you need any money, Wilf, for lawyers, or whatever?'

'It'll be OK, Joe. But thanks all the same.'

Before he rang off, Joe said that he had no idea how he would break the news about all this to Theresa.

'Just do me a favour, Joe. Just don't say anything at all until we know the outcome of the trial.'

Despite his telling off, Wilf felt better when he'd talked to Joe. As usual, when it mattered, he was there for him.

★

Summer had come by now and apart from the case still hanging over him, life continued to look up for Wilf. Not only had he come to his senses, but his family was happy, 'and I now had a beautiful young woman on my arm. She was always there and she had suddenly become my life.'

Wilf had almost forgotten about the trial when out of the blue his solicitor rang to tell him that they were just about to fix a date for it.

'I'm not going to be tried on the Isle of Wight, am I?'

'Of course you are. Every serious case ends up here in the Crown Court.'

'In that case I haven't a hope in hell of getting a fair trial. I'm too well known on the island. How are you going to get twelve good honest citizens sitting there and giving an unbiased verdict on the likes of me?'

'You're right,' she said. 'I'll see what I can do.'

A day later she rang back. 'I've had a word with the Crown Prosecution Service. and they've agreed to let you stand trial at Winchester Assizes.'

The summons to appear arrived a few days later.

By now it was mid-August. 'Ros, thank God, had promised to stand by me and told me not to worry, as she'd take good care of the children.' But even so, Wilf had a heavy heart on the morning when he left for Winchester, knowing full well that he might not be coming back for several years. But as he kissed Ros goodbye, he felt as if she'd been there all his life.

Now Wilf had another stroke of luck. On the evening before the trial an old friend from the East End called Fred Toomey, aka Fred the Bed, had paid him a visit.

'Can I ask you something, Wilf? Just how bad is your record?'

'It ain't that good, but it ain't that bad. I've been up before the magistrate plenty of times, but I've not had that many convictions – and those I did have were small things like a fine or a probation order.'

'Good. Now another question, Wilf. This Ronnie Morris. How many convictions has he had for violence?'

'Forget it. The guy's an animal. The list is as long as my arm and then some.'

'That's your answer, then, Wilf. What people don't know is that when you go to trial, as long as your counsel says that you're willing to open your criminal record to the other side, then automatically their client has to do the a same, and your barrister can use this to attack him.'

At Winchester Assizes, before the trial, Wilf had to surrender his bail and go down to the cells, where his barrister, Jonathan Smythe, came down to see him. He was an intelligent young man, very bright and clearly determined to fight the case every inch of the way.

Wilf mentioned the advice Fred the Bed had given him. 'What is Morris's record like?' 'Pretty horrendous,' Wilf replied. 'Then I'll see what I can do to get hold of it,' he said.

At the beginning of the trial, the prison warders who brought Wilf up into court, seemed very hostile towards him, but once they realised who he was up against their attitude changed completely. 'He's not *that* Ronnie Morris, is he?' one of them whispered to him in he dock. 'We know him. We've had him here in Winchester Prison. He's a psychopath.'

When Ronnie Morris took the stand, Wilf's barrister went straight into the attack on his criminal record. 'Would you tell me where you were on such and such a date?' he asked.

'No, I can't.'

'But it says here that you were up in court at that time. Can you tell me what you were charged with?'

'Malicious wounding,' he admitted.

'I see. Malicious wounding. Now, wasn't the truth that on that occasion you used a broken beer bottle to shave your victim's head?'

'Well, not exactly.'

'Were you found guilty?'

'Yes, I was.'

This went on and on for about twenty minutes as Jonathan Smythe read out Ronnie Morris's violent record.

By the time he'd finished, Ronnie Morris lost his temper and shouted out: 'That was when I was thirteen, for Christ's sake!'

'So you started early and you haven't changed much over the years, have you?' said Jonathan Smythe.

Wilf had no intention of going in the witness box, since he claimed that he remembered nothing, including the identity of his assailant. Besides, the jury had his answers to the police questions on his questionnaire. With this, the first day's hearing ended. The judge renewed Wilf's bail, and he was able to go home.

The second day, much the same routine continued. Now the prosecution started to produce their witnesses, but none of them could say that they had actually seen Wilf commit the crime. But on the third day it was time for a witness for the defence – the boy who told Wilf that Ronnie Morris was out to get him in the first place. But because Ronnie Morris was sitting there watching what was going on, this boy was too frightened to go into the witness box.

Wilf's lawyer told the judge, who immediately ordered Morris out of the court. Then the boy was brought in and gave his evidence. Finally it was time for the defence counsel to exercise his right of a final plea before the judge's summing up and here Jonathan Smythe excelled himself. He said: 'Gentlemen of the jury, there is little point in my calling my client, as you have read, in his answers to the police questionnaire, that he can't remember a thing. I'll call him if the jury wishes it, but I think that it will be a waste of the court's time.' To which the judge said: 'I don't think it will be necessary.'

But it was Jonathan Smythe's closing statement that clinched the case.

'Gentlemen of the jury, just look for a moment at these photographs of my client's hands taken in hospital on the morning after the incident. To me it looks as if they're ripped to pieces, but if the wounds are that clean the injuries had to have been inflicted by a knife. So, gentlemen of the jury, the question you must decide is this. Who was holding that knife in the first place and who was trying to take it from him? I rest my case for the defence.'

The jury retired, but several times the foreman of the jury returned to ask the judge a question. While this was going on, Jonathan Smythe said: 'Listen, Wilf. You must be prepared. If the case goes against you, I don't want to hide the fact that you'll be looking at a minimum of eight years. So let's just keep our fingers crossed.'

Finally the jury seemed satisfied and the foreman said that they had reached their verdict.

'Gentlemen of the jury,' said the judge. 'On the first charge of malicious wounding with intent, do you find the prisoner guilty or not guilty?'

'Not guilty.'

'And on the second charge of causing grievous bodily harm, how find you?'

'Not guilty.'

'Prisoner at the bar,' said the judge. 'You are free to go.'

It was a homecoming Wilf had never dared hope for and would never forget. Back on the island, Ros was waiting for him with the children and as soon as he opened the front gate little Sammi rushed into his arms to welcome him home and both his boys hugged him.

To celebrate, that evening they decided they would go to the Ryde Pavilion for a meal, 'and bugger me,' says Wilf, 'who should be sitting at the next table but the young cop attached to the CID who nicked me.' He was with a couple of the other cops from the case for a night out with their wives.

So I said to Ros: 'I'm not in the mood to be petty minded. So I called the waiter over and said: 'What champagne have you got? Bring me a bottle of the best you have, together with six glasses and take it over with my compliments to the next-door table.'

Ros says: 'Don't you think you're pushing your luck?'

'No, not really. They're all good guys at heart.'

By then all of us were laughing and they raised their glasses. 'Cheers Wilf. Well done,' they said as they drank my health.

After this, they had no intention of being outdone and returned the compliment and sent a bottle of the same champagne over to our table.

The following day I had a talk with Ros and I said: 'Before all this thing happened, I was planning to leave the island with the kids. The Island and me no longer seem to get along together. As much as I love the place and I do to this day, but with the things I've been doing and the life I've been leading, how could I fit into this community again?'

Most people weren't even aware of what I was doing. All the time I was in London in the music business. They only think of me as a vicious thug. It will always be like that. Nothing will change. I don't want my two sons and my daughter being brought up under the shadow of the sins of their father.

'Are you serious, Wilf?' she said.

'I'm absolutely serious, but only if you'll come with me.'

'Give me a little while to think about it.' she said.

But it didn't take her long. 'I've thought about it, Wilf,' she said. 'Of course I'll come.'

So then I sat the children down and told them what was happening. I explained how they would be uprooted from their school and that they'd have to leave their friends behind as all of us would be starting a new life. I asked them how they felt about it.

Sean was the first to speak. 'What about Ros?' he asked.

I said she'd just promised me that she'd be coming with us.

'Oh, that's OK, then, Dad,' said Sean. 'That's fine by us. So long as Ros comes, there's no problem.' And there wasn't.

There and then we decided we'd go back to Ewell in Surrey. We'd rent a house there. The children would like it and it was close enough to London for me to get around and do whatever I had to. We soon found a house we liked and Ros was wonderful the way she took over, organising schools for the kids and creating a home for us all.

Finally the day of our departure dawned, and when we were going over to Portsmouth on the car ferry I went up on deck to have a breath of fresh sea air and take a last look back at the island. I saw that we were being followed by the usual flock of seagulls, but this time there was something different. In the past they'd always seemed to make the same screeching noise. But something had changed, and now they seemed to be making a different sound. Were they telling me something?

To this day I could swear those Isle of Wight seagulls following that ferry were saying 'Fuck off! Fuck off! Fuck off!' all the way across the Solent.

It is now twenty-five years since Wilf, Ros and the children left their beloved Isle of Wight.

17

Contentment – Then One by One the Lights Go Out

WHEN WILF ARRIVED in Ewell he found that his past success in the record business had gone before him. He may have finished with the music industry but the music industry had not quite finished with him and offers started rolling in. Some came from record companies and some from individual artistes, many of them big-name stars, asking him to be their manager. Others wanted him to put another band together, as he did with Judas Jump, and he was even asked to work as a freelance record producer or arranging tours for various artistes. It was flattering and it could have brought him in a lot of money. But he'd been there and done it all too many times before by now and the past was over.

For old times' sake the framed gold discs of the artistes he had managed (Black Sabbath, Stray and the Groundhogs) still hung on the wall of his sitting room, but apart from this he was no longer really interested. He was back in the streets where he felt comfortable and he says that to meet the bills he turned the skills he had learned managing his acts into running an interior decorating business.

It was in 1979 that Charlie Kray paid Wilf a visit and asked if he had seen the news about his brother, Ron, who had just been certified criminally insane and sent to Broadmoor.

'Sure,' said Wilf. 'I heard about it. It's a crying shame. I'm really sorry.'

'You could say that. But the truth is that Ronnie really worked at it.'

'Worked at it?'

'Well,' said Charlie. 'As you know, Ron is a paranoid schizophrenic, and he was smart enough to forget to take the right amount of his medication so that he would go crazy and get himself in trouble. Then someone would get hurt and more trouble would follow, with someone else getting hurt and in the end the prison authorities got fed up with him, as he had intended from the start. Now he's where he wanted to be all along – in Broadmoor. Life's easier for him there in all sorts of ways.'

Wilf said that he was glad to hear this and hoped everything would now work out for him.

'Yes,' said Charlie, 'but it might not work out quite so well for you, my friend. Until now, you've been able to avoid visiting him, but you won't be able to much longer. In Broadmoor there aren't the same restrictions on visiting that there were in Parkhurst. Parkhurst was a prison, but Broadmoor is a hospital for the criminally insane, so it's just like visiting a patient. All you have to do is turn up at the gate, where they check that whoever you're visiting has asked to see you. Then you sign the book and in you go. I warn you, Wilf, Ron's set his heart on seeing you, so be prepared.'

Until now, Wilf had continued meeting Charlie Kray from time to time and sometimes Charlie passed on requests to him from Ronnie – usually some small favour, or someone he wanted him to see. Wilf invariably did his best to oblige and whenever he did Charlie would always convey Ron's thanks to him later. But apart from this, the truth was that with all the changes now going on in Wilf's life, he had more important things to think about than Ron, particularly as Ros had just given him the news that she was pregnant.

Wilf always says that this was one of the happiest moments in his life and when he told the children they were overjoyed as well. So it wasn't until later, when he had given it some thought, that he realised that this presented him with a slight problem. He mentioned it to Ros.

'What problem?' she replied.

'A practical one. I don't know if I'm divorced or not.'

'Why? Are you going to marry me?'

'If you'll have me,' he said.

Wilf has never forgotten her reply. 'I'd love to,' she said. This was very different from the time when he had asked Lesley the same question and her reply had been: 'Why not?'.

But the problem still remained. Wilf believed he was still legally married to Lesley, but as he'd lost touch with her he had never bothered to sort things out. So now he told Ros that he'd ring her parents, find out where she was and try to sort out a divorce. He telephoned them that same evening and was lucky to get his father-in-law, with whom he had always got on well in the past. He couldn't have been more helpful.

'My God, Wilf, we've been trying to get hold of you for months,' he said.

It seemed that Lesley had been trying to complete a do-it-yourself divorce on the grounds of the irretrievable breakdown of their marriage and all it needed now was Wilf's signature to the papers.

He gave him his address and promised to sign them the moment they arrived, which they did next morning. The divorce followed quickly, leaving Ros and Wilf now free to marry.

The marriage took place on 26 July 1980 in Newport Register Office on the Isle of Wight. Wilf had Scots Billy, the man he had once meant to bury, as one of his witnesses and Dave the Rave, who had tried to sew his hand up two years before, as the other. Obviously Dave Farley had to be his best man – except that he very nearly wasn't. Dave being Dave, he mistook the time, and angry couples waiting to be married were already queuing up outside when Dave finally arrived, dressed up to the nines and the exasperated registrar was about to insist on performing the ceremony without him.

'What's up?' said Dave. 'Anything the matter?'

Wilf says that had he not been getting married, he'd have killed him.

The register office was opposite Newport's police station and as the happy couple came out to have the wedding photographs taken,

313

policemen were leaning out of the windows and several of them were taking pictures while others shouted out 'Good luck, Wilf' as they drove away.

When six months later their baby son Alex was born, Wilf seemed finally to have achieved what he had always wanted – contentment and a stable family of his own.

With so much on his plate, he put off visiting Ron Kray for as long as possible, but Ron persisted. Then one day, late that summer, Wilf found himself with Charlie, driving up the road from Bagshot over miles of Surrey heathland towards one of the most forbidding-looking buildings in the land, the Victorian institution known as Broadmoor Hospital for the Criminally Insane, to visit its most famous inmate.

But at Broadmoor, appearances were deceptive. However grim it may have looked from outside, Charlie had been right about the ease of entry and, once inside, the atmosphere was equally relaxed. A male nurse took Wilf and Charlie to the enormous visiting room, which could have come straight out of a Victorian lunatic asylum. So could some of the patients, who were under heavy medication. But there was one exception.

As soon as Wilf and Charlie Kray appeared, an upright figure in a dark blue, Savile Row suit stood up and came to greet them. It was Ronnie Kray, complete with his gold wristwatch and jewelled cuff-links, his freshly laundered snow-white shirt and neatly tied, expensive dark silk tie. Far from appearing like an inmate, Ronnie looked as if he owned the place.

'You took your fucking time coming to visit me,' were his first words of greeting.

For a moment there was an awkward silence, then he started laughing and, rather nervously at first, the other two joined in.

Ron and Wilf shook hands, and by now he was appearing very genial, thanking Wilf for all he'd done, then saying they would have a chance to get to know each other better in ten or fifteen minutes' time. This remark puzzled Wilf, as Ron abruptly turned his back on him and began an earnest conversation with his brother. This was Wilf's first glimpse of the sort of ceaseless pressure Charlie had always been under from Ron and Wilf soon heard him subjecting poor Charlie to a tirade of abuse.

'You did this . . . you didn't do that . . . why didn't you do so-and-so?' It was nothing but complaints from Ron from start to finish. And no matter how hard Charlie attempted to appease him, Ronnie wouldn't listen.

Wilf had grown fond of Charlie and was so put out by this that he was on the point of leaving rather than having to endure similar treatment himself. But as soon as Ronnie had finished berating Charlie, he took a deep breath, turned to Wilf and said quite calmly: 'Sorry about all that.'

Ronnie had swung right around by now and was holding Wilf transfixed by the gaze of his dark eyes through blue-tinted rimless spectacles. He spoke rather softly with a touch of old-fashioned formality.

'First of all, Wilf, I'd like to say how glad I am that you won that case against you on the Isle of Wight. Charlie told me all about it at the time.'

Wilf replied that he was too, then asked what he could do to help him.

Ronnie didn't beat about the bush. 'Wilf, we do all right for money. We get by. But things seem to be costing more and more all the time and we have our expenses. Now Charlie here has explained to us how good you were in the record business. He says you're very clever. Is there any way that you can work some magic deals for us to bring us in some cash? It's cash we always need.'

Somewhat taken aback by this, Wilf played for time and said he'd have to think about it. 'What have you in mind? Are we going out on an armed robbery or something?'

'No, Wilf. That would be silly. Nothing like that. Nothing so crude. But we've been thinking about it and there's got to be a way to make some money out of our name.'

Wilf saw what he was getting at. 'You could be right,' he said, 'but I'll need time to think about it. Then I'll get back to Charlie.'

'No, no, no,' he said. 'Don't get back to Charlie. Now that you've visited me here, you can always come again.'

'With that he gave that funny smile of his, which always made me feel as if I wasn't sure if he was going to kiss me or hit me.'

'Just give me a few days to think about it, Ron and I'll get back to you,' Wilf said.

'Yes, back to me. That's the word, Wilf. Back to *me*. All you have to do is turn up here. It's as easy as that. I'll put your name on my list of visitors, so you can come here when it suits you.'

'Then all three of us started talking about this and that and nothing in particular,' says Wilf. 'By the end of it I was thinking that if Ronnie Kray was as mad as the authorities claimed he was, he had to be the smartest madman I had ever met. He was talking coherently and fluently all the time by now and asking all sorts of questions, particularly about my friends in America. I mentioned my meeting with Angelo Bruno.'

'My God, Wilf. Angelo! How's he looking?'

'He looks good. He looks real good, 'said Wilf, which seemed to satisfy Ronnie. All he said in reply was: 'What a nice man he was.'

'In the circumstances I thought it best not to tell him Angelo Bruno's remark about having told the twins that if they put their hands in shit, some of it would always stick,' says Wilf.

When the time came for the patients to return to their wards, Ronnie rose, shook hands and made Wilf solemnly promise to come back soon to see him. With this he left. Wilf looked at Charlie and Charlie looked at Wilf.

'You see?' said Charlie.

'See what?'

'Now you can see what I've been putting up with all my life.'

Wilf tried reminding him that Ron was stuck inside this place, day in, day out.

'Yeah, but you don't know the half of it. From now on it's you I feel sorry for.'

'Why me?'

'You'll soon see. Up until now I've protected you as much as I could, but once Ronnie gets into you you're trapped,' he said.

On the way back they stopped at a pub in Bagshot for some lunch and while they were eating and talking about Ron Wilf had a bright idea. 'Hang on,' he said to Charlie. 'There are plenty of T-shirts out there with logos by people like Armani and Versace. Have you ever thought of T-shirts with the Kray twins on them? All we have to do is find the right printer and the right outlets and – you know what? it could work. Then there's a lot of other stuff that we could market – like pictures of the twins which could go on mugs and postcards. There's photographs of them, too and Christ knows what besides.'

After that conversation over lunch with Charlie, Wilf's mind started working overtime. Back home that evening, he took pen and paper and began listing all the things that might provide a way for the twins to earn money. He ended up with over twenty separate possibilities. Ideas were one thing, but getting them to work was another and Wilf began enquiring among several print firms he had got to know in his time in the record business about the feasibility of printing the twins' faces on T- shirts.

When Wilf mentioned this to Charlie, his reaction was: 'Please leave me out of it. This is your problem now.' So he made a second trip to Broadmoor, this time on his own, 'and Ronnie greeted me as if he'd known me a hundred years'.

He clearly knew a lot about Wilf's private life and was soon enquiring about Ros and the children and the baby. 'After twenty minutes or so of social gossip, it was back to that stare of his again. "Well, what have you come up with? Charlie says you've something to discuss." '

When Wilf explained about the T-shirts, he saw the point at once, but wanted to know how Wilf could get it done. He replied that it was perfectly possible, but that he'd need to bring in some of the people involved to meet him.

'Why?' he asked at once. 'I'm not some puppet sitting here for anyone to come and have a look at.'

It took Wilf quite a while to explain that to get these projects off the ground, the people they relied on would need to be convinced that the idea had his blessing. Once they knew this, Wilf could then go ahead and arrange the deals on the twins' behalf. Ron finally agreed to this and over the next few months Wilf took a number of printing executives and businessmen and publicists on that memorable drive to Broadmoor to meet its even more memorable inmate. Wilf's 'magic' had begun to work and what he calls 'the Kray twins' cottage industry,' started. Soon all sorts of people were visiting Broadmoor to organise fresh deals with them, and Wilf began to feel his work was over. As the twins were making money, he was happy to leave the deals to others and although he went on seeing Ronnie the visits became increasingly social in character.

Throughout this period, although Reg was still in Parkhurst, he, too, was seeing quite a lot of visitors of his own and Ron kept on at Wilf to visit him as well. But he had no intention of doing so. This was not because he had anything in particular against Reg. 'All I felt at this stage was that, as I was dealing with Ron, I didn't want to get mixed up with the other one.' He had heard from several people and especially from Charlie, that once you got involved with both the twins together one would play you off against the other all the time. 'This would lead to fuck-ups, it would lead to confusion and frankly I wasn't that sort of guy. I wanted life kept simple.'

But by now Wilf was regularly receiving letters from Reg. He didn't want them, but nor could he ignore them, and in the end he started writing back. Soon Reg had started not just asking Wilf to do this and that for him but telling him to, which didn't go down too well. 'Nobody *tells* me to do anything,' says Wilf and that included Reg. Things came to a head when, during his next visit to Broadmoor, Ronnie told him that the last of his monthly visits from Reg had ended with one almighty row about him.

'Why about me?' Wilf asked. 'What have I done wrong?'

'It was your reluctance to go and see him. He said he wouldn't be bothering with you any more because you were *my* fucking man.'

'In fact, what Reggie said was true,' says Wilf. 'From that day until the day he died, I was always Ronnie's man. Reg had his own. And when eventually I did get to visit Reg, there was a wall between us from the start. I sensed he didn't like me and at that stage I sure as God didn't like him. But with Ronnie, nine out of ten of the visits I had with him were what you might call "friendship visits" – and had nothing at all to do with business. We would talk about this and that and through these visits I got to know a very different man from the one portrayed in the media. I found him kind, caring and considerate – but I won't deny that at certain moments he was also fucking scary.'

Wilf may have found contentment now with Ros and the children, but time and life were catching up with him – and with those he loved. While he was getting to know Ron Kray, he had been keeping in as close touch as ever with Joe Pagano. No week went by without at least three or four telephone calls between them, but early in 1981, when Wilf rang Joe as usual, he spoke to Theresa instead. She had bad news. Joe had had a heart attack, a mild one, but it had been enough to scare everyone involved except for him. Theresa put him on the line and he told Wilf at once that there was nothing at all to worry about. However, when Wilf said that he'd be flying in immediately to see him, he told him not to, as the doctors had banned visitors for a while. But Wilf went on calling every day until he knew for sure he was fine. Once he was, he decided not to tell Joe that he was coming and took a night flight to New York, booked himself into the Sheraton, then took a cab out to the house.

'To be honest, Joe was looking as good as I'd ever seen him. He was glad to see me and told me he was feeling fine. He was even trying to give up smoking, but said he was sneaking the odd one here and there.' As usual, he wanted to know everything that Wilf was up to, and when he started telling him the latest about Ronnie Kray, he became really interested and wanted to know how he was managing in Broadmoor. Wilf told him he was fine and mentioned that Ronnie had been anxious to know all about Joe himself, together with his various friends in America.'When you're locked up in a place like that, surrounded by crazy people, you really long for news from friends in the world outside,' he said.

This remark evidently made Joe Pagano think. Wilf knew that Joe had never been a letter writer, so he was surprised when he suddenly remarked: 'I tell you what, Wilf. I'm going to make an exception of Ronnie Kray. If I write him a letter, will you give it to him for me?'

Wilf said that of course he would and that Ronnie would be really pleased to hear from him. But Joe didn't write the letter straight away. First they had to have a drink in his famous bar. He was trying to cut back on hard liquor and was drinking sherry instead, believing it was better for him than spirits, until Wilf told him otherwise. He was also taking a rest in the afternoon, so he went off to his room for a couple of hours while Wilf sat talking to Billy and two or three other old friends, catching up on the gossip.

When Joe reappeared he handed Wilf a letter addressed to Mr

Ronald Kray. Two days later, satisfied that Joe was really getting well now, Wilf flew home with it.

He never discovered what was in the letter and when he presented it to Ron, in Broadmoor, two days later, he knew better than to ask him. But Ron was clearly excited by it and asked Wilf to come and see him the following weekend as he wanted him to take back a reply.

For some time now Ronnie had also been asking Wilf to bring Ros in to see him, together with their baby, Alex. When the weekend came, they did so.

Almost as soon as they arrived, Ron began paying more attention to the baby than to them, and they saw an unsuspected side of Ronnie Kray. As Wilf says: 'He obviously loved kids and they loved him.' Quite a number of families visited Broadmoor at weekends and a playpen was provided for the very young children. When they placed Alex in it, it was Ron who insisted on looking after him as if he was his own.

'When Alex got a little out of hand with one of the other kids, it would be Ronnie who got up, pulled him back, told him to behave and proudly said to us: "Look at him. He's a born fighter, this kid."'

As they left, Ron gave Wilf a letter to mail back to Joe Pagano and within a week or two Joe was writing back to him. The two of them continued to correspond, via Wilf, until Joe's death and through their letters a genuine friendship grew up between them. At this time, Reg Kray was in Gartree Prison with Harry Roberts, who was serving life for killing a policeman. Roberts was also an accomplished carpenter who was known for the lacquer boxes he produced in the prison workshop and, through Reg, Ron asked him to make Joe a specially inscribed cigar box, which Wilf took with him on his next visit to New York. Although he had all but given up cigars, Joe was immensely touched by this and reciprocated by sending Ron an old-style diamond agate and gold pinkie ring, which he asked Wilf 'to give to my friend Ronnie Kray, on your next visit into Broadmoor.'

Until the age of thirty eight Wilf had always taken his health for granted, despite the fact that he had always had trouble with his hips, having been born with both hip joints out of alignment. In 1983 a pelvic osteotomy operation to correct this ended by making the condition worse. But although he suffered pain when he walked, he remained as strong as a bull and it never struck him that the life that he had led would take its toll on him one day. Early in 1982, that day arrived.

What happened was as sudden as it was unexpected. On returning from a walk with Ros and Alex, he was pottering around the kitchen when he was hit by an excruciating pain in his chest. The pain was so extreme that he passed clean out. When he recovered, the doctor was bending over him and telling him that he suspected he had had a heart attack and was just about to call an ambulance. By now the pain had gone as swiftly as it had come, so Wilf refused to go to hospital, but to be on the safe side the doctor insisted on taking a sample for a blood test. A few days later he returned with the news that, as suspected, Wilf had definitely had a heart attack and was suffering from angina. He also said that, as a precaution, Wilf should cut out drinking, stop smoking and take things easy. But, of course, he did none of these things, rapidly recovered and more or less forgot about it.

For as he says, married life with Ros and the children was giving him a contentment he had never known before and 'everything in the garden was rosy'. He was still in close contact with Joe Pagano and saw Ronnie fairly regularly in Broadmoor. The various deals he had put in place for him were bearing fruit, and he seemed as happy now as he ever would be. Then, once again, in 1983, disaster struck. Theresa rang to say that Joe had had a stroke.

He had been lunching at the Marigold Restaurant in Manhattan with his old friend Bobby Bumps and another friend, called Jerry Castle, when he rose from the table and suddenly collapsed. As this was obviously something serious, his two friends rushed him to a nearby hospital, where after tests the doctors told him he had had a stroke. As soon as Wilf heard this, all he wanted to do was to fly to New York straight away to see him, but Theresa put him off, saying Joe was far too ill for visitors. Within a month, however, Theresa told Wilf that Joe was fighting back and seeing a speech therapist. Then, a few weeks later, as soon as Joe was strong enough, Wilf flew in.

'To be honest he was looking good. His speech was slow, but it was coming back, although he had to pronounce his words very slowly and deliberately. One thing I did notice was that when he walked he had to use a stick.'

Because of his hips, Wilf had been using a walking stick himself for quite some time by now, but the stick he used was a very ordinary one. Joe noticed it at once. 'My God, Wilf, what's that?' he said. 'Do you call that thing a stick?' With that he picked up his own stick, saying proudly: 'Now this really is a stick! It's a Gucci.'

'It's a what?'

Because of the slight impediment in his speech, Joe repeated the words very slowly and clearly – 'IT'S . . . A . . . GUCCI,' – in the way his therapist had told him to.

In a friendly, mocking sort of way, Wilf answered: 'IS . . . IT?'

With that Joe got mad and hit him across the head with it.

'You disrespectful . . .'

'Whoa, calm down!' said Wilf.

'I'm only kidding you,' said Joe.

But by now Wilf was looking at his walking stick. 'It's a beauty. Where'd you get it?'

Joe said a friend called Charlie had bought it for him when he heard he had to use a stick to get around. 'Anyway,' he said. 'Who knows? If you're a good boy, Wilf, I might buy one for you, one of these days.'

Wilf spent the next ten days or so with Joe. During the day Danny would usually be out working, so Wilf would stay at home to be with him and Danny would say: 'I'll leave you two old guys here to reminisce. Us younger guys have got to go to work.'

By the time that Wilf was ready to leave, he guessed that Joe was set to make a full recovery.

But while he was still in New York, Wilf spent time with his old friend Wassel and some of the other guys on East 115th Street in the old neighbourhood. 'If anyone can restore your spirits and cheer you up, it's them. Nothing seems to get them down,' he says. Back in England, the good life continued for Wilf and for his family. In 1984, keen for a change, they moved from Ewell to a house in Staines and the following year, when Ros had a daughter called Emma, it seemed as if their happiness was now complete.

It was in 1986 that Joe Pyle, who had been a friend of Wilf's for years, approached Wilf for advice. Everyone in Wilf's world knew that Joe Pyle had been the nearest thing to a godfather of British crime for more than three decades, but now he said he wanted to go straight and to make a new career in the record business.

'My advice to Joe was to fucking forget it. Luckily he didn't take it, and today he is a very successful agent and promoter in the music industry.'

But what Joe really wanted out of Wilf were business contacts in New York and anywhere else in America for that matter.

'It's your back yard,' he said. 'How's about you coming over with me and introducing me to a few people?'

Wilf would not have done this for anyone, but the former godfather has a special place in his affections. 'As far as Joe's concerned, I just love him to death. No question about it. Joe Pyle is my favourite kind of guy. He's a big man but he's also gregarious, outgoing and fantastic company. So all I could say was: "Fine, Joe. When are we going?"'

Before leaving, Wilf had automatically told Joe Pagano he was coming and that this time he'd bringing 'a good friend of ours', knowing that Joe would understand what he meant. As Wilf puts it: 'to say that someone is a good friend of ours means he's one of us. That's the way they use it over there.

'Now Joe Pyle was not unknown in America through associates of associates and I had spoken to Joe about him quite frequently in the past.' Joe said that he would book them both rooms in the newly opened Holiday Inn nearby and said that once they were settled in they should come and see him at the house.

They took an overnight flight from London to New York and as usual the faithful Charlie was there to meet them, this time with a brand-new midnight-blue limo and drove them straight to their hotel. And later that morning, when they took a cab to the Pagano house, they found it full of people. Since his stroke, Joe no longer went out much and had effectively made his house his office. This meant that Wilf was able to introduce Joe Pyle to a number of other good friends there, including Danny, whose father was upstairs when they arrived. When he came down to greet them, he gave Wilf his customary hug and kiss. Among his friends, Joe Pagano was always known as 'Joe P', so when Wilf now introduced them he could not resist saying: 'Joe P, I want you to meet Joe P.' ('I knew it was corny, but what the hell?' he says.)

Luckily the two Joes got on famously together and when Joe Pyle explained that he wanted to get into the music business, Joe Pagano said: 'Then the man you have to meet is a mutual friend of ours called Wassel. If there's anyone in the music business Wassel doesn't know, then they're not worth knowing.'

During their stay in New York, Wilf also introduced Joe Pyle to various agents and useful contacts and towards the end of their visit Joe took himself off for a day's gambling in Atlantic City with an old friend he'd known in London in the days of the Colony Club called Robbie. That same evening, Wilf had arranged to meet Joe for dinner back in New York at the Columbus Restaurant, on the corner of 70th Street and Columbus Avenue. It was very much the in place at the time and, while he was waiting, Wilf enjoyed talking to another old friend who was now part-owner of the restaurant, called Charlie Herman.

'While I was talking to Charlie, who should come through the door but John Gotti. He was looking slightly older and his hair was greyer than when I saw him last, but he was smarter than ever, looked a million dollars and still had the same old twinkle in his eye.'

Since that afternoon when he had first met him when driving back with Lesley from Long Island, Wilf had gone out clubbing with John Gotti several times and had grown to like him. But that was several years ago, since when John Gotti's life had changed dramatically. In December 1985 he is credited with having organised the shooting in Manhattan of the millionaire racketeer and businessman, Paul Castellano and had reputedly succeeded him as boss of the Gambino family. If this was true, this would have made him the most powerful mobster in the country. But unlike most gangsters, the flamboyant 'Dapper Don' enjoyed his notoriety and in the year following this meeting with Wilf he would achieve the publicity coup of his career, when he was acquitted in a major conspiracy trial and became something of a folk hero among his own. He was finally sentenced to life imprisonment without parole in 1992, but, according to one obituary, even when he died in prison, ten years later, 'his status as a latter-day Robin Hood and keeper of the Mafia myths remained for some undiminished.' It was this that makes Wilf's meeting with him that evening in New York so eerily prophetic.

'He looked at me and said: "My God, it's Wilf. How are you, buddy? Come and have a drink and talk to me. What's been happening with you?"

'It's not what's been happening with me that matters. It's what's been happening with you,' said Wilf.

'Even as I said this to him, he retained that twinkle in his eye.'

'Now, what have you been hearing about me?' he replied.

'What have I been hearing? Let me tell you something, John. You're all over the newspapers in my country. You're all over the TV. That's what I've been hearing.'

Wilf's words clearly pleased him. 'Am I really that well known over there?' he said.

'I'm telling you, your face is everywhere. But just between me and you, John, how do you really feel about all this?'

'As it's between me and you, I'll tell you, Wilf. One thing's for sure, I've never been a lay-down Sally in my life. But guys like me usually end up in the gutter with two ounces of lead in the back of the head, or spend the rest of their lives in jail and then they're forgotten. But when I go, Wilf, everybody in the world is going to remember who John Gotti was.'

Back in England, Wilf began suffering from chest pains again, which proved to be angina, although he refused to believe it, insisting it was only indigestion and would go away. But soon he had a fresh attack, this time a bad one, ending up in hospital in intensive care, where a second attack resulted in cardiac arrest. When he came to, everything in his body was aching and the doctor said that he had had to punch and pummel him back to life as the electrical treatment on his heart had failed to get it going.

The state of his heart meant that for several years to come Wilf's days of travelling by air were over, since no doctor would give him a clean bill of health to fly. Besides, he was beginning to accept that he had responsibilities for a wife and children and that the time had come to do something he'd never really done before – calm down and start enjoying a quieter way of life.

As far as Joe Pagano was concerned, the ban on flying meant that they could meet no longer and they kept in contact entirely by telephone, which they did as much as ever.

But death was dogging Wilf by now. His brother Bernie had become something of a loner since the recent break-up of his marriage and was living by himself in a house in Coulsdon. Then, just before his forty-seventh birthday, Bernie died of a massive heart attack. His death affected Wilf far more than he'd expected and it was only when he'd gone that he realised how much he missed him and how much he had relied on his brother always being there.

It was early in April 1988 that Wilf received one of his regular morning calls from Joe Pagano, but this was not the Joe he knew. Something had vanished from that resonant voice of his and he was no longer giving Wilf advice. This time Joe was asking for advice instead.

'Wilf, you remember all that coughing and that stuff I was bringing up in the mornings a few years back? Well, I didn't tell you at the time, but I had blood tests and as nothing showed up I forgot about it. But recently the coughing started up again and I had fresh tests at the hospital.'

Wilf knew what was coming and felt sick in the pit of his stomach. 'What did they show?' he asked.

'What did they show? They showed that I've got cancer. But they tell me at the hospital that if I have the lung removed it will be a dangerous operation but there's at least a chance of survival.'

Wilf tried sounding hopeful. 'That's great, then, Joe. At least that's something.'

'Yes, but I can't quite make up my mind about it. What do you think I should do?'

It was an impossible question to be asked by someone else, particularly by someone as important to Wilf as Joe Pagano.

'I don't know, Joe,' he stammered. 'Honestly, I just don't know.'

'Wilf, I'm asking you as my friend. What should I do?'

By this point in the conversation, Wilf was feeling so emotional that he couldn't answer. As he says: 'Here was this guy who was the nearest thing to a father I had ever had suddenly asking me this life-and-death question.' Joe must have understood this, for instead of pressing for an answer all he said to Wilf was: 'Well, let's sleep on it and talk about it tomorrow.'

That night, of course, Wilf couldn't sleep, but during the night he managed to think out what to say and when Joe rang and asked if he had come to a conclusion he said that, yes, he had.

'All I'll say to you is this, Joe. You are your own man and you've always been the one who made the decisions. And even now you're still the only one who can.'

To Wilf's surprise, Joe laughed at this. 'Well, I'll be honest with you, Wilf. I've been kidding with you. After I spoke to you yesterday, I naturally discussed it with Theresa and the children and you're right. It is my decision and there's only one thing to be done. I know I have to have that operation.'

Having said this, suddenly all that Joe seemed to be concerned about was Wilf.

'Now, Wilf, I don't want you trying to be a smartarse and jumping on a plane to come and see me. I'll be fine. Remember I'm a tough guy. You and me, we'll stay in touch through Theresa and she'll let you know what's going on.'

Next day Joe entered the Nyack Hospital in New York, where he was operated on the following day. The operation was successful, although it took him some time to come around from the anaesthetic. Wilf had a direct line to the private ward where he was recovering. 'Hang on a minute,' said the nurse when he rang and to his amazement he heard Joe's voice answering.

'Joe. How are you doing? This is great,' said Wilf.

'Yeah, yeah, yeah. Now get off the phone,' said Joe.

'Later, when I got back to the nurse, she told me: "That was marvellous. He'd only just come around. He'll be fine now. Call again tomorrow, and I'll tell you how he is."'

Wilf did call the following day and Joe spoke to him for a short time, and over the following weeks and months every time they

327

spoke he sounded just a little stronger. Then just as it seemed that he was out of the woods, Wilf received a call from Danny, on 22 March 1989, telling him that his father and Wilf's friend, Joe Pagano, had died on the evening of 20 March. Joe had lived for nearly a year after the operation.

Danny said that one minute he had been fine and the next he suddenly collapsed with a massive heart attack. Ever since, one of the biggest regrets of Wilf Pine's life has been that he didn't fly over straight away.

A part of me died when I heard the news and I couldn't control my grief. A light had been extinguished in my life. It was horrible and what made it worse was that even now, because of my heart condition, I couldn't fly in for the funeral. Joe was laid to rest in the same grave as his son Jimmy, in the Cemetery of the Assumption in Monsey.

After the funeral I spoke to Danny and I knew that if anyone was really suffering now it was him. Joe had always said that Danny wasn't just his son but also his best friend; in the same way Joe was the best friend in the world to Danny. He told me that over three thousand people from all over the country came to the funeral. This says a lot about the man who had been my dearest friend and mentor.

On 31 May 1989 Wilf had successfully negotiated and concluded, on Ronnie's and Charlie's behalf, a deal with the Parkfield Group plc to sell their rights to the film *The Krays*. The film would in fact be made later by Fugitive Films and finally, for once, all three Kray brothers were delighted with the outcome.

A few days later, on his next visit to Broadmoor, Ron told Wilf that he had just decided to marry a friend called Kate Howard. Wilf's first reaction was to laugh. Ronnie asked him what he found so funny about it.

'Well, Ron,' said Wilf, 'you're still married to your first wife, Elaine, aren't you? And surely Kate is still very much married to her husband, Harry.'

Instead of replying, Ronnie gave Wilf a look that stopped him making any further comment. Then he took a sharp intake of breath, which was usually an indication that Ronnie was about to say something serious.

'Wilf,' he said. 'You know that I've not had any contact with Elaine for nearly two years, so I've just instructed my solicitor, Stephen Gold, to obtain a divorce for me on the grounds of the irretrievable breakdown of our marriage.' As as an afterthought, he added that anyhow the marriage had never been consummated. At this they both started laughing. Even if the Broadmoor authorities had allowed it, Ron had never disguised the fact that he was homosexual. Then Ronnie said that there was something he would like Wilf to do for him. This turned out to be one of the most bizarre things he had ever had to do for a friend: Ronnie wanted him to appear in court on his behalf to give evidence for his divorce.

Until now Ron had not discussed the matter with anyone except his solicitor, Stephen Gold, but now that divorce proceedings were about to start, Stephen Gold had advised him that it would be better for his case if he could call a witness, provided the judge allowed it. Although divorce papers had been served on Elaine and a date fixed for the hearing, she had neither replied nor given any indication whether she wanted a divorce or not.

A few weeks later Wilf went to the Law Courts in Portsmouth to attend the hearing. At first the judge was unwilling to consider the petition, but finally allowed Stephen Gold to submit his case. Gold explained to the judge why Ronnie Kray could not be present but told him he would like to call Wilf Pine to give evidence on his client's behalf. The judge agreed and, under oath, Wilf explained how Elaine had refused to have any contact whatsoever with her husband for the last two years. After Wilf had given his evidence, the judge said he would take the most unusual step of granting the divorce, but that this case was not to set a legal precedent.

So Ronnie Kray was free to marry for the second time which he did, early that October, in the chapel at Broadmoor, in the presence of Wilf, Joe Pyle, Johnny Nash, Alex Steyne, Charlie Smith, Charlie Kray, Nick Treeby and Paul Lake. Kate was allowed one female guest as her matron of honour and her ex-husband Harry drove her to the wedding.

At the end of that month, because Ros was worried about Wilf's continuing ill health and wanted their two young children to grow up near the coast, they moved to their present house near Bournemouth. By now Sean had moved away from home and was living in Greenford, Middlesex, with his future wife, Dawn, and Scott had married his girlfriend, Julia, and was living in Chertsey, Surrey. Their daughter Sammi was working and living with a friend of hers near Staines. Over the years, Ros's decision to move the family to Dorset proved to be a good one. For the next two years, life seemed pretty good for him and his family.

But their happiness was not to last. A phone call at five minutes past two in the early morning of 16 February 1991 from Dave Farley brought it to a shattering end. Wilf took the call, but Dave asked to speak to Ros. Wilf said she was sleeping, but Dave insisted that he woke her up as he had to speak to her urgently. Sensing that something was terribly wrong, Wilf did wake Ros then and as she listened to what Dave was saying, tears started streaming down her cheeks. All she said was, 'I'll tell him', then she put the phone back. Almost beside himself by now, Wilf said: 'What is it? Ros, what is it?'

Sobbing uncontrollably, she told him that his son Scott was dead.

Wilf still finds the subject of his son's death so painful that he cannot bear to talk about it. What he did tell me was how wonderful his friends and family had been and what support they gave him and Ros throughout this nightmare. His dear friend Theresa Pagano understood their agony all too well. The letter she wrote to him and Ros they treasure to this day.

Scott's funeral took place on Thursday 22 February, the day before Wilf's forty-seventh birthday, and was attended by many friends, including some from America. He was laid to rest at St Jude's Cemetery in Englefield Green, Surrey, in the very plot that Wilf had bought only the year before for himself. Scott was only twenty-three years old when he died.

That was the day for Wilf Pine and his family when the brightest light of all went out.

Later I learned that an inquest was held on 1 March 1991, at the Coroner's Office, Redhill, Surrey and the cause of death was given as 'death by hanging, while the balance of his mind was disturbed'.

I couldn't help thinking how sadly and uncannily Wilf Pine's life seemed to have run on a parallel with that of his late friend, Joe Pagano, whose young son Jimmy also died in similar tragic circumstances in 1973.

Scott's untimely death brought this already close and loving family even closer. Wilf said: 'None of us will ever get over our loss, but the grieving had to end and as difficult as it was, our lives had to go on.'

One indirect result of Scott's death was to improve relations between Wilf and Reg Kray. Up until then, they had had a mutual dislike for one another, but Reg as well as Ron had shown such care and consideration for Wilf and his family that their relationship started to improve. This did not mean that they would ever be the greatest of friends, but now Wilf's visits to Reg were no longer as hostile as before. Throughout this period, Ron was a tower of strength for Wilf, who continued to visit him regularly and took care of his business on a day-to-day basis.

Then, in September 1993, it was Ron's turn. He suffered a suspected heart attack. The staff at Broadmoor informed Wilf straight away, and within a few hours, after being cleared by the police officers who were guarding him, he was by his bedside in Wexham Park Hospital, Berkshire. Wilf was shocked to see Ronnie looking so grey and drawn, but to cheer him up he told him he looked fine.

'Well, I don't bloody feel it,' was Ron's reply.

While they were talking, one of the nurses interrupted them, saying that his brother Reg was on the line. He handed him the telephone and while they were talking Wilf discreetly moved to the far side of the room. But after a couple of minutes, Ronnie called him over, saying that Reg wanted a word with him.

He began by thanking him for getting to the hospital so quickly, but his main concern was for his brother. Wilf tried to reassure him, saying that he could only repeat what he had been told; at the moment he seemed weak but stable.

'Reg then made me promise to look after his brother while he was in hospital . . . 'That goes without saying,' Wilf replied.

After Wilf had hung up, Ronnie asked Wilf what his brother had said to him. Wilf repeated their conversation. Ron then took Wilf's hand and, sick though he was, his vice-like grip had not diminished.

'Wilf,' he said, 'I want you to give me your solemn promise that if anything happens to me, you'll look after Reg'.

'Of course I will,' said Wilf.

At that moment, Ron's wife Kate came into the ward. She had heard on the radio the news of Ronnie's heart attack and had rushed up to see him from her home in Kent.

'Things had been bad between her and Ronnie ever since she published her book, *Murder, Madness, Marriage*, very much against his wishes. The worst thing about the book for Ronnie was that he felt that it had made him look a fool and he had made it clear that he wanted nothing more to do with her. Before she could say a word, Ronnie was yelling at her and telling her to get out of the room, as he had no wish to see her.

'When Kate tried to speak to him, Ronnie grew even angrier. By now the lines on the screen of his heart monitor were going berserk and one of his nurses from Broadmoor asked Kate to leave at once. Clearly she didn't know which way to turn and she told me that when she came in she had been spotted by the crowd of reporters and photographers that had gathered at the hospital gates. She was anxious to avoid them now at all costs.'

By now Ronnie, who was breathless from shouting, asked Wilf to see Kate out to her car. Kate tried once more to speak to him, but he closed his eyes and turned his head away. As Wilf left with Kate, someone from the hospital's administration department stopped them and asked Kate if she would mind speaking to the press. Kate, in tears by now, said she would, but only if Wilf would accompany her. The press conference that followed was an emotional affair and once it was over he walked a still-sobbing Kate to her car and wished her good luck.

'I never saw her again until Ron's funeral in 1995 and I have not spoken to her since. When I returned to Ronnie's room, in spite of sedatives, he was still agitated, but when I told him that Kate had left and was on her way back to Kent, he became calmer.' When he heard that his brother Charlie and his lifelong friend Laurie O'Leary would soon be coming in to see him, Ron perked up and Wilf told him that he would leave him now to get some rest but that he would ring him later.

In the next couple of days Ronnie's condition had improved so much that he was sent back to Broadmoor, but Wilf says that the last eighteen months of Ronnie's life were one big nightmare. Wilf believes that Ronnie never recovered from that heart scare or his break-up with Kate. He says that almost every visit ended with getting back to he subject of Kate and 'that bloody book' and the question of whether he should or should not divorce her.

Whenever the subject of divorce came up, Wilf staunchly stood his ground and refused to give an opinion either way. He told Ronnie that it was his decision and his alone.

Ronnie told Wilf that in the early part of 1994 Kate had visited him to talk things over but that he couldn't find it in his heart to forgive her and intended to divorce her. Kate did not contest the divorce and within three months both of them were free of one another. Ronnie was now sixty.

From then on Wilf had the melancholy task of watching his friend's mental and physical decline. Even so, when Charlie Kray telephoned him on the morning of 17 March 1995, telling him that Ronnie was dead, it took a while for Wilf to grasp it and realise that what he said was true. 'I was numbed and I was sad, but in a way I was relieved that Ron was finally at peace.'

Wilf kept the promise he had made him to look after his twin brother and did all he could to console him. But almost at once, Reg threw himself into making the arrangements for his brother's funeral and finally arranged to meet Wilf on the day of the funeral at English's Funeral Parlour in Bethnal Green. It was there, on 29 March, that Wilf joined Reg in the room that was set aside for him and his prison escort. According to Wilf, any barriers that remained between them disappeared the moment they set eyes on one another.

Accompanied by Reg's escort of two prison officers, he and Wilf then entered the room where Ron was lying in his coffin. 'We spent a last few minutes there, saying our farewells, Reg to his twin, me to my friend. Then we both kissed Ron goodbye.'

After Ronnie's death and with 1996 well under way, everything seemed calm at last in the Pine household. But, as usual, their happiness didn't last for long. Wilf, who had been keeping in close contact with the Pagano family, suddenly heard that Theresa had been diagnosed with inoperable cancer. He was shattered by the news. He had always loved Theresa, who had shown him such kindness and understanding, especially after the death of Scott.

Wilf asked himself what kind of God this was who could inflict such a cruel disease on somebody as good and kind as Theresa. After a brave fight, Theresa died on 11 August 1996 and was buried with her husband Joe and their son Jimmy in the Cemetery of the Assumption in Monsey.

But the sad and sorry tale of Wilf Pine continued to roll on. Barely five weeks had passed since the death of Theresa before bad luck struck again. On 16 September Ros celebrated her fortieth birthday, and they both woke up to a bright and sunny morning. Wilf didn't feel too good, but he wished Ros a happy birthday and jokingly told her that she was the oldest woman he'd ever been married to. (Both her predecessors were in their twenties when they split up.)

After breakfast, Ros left for a hair appointment, as they planned to celebrate her birthday by going out to dinner. Wilf was expecting a friend of his called Big Jon Stephenson to take him to the garage to collect his car, which had been in for repairs. Wilf remembers walking out of the back entrance to the house to meet him, but as he was closing the gate behind him he felt the most horrendous pain across his chest. But luck was with him. Jon arrived slap on time and the moment he saw Wilf he realised that there was something terribly wrong. Before Wilf could say a word, Jon had bundled him into his car and was on his way to Bournemouth Hospital.

Jon realised that every moment counted now and he broke every rule in the Highway Code to get him there as soon as possible. Luckily Jon is immensely strong and he lifted Wilf bodily out of the car and carried him into casualty. Wilf doesn't remember much except the excruciating pain and Jon's voice shouting for a doctor to do something for him. He was put on a trolley, and a doctor came and gave him an injection to ease his pain. Wilf thought that it was all over for him now.

'For some reason,' says Wilf, 'I asked Jon to lift me up. I've no idea why. Maybe it was to look the world in the eye for one last time. Then the lights went out.'

He came to in the intensive care unit with a nurse leaning over him and calling his name. She told him he had had another heart attack and then Ros was there. Although she was obviously deeply distressed, she managed to make Wilf smile by saying: 'Trust you to ruin my birthday.'

Then Jon came in. 'When I saw him I felt such gratitude towards him. For I knew that he had saved my life.' Later the doctors told Wilf that he had been clinically dead for two minutes, fifteen seconds, before they had managed to persuade his heart to beat again.

Since his previous cardiac arrest, Wilf had, in fact, suffered no fewer than four relatively minor heart attacks and had been diagnosed as suffering from a hereditary heart disease, which had taken its toll of many male members of the Pine family, including a cousin who died at twenty-two. In the first weeks after the attack, Wilf remained in Bournemouth Hospital. He was very weak and the truth, which he and Ros both knew, was that he was dying. Resigned to his fate, Wilf asked a doctor if he could go home to die and the doctor promised that, should it come to it, Ros could take him home.

'To be honest, the doctor's promise cheered me up, as I've always dreaded dying with strangers.'

Then Dr Adrian Rozkovec, a brilliant young cardiologist, entered Wilf's life and saved it.

'I see here that you have been a patient of Dr Kim Fox and Professor Magdi Yacoub at the National Heart Hospital in London, and have been considered for a heart transplant,' he said to Wilf.

'Shall we take him on?' Dr Rozkovec asked the registrar who was with him at Wilf's bedside. The registrar nodded and Dr Rozkovec said he would come back and talk to him later.

During the next few days, Wilf had extensive tests and was then moved to Southampton General Teaching Hospital, where, according to the doctor, 'they have a wonderful team of plumbers'. It was here that they discovered that a part of his heart muscle, which had shown up as dead on the last test in London a few years before, had by some miracle kick-started itself. This was important, for it meant that he was now considered a suitable patient for a heart bypass, which Wilf had been previously told was out of the question.

When he had the operation, it lasted ten hours, and when he came round from the anaesthetic the doctors told him it had been successful and, provided all went well, he should be able to go home in two weeks' time.

Ros collected Wilf from the hospital and drove him home on a fine November morning. Having been so near to death, everything that happened to him now seemed like a bonus and he appreciated Ros more than ever and could not imagine life without her.

He began to grow stronger by the day but was still wary of long journeys.

Then one evening he received a phone call from Joe Pyle, whose career in the music business had been rudely interrupted by a six-year spell in prison. Joe was only one of many of Wilf's close friends who had kept in close touch with Ros while Wilf was in hospital. But this was something different. Joe explained that he had been granted a day release from HM Prison Coldingly, where he was serving the last part of his sentence. He asked Wilf if he could pick him up next morning, as the prison governor had agreed that if he was returned to the prison by six o'clock that same evening all would be well.

Wilf's reply was: 'What time should I be there?'

Big Jon Stephenson drove him to the prison, where he and Joe Pyle had an emotional reunion. They enjoyed their day together so much that by the time they dropped Joe back at Coldingly Wilf's fear of travelling far from home had left him.

Less than six months later, Wilf received the news that he had most hoped to hear. His doctors told him that they now considered him fit to fly. Armed with that precious piece of paper, he immediately booked a New York flight for him and Ros. By the end of April, feeling better than he had for years, Wilf was once again back in New York, looking forward to showing Ros around his favourite city.

Although he had long ago fallen out with the Catholic Church, he still believed in God, but could never understand why God had allowed Theresa to suffer so much, any more than he could understand why God had taken away his son, Scott, while he was still so young. The more he reflected on his life, the more difficult it was for him to find an answer.

The first thing he did after settling in to their hotel was to ring his old friend Danny Pagano, with the news that they had just arrived. Danny immediately invited them for dinner at his house the next day. He told him he would be sending his son Joseph to pick them up.

Next morning Joseph collected them in his car and the first thing Wilf had to do was to buy flowers, lots of them: a bunch for Gina, Danny's wife, and more to place on the grave of Joe and Theresa. Because of his illness, he had had to wait so long to visit the cemetery, but as soon as young Joseph drove them through the gates Wilf felt a sudden sense of calm come over him. When they parked the car, Ros whispered to Wilf that she would be along in a minute, which was her way of saying that this moment was his.

Wilf's old friend Wassel had joined them that morning and they stood together at the graveside of the two people both of them had loved and now missed so much. Afterwards they drove to Danny's house, where Wilf was overwhelmed to see so many people whom he hadn't seen for years. There was Danny's brother Joseph, together with his two small children; there were his sisters Fran and Toni, with their husbands and their children; there was his old friend Bobby Bumps, who hadn't changed a bit; and finally there was his friend Anthony Colombo, the eldest son of the legendary crime boss, Joe Colombo. And, of course, there was Danny, looking just the same as ever, except for a touch of grey in his hair.

When Ros had been introduced to everyone, Danny's wife Gina emerged from the kitchen. Wilf describes her as 'a stunningly beautiful brunette'. Her youngest son Vincent was with her. Vincent needed no introduction. He was the spitting image of his grandfather, Joe Pagano. As they sat around the table with so many people Wilf remembered, for a moment it seemed to him just like those happy days when Joe and Theresa had entertained him at their home.

Because of his hips, Wilf walked with a permanent limp by now and at the end of dinner Danny turned to him and asked him if he always used a walking stick. When Wilf told him that he did, Danny got up and left the room. A few minutes later he returned and said to

Wilf in front of everyone: 'When my father died, I kept just a few of his personal things. And there's one thing I know he would have liked you to have to remember him by.' With this, Danny handed Wilf Joe Pagano's Gucci walking stick.

18

A Wedding and Two Funerals

WILF AND ROS returned from a happy, if at times emotional, fortnight in New York, Wilf supported now by Joe Pagano's walking stick.

Back home, some unexpected news awaited them. Dave Young, an old friend from the music business, rang Wilf out of the blue with a strange request. Would he be best man at his wedding in two weeks' time? Although Wilf was pleased to hear the news, he couldn't have been more surprised. He had always know Dave as something of a womaniser and a confirmed bachelor, and the thought of him settling down to married life was almost a joke. Dave, of all people!

The wedding would take place at Kensington Register Office with only a few close friends. This would be followed by lunch in a private room at a nearby Italian retaurant. Because of the short notice they were given, there was no chance for Wilf and Ros to meet the bride beforehand. But Wilf, in his wicked way, was looking forward to doing everything he could in his best man's speech to embarrass the old Don Giovanni on the subject of his former conquests.

He took a lot of trouble to prepare his speech, although he had to promise Ros to keep it clean, and throughout the wedding he was going over in his mind all the shocking exploits he would soon divulge.

But then something happened. There was something about the bride that made him pause. She was not at all what he had been expecting. Far from the glamorous brittle women Dave had been invariably seen with in the past, Linda, the bride, seemed shy and was far from glamorous, but she clearly loved him. And Dave had changed as well from the ruthless womaniser Wilf remembered. Could it be possible that he, too, was in love?

Wilf pondered this throughout the lunch and at the very last moment he knew the answer. This unlikely pair really were in love. And so much for that shocking speech that Wilf had spent hours preparing and chuckling over in the silence of his room.

Instead it was a deeply sentimental Wilf who gave the pair his blessing.

As they were driving home, Ros asked: 'What on earth came over you?'

He didn't answer, but it was then that he realised that he must be mellowing with age.

Just a few weeks later, early in April 1996, came another all-important event in the unexpected mellowing of Wilf. He and Ros became grandparents when his elder son Sean and his wife Dawn presented him with a grandson, Harry Pine. In no time at all, Wilf became a doting grandfather.

But while life was looking up for Wilf, things were not so good for another of his friends. Around the same time that Wilf became a grandfather, Charlie Kray had been arrested and was now in prison on a serious drugs charge.

At first Wilf was baffled by the news, as he knew that drugs had never been Charlie's thing. This was so unlike the Charlie Kray he knew that the only explanation Wilf could offer for such sheer stupidity had to be his age coupled with the fact that he was still grieving for the recent death of his only son, Gary.

But none of this carried any weight when, eleven months after his arrest, Charlie was found guilty and Judge Michael Carrol imposed the maximum sentence of twelve years' imprisonment.

By then, Charlie Kray was seventy. 'Judge Carrol might as well have put the black cap on his head and sentenced him to death,' says Wilf.

He should certainly have been more careful, and he should have known that the law would always be out to get him with a name like

Kray. But for the police it was good publicity in their failing 'war on drugs' to secure a conviction against somebody called Kray – even at the age of seventy.

The truth was that, unlike his brothers, Charlie Kray had never been a serious criminal but had suffered all his life from the curse of the name of Kray. He wasn't violent, but he was a Kray.

It wasn't just the length of Charlie's sentence that seemed so wrong to Wilf. Worse than this for Charlie was the fact that he was immediately made a rigorously guarded category-A prisoner in maximum security. This made him by far the oldest serving maximum-security prisoner in Britain.

Throughout the early years of Charlie's sentence, Wilf kept in touch with him in Long Lartin Prison. Then he began hearing worrying reports about his health. including the news that he had been suffering from breathing difficulties. Then Wilf heard that Charlie had been moved to Parkhurst on the Isle of Wight, where there was an up-to-date hospital wing and the prison was two hundred yards away from St Mary's Hospital.

It was just before Christmas 1999 that Wilf's old friend Joe Pyle rang to tell him that he had a visiting order to see Charlie Kray in Parkhurst. Would Wilf go with him? Wilf agreed to go, but when he saw his friend he was shocked to see what had happened to the once good-looking Charlie Kray. He still had the head of blond hair he had inherited from his mother Violet, but it had been cut very short. 'He also had those wonderful white teeth that had cost him so much money', but his face was drawn and gaunt and when Joe and Wilf tried to raise his spirits he failed to respond. All he could say was: 'I don't know what it is. I guess it has to be old age. But things just aren't right with me. My legs are swelling up and I'm getting breathless.' While the doctors were puzzled, Charlie Kray seemed to be confused by it all.

By now, faithfully keeping the promise he had made to Ron, Wilf had been trying to look after Reg. Their old animosity was over. Wilf visited him and corresponded with him from time to time. In February 2000 Reg rang to say that he was seriously worried by the news that Charlie had been moved from Parkhust Prison into nearby St Mary's Hospital, Newport and asked Wilf if he could possibly find out what was going on. First thing the next morning, Wilf was back on the familiar Isle of Wight ferry and heading for the hospital.

It was three months since Wilf had last seen Charlie with Joe Pyle and now 'the former playboy had become a little old man in handcuffs, lying in a hospital bed chained to a prison officer'.

'Thank God you've come!' he said when Wilf appeared. 'Didn't I tell you Wilf would come?' he said to the prison officer sitting by his bed. Like most of the prison staff who had to deal with Charlie, the officer was kind to him, but nothing could disguise the fact that he and Charlie were chained together by the wrist. Wilf enquired if this was really necessary for someone as old and obviously as sick as Charlie.

'D'you think we like it either, Wilf?' the officer replied. 'But it's laid down in prison regulations, so what can we do?' Luckily the chain was fairly long, and the officer discreetly left the room and stood outside so that Charlie and Wilf could have a few minutes' talk in private.

'I'm in real trouble, Wilf,' said Charlie when they were alone. 'The doctors don't know what it is, but just look at this.'

With this, Charlie pulled back the bedclothes to reveal his legs, and Wilf was horrified by what he saw. In the old days, Charlie Kray was proud of his figure and never weighed more than eleven stone. 'But now his legs were as thick as tree trunks and his feet were so swollen that he could barely walk.'

This disturbed Wilf as he remembered seeing similar symptoms with his mother shortly before she died, and before he left he promised Charlie that he would be back the next day. Charlie's eyes lit up. 'God bless you, pal!' he said. 'I knew that you'd be here when I needed you!'

Knowing that relations between Charlie and his brother Reg were still strained, before he left Wilf made a point of saying that it was entirely thanks to Reg's phone call that he had come so soon. Charlie seemed surprised at this.

'Oh, Reg!' he said. 'How is he? He's still giving me a pretty rough run around, with all those bloody letters he keeps sending. But what can I do? That's Reg for you. You can't change somebody like him after all these years.'

Next morning, when Wilf returned to the hospital, he found Charlie more upset than ever. The doctors who had seen him had just told him that they would treat his condition with medication, and had recommended him to be returned to Parkhurst later that day.

Although the thought of such a swift return to prison was obviously a blow for Charlie, Wilf was relieved to know that the doctors had said he could be treated. As he told Charlie, this should mean that he would soon be well. 'Keep your chin up!' he told him as he left, promising he would soon be back to see him.

During the next few days there was no further news. Then Wilf received another worried call from Reg, who had just heard that Charlie was once again in hospital and undergoing tests. Could Wilf get there as soon as possible and find out what was going on? This, of course, he did.

This time he found Charlie sitting propped up in bed, in a side room off the main ward. Sunlight streamed in through the window, there was a view of trees outside and Charlie was looking relatively relaxed, although he still had no idea what was wrong with him, until he knew the results of his tests. Wilf enquired about Diane and it seemed that she was in London, working, as she always did at this time of year, for a few weeks at the Ideal Home Exhibition. Of course, she had been in constant touch with Charlie and the hospital by telephone.

One thing still upset Wilf when he looked at Charlie. As he says: 'He had always been a dapper man and I hated seeing him stuck there in bed in a pair of grotty prison pyjamas.' So he told Charlie that he had to leave him for an hour or so but would soon be back. Was there anything special he would like to eat?

'Any chance of some brown–bread prawn sandwiches?' he asked. 'I've been lying here dreaming about them.' Wilf said he'd see what he could do.

His first stop was Marks & Spencer in Newport, where he bought two pairs of smart pyjamas, together with matching dressing gowns and a pair of the biggest slippers he could find, 'hoping they would fit poor Charlie's swollen feet'.

343

Then at the sandwich counter he bought Charlie his prawn sandwiches and, remembering that he loved all sorts of seafood, he also got him crab and smoked salmon and every sort of sandwich filled with seafood he could find.

All this shopping took a little longer than expected, and Wilf returned to the hospital to find an anxious Charlie asking where on earth he'd been. But when he saw what Wilf had brought, 'his whole face seemed to come alive and the look he gave me was worth a million pounds'.

Then Wilf and the two prison officers helped dress him in his new pyjamas and his dressing gown. 'My friend had some dignity now. I can't tell you how pleased this made me.'

Shortly afterwards, Wilf left the room and waited while the doctors came in and talked to Charlie about the results of the tests. On their way out, one of them stopped and told Wilf that Charlie had given him permission to talk to him about his case.

'I'm afraid things don't look good,' the doctor said.

Wilf said that he wasn't surprised.

'Whatever happens, he's going to be in here some time, and we'll just have to see what can be done.'

From then on Wilf appeared to spend his time going backwards and forwards to the Isle of Wight. And day by day, he watched Charlie Kray grow weaker. Then, by the second week, he knew for certain he would die.

But although Wilf knew that there was no hope left for Charlie, he was determined to keep his spirits up to the end, even if this meant giving him false hope. And here, without intending to, the doctors helped Wilf to do this by the very way they broke the news to him that he was dying.

What happened was that one of the doctors told Charlie that he would try to get him a compassionate release on the grounds that he was terminally ill. When Charlie heard this he was stunned, and when Wilf saw him soon afterwards he asked him bitterly why he had lied to him. 'Why did you keep on telling me that I wasn't dying? Why did you promise me that I was going to get better?'

Wilf had to think fast; for the right reasons, he had to con his friend. When the doctor left the room, he said: 'Listen, Charlie. Use your brains. There's no way on God's earth that you, at the age of seventy-plus, are going to have the authorities pay out lots of money for a heart bypass operation. But once that doctor gets you home on compassionate grounds, I've arranged for friends of yours and mine to hold benefit nights all over the country – Birmingham, Manchester or wherever. These will raise enough money for us to get you the best surgeon in the land to operate privately and give you what you need.'

'Jesus! You're a smart bastard, Wilf,' said Charlie. 'I'm sorry to have doubted you. Just get me out of here and get me that operation. That's all I need.'

'I knew that I had conned him and that he was too far gone by now for any surgeon in the world to save him. But the look on Charlie's face at that moment made it worth the lie.'

As he left the room, one of the prison officers saw him out. 'That was some move, Wilf,' he murmured. 'Well done.'

During Wilf's next visit, he and Charlie got down to discussing which visitors, out of all his many friends, he would most like to see. By now his brother Reg was visiting him regularly, with the prison authorities bringing him down from Wayland Prison, in Norfolk, almost every day. And a regular visitor was his childhood friend, Laurie O'Leary, who had a magical way of cheering him up and making him laugh. Among the others Charlie wished to see were two of their mutual friends, Keith Smart and Big Albert Chapman from Birmingham. But at the very top of his list was Joe Pyle and, of course, he wanted to see Diane, whenever she could get away.

Joe's visit proved to be an emotional one, as he couldn't bear to see his old friend now reduced to such a state. To make things worse, Joe had brought along another of Charlie's friends, someone called John Nielsen, but although they had known each other for at least fifteen years, Charlie didn't recognise him.

'It's very nice of you to come and see me,' Charlie said, 'but what's your name again?'

This was the first indication that Charlie's memory was going.

By now the prison authorities had moved Reg into Charlie's

former cell at Parkhurst to be near him and although the two brothers didn't have much to say to one another, Charlie knew at last that Reg was there for him. Reg also did his best to cheer him up by reminiscing about their childhood days in Bethnal Green.

But although it was thoughtful of the authorities to allow Reg to stay so close to his brother, every visit to him was a considerable ordeal. For once again, prison regulations insisted that on leaving the prison for the hospital, Reg's wrists had to be handcuffed together in front of him and his legs chained at the ankles. This meant that on every visit he made to Charlie, Reg had to shuffle through the hospital in chains in front of all the staff and patients. This upset Reg; it also upset Charlie. But once again, rules were rules, and there was no alternative.

For Wilf there was another problem over Charlie's visitors. For over a year there'd been a deep misunderstanding between Reg and Freddie Foreman over a television programme. Wilf had done his best to make peace between them, but Reg had always refused to listen. Wilf tried again, but when he told Reg that Foreman would be visiting Charlie the next day, Reg still refused to be in the same room as him and there was no way of getting him to change his mind.

Not that this stopped Freddie Foreman's visit and next morning Wilf met him and Diane off the Ryde ferry and brought them to the hospital. Throughout the drive Freddie showed considerable concern for Charlie, whom he had known for more than forty years. And once they were in the room, Diane tactfully made an excuse to leave Charlie, Wilf and Freddie on their own. Wilf has never forgotten what happened next.

'I've witnessed some things with tough guys in my life, but I've never seen anything quite like this before or since. Freddie was sitting down with Charlie, who was now in a wheelchair, and he leaned over him and took his hand. 'My pal,' he said. 'It breaks my heart to see you like this.'

For a while Charlie just looked at him as if he hadn't heard him; then at last he spoke. 'You know what breaks *my* heart, Freddie?'

'No,' said Freddie.

Speaking in a low voice now, Charlie answered. 'That I ever introduced you, my dearest, dearest friend, to those twins of mine. Just look at all the trouble it has caused you ever since.'

At this, Freddie Foreman shook his head. 'No, Charlie, no,' he said. 'You've got it wrong over me and your twins. You don't understand, Charlie.'

Charlie said: 'Understand what, Fred?'

'You don't understand that I was with *you*, Charlie. Always you. Never your twins.'

When he heard this, Charlie became tearful and Wilf got up and walked away. 'But I realised,' he says, 'that with those few words, Freddie Foreman had just given Charlie something he had needed to hear all his life. In saying this, Freddie gave his friend and mine his self-respect back. I will always love Freddie for that.'

After this visit Wilf had to drive Diane and Freddie Foreman back to catch the ferry. As they said goodbye, Wilf promised he would keep in close contact with Diane on her mobile. Then he returned to the hospital to say good night to Charlie. He found him calmer and happier than he'd been for several days and, although he never mentioned what Freddie had said to him, Wilf could tell how much it had meant to him.

But from then on Charlie started going downhill fast. Guessing that Charlie had little time to live, Wilf was staying on the island now and it was soon after Freddie's visit that the doctors told him that Charlie's death would come even sooner than expected and that Reg should be summoned quickly from the prison. Wilf informed the escort and in less than half an hour Reg was with him. Wilf explained the situation and told him that one of the nursing sisters had asked if Charlie should have resuscitation. Wilf said that the decision had to lie with Reg, as next of kin and after a short discussion Reg decided: 'No resuscitation.'

Then Reg was asked about religion. Was Charlie Catholic or Church of England? Did Reg want a priest to be present?

Wilf was taken aback by Reg's answer. 'No priests. No vicars. Nothing religious,' he said.

Wilf was to remember Reg's words when, at Reg's own funeral later that year, the evangelical chaplain, Dr Ken Stallard would eloquently tell the mourners that in his opinion Reg, like Ron, had become a devout Christian while in prison.

Then Reg said to Wilf: 'We must be realistic now. What do you think we should do about Charlie's funeral?'

Wilf replied: 'All I can do is tell you, Reg, what Charlie told me just a few hours ago before he started drifting. He made it very clear that all he wanted was to be taken back to Diane's home and from there to be taken quietly, with just Diane and a few close friends, to be buried at Chingford beside his son, Gary. He doesn't want any fuss. He doesn't want any of the razzmatazz of Ron's funeral either. That's just the way he wants it.'

Reg looked puzzled at this but said: 'All right, then. If they're his wishes, that's what he'll have.'

Reg spent the next fifteen minutes sitting quietly alone with his brother. Wilf saw Reg clasp his hands and kiss him on the forehead. Then they took Reg back to prison.

By now it was mid-afternoon and Wilf finally got through to Diane on his mobile, telling her that there was little time and that she must get to the hospital as fast as possible. As she was still in central London, he promised to keep in constant touch with her by mobile phone.

Charlie was fading fast by now, but he knew that somehow he must stay alive long enough to see Diane. Refusing to lie down, he desperately struggled to stand up, although his feet were now the size of footballs.

'Hold me! Hold me!' he repeated.

In spite of his arthritic hips, which were causing him agony, Wilf held him upright for the next twenty minutes, when luckily for him the prison governor, Governor Monro, appeared.

'Charlie, how are you?' said the governor.

'Somehow Charlie just managed to recognise him and said: 'I'm fine.'

Under his breath Wilf said, 'Ask him to sit down. I can't hold him up any longer.'

Governor Monro obliged. 'Charlie, can you do me a favour and sit down so that I can sit beside you on the bed and talk to you?' he said.

Then suddenly Charlie found his voice. 'Yes, sir,' he said, and the governor sat beside him.

Charlie Kray may have been dying, but he was still a prisoner and although he was no longer chained or handcuffed there was still a prison guard, in the form of a female officer outside the door, to prevent any unwanted visitors from entering.

The governor asked Wilf how much longer he thought he had.

'The doctors say he can go any time now,' said Wilf. 'Reg was over earlier, but he wasn't as bad as this and I'm fighting against time to get Diane here before he goes.'

According to Wilf, what followed 'shows the humane side of some prison governors that you rarely hear about'. The Governor and Wilf went outside the room and he borrowed the female officer's walkie-talkie. Speaking into it, he gave a code and said it was Governor Monro speaking. By then it was six-thirty and the prison had officially been shut down at six. But he asked to be put through to Reg's wing and asked for two volunteers to bring prisoner Kray over to the hospital straight away.

Wilf swears that in less than fifteen minutes Reg and two prison officers were in the room. All three of them were out of breath and, as it was raining heavily, they were all soaking wet.

Thanks to the humanity of Governor Monro, Reg now had his chance to say farewell to his brother in private. But there was still the problem of getting Diane to the hospital in time and the dreadful weather made things worse. Thanks to his mobile phone, Wilf knew by now that Diane was on the ferry. He rushed to meet her at Ryde, only to be told that owing to the storm the ferry had been diverted to Fishbourne, which meant yet more delay and a desperate drive by Wilf.

To make matters even worse, during that drive his mobile rang again. It was Ros, almost hysterical with the news that her father had just died. This was almost too much for Wilf. At this stage there was nothing he could do himself, but luckily he was able to contact Big Jon Stephenson, who picked Ros up and drove her straight to her mother. Wilf promised Ros to join them as soon as possible.

The ferry finally arrived. Diane was now with him in the car and Wilf was racing back to Newport. Over his mobile he heard the voice of Governor Monro telling him that Charlie was still alive, but only just, urging them to hurry. While Wilf was away, an unexpected friend of Charlie's had arrived to see him. This was Stephen, his young black driver, who, hearing of his plight, had also come to say farewell.

Diane and Wilf arrived at the hospital and rushed to Charlie's room to find him almost gone, with young Stephen and Governor Monro keeping watch beside him. Charlie appeared to be unconscious. But as soon as Diane took him in her arms and whispered to him, 'Charlie, I'm here', he opened his eyes and spoke to her. For the next twenty minutes of Charlie's fast-ebbing life, there was what sounded like a perfectly normal conversation between Charlie, his friend Stephen and Diane. Then suddenly he faded as if leaving them.

'How much do you love me, Charlie Kray?' Diane whispered.

He answered her in their secret code. 'Twenty-two bob,' he murmured, as if to tell her he was still alive.

Wilf thought he should leave the two of them alone together, but as he went towards the door Charlie called out in a feeble voice: 'Where are you going?'

'I'm just going for a breath of air,' he said. 'I'll soon be back.'

'I love you, Wilf Pine,' he said.

'I love you too, Charlie Kray,' replied Wilf.

Within seconds of closing the door behind him, Steve called him back in. Charlie has passed away in Diane's arms.

The funeral that Charlie Kray had wanted for himself was not to be. The first hint Wilf got of this came when Reg rang him the next day and told him he'd thought about it and decided that a private funeral would disappoint too many people who wanted to pay their last respects to Charlie, 'so I'm going to give him the kind of funeral I think that he deserves'.

'Which went to show,' says Wilf, 'that even in death Charlie's wishes always came second to the twins'.'

Reg decided to take over Charlie's funeral and turn it into his own personal spectacular. He knew how to do this better than anyone, as he had shown by the way he had organised and planned Ron's funeral. Through ceaseless phone calls from prison, he had carefully arranged the details of the black-plumed horses pulling the old glass-sided hearse, the black-coated minders lining the route like members of a private army and the sea of flowers. When East Enders turned out in their thousands, jamming the length of Bethnal Green Road, Reg had made Ronnie's funeral the most memorable the East End had ever seen.

Reg knew quite well that he could do much the same with Charlie's. The pattern was already there for him to follow. Those last wishes for a private funeral which Charlie had whispered to Wilf as he lay dying could be treated much as Reg had treated Charlie's wishes all his life. As Wilf put it later, all that really mattered now was what he called 'the Reg Kray road-show'.

No one who witnessed the extraordinary scenes in Bethnal Green towards eleven on the morning of 19 March 2000 will ever forget the moment when a dark blue 'people carrier' with blacked-out windows, preceded by a presidential-style escort of police motor-cyclists in bright yellow jackets, drew up outside Mr English's funeral parlour to bring the principal mourner to the funeral.

There was an air of great excitement in the waiting crowd. Cheers went up, a banner was unfurled proclaiming 'Good Old Reg', as a grey-haired, frail figure in a dark blue suit walked slowly past the cheering throng. The uncrowned gangster king of Bethnal Green was all too briefly back among his own, and during the rest of that extraordinary day Charlie lay more or less forgotten in his coffin while Reg was fêted all the way from Bethnal Green to Chingford Mount Cemetery. The one Kray everyone was interested in now was Reg, as he took his place of honour in the front row of St Matthew's Church, standing beside his wife, Roberta and flanked by the leading figures of London's criminal fraternity. If anything the interest grew when the service ended and the long cortege of nearly thirty gleaming limos followed Reg and Charlie through the crowd-lined streets of the old East End, then out to the cemetery at Chingford Mount for burial in what was already being called 'Kray Corner'.

After the coffin had been lowered into the grave, and it was time for Reg to be driven back to prison, just as he was about to climb into the prison van a voice from the crowd shouted out, 'Three cheers for Reg!', then hundreds of voices joined in: 'Three cheers for Reg!'

Thus Charlie's funeral turned into his brother's grand finale as a legend and a living celebrity.

After Charlie's funeral, all that life had left to offer Reg was the hope of freedom. But despite thirty-one years in prison, he would never be a free man until it was too late. For although he didn't know it, by now he was terminally sick himself and had only seven months to live. During this period, Wilf felt he had a duty to support Reg as much as possible in accordance with the promise he had made to Ronnie. He also tried to help Roberta fight her lonely battle for her husband's freedom. But his true test came late that summer when they discovered that Reg had cancer.

Wilf could only admire the bravery with which Reg endured the two major operations that followed. During this period he was perpetually driving up and down to Norwich and visiting the private room on the seventh floor of the Norfolk and Norwich Hospital where Reg was being treated. Whenever Wilf was needed, he was there.

For along with the toughness and the violence that would never change in Wilf's complicated nature went an unexpected streak of kindness and compassion for any friend in trouble. During these days when Reg was fighting a losing battle for his life, this kindness inevitably extended to the much-put-upon Roberta, who in her difficult role as Reg's second wife, had need of all the help and the support that she could get. Along with her desperate anxiety for her stricken husband, she had to deal with intrusion by the press and jealousies within the criminal community.

During this potentially explosive period, Wilf played an all-important part in trying to keep everyone as calm as possible and here he showed another facet of his personality in his surprising tact and diplomatic behaviour. And after Reg's death it was largely thanks to him that his funeral went as smoothly as it did.

As Wilf expected, Reg's own funeral was something of an anticlimax, for nothing could equal that spectacular occasion he had staged for Charlie. Ironically, far fewer people bothered to turn out to mourn him now that he was dead than had cheered him so wildly at Charlie's funeral when he was living. But even here, as I witnessed for myself, Wilf's role was crucial. At the beginning of this book I described how I saw him standing at Roberta's side, leaning on his Gucci walking stick. I understood even then that his presence was a guarantee that none of the bitter animosities that had been building up over Reg's last wishes would erupt and that he would be buried on that day with dignity.

What I didn't understand was how he did it. Now I think I do.

At least I understand the way in which he fulfilled the promise he had made to Ronnie Kray before he died. I know about that famous Gucci walking stick and the importance to him of the man it had belonged to, Joe Pagano. I also understand why so many London gangsters there that day held Wilf Pine in such awe. He still is feared by many, but he is also loved by quite a few.

Postscript

WHAT WAS SO interesting about that day at Chingford
Mount Cemetery by the graveside of Reg Kray was that none
of the other former big-time criminals could have done what Wilf
did. Certainly not Frankie Fraser, not even tall good-looking Johnny
Nash who, in fact, did come and stand beside Wilf in the church to
give him his support.

It was only sometime afterwards that I remembered a remark made
by the ex-villain, Dave Courtney, saying that Wilf is unique in the way
he could walk into a room where there were men with guns drawn,
and say, 'Now, now, boys. Don't be silly. Put those things away'.
Courtney also says, that in terms of the criminal pecking order, 'Wilf
Pine has been up there with the gods as long a I can remember,' and
his prestige extends to most corners of the United Kingdom.

But as Wilf's story shows, there is more to him than that. Only a
very unusual character could possibly have crammed into one short
life-time a successful career in the music business, a trusted role
among some of the legendary names in the American Mafia, and an
intimate relationship with all three members of the most notorious
crime family in Britain, the Krays. To have done all this, while still
keeping out of prison, puts him among the most improbable and
extraordinary villains of our time.

I am still not absolutely certain how he did it. But having worked
closely with him on this book, I have come to the conclusion that
really there are two Wilf Pines. One is the person who was abused as
a child and who learned all too well the dangerous lessons from the
institutionalised violence and bullying he encountered at the nautical
training school during that crucial period of his adolescence. This is

354

the Wilf that he himself describes as 'a hoodlum', rejecting authority, enjoying violence, feeling at ease only with other criminals.

But the second Wilf Pine is the intelligent and practical individual who, virtually without any formal education, reached the top of the demanding world of the music business, coping single-handed with complicated contracts, long recording sessions, and the personal problems of assorted artistes. This Wilf Pine is almost everything the hoodlum Wilf is not – devoted to his family, and one of the kindest men I've ever met.

Divided natures such as his are not infrequent among criminals. But what makes Wilf unusual, and povides the true theme of this book, is that for much of his life, he has been in search of the two things he had never known as a child but had always longed for – a father figure and a family he could feel at home with.

As we have seen, it was a mere chance that led him to find both of these within the Pagano family in the early 1970s. But the point of this discovery, and why it had such a profound effect upon him at the time, is that almost everything about that family fitted in with his own divided personality. Like so many Italian-American families at that time, the Paganos really were immensely kind and loving, and because Wilf entered their circle at a time of sorrow and bereavement, he truly did become 'one of the family.'

But the Paganos had two sides to them just like Wilf. Joe Pagano was concerned and wise and almost everything that Wilf could have asked for in a father, but as 'The Valachi Papers' show, he and his brother Pat had both been ruthless killers. So were many of their friends and associates, and clearly Joe did not take the interest that he did in Wilf, just because he and his wife, Teresa, were so touched by his deep concern after the death of their young son, Jimmy. From the start, Joe must have recognised Wilf as 'one of his own,' and realised his worth.

In many ways their backgrounds were strangely similar – both were cradle Catholics, both were natural fighters, and both took to crime following deprived childhoods. More than this, at that gathering at Captain's Cove, following the killing of his brother, Joe Pagano must have understood from the start that he could trust Wilf Pine, as much as he would have trusted his own son.

As Wilf's story shows, trust him he did, on many subsequent occasions. Quite how far this trust extended I genuinely do not know. When we began this book Wilf made it clear that he would say nothing that could conceivably incriminate himself or any living associates. This is something he has rigidly adhered to.

But our agreement does not stop me mentioning information which I gained from various sources, and with which I am able to fill in certain gaps which Wilf can not.

For instance, a wall-chart from the Seventies which I was shown in the offices of the New York Police Department's Task Force on Organised Crime, showed both Joe Pagano and his brother, Pat, as joint capos in the Genovese crime family. A federal agent also once went on record describing the Genoveses' as 'The Ivy League family among the five crime families of New York', and as rising young Genovese capos, the Pagano brothers would have been treated as Mafia royalty, with easy access to some of the key figures in the world of American organised crime in the Sixties and Seventies. This makes sense of the remark Joe made to Wilf about how he got to know Frank Sinatra, when Vito Genovese gave him that 'sizeable piece of the action at the Copacabana Club,' after ousting Frank Costello as reputed boss of the Genovese. And logically the Paganos should have earned Vito Genovese's favour, if Valachi's testament is true, and Pat Pagano killed the unfortunate Steve Franse, on Genevese's orders.

Certainly as young, ambitious capos in the late Sixties, both Paganos would have been well placed to succeed and prosper in what, in retrospect, appears a last brief golden age of the American Mafia. Much of the importance of Wilf's story comes from the way it coincided with the conclusion of that long-gone period, and it was thanks to the favoured position of the Paganos that Wilf had the chance to become involved with so many characters of importance in the history of organised crime in America.

In this way the most significant of those he met was the hunched old man with the heavy spectacles for whom he delivered his very first message as a courier for the Mafia, Joe Pagano's friend and patron, Alfonse, 'Funzi' Tieri. Some journalists have claimed on dubious evidence that by the Seventies Funzi was the mythical 'boss of bosses' of organised crime in America. But his real power came in

1972, when in his late sixties, he effectively took control of the Genovese family which he ruled with continuing success until his death by natural causes in 1981. Immensely rich himself, he was widely considered 'the wisest of the godfathers', thanks to the way he enriched those beneath him, including undoubtedly his younger friend, Joe Pagano.

Another important old-timer Wilf became involved with was the little man he met with Irwin Schiff in the cafe at Grand Central Station. 'Jimmy Nap' Napoli, was a devoted underling of Funzi's, who is said to have made a sizeable fortune from casinos, race-tracks and ambitious financial operations, of which the attempted takeover of Worldwide Artists was typical. As Wilf suspected at the time, the fat man, Irwin Schiff was finally revealed as a police informer and was gunned down while eating the last meal of his life at the Sergio Brava Restaurant in Manhattan.

A number of other friends and associates Wilf met through Joe Pagano became important later in his life. These included the cigar-chewing 'Fat Tony' Salerno who reputedly succeeded Funzi Tieri on his death in 1981 and, according to 'Fortune' magazine, as the aged head of the Genovese crime family, ranked as 'America's top gangster for power, wealth and influence'. He was certainly extremely rich, and as well as the estate in upstate New York where Wilf first met him, he owned a lavish property on Miami Beach, and an apartment on smart Gramercy Park, Manhattan. At the famous Commission Trial, Fat Tony was convicted and sent to prison for a hundred years, where he died of natural causes.

One of my informants with the FBI believes that Fat Tony's underboss with the Genovese was another friend of Wilf's, good-looking Vinnie Mauro. Most of this sort of talk of 'bosses and underbosses', Wilf himself dismisses as 'usually a load of bullshit', but bullshit or not, such rumours seem to have a way of following two further friends of Joe Pagano who Wilf first got to know in New York in the early Seventies. The first of these is Arnold 'Zeke' Squitieri, who at the time of the death of John Gotti was widely rumoured to have been underboss of the Gambino crime family, and for a period Gotti's actual successor.

The second of these friends is the ever cautious Dominic 'Quiet

Dom' Cirillo. Here Wilf is even more insistant that the reports I heard are so much nonsense, but my contact in the Organised Crime Task Force in New York City states categorically that since 1997 'Quiet Dom' has been the official boss of the Genovese crime family.

But for me the biggest mystery of all remains Wilf himself. Despite his failing health and the fact that he is more or less crippled now, I feel that deep down he has never really changed and that, with sufficient aggravation, he might still throw someone through the window. On the other hand, these days he demonstrates his feelings for his friends by cooking for them. One of the incidental benefits of his contacts with the mob was that he learned cooking from their wives, and while working on this book, I have particularly enjoyed his *lasagne alla Romana*, his meatballs with tomato and oregano sauce, his Parmesan bread, and a speciality known as *pasta Vazzu*, for which he got the recipe from Joe Pagano's sister, the redoubtable Aunt Rose. As I had been unable to trace this in any Italian cookbook I imagined it must come from some Pagano forbears in Naples, but Luigi di Franco of la Famiglia Restaurant in London tells me that it is a New York Italian shortening of 'pasta vegetal' which seems more than likely.

As for Wilf's more questionable activities these days, the answer has to be that I simply do not know what, if anything, he is up to. According to our original agreement, I don't ask and I realise that if I did he wouldn't answer. Wilf himself makes no secret that he has visited the Federal Correctional Institution at Otisville in New York State, where Danny Pagano is halfway through an eight-year sentence for his part in the so-called 'Daisy Chain' conspiracy. According to the evidence at his trial, at the time of his arrest as a reputed capo in the Genovese crime family, he was allegedly involved in a racket in conjunction with the Russian Mafia in New York, by which he was supposedly receiving one penny for every gallon of petrol that went into the tanks of most of New York's unsuspecting motorists.

Wilf likes to keep in touch with his old friends, and a few mean more to him these days than Danny, the son of Joe Pagano. Whether anything more than friendship lies behind these visits, the reader must, like me, decide for himself.

Index

index

index

The Gamblers

John Pearson

Britain's foremost writer on crime turns to the disappearance of Lord Lucan

For over thirty years, John Pearson has provided us with literary exposures of some of the most enigmatic people and underground organisations of our modern world. *The Gamblers* follows the fortunes of five men at the centre of the ultra-fashionable Clermont Set: the Clermont Club's eccentric founder John Aspinall; Dominic Elwes, who was to betray the Set's code of silence; the socialite owner of Annabel's, Mark Birley; the womanising, multi millionaire James Goldsmith; and the infamous Lord 'Lucky' Lucan.

At the heart of the Set lay a belief that risk-takers are the people who make civilisation tick. Cruel, heartless and snobbish, they gambled with their fortunes and kept a stiff upper lip when they lost. This and a loyalty to each other that transcended everything else enabled them to rise above crises such as the long affair between Birley's wife and James Goldsmith, and the facial mutilation of the Birley's son by one of Aspinall's tigers. Pearson revels in the charisma, charm and wit of these dastardly but debonair millionaires, and reveals how their code led to one of the great unsolved mysteries of the twentieth century.

'A riveting portrait of the notorious Clermont set . . . reads like a galloping Mayfair noir thriller' *Sunday Times*

arrow books

ALSO AVAILABLE IN ARROW

Respect

Autobiography of Freddie Foreman

Freddie Foreman with John Lisners

Freddie Foreman's admission in this book that he was responsible for the gangland killings of Ginger Marks and Frank 'the Mad Axeman' Mitchell, who had been sprung from Dartmoor Prison by the Kray twins, made deadlines around the world.

To Britain's criminal underworld, Freddie Foreman is the Godfather. His name inspires more fear than any other. 'Don't mess with Brown Bread Fred or you're dead!' Throughout his career Freddie has ruthlessly upheld the underworld code of conduct. The 'comeback' for those who transgressed was mercilessly applied.

Freddie's chilling but often humorous account of his life is a story from the inside of how some of Britain's most famous and daring robberies were committed, of bent coppers and the criminally insane, of loyalty and betrayal, and above all, of killing.

'Sensational!'
News of the World

arrow books

The One That Got Away

Chris Ryan

**The number one bestseller that has now become a classic
from the true hero of the Brave Two Zero mission.**

The SAS mission conducted behind Iraqi lines is one of the most
famous stories of courage and survival in modern warfare. Of
the eight members of the SAS regiment who set off, only one
escaped capture. This is his story.

The One That Got Away is a breathtaking story of extraordinary
courage under fire, of hairbreadth escapes, of the best trained
soldiers in the world fighting against the most adverse conditions, and, above all, of one man's courageous refusal to lie
down and die.

'You have personally made SAS history'
General Sir Peter de la Billière

'It's a thrill-a-minute story of terror, hardship, heroism, bravery
and sheer guts'
Sun

'Raw and brutal'
Daily Express

arrow books

The Good Guys Wear Black

Steve Collins

The top ten best-selling story of the true-life heroes of Britain's armed police

SO19, the Metropolitan Police Special Firearms Wing, is an awesome squad of gunfighters who daily defend the public from evil. Here, Sergeant Steve Collins, who led Black Team, the hardest and most renowned team within the unit, tells their story. Yardies, international drug barons, IRA enforcers and celebrity South London gangsters and hitmen have all been taken off the streets by the true-life heroes of SO19 either in handcuffs or in bodybags. The tensions and camaraderie of a team who daily risk death has never been captured so vividly on the page.

'Gripping . . . action-packed . . . compelling' *Sun*

arrow books

Bringing Down the House

Ben Mezrich

How Six Students took Vegas for Millions

Liar's Poker meets *Ocean's Eleven* in Ben Mezrich's riveting story of a team of brilliant card counters who developed a system to take some of the world's most sophisticated casinos for millions of dollars. *Bringing Down the House* is a real-life thriller, utterly gripping and a fascinating insight into a tightly closed, utterly excessive and utterly corrupt world.

'In this high-octane tale with rich, sharp dialogue, bordering on Elmore Leonard turf, the plot races by at a Nascar pace and the characters on both sides of the table are as real as an inside straight . . . *Bringing Down the House* is a can't-miss deal.'
Lorenzo Carcaterra

'An extraordinary story . . . [I read] this thrilling book in almost one sitting – it is, to use that cliché, "unputdownable" . . . a book that will surely become a classic of its genre.'
Sunday Express

'A surreal cacophony of glamour, suspense and, eventually, terror. Part Tom Clancy, part Elmore Leonard . . . Gripping'
The List

'The tale laid out in *Bringing Down the House* is so beguiling, so agreeably reminiscent of, say *Ocean's Eleven* or *House of Games* that you find yourself mentally casting the parts as you read along . . . A fine yarn'
Sunday Times

arrow books

Born Fighter

Reg Kray

Reg Kray was one of Britain's most notorious criminals. Together with his brother Ron, he rose through the ranks of London's East End gangland to run an evil empire of vice and villainy. Here, in his own words, is the true story of his life with Ron, the chilling career of two streetwise kids who became standard-bearers of violence – from fire-bombings, to shootings and cold-blooded murder.

But here too is the inner voice of a one-time mobster who learned compassion through his own struggle to come to terms with a life sentence. As Reg says, 'We were better at violence than the others . . . but I believe that our lives were better for the saving'.

Candid, compelling and often shocking, *Born Fighter* is the definitive book on the life and times of the Krays.

arrow books

**Order further Arrow titles
from your local bookshop, or have them delivered
direct to your door by Bookpost**

☐ **Respect** Freddie Foreman 9780099699514 £7.99
☐ **The One That Got Away**
   Chris Ryan   9780099460152 £7.99
☐ **Journey Into Darkness** John Olshaker & Mark Douglas
                                9780099427940 £7.99
☐ **The Good Guys Wear Black**
   Steve Collins   9780099186823 £6.99
☐ **Bringing Down the House**
   Ben Mezrich   9780099468233 £6.99
☐ **Born Fighter**
   Reg Kray   9780099878100 £5.99

Free post and packing
Overseas customers allow £2 per paperback
Phone: 01624 677237
Post: Random House Books
c/o Bookpost, PO Box 29, Douglas, Isle of Man IM99 1BQ
Fax: 01624 670923
email: bookshop@enterprise.net
Cheques (payable to Bookpost) and credit cards accepted

Prices and availability subject to change without notice.
Allow 28 days for delivery.
When placing your order, please state if you do not wish to receive any
additional information.

www.randomhouse.co.uk/arrowbooks

arrow books